This is a fascinating book. It really covers the state of the art in IR research that is at the intersection with work in other fields that consider the intersections of science, technology, and society. The introductory chapters on different approaches to technology studies will be useful to anyone in IR who is unfamiliar with the broader field and most of the chapters on specific technological issues are outstanding.

Craig N. Murphy, Wellesley College, USA

This superb volume strikes new ground in its interdisciplinary approach to technology and global politics. It advances productive intellectual engagements with the sociotechnical systems that characterise our world. Essential reading for anyone interested in the complexities of technology, society and international relations in the 21st century.

Tim Stevens, King's College London, UK

This fascinating collection showcases recent approaches to theorizing the material in world politics in a manner that is both accessible and highly informative. Essential reading for anyone interested in how technology is shaping, and being employed to shape, ever greater domains of human life. A benchmark work in the renewal of materialism in the study of international relations.

Daniel H. Deudney, Johns Hopkins University, USA

TECHNOLOGY AND WORLD POLITICS

This edited volume provides a convenient entry point to the cutting-edge field of the international politics of technology in an interesting and informative manner. *Technology and World Politics* introduces its readers to different approaches to technology in global politics through a survey of emerging fusions of Science and Technology Studies and International Relations. The theoretical approaches to the subject surveyed include the Social Construction of Technology, Actor-Network Theory, the Critical Theory of Technology and New Materialist and posthumanist approaches.

Considering how such theoretical approaches can be used to analyse concrete political issues such as the politics of nuclear weapons, Internet governance, shipping containers, the revolution in military affairs, space technologies and the geopolitics of the Anthropocene, the volume stresses the socially constructed and inherently political nature of technological objects. World order is subsequently understood as always socio-technical.

Providing the theoretical background to approach the politics of technology in a sophisticated manner, alongside a glossary and guide to further reading for newcomers, this volume is a vital resource for both students and scholars focusing on politics and international relations.

Daniel R. McCarthy is Lecturer in International Relations in the School of Social and Political Sciences at the University of Melbourne, Australia.

TECHNOLOGY AND WORLD POLITICS

An Introduction

Edited by Daniel R. McCarthy

Routledge
Taylor & Francis Group

LONDON AND NEW YORK

First published 2018
by Routledge
2 Park Square, Milton Park, Abingdon, Oxon OX14 4RN

and by Routledge
711 Third Avenue, New York, NY 10017

Routledge is an imprint of the Taylor & Francis Group, an informa business

British Library Cataloguing in Publication Data
A catalogue record for this book is available from the British Library

Library of Congress Cataloging in Publication Data
A catalog record for this book has been requested

ISBN: 978-1-138-95583-7 (hbk)
ISBN: 978-1-138-95587-5 (pbk)
ISBN: 978-1-31566-601-3 (ebk)

Typeset in Bembo
by Taylor & Francis Books

CONTENTS

PART II
Illustrations   **101**

CONTRIBUTORS

Antoine Bousquet is Senior Lecturer in International Relations at Birkbeck College, University of London. He is author of *The Scientific Way of Warfare: Order and Chaos on the Battlefields of Modernity* (Hurst, 2009), and has published in *Millennium: Journal of International Studies, Cambridge Review of International Affairs* and the *Journal of International Relations and Development*.

Christian Bueger is Reader in International Relations in the Department of Politics and International Relations, Cardiff University. In 2013 he was a visiting fellow at the Centre for Advanced Security Theory, University of Copenhagen; in 2011 a Leverhulme Fellow at the Greenwich Maritime Institute, London; and, prior, a research fellow at the Institute for Development and Peace, Duisburg, Germany (2010). He obtained his PhD in Political and Social Sciences from the European University Institute, Florence, Italy (2010). He has published in *International Studies Quarterly, Contemporary Security Policy, European Political Science Review, Global Policy, International Political Sociology, International Studies Perspectives, Journal of International Relations and Development* and *Third World Quarterly*.

Alejandro Colás is Reader in International Relations at Birkbeck College, University of London. He is the author of *International Civil Society* (Polity, 2002), *Empire* (Polity, 2007) and editor (with Bryan Mabee) of *Mercenaries, Pirates, Bandits and Empires: Private Violence in Historical Context* (Hurst, 2011). He has published in the *European Journal of International Relations, Millennium: Journal of International Studies* and *Review of International Studies*.

Jairus Victor Grove is Assistant Professor in Political Science at the University of Hawai'i Manoa and Director of the Hawai'i Research Center for Futures Studies. His research centres on ecology and the future of global warfare. He has published in *International Political Sociology*, *Theory and Event* and *Critical Studies on Security*. His book *Savage Ecology: Geopolitics at the End of the World* is forthcoming from Duke University Press.

Mary Manjikian is Associate Professor in the Robertson School of Government, Regent University. She is the author of *Threat Talk: The Comparative Politics of Internet Addiction* (Routledge, 2012) and *The Securitization of Property Squatting in Western Europe* (Routledge, 2013), in addition to articles in *Alternatives*, *International Studies Quarterly* and the *International Feminist Journal of Politics*.

Joseph P. Masco teaches Anthropology and Science Studies at the University of Chicago. He is the author of *The Nuclear Borderlands: The Manhattan Project in Post-Cold War New Mexico* (Princeton University Press, 2006), which won the 2014 J.I. Staley Prize from the School of Advanced Research, the 2008 Rachel Carson Prize from the Society for the Social Studies of Science and was the co-winner of the 2006 Robert K. Merton Prize from the Section on Science, Knowledge and Technology of the American Sociology Association. His latest book is *The Theater of Operations: National Security Affect from the Cold War to the War on Terror* (Duke University Press, 2014).

Daniel R. McCarthy is Lecturer in International Relations in the School of Social and Political Studies, University of Melbourne. His research examines technology as a form of power in global politics and the politics of global transparency, drawing on Critical Theory and historical materialism. He is the author of *Information Technology, Power and International Relations Theory: The Power and Politics of American Foreign Policy and the Internet* (Palgrave Macmillan, 2015), and has published in *Review of International Studies*, *Millennium: Journal of International Studies* and the *European Journal of International Relations*.

Columba Peoples is Senior Lecturer in International Relations in the School of Sociology, Politics and International Studies, University of Bristol. He is the author of *Justifying Ballistic Missile Defence: Technology, Security and Culture* (Cambridge University Press, 2010), and, with Nick Vaughan-Williams, is co-author of *Critical Security Studies: An Introduction* (Routledge, 2010, 2015) and co-editor of *Critical Security Studies, Volumes 1–4: Critical Concepts in Military, Strategic and Security Studies* (Routledge, 2013). He has also published multiple articles on nuclear and space security in journals that include *Security Dialogue*, *Millennium: Journal of International Studies*, *Cold War History* and *Contemporary Security Policy*.

Monroe Price is the Director of the Center for Global Communication Studies at the Annenberg School, University of Pennsylvania. He is also the Joseph and Sadie Danciger Professor of Law and Director of the Howard M. Squadron Program in Law, Media and Society at the Cardozo School of Law. He directs the Stanhope Centre for Communications Policy Research in London and is Chair of the Center for Media and Communication Studies of the Central European University in Budapest. His recent books include *Media and Sovereignty: The Global Information Revolution and Its Challenge to State Power* (MIT, 2002) and *Free Expression, Globalism, and the New Strategic Communication* (Cambridge University Press, 2015.

Nick Srnicek is author (with Alex Williams) of *Inventing the Future* (Verso, 2015) and *Platform Capitalism* (Polity, 2017) and of numerous contributions to edited collections on technology, assemblage theories, complexity and global politics.

Jan Stockbruegger is a graduate student in International Relations at the Department of Political Science at Brown University, USA. Before joining Brown, he was a research assistant in the Department of Politics and International Relations at Cardiff University, UK, and at the Institute for Development and Peace, University Duisburg-Essen, Germany. Jan holds an MA in African Studies (research) from Leiden University in the Netherlands, and a BA in African Studies from Bayreuth University in Germany. His research centres on the role of the oceans in international affairs, including order and security competition at sea and maritime piracy in the Western Indian Ocean.

ACKNOWLEDGEMENTS

Edited volumes are the work of many hands, so many thanks to each of the contributors for their hard work and their patience with the finalization of the book. Thanks to Mathias Koenig-Archibugi, Campbell Craig, George Lawson and Trevor Findlay for helpful advice at various stages. Ashley Barnwell, Clayton Chin and Lisa Denney generously read drafts of my chapters, saving a few howlers from finding print. The anonymous reviewers of the book offered very helpful suggestions, particularly around issues of writing clarity, and their time is appreciated. Lydia de Cruz at Routledge has been a very patient editor, particularly through a couple of hiccups in the development of the manuscript.

Finally, this book is dedicated to Lisa. She is a constant source of encouragement, serenity and good humour, and I could not have completed the project without her support.

1

INTRODUCTION

Technology in world politics

Daniel R. McCarthy

It would be difficult to overestimate the place of technology in our daily lives. From the moment we wake in the morning (assisted by alarm clocks) to trips to work or school on trains, buses, cars and bikes (where we use laptops or coal-diggers or barcode scanners, before enjoying an increasingly mediatized leisure time), technological objects structure and shape every aspect of our existence. Indeed, simply trying to imagine human existence without the material objects that extend our reach, augment our eyesight, aid our strength, create our clothing or cook our food is a near impossibility. An indication of the centrality of the non-human world to our everyday lives is found in the often-noted – if slightly misleading – attempt to define the human species as the 'tool-making animal'.[1]

Practices in world politics are, similarly, always composed of our relationship to and use of technological objects and systems.[2] A cursory examination of news headlines illustrates how deeply international politics is inflected by the politics of technology. American shuttle diplomacy relies upon jet technologies that were the product of massive geopolitical upheaval during the Second World War. European Union (EU) reactions to crises in Eastern Europe and Russia are inflected by the natural-gas pipelines bringing heat to European homes. Deeply integrated production networks – reliant on heavily automated just-in-time manufacturing technologies and shipping container, road and rail complexes – connect Western consumers to developing state producers ever more tightly. The interdependence of these networks shapes the macroeconomic policy range of governments across the world. Warfighters extend their reach from Nevada to Afghanistan, Iraq, Somalia and Yemen by means of drone technologies, while those targeted respond via propaganda campaigns on YouTube, Twitter and Facebook. Telling any story about international relations requires paying significant attention to the technological objects and **large technical systems** (LTS) that comprise it. Given our inescapably technological existence, studying how technological objects come into being and their role in social action is a central task of social inquiry.

The past 30 years have witnessed an explosion of interest in these issues. Emerging from the Sociology of Scientific Knowledge (SSK), the history of science and post-positivist philosophy (Kuhn 1962; Berger and Luckmann 1967; Bloor 1976; Latour and Woolgar 1979; Hughes 1983; Shapin and Schaffer 1985),[3] interest in the social shaping of technology has resulted in the creation of a distinct subfield of sociology, Science and Technology Studies (STS), with its own professional associations, journals, conferences, academic departments and disciplinary debates. STS has become one of the most theoretically dynamic and empirically productive fields in the social sciences; its interdisciplinary approach has encouraged fruitful exchanges across academic boundaries. One result of this process is that theories and methods developed within STS are increasingly influential in studies of world politics. International historians and International Relations (IR) theorists are drawing upon STS approaches in an effort to develop holistic accounts of how global political conduct creates, and is created by, the politics of technological artefacts.[4]

This is a positive development, and students of International Relations will benefit from the influence of STS in IR. For most of its history as a discipline the study of technology has been of marginal interest to IR, resulting in under-theorized treatments of non-human objects. Empirically, technology has primarily been treated as an already given variable, with the politics of technological design sidelined. The result has been ahistorical and deterministic readings of technology, with the social and the technological kept resolutely separate. Technology is more than a variable, though. Social practices are not caused by technology in a linear temporal sequence: driving a car or fighting a war are human actions that not only use cars or tanks but also are composed of them. Technology is, to use the favoured clichéd expression of the 1990s, socially constructed (cf. Hacking 1999). Acknowledging this does not settle the issue of how we should think about the relationship between technology and global politics. It does, though, point readers away from simple **technological determinisms**. To this end, the approaches surveyed in this volume engage with STS scholarship and its related strands in social and political theory in order to examine how we can begin to think about the materiality of global politics beyond the traditional coordinates set by International Relations.

STS has been a beneficial source of inspiration and engagement for IR scholars, but we should be wary of casting aside the insights of IR *tout court*. If IR has not adequately theorized or studied the role of technological objects in world politics, STS has largely neglected the specific role of 'the International' in processes of social development (Rosenberg 2006). Competition and cooperation between multiple political communities, the place of foreign policy interests, the norms of international society; all of these are central to the character of technology and science. For example, the shift from 'small science' to 'big science' in the field of particle physics had a significant impact on the course of its development, altering the kind of problems that scientists would, and could, pursue and their access to cutting-edge technologies that enabled this (Pickering 1993). This process emerged from the transition in government funding for scientific research in the United States during the Second World War, a shift that favoured large and expensive research projects and equipment over the 'small science' that 'was the traditional work style of experimental physics' (Pickering 1993: 572). The role of inter-state competition and war was central to this development, as was the subsequent prestige attached to science in the Cold War. Yet geopolitical competition and the presence of multiple political communities are not theorized in the classic STS account of this process. Technological development is always modulated by the specific dynamics of cooperation and competition between political communities within a global system of states. Various traditions of IR theory offer resources for a sustained interdisciplinary dialogue with STS centred on the global politics of technology.

With these thoughts in mind, this volume is designed to provide students and scholars of International Relations with an introduction to the emerging interdisciplinary scholarship in this area. The remainder of this introductory chapter will outline these preliminary remarks in greater depth, before turning to discuss the structure of the book as a whole. First, we will note the twin technological determinisms that have dominated IR theory until quite recently – **instrumentalism** and **essentialism**. A brief discussion of these determinisms points to the elaboration of alternative perspectives in Part I of the book. Second, the introduction will outline some shared **epistemological**, **ontological** and methodological guidelines central to Science and Technology Studies. This will allow us to locate where STS-IR sits in relation to other approaches to International Relations. Finally, we will outline how the volume as a whole fits together. This section will clarify the relationship between the theoretical sections of the book and the chapters dealing with empirical issues, noting how the former informs the latter, and vice versa.

'God from the machine': traditional approaches to technology in International Relations

It may seem a bit unusual to claim that the field of International Relations has neglected technology as an important element of global politics. Since the inception of the discipline of IR in the second decade of the twentieth century, technology has been of central concern to the field. Alfred Zimmern, holder of the world's first chair in International Politics (created in 1919), was not alone in placing his theorization of the international within the context of rapid technological change (Zimmern 1928). Norman Angell, E.H. Carr, Halford Mackinder, Hans Morgenthau, Reinhold Niebuhr and Leonard Woolf all stressed the central role of technology in shaping international political life (Carr 1939: 228–230; Niebuhr 1932; Morgenthau 1946, 1949; cf. Ashworth 2011; Craig 2003; Osiander 1998; Scheuerman 2007). Technology – and particularly transport and communications technologies – were viewed as a force driving global politics towards greater integration (although not necessarily greater harmony). Carr, in an argument echoed by other authors, asserted that ongoing industrialization, new military technologies and the expanding reach of transportation and communications posed a profound challenge to existing forms of territorial state sovereignty. A technologically driven reshaping of the size and nature of political units was 'perhaps likely to be more decisive than any other for the course of world history in the next few generations' (Carr 1939: 230).

Understood as a causal variable or as a background context, technology has never really lost this central place in IR. Barring the occasional claim that material objects are entirely indeterminate, and that IR theory should concentrate on ideas as the driving force of social action (Wendt 1999: 256),[5] technological artefacts and systems continue to be recognized, both theoretically and empirically, as an important factor influencing actors' decisions and their subsequent outcomes. Indeed, at times certain prominent approaches to IR have been criticized for being far *too* focused on technology, such as neorealist international security studies or 'globalization theory' (Buzan 1991; Rosenberg 2005: 3, 6, 55). Critics suggest that, in paying too much attention to the number of tanks, bombs and bullets a state possesses, we miss other, equally important, forms of power or sources of social action. The determining quality of technology is, it is claimed, overrated. Culture, ideas, institutions – or any number of other aspects of social life – should be granted far greater attention in accounting for the character of global politics.

How is it possible, then, to suggest that technology has been neglected as an area of study in International Relations? This rests on the argument that a predominantly determinist theory of technology has been held by IR scholars. Two examples of how IR theorists have studied technology and international politics are helpful in illustrating this claim. First, IR scholars have argued, over a long period of time, that new information technologies are changing the shape of global politics (Keohane and Nye 1977; Scholte 2005; Schweller 2014). Claiming that satellite television, mobile communications and the Internet were overcoming geographical distance, such work has asserted that 'traditional' structures of global politics – anarchy, sovereignty and the primacy of inter-state relations – were, and are, being eroded.

Information technology is cast as an agent in this process, driving forward social change. Yet this work has not investigated the innovation process itself – the micro-politics of design that shaped how these large technological systems came into being. Artefacts and their (purported) properties have been taken as given, with analysts treating them as established facts rather than objects subject to ongoing contestation and interpretation of their design, purposes and uses. Not accounting for the social, political, economic and cultural dynamics that have shaped the design of new information technologies leaves the story of globalization incomplete. Technological responses to reconstitute sovereignty, such as Internet filtering (see Deibert et al. 2012), illustrate this effectively.

Second, there has been sustained examination in IR and the subfield of strategic studies of nuclear weapons and the revolutionary impact they have had on inter-state relations (Herz 1950; Waltz 1981; cf. Buzan and Hansen 2009: 66–100; Craig 2003; cf. Sylvest 2013). But, despite all this attention, the majority of scholarship on this topic has not considered the politics of nuclear weapons creation and reproduction – the 'laboratory politics' of weapons creation (see Chapter 6). Nuclear weapons require continuous efforts to maintain them, and the weapons themselves can take any number of different forms depending on the strategic, cultural or economic goals they are designed to meet (Mackenzie 1990; Masco 2006; Peoples 2010; Sims and Henke 2013). Attending to the large-scale systemic impact of nuclear weapons – treating them as a variable in altering the trajectory of world order – as IR has conventionally done is very important (e.g. Waltz 1981); but the precise shape of this altered trajectory is dependent on the micro-politics of technological design and development.

In sum, until quite recently, technology featured in explaining outcomes in global politics; but analysis never extended to ask how technology artefacts are created, why they are created, by whom and what norms or values objects embody. To use a favourite expression of STS scholars, technology remained the unopened **black box** that could be used in explanation but was never itself explained – a *deus ex machina*, as it were.[6] A generic understanding of the generative forces of technological development has certainly been present in International Relations, with, for example, inter-state security competition theorized as the structural pressure pushing states to pursue technological innovation. Grasping such generative mechanisms is certainly important. However, it is equally important to also understand how structural pressures interact with the micro-politics of innovation and technological design to produce world orders that are, at their foundation, always socio-technical.

What accounts for this blind spot? Numerous possible factors present themselves: the generic **reification** of technology in contemporary social usages (Marx 2010: 576–577); an understanding of science in IR derived from physics rather than, say, biology; the dominance of positivist epistemology in defining 'theory' in IR; and the centrality of Humean accounts of causation. We will examine these in more detail shortly.[7] Regardless of the root causes of IR black boxing technology, the general result has been ahistorical, technologically determinist positions (Herrera 2006; Fritsch 2011).[8] Technological determinism may be 'patently bizarre' on the surface (Winner 1977: 13), but determinist ideas have guided most IR treatments of technology, if often only implicitly. At its core, the basic claim of technological determinism is that technology is beyond the control of human agents (Winner 1977: 15; Wyatt 2008: 168).[9] Technology is treated as separate from society: it may or may not influence the course of social development, but it is not itself the product of social construction as such.

Determinism has two primary variants, technological instrumentalism and technological essentialism. These perspectives occasionally feature as opposing points of contention in IR debates, as in the structural realist dispute over the importance of the 'offense–defense balance' of military technology on state conduct and the structure of international politics (Jervis 1978; Levy 1984; Lynn-Jones 1995; Lieber

2000; Glaser 2010). In this literature, the 'offense–defense' balance of military technology is claimed, by proponents of the theory, to be a central factor in deciding both whether the international system as a whole is more violent or more stable and whether individual states act aggressively or defensively. New military technologies are asserted to alter the 'relative ease of attack or defense', a 'concept meant to capture the objective effects of military technology on war and politics' (Lieber 2000: 75). Detractors suggest that weapons are ultimately neutral in their effects, only attaining a purpose in the context of a military strategy or culture. The former position is essentialist, claiming that weapons have inherent properties that drive social outcomes towards aggressive or defensive action – the weapons' **biases** are independent of human control or intention. The latter viewpoint is instrumentalist in that it treats these objects as tools or instruments that have no bias towards offensive or defensive military postures. A similar set of positions implicitly defines contemporary debates over the impact of drones on the international system (Horowitz et al. 2016: 13–17).

It may seem like these options exhaust how technological objects can be conceptualized. After all, how could a technological system cause political outcomes *and* be neutral in its political impacts? It seems that choosing one of these options rules out the other. This is a false dichotomy underpinned by a shared picture of technological rationality as natural. This ultimately suggests that technology is autonomous. We will now look at instrumentalism and essentialism in greater detail.

In the instrumentalist viewpoint, technology is neutral, a tool that can be turned to whatever use a user desires. For scholars embracing an instrumentalist approach this seems to avoid the issue of determinism entirely (Rosenau 2002: 275; Rosenau 2005: 78). The classic form of such claims is embodied in the US National Rifle Association (NRA)'s claim that 'Guns don't kill people' (Latour 1994; Selinger 2012). Here, the NRA is suggesting that guns are neutral in their design: guns do not favour any specific social outcome. Rather, guns are only given purpose in use by human beings. The parallel of this claim in the offense–defense literature in IR, or treatment of drones, nuclear weapons and so forth, should be clear: weapons are only offensive in the hands of offensive states. The limits of this claim are effectively, and humorously, illustrated in an episode of *The Simpsons* entitled 'The Cartridge Family'. In this episode, Homer purchases a gun to protect his family. Typically, he is not responsible in his gun ownership, and attempts to use the gun to complete all kinds of tasks for which it is not suited – getting a basketball off a roof, opening a beer can, hanging a picture on the wall, turning out the lights and changing the channel on the television. Needless to say, things do not work out as Homer planned, and he leaves a trail of destruction in his wake. By the end it is clear to Homer and the audience that a gun cannot be put towards any end. The technology has been created for a particular purpose – to kill things, whether in the hands of 'good' or 'bad' people – and cannot be used to accomplish any task a user desires.[10]

This example may seem facetious, but a serious theoretical point is at stake here. In instrumentalist accounts, human agency is bracketed in the *design* of technology and the ability of people to *create* objects to meet specific social purposes. Instrumentalists can, of course, study how technological innovation occurs with varied levels of success according to the configuration of economic and political institutions within and between countries, and across time periods. This approach is exemplified by the national systems of innovation literature and economic historical sociology, and in 'mild' variants of constructionism in STS (see, respectively, Freeman 1995; Gerschenkron 1962; Bijker 2010: 65). While doing a fine job of accounting for the scope and pace of change, such work cannot tell us much about the nature or form that such change takes – what kinds of objects are being created, why they are being created, what purposes they serve and so forth. This undermines its claims to emphasize agency via the suggestion that people cannot design technological objects to have biases towards particular social ends. At a basic level, a sceptic of instrumentalism could rightly query whether gun designers and manufacturers actually conceptualize their labours as neutral, as the production of objects without any specific end in mind, or whether the presence of handguns in society does not structure social choices at all, remaining truly neutral (Selinger 2012).[11]

More tellingly, instrumentalism relies on the assumption of an ahistorical technical logic. Wyatt (2008: 168) summarizes this facet of instrumentalist determinism: 'New or improved products or ways of making things arise from the activities of inventors, engineers, and designers following an internal, technical logic that has nothing to do with social relationships'. In the instrumentalist position, technological objects are clearly made by people and are in this sense 'socially constructed', but the objects take a form determined by an abstract non-social nature (see Demeritt 2002: 777–778). Claims that a 'technical' logic exists outside a social definition of this logic removes the technical from its creation by human action. The product of innovation is not theorized as subject to social shaping, and is thereby – often unintentionally – determinist. Instrumentalist approaches have the significant merit of focusing on technology in use, thereby allowing analysts to examine how social practice at one level is socio-technical; but, overall, in instrumentalist accounts the black box remains closed.

Essentialist determinism is more straightforward as a variant of determinism. Essentialism is present in many different strands of social theory, including Marxist, Liberal and Conservative variants (Marcuse 1968: 201–220; Winner 1977). It is also present in a diverse range of IR scholarship, from liberalism and realism to post-structuralism and 'eclectic' theories of globalization (McCarthy 2015: 19–42). For essentialists, technological development is not merely bracketed; it is also claimed that technology continually develops throughout human history (Cohen 1978; Deudney 2008). Technology is thought to evolve from less advanced to more advanced objects. As technological progress occurs, technological systems pressure human social organization to change and adapt to the capacities new objects possess. Technology is thereby conceived as the driving force of social change (see

Chapter 4). Essentialist claims have been used to explain large-scale social change, such as the shift from feudalism to capitalism (White 1962; Parker 1996) or the shift from 'old wars' to 'new wars' in the era of globalized production networks (Kaldor 2007). The central tenets of essentialism are effectively captured by Andrew Feenberg (2002: 138–139):

1. The pattern of technical progress is fixed, moving along one and the same track in all societies. Although political, cultural, and other factors may influence the pace of change, they cannot alter the general line of development that reflects the autonomous logic of discovery.
2. Social organization must adapt to technical progress at each stage of development according to the 'imperative' requirements of technology. This adaptation executes an underlying technological necessity.

These claims are so widespread in popular culture as to be nearly ubiquitous. To take one small example, arguments that society must adjust to a new digital environment rely on an understanding of technological development as outside human control. Digital technologies – developed to meet certain social and political aims (Herrera 2002; DeNardis 2009; McCarthy 2011, 2015; Carr 2012) – are instead portrayed as the outcome of an unstoppable, linear and evolutionary process of technological change. Disruption caused by these transformations instigate social change, such as higher levels of unemployment. People do not make their own history.

There are quite considerable problems with essentialism. The claim that technology continuously develops throughout human history is at least overstated in essentialist work. Certainly, current levels of technological sophistication are very high in historical comparison; but to read back our current situation as the outcome of linear historical progression of science is misleading. Things could have been different. Contrary to a common-sense understanding of scientific and technological knowledge as cumulative, both can be, and have been, forgotten historically (Hacking 1983; Headrick 2009: 87–90; Wickham 2009). Moreover, the potential to lose technical know-how remains an ever-present possibility, as American nuclear weapons programmes have learnt in the post-Cold War era (Henke and Sims 2012). Essentialist claims to identify sequential technological development in history and portray the history and practice of technological innovation as the realization of an external natural logic. The political and moral judgements that result from such a position are evident (see Chapter 4). Nevertheless, just as instrumentalism captures an important aspect of human agency in the use of technologies, essentialism is valuable in highlighting the constraints technological systems place upon our political horizons. Retaining both of these insights is important for a reconfigured understanding of technology in world politics, and each approach outlined in this book does so in some measure.

Determinism, in its two variations, has operated as the primary conceptualization of technology in International Relations. Both perspectives have excluded the technological from our field of vision. The approaches outlined in this volume are driven, in part, by a concern to overcome these problems and return technological development and use to its place as a thoroughly social and historical phenomenon. Determinism remains signally important in the pursuit of technological closure; and, though determinism cannot provide a suitable framework for the study of global technopolitics, we should continue to study why this broadly discredited view of social life remains so prominent (Wyatt 2008; Winner 1977). The following discussion will outline some of the intellectual assumptions within IR that underpin determinist thought, before turning to consider the STS challenge to such approaches.

Things can be different: epistemological and ontological challenges to determinism

As noted above, precisely why the determinist vision of technology has dominated IR is not entirely clear, but three preliminary suggestions can be forwarded. First, determinist arguments often coincide with the dominant Humean or regularity view of causation in IR theory (Kurki 2008; Jackson 2011: 63–71; McCarthy 2015: 27). The regularity theory of causation defines cause as the constant conjunction between X and Y, in which X and Y do not stand in a necessary relationship. As necessity is not empirically observable in this view, we do not have grounds to know when a relationship is necessary or not (Kurki 2008: 33–59, *passim*; Manicas 2006). Offense–defense theory uses this form of explanation: it takes weapons technology as a given variable and then determines its impact on security competition. Without question, this form of explanation has its place in international relations when applied to specific problems with well-defined scope conditions; but in the study of technology and world politics it becomes problematic. It separates social life into distinct variables that exist prior to interaction with each other. As a result, questions around the constitution of the variables, their powers, their history and so forth, are not the focus of study (Kurki 2008: 36–39). Approaching the politics of technology in International Relations as if the social and the technological are atomistic variables – as we do when we ask whether certain weapons make warfare more or less likely – sidelines how the capacities of specific weapons are created, or how they are embedded and constitute specific forms of warfare. With society and technology viewed as variables, determinism becomes conceptually plausible.

Second, IR has often been guilty of ahistoricism, as scholars working at the intersection of historical sociology and IR theory have noted for some time (Buzan and Little 2000; Lawson 2012). IR theorists have traditionally not engaged with the sociological or historical study of science and technology – although, as this volume illustrates, this is changing. Failing to attend to the history of science and technology and their controversies leads to a presentation of technological development as linear and smooth (Collins and Pinch 1998: 155–177). As historians of science and technology have been documenting since the mid-1970s, the development of any given technology is fraught with personal conflicts, political disagreements, financial burdens, normative hurdles and any number of other problems that shape how technological objects come into being (Shapin and Schaffer 1985; Shapin 2010). The process of technological development is thoroughly political. We should ask not only whether drones or dreadnoughts make war more or less likely, but how they have come into being in the first place and what wider socio-technical reordering has occurred alongside their development.

Finally, and perhaps most significantly, International Relations has operated with an understanding of what constitutes scientific knowledge based upon a picture received predominantly from the positivist philosophy of science (Jackson 2011: 68–69). This understanding has relied upon a hierarchy of scientific practices in which physics, 'queen of the sciences', served as the model of scientific practice, while other equally established scientific fields, such as biology, did not (cf. Rose 1997: 4–20). 'Science', for mainstream positivist-inspired IR scholarship and for its critics (e.g. Booth 2008: 31), is generalized from one quite specific area of scientific practice in which 'law–like' predictive theories held sway, rather than from the contingency that characterizes biology's explanations.[12] There is a strong assumption in IR positivism that knowledge and the object of knowledge – what we know about a world that is independent of our minds – are separate. For positivists, our concepts and theories explain the world either more or less effectively; but they do not construct or produce the objects that are under study. An approach appropriate for one branch of science is thereby generalized as the required way to study the social sciences and humanities. 'Mind–world' dualism has significant implications for how we think about the relationship between science and culture, humans and nature, depending on where these lines are drawn.

Such an image of science is, at the very least, contestable. It ignores the practical, material process by which scientists produce results in the laboratory. Research scientists must gain skills in the manipulation of their objects of study – training worms and rats, honing biological assay abilities, carefully manufacturing technical apparatus (Collins and Pinch 1998; Shapin and Schaffer 1985). Technological artefacts are a central part of this social production, shaping what is investigated, how it is investigated and the findings that result (Bijker and Pinch 1987; Shapin and Schaffer 1985). Thus, if positivism prevents us asking questions about how successful scientific knowledge is created within given historical conditions, it also prevents us from inquiring into the technology–science relationship in any detail (Jackson 2011: 60). This has significant repercussions for how we consider the relationship between the technical and the social in global politics. Specific technological capacities produce certain images or understandings of the international, as illustrated in the impact of maps on notions of sovereignty (Branch 2013). For academics and policy-makers, knowledge of global politics is mediated by the objects we create.

Overcoming technological determinism in STS and STS-IR has required rejection of many of the causal and philosophical claims outlined above, claims that underpin the majority of scholarship in political science and IR (Jackson 2011: 60).

Indeed, one of the central goals of STS-IR has simply been to displace determinism as the common-sense position in IR theory. As we will see in the following chapters, there is no uniform approach to how we should displace determinism. Still, a few key shared claims of STS approaches to technology and their relevance to IR are worth emphasizing at the outset, both to set out its focus and to highlight how these generic arguments differ in their specific manifestations in the first half of the book. First, the STS approaches outlined in Part I are broadly constructivist in their approach to knowledge (Bijker 2010: 66). The basic thrust of constructivist perspectives in social theory is, of course, to stress the idea that things could be different – a perspective incompatible with technological determinism (Hacking 1999).

However, to claim that technology is socially constructed is not as simple as it sounds, and readers should be wary of drawing any straightforward epistemological or ontological conclusions from this statement. 'Social construction' can mean many things, and depends on many divergent understandings of 'nature' (Demeritt 2002). This is tricky terrain, and there is substantial disagreement in STS and SSK on precisely what is and what is not constructed in practices of science and technology, although this is perhaps less contentious for technology studies than for studies of laboratory science. The remarks offered here should be taken as the slightest sketch of a very large literature.

STS analyses of technology are broadly epistemologically constructivist because, drawing on SSK, they emphasize that the 'success' or 'failure' of objects – whether or not they are taken up and used – is not determined by laws of nature or a pre-social technological rationale (Bloor 1976; Latour and Woolgar 1986: 237). Rather, success or failure, often expressed in relation to whether or not a technology 'works', is produced by actors; or, to paraphrase a famous quote from International Relations, technology is always for someone or some purpose (Cox 1981).[13]

This claim is not all that radical, but it does overturn some ways of speaking about technology in IR, such as analysis of the 'objective' properties of military technologies undertaken by offense-defense theory mentioned above. Actors know a technology works not because it mirrors what is required by nature but because they define what working means. STS stresses that we should embrace the methodological principle of **symmetry** as a result. This entails that we explain *both* the success and the failure of objects as due to social factors. This does not mean that the natural world does not play a role in what we can plausibly say about such humanly created objects (Bloor 1999). After all, you can use a technological artefact to see its effects – either a gun fires or it does not. Rather, it means that the natural world is underdetermining how we understand, design, develop and use technological artefacts and systems. STS focuses on how scientific and technical knowledge is produced. Understood in these terms, the general epistemological claims of STS are directed against correspondence theories of truth, the idea that knowledge is defined by our ideas mirroring reality. However, if this accounts for how the groups of designers and users know when a technology works, it also raises questions about the theoretical **reflexivity** of STS scholarship: how is valid knowledge defined within social studies of science? How should social scientists judge whether an explanation succeeds or fails? We do not need to engage this question here – it has been well covered in IR (e.g. Booth et al. 1996) – but it is important to note given its heavy emphasis in STS.

Second, breaking down the division between the human and the non-human, or the social and the technical, requires that we reconsider how we understand the ontology of the social world – how we describe and analyse even basic social practices and what they are made of. While debates over philosophical realism and anti-realism have been important to SSK, they are less so for social studies of technology. Debating the reality of a technological artefact or system is implausible, hindering philosophically idealist claims in a way that debates over the very existence of the quarks do not (cf. Bijker 2010: 65–67). How we give meaning to an object does not change the existence of that object itself (but see Chapter 2). In changing our understanding of social ontology to include non-human artefacts and systems we begin to rethink how we talk about human practices. For instance, work becomes something no longer something done *on* laptops but *with* them: this introduction is being written by a human being, a computer processor, a keyboard and some software working together. Re-describing our social practices to account for the inevitably socio-technical character of human existence requires that some central categories of social theory are subsequently subject to significant revision. If social actions are socio-technical, fundamental social scientific concepts such as agency, system, power or structure may require serious reconsideration. To give one example, Actor-Network Theory (ANT) and New Materialist approaches have asserted that our understanding of social agents must be extended to include non-human objects; the resistance or assistance of artefacts cause social outcomes as much as human action (Latour 2005; Connolly 2010). It becomes important to consider how analytical categories built upon a division between the technical and the social may need to be rethought once this ontological divide is overcome.

Third, arguing for the dissolution of the divide between the technical and the social on constructivist grounds requires reconsideration of how we study the social world. Following the principle of symmetry requires using hermeneutics, ethnography, participant observation, discourse analysis, 'following the actors' and other interpretivist approaches to accounting for socio-technical practices. Similarly, historicizing technological design, development and use is of critical importance; as noted, a historical approach undercuts the tendency to determinism. Again, how these general methodological impulses are carried out varies between the approaches surveyed in this volume.

In sum, Science and Technology Studies presents epistemological, ontological and methodological points of engagement with International Relations. Broadening our understanding of science as a human practice entails describing the success or failure of scientific and technological endeavours in constructivist terms. STS is post-positivist and qualitative in orientation, sensitive to historical contexts and processes, and draws its ideas of science and technology from observation of what happens in the laboratory or the shop floor rather than from *a priori* theorizing (Bloor 1976; Shapin 2010). If this undercuts a level of certainty about scientific knowledge claims, it also opens up the material constitution of the social world for more sophisticated and nuanced treatment. Different configurations of these broadly shared analytical underpinnings carry distinct moral and political commitments, as the first half of this book demonstrates. Still, the core claim remains shared. Global politics is thoroughly socio-technical; anarchy is the product of people and machines; war is a practice of users and artefacts; and the politics of technological design are central to international political life. While this presents a serious challenge to some approaches in International Relations, it connects well with other strands of the field.

Locating STS-IR in the field of International Relations

As noted, STS-IR approaches to the study of world politics are epistemologically post-positivist (an admittedly problematic label), focused on rethinking the ontology of the international and qualitative in methodological orientation. This is a rather broad set of coordinates to be useful in situating where STS-IR approaches stand in a field traditionally defined in terms of 'isms' – realism, liberalism, Marxism, constructivism, feminism and so on, so a few brief remarks about where STS-IR is located in the larger field of International Relations are required.

Perhaps the first point to stress is that, with the partial exception of Critical Theories of Technology and Critical International Relations Theory, there is no direct mapping of any of the approaches studied here to any textbook framework of IR. No cohesive Realist or Liberal theory of technology in global politics exists. So, for instance, the Social Construction of Technology (SCOT) framework has been predominantly linked to the English School approach to global politics (e.g. Herrera 2006; Fritsch 2011); but SCOT approaches have equally been used to examine IR from feminist perspectives (Manjikian 2014). ANT represents a significant challenge to positivist IR theory and to substantive claims that assume the state-system as the principal object of study in IR, as in neo-realism (see Chapter 3). At the same time, the politics of ANT – its emphasis on struggle and strength in the creation of networks echoing Hobbes (Latour 1993) – is potentially closer to Realist IR theory than any other STS-IR alternatives. Both New Materialism and **posthumanist** approaches share an affinity with strands of IR – poststructuralist and systems theory-influenced scholarship, respectively – but neither is strongly wedded to any preconceived model of global politics in the IR 'schools of thought' understanding. The Critical Theory of Technology (CTT) approach is the lone standout in this regard in that it is explicitly located within and as a contribution to Critical IR Theory (see Chapter 4).

STS-IR is also not limited to a focus on any specific issue areas, even though its primary focus to date has been on issues that may be understood as 'technological'. STS-IR has empirically engaged with a range of empirical issues, including:

Internet governance and digital politics (Carr 2012; Ansorge 2015; McCarthy 2015); drone warfare (Holmqvist 2013); nuclear weapons (Peoples 2010; Sylvest 2013); border security technologies and data surveillance (Salter and Mutlu 2012); the politics of mapping technologies (Branch 2011), and so forth.[14] However, as the perspectives in this volume assert, all of global politics is necessarily socio-technical. As a result, STS-IR is not limited to the study of narrowly defined 'technological' issues, as illustrated by research on piracy, intervention and conflict, or financial markets (Bueger 2015; Smirl 2016; Porter 2013). Another way to say this is that STS-IR stretches across IR subfields such as Security Studies, International Political Economy, International Communication and International Organization. Technology and world politics is not itself a subfield of study. Any account of global political phenomena needs to account for its socio-technical character.

The best way of locating STS-IR may be to understand it as part of a shift within International Relations from a focus on epistemology to a focus on ontology. As noted above, STS is not terribly interested in setting out a priori grounds to define science or knowledge, preferring to study how actors define these in practice (see Chapter 3). STS-IR has emphasized substantive claims about the objects and processes of global politics. It has accentuated the development of concepts to study empirical aspects of global politics, rather than establishing deductive theoretical frameworks for testing. As a result, theory remains important to STS-IR (and IR in general), but it is increasingly focused on how to theorize the ontology of 'the International' (Rosenberg 2016; Wight 2006). As Jackson and Nexon note, the dividing lines within IR are increasingly divided by more fundamental claims about basic social ontologies, rather than the epistemological or methodological differences that characterized previous 'paradigm wars' in IR. In their re-classification of theory in IR, they suggest three potential overarching theoretical categorizations: choice-theoretic, experience-near and social-relational accounts (Jackson and Nexon 2013: 553–560). The first category, choice-theoretic approaches are generally positivist, rationalist and quantitative in orientation. No STS approaches fit comfortably within this ideal-type. By contrast, the other two categories capture important commonalities and distinctions between STS-IR frameworks. 'Experience-near' approaches are idiographic, interested in explaining specific events and process rather than making generalizable claims about world politics as a whole. Actor-Network Theory and New Materialisms can be located as 'experience-near' approaches given their stress on thick contextual description and distaste for the theoretical abstraction (Jackson and Nexon 2013: 556–557; see Conclusion). Critical Theories of Technology, Social Construction of Technology and (some) approaches to posthumanism embrace social-relational accounts that abstract from micro-level processes to account for large-scale, enduring social structures. Jackson and Nexon stress that there is clear overlap between these idealized categories and the same point applies to STS-IR – each STS approach is relational in some sense – but these points of distinction remain salient. Making sense of different STS-IR approaches in this manner helps us focus on substantive claims about international politics (see also Conclusion). If STS-IR is not easily understood through an emphasis on the relative importance of power politics or cooperation in anarchy, as per traditional Realist–Liberal debates, it is nevertheless embedded within the central dynamics of a changing field.

Plan of the book

With these ground-clearing remarks in mind we can now proceed to outline the format of the book. This volume is comprised of two complementary halves. The first half presents readers with an introduction to the various theoretical perspectives that IR scholars have drawn on while studying the place of technology in international politics – the Social Construction of Technology (SCOT), ANT, Critical Theories of Technology and New Materialisms. These chapters present an introduction to each approach and their relationship to IR. They draw out the affinities and the differences that exist between STS-IR perspectives, distinguishing, for example, the anti-humanist New Materialisms from the humanist emphasis of the Critical Theory of Technology. These distinctions are important; the temptation to import concepts and categories wholesale from Science and Technology Studies risks overlooking the debates and disputations within that field. Each of the theories reviewed has its own distinct intellectual history and its own problems, gaps and shortcomings. Careful attention to these issues will help avoid the simple 'bolting on' of sociological categories to International Relations theory, and vice versa.

Part I, 'Theories', begins with Mary Manjikian's introduction to SCOT perspectives. SCOT approaches have been foundational in the development of sociological studies of technology, and were one of the first explicit points of engagement for IR scholars interested in the question of technology (Herrera 2002). Manjikian's chapter outlines the different bodies of scholarship that fall under the SCOT banner, from those integrating determinism and constructivism to more radical constructivist approaches. In Chapter 3 Christian Bueger and Jan Stockbruegger introduce Actor-Network Theory (ANT). ANT is perhaps the most high-profile approach from STS now employed in International Relations, with a more clearly defined research community than the other approaches examined. ANT may present the most radical theoretical challenge to traditional International Relations theory, as Bueger and Stockbruegger highlight in their consideration of the power of scallops and the centrality of the bush pump to Zimbabwean nationalism. Together, SCOT and ANT have been the primary points of intellectual engagement for IR scholars.

If ANT is (possibly) the most theoretically disruptive approach surveyed, the most politically radical is outlined in Chapter 4, covering the Critical Theory of Technology. Informed by the critique of political economy and the diverse philosophical heritage of Marxism, it stresses the centrality of capitalism in the generation and shaping of technological innovation. The final theoretical offering, Chapter 5 by Nick Srnicek, introduces readers to 'New Materialisms' – a diverse set of perspectives influenced by Continental philosophy. This chapter represents a slight departure from the previous chapters, as its primary source of inspiration is not the field of Science and Technology Studies. Instead, New Materialist scholarship is inspired by a creative combination of social theory and Continental philosophy, neurobiology and complexity theory. Each of the theoretical chapters will note how the integration of social theories of technology improves our understanding of world politics empirically but, crucially, also how these theories can help readers rethink key concepts in International Relations, such as power, anarchy, law, sovereignty, agency, structure and international system/society. Introducing readers to cutting-edge theoretical debates in the social sciences, the first half of the book should also prompt reflection on where future theoretical work in this area may lead. To this end, readers should think of Part I as the beginning of a conversation for STS-IR rather than an accounting of its aftermath.

Part II of the volume is, for lack of a better term, the operationalization of the theoretical introductions. That is, each of the issue-specific chapters employs analytical tools outlined and discussed in at least one of the theoretical chapters. As a result, each theoretical chapter has at least one empirical counterpart. Roughly – for there is overlapping use of different theoretical approaches within certain empirical chapters – this correspondence is as follows. Joseph P. Masco's Chapter 6 on nuclear weapons, while rooted in anthropology, has shared theoretical kinships to ANT, Critical Theory and New Materialisms. Monroe Price's piece on Internet foreign policies in Chapter 7 draws on both SCOT and CTT, although with greater emphasis on the former. Chapter 8 by Alejandro Colás on the infrastructure of the global economy, exemplified by the shipping container, resonates with both Chapters 3 and 4 on ANT and Marxism, respectively. Antoine Bousquet's Chapter 9 on the revolution in military affairs and the application of techno-science to warfighting echoes some of the theoretical and conceptual approaches discussed in Chapter 5. Chapter 10 on space politics, written by Columba Peoples, is linked to Chapter 4's discussion of CTT. The final issue-focused contribution, Chapter 11, presents Jairus Victor Grove's New Materialist and Posthumanist-inspired approach to the geopolitics of the **Anthropocene**.

While the first and second halves of the volume complement each other, and while engagement with each half will be of particular benefit to readers new to this area of scholarship, the second half of the volume may also be read as a set of stand-alone essays one can dip into without recourse to the other parts of the book. Readers familiar with the theoretical apparatus of SCOT can engage directly with Price's chapter on Internet governance, for instance, or seasoned ANTs can see what Colás has to say about shipping containers. Throughout, theoretical terms that may be novel to readers unfamiliar with Science and Technology Studies are in bold text and can be found in the Glossary at the end of the book. This sets out key concepts in STS and social theory that may be unfamiliar to students of International Relations, such as symmetry or **actant**. If readers encounter a term in a given chapter that is confusing or unfamiliar this should be the first port of call. The second appendix provides a series of suggestions for further reading. Areas covered in this list include seminal readings from SSK, key texts from specific theoretical approaches in STS, and a list of introductory textbooks in STS. The further reading list, while detailed, is not comprehensive by any means, and serves as a prompt to further investigation alongside the references listed at the end of each chapter.

The Conclusion summarizes the contents of the book. In the process of undertaking this reflection, it will also suggest possible future areas of research and study that scholars and students of technology and IR may pursue. Rather than recapping the contours of a settled area of study, it will outline where this dynamic area of scholarship may head next. This decision is partly pragmatic – no settled area exists at the moment – but is also driven by a desire to open up further areas of debate and research. The STS-IR synthesis remains at a very early stage of development; readers of this volume will, hopefully, find their own thoughts on how this project should proceed enriched through engagement with its arguments.

Notes

1 The phrase is commonly attributed to Benjamin Franklin. This designation of humans as unique in being tool-making animals is inaccurate – bonobos, for example, craft and use rudimentary tools.
2 It is sufficient for our purposes to define technology as objects, artefacts and systems in keeping with its general use in IR. STS definitions such as Bijker's – 'Technology comprises, first, artefacts and technical systems, second the knowledge about these and, third, the practices of handling these artefacts and systems' (Bijker 2010: 64) – put the cart before the horse for this chapter.
3 SSK formed part of a general reaction against 'high modernist' orthodoxy in the social sciences – typified by Talcott Parsons' structural-functionalism, Walt Rostow's stagist modernization theory of development, and various 'end of ideology' theses – and its political quiescence in the face of the ruptures of the 1960s and early 1970s, with Vietnam, Algeria, decolonization, the civil rights movement and May 1968 foremost among these. See Bernstein (1976) and Feenberg (1999: 21–43).
4 Indicative of this are the number of journal special issues devoted to these approaches – see *Cambridge Review of International Affairs* (2009), *Millennium* (2013) and *International Political Sociology* (2013).
5 It should be noted that Wendt is inconsistent on this claim, as he also stresses a 'rump materialism' as important to his account of international politics and notes that technology is a social and historical product (1999: 110–113).
6 Latin meaning 'God from the machine', this refers to the dramatic device whereby a person or thing is dropped into a plot in order to resolve an irresolvable problem.
7 This ground is deeply contested within STS and the philosophy of science – key arguments are laid out in Pickering (1992) and Hollis and Lukes (1982). Booth et al. (1996) is an edited collection featuring various perspectives on these issues as they apply to International Relations. More recent book-length treatments of philosophy of science in IR include Wight (2006), Kurki (2008) and Jackson (2011).
8 Authors working in IR, including the present author, have repeated these criticisms in nearly every article or book on the integration of STS and IR. See Wyn Jones (1999), Herrera (2006), Peoples (2010), Carr (2012), Fritsch (2011), McCarthy (2013) and Sylvest (2013).
9 But see Edgerton (1999: 120–122) for a brief discussion of how determinism can be differentiated between *innovation* determinism and *technological* determinism.

10 While guns may not be able to discern good or bad intentions, this being difficult enough for people, this does not mean that the technology does not express specific social norms, such as the ability to end lives quickly and effectively at a distance.

11 Gun manufacturers list the purposes of their weapons in their catalogues – hunting, law enforcement, personal protection, home security and so forth. See www.smith-wesson.com and www.remington.com for examples.

12 Jackson (2011) provides an excellent discussion. See also Wight (2006), Kurki (2008) and Smith (1996).

13 It is this claim that vexed certain scholars and scientists during the 'Science Wars' of the 1990s. Turner (2003) offers a good critical recapping of these debates.

14 Please note this list is far from exhaustive.

References

Ashworth, Lucian M. 2011. Realism and the Spirit of 1919: Halford Mackinder, Geopolitics, and the Reality of the League of Nations. *European Journal of International Relations* 17(2): 279–301.

Berger, Peter and Thomas Luckmann. 1967. *The Social Construction of Reality: A Treatise in the Sociology of Knowledge*. London: Penguin.

Bernstein, Richard J. 1976. *The Restructuring of Social and Political Theory*. Oxford: Blackwell.

Bijker, Wiebe. 2010. How is Technology Made? That is the Question! *Cambridge Journal of Economics* 34(1): 63–76.

Bijker, Wiebe E., Thomas Hughes and Trevor Pinch (eds). 1987. *The Social Construction of Technological Systems*. Cambridge, MA: MIT Press.

Bloor, David. 1976. *Knowledge and Social Imagery*. London: Routledge.

Bloor, David. 1999. Anti-Latour. *Studies in the History and Philosophy of Science* 30(1): 81–112.

Booth, Ken. 2008. *Theory of World Security*. Cambridge: Cambridge University Press.

Booth, Ken, Steve Smith and Marysia Zalewski (eds). 1996. *International Theory: Positivism and Beyond*. Cambridge: Cambridge University Press.

Branch, Jordan. 2011. Mapping the Sovereign State: Technology, Authority, and Systemic Change. *International Organization* 65(1): 1–36.

Bueger, Christian. 2015. Making Things Known: Epistemic Practices, the United Nations, and the Translation of Piracy. *International Political Sociology* 9(1): 1–18.

Buzan, Barry. 1991. *People, States and Fear: An Agenda for International Security Studies in the Post Cold War Era*. Brighton: Harvester Wheatsheaf.

Buzan, Barry and Lene Hansen. 2009. *The Evolution of International Security Studies*. Cambridge: Cambridge University Press.

Buzan, Barry and Richard Little. 2000. *International Systems in World History*. Cambridge: Cambridge University Press.

Carr, E.H. 1939. *The Twenty Years' Crisis, 1919–1939: An Introduction to the Study of International Relations*. New York: Harper.

Carr, Madeline. 2012. The Political History of the Internet: A Theoretical Approach to the Implications for US Power. In Sean S. Costigan and Jake Perry (eds) *Information Technology and International Affairs*. Farnham: Ashgate.

Cohen, G.A. 1978. *Karl Marx's Theory of History: A Defence*. Princeton, NJ: Princeton University Press.

Connolly, William. 2010. *A World of Becoming*. Baltimore, MD: Johns Hopkins University Press.

Cox, Robert W. 1981. Social Forces, States and World Orders: Beyond International Relations Theory. *Millennium: Journal of International Studies* 10(2): 126–155.

Craig, Campbell. 2003. *Glimmer of a New Leviathan: Total War in the Realism of Niebuhr, Morgenthau and Waltz*. New York: Columbia University Press.

Demeritt, David. 2002. What is the 'Social Construction of Nature'? A Typology and Sympathetic Critique. *Progress in Human Geography* 26(2): 767–790.

DeNardis, Laura. 2009. *Protocol Politics: The Globalization of Internet Governance*. Cambridge, MA: MIT Press.

Deudney, Daniel. 2008. *Bounding Power: Republican Security Theory from the Polis to the Global Village*. Princeton, NJ: Princeton University Press.

Edgerton, David. 1999. From Innovation to Use: Ten Eclectic Theses on the Historiography of Technology. *History and Technology* 16(2): 111–136.

Feenberg, Andrew. 1999. *Questioning Technology*. London: Routledge.

Feenberg, Andrew. 2002. *Transforming Technology: A Critical Theory Revisited*. Oxford: Oxford University Press.

Freeman, Chris. 1995. The 'National System of Innovation' in Historical Perspective. *Cambridge Journal of Economics* 19(1): 5–24.

Fritsch, Stefan. 2011. Technology and Global Affairs. *International Studies Perspectives* 12(1): 27–45.

Gerschenkron, Alexander. 1962. *Economic Backwardness in Historical Perspective*. Cambridge, MA: Belknap Press of Harvard University Press.

Glaser, Charles L. 2010. *Rational Theory of International Politics: The Logic of Competition and Cooperation*. Princeton, NJ: Princeton University Press.

Hacking, Ian. 1999. *The Social Construction of What?* Cambridge, MA: Harvard University Press.

Headrick, Daniel R. 2009. *Technology: A World History*. Oxford: Oxford University Press.

Herrera, Geoffrey. 2002. The Politics of Bandwidth: International Political Implications of a Global Digital Information Network. *Review of International Studies* 28(1): 93–122.

Herrera, Geoffrey. 2006. *Technology and International Transformation: The Railroad, the Atom Bomb, and the Politics of Technical Change*. Albany: State University of New York Press.

Herz, John. 1950. Idealist Internationalism and the Security Dilemma. *World Politics* 2(2): 157–180.

Hollis, Martin and Steven Lukes (eds). 1982. *Rationality and Relativism*. Oxford: Blackwell.

Holmqvist, Caroline. 2013. Undoing War: War Ontologies and the Materiality of Drone Warfare. *Millennium: Journal of International Studies* 14(3): 535–552.

Horowitz, Michael C., Sarah E. Kreps and Matthew Furhmann. 2016. Separating Fact from Fiction in the Debate over Drone Proliferation. *International Security* 41(2): 7–42.

Hughes, Thomas P. 1983. *Networks of Power: Electrification of Western Society, 1880–1930*. Cambridge, MA: MIT Press.

Jackson, Patrick Thaddeus. 2011. *The Conduct of Inquiry in International Relations*. London: Routledge.

Jackson, Patrick Thaddeus and Daniel Nexon. 2013. International Theory in a Post-Paradigmatic Era: From Substantive Wagers to Scientific Ontologies. *European Journal of International Relations* 19(3): 543–565.

Jervis, Robert. 1978. Cooperation under the Security Dilemma. *World Politics* 30(2): 167–214.

Kaldor, Mary. 2007. *New and Old Wars: Organized Violence in a Global Era*, 2nd edition. Stanford, CA: Stanford University Press.

Keohane, R.O. and J.S. Nye. 1989. *Power and Interdependence*, 2nd edition. Boston, MA: HarperCollins.

Kuhn, Thomas. 1962. *The Structure of Scientific Revolutions*. Chicago, IL: University of Chicago Press.

Kurki, Milja. 2008. *Causation in International Relations: Reclaiming Causal Analysis*. Cambridge: Cambridge University Press.

Latour, Bruno. 1993. *We Have Never Been Modern*. Cambridge, MA: Harvard University Press.

Latour, Bruno. 1994. On Technical Mediation: Philosophy, Sociology, Genealogy. *Common Knowledge* 3(2): 29–64.

Latour, Bruno. 2005. *Reassembling the Social: An Introduction to Actor-Network-Theory*. Oxford: Oxford University Press.

Latour, Bruno and Steve Woolgar. 1979. *Laboratory Life: The Construction of Scientific Facts*. Beverly Hills, CA: SAGE.

Lawson, George. 2012. The Eternal Divide? History and International Relations. *European Journal of International Relations* 18(2): 203–226.

Levy, Jack S. 1984. The Offense–Defense Balance of Military Technology: A Theoretical and Historical Analysis. *International Studies Quarterly* 28(2): 219–238.

Lieber, Keir. 2000. Grasping the Technological Peace: The Offense–Defense Balance and International Security. *International Security* 25(1): 71–104.

Lynn-Jones, Sean M. 1995. Offense–Defense Theory and Its Critics. *Security Studies* 4(4): 660–691.

Mackenzie, Donald. 1990. *Inventing Accuracy: A Historical Sociology of Nuclear Missile Guidance*. Cambridge, MA: MIT Press.

Manicas, Peter. 2006. *A Realist Philosophy of Social Science*. Cambridge: Cambridge University Press.

Marcuse, Herbert. 1968. *Negations: Essays in Critical Theory*. London: Penguin.

Marx, Leo. 2010. Technology: The Emergence of a Hazardous Concept. *Technology and Culture* 51(3): 561–577.

Masco, Joseph P. 2006. *Nuclear Borderlands: The Manhattan Project in Post-Cold War New Mexico*. Princeton, NJ: Princeton University Press.

McCarthy, Daniel R. 2011. Open Networks and the Open Door: American Foreign Policy and the Narration of the Internet. *Foreign Policy Analysis* 7(1): 89–111.

McCarthy, Daniel R. 2013. Technology and the 'International', or How I Learned to Stop Worrying and Love Determinism. *Millennium: Journal of International Studies* 41(3): 470–490.

McCarthy, Daniel R. 2015. *Power, Information Technology and International Relations Theory: The Power and Politics of US Foreign Policy and the Internet*. Basingstoke: Palgrave Macmillan.

Morgenthau, Hans. 1946. *Scientific Man vs. Power Politics*. Chicago, IL: University of Chicago Press.

Morgenthau, Hans. 1949. *Politics among Nations: The Struggle for Power and Peace*. New York: McGraw-Hill.

Niebuhr, Reinhold. 1932. *Moral Man and Immoral Society*. London: Bloomsbury.

Osiander, Andres. 1998. Re-Reading Early Twentieth-Century IR: Idealism Revisited. *International Studies Quarterly* 42(3): 409–432.

Parker, Geoffrey. 1996. *The Military Revolution: Military Innovation and the Rise of the West, 1500–1800*. Cambridge: Cambridge University Press.

Peoples, Columba. 2010. *Justifying Ballistic Missile Defence: Technology, Security and Culture*. Cambridge: Cambridge University Press.

Pickering, Andrew (ed.). 1992. *Science as Practice and Culture*. Chicago, IL: University of Chicago Press.

Pickering, Andrew. 1993. The Mangle of Practice: Agency and Emergence in the Sociology of Science. *American Journal of Sociology* 99(3): 559–589.

Porter, Tony. 2013. Tracing Association in Global Finance. *International Political Sociology* 7(3): 334–338.

Rose, Steven. 1997. *Lifelines: Biology, Freedom, Determinism*. London: Allen Lane.

Rosenau, James N. 2002. Governance in a New Global Order. In David Held and Anthony McGrew (eds) *Governing Globalization: Power, Authority and Global Governance*. Cambridge: Polity.

Rosenau, James N. 2005. Illusions of Power and Empire? *History and Theory* 44(4): 73–87.

Rosenberg, Justin. 2005. Globalization Theory: A Post Mortem. *International Politics* 42(1): 2–74.

Rosenberg, Justin. 2006. Why is There No International Historical Sociology? *European Journal of International Relations* 12(3): 7–40.

Salter, Mark B. and Can E. Mutlu. 2012. Psychoanalytic Theory and Border Security. *European Journal of Social Theory* 15(2): 179–195.

Scheuerman, William. 2007. Was Morgenthau a Realist? Revisiting Scientific Man vs. Power Politics. *Constellations* 14(4): 506–530.

Scholte, Jan Art. 2005. *Globalization: A Critical Introduction*. Basingstoke: Palgrave Macmillan.

Schweller, Randall. 2014. *Maxwell's Demon and the Golden Apple: Global Discord in the New Millennium*. Baltimore, MD: Johns Hopkins University Press.

Selinger, Evan. 2012. The Philosophy of the Technology of the Gun. *The Atlantic*, 23 July. Available at: www.theatlantic.com/technology/archive/12/07/the-philosophy-of-the-technology-of-the-gun/260220/. Accessed 19 September 2014.

Shapin, Steven and Simon Schaffer. 1985. *Leviathan and the Air-Pump: Hobbes, Boyle and the Experimental Life*. Princeton, NJ: Princeton University Press.

Sims, Benjamin and Christopher R. Henke. 2012. Repairing Credibility: Repositioning Nuclear Weapons Knowledge after the Cold War. *Social Studies of Science* 42(3): 324–347.

Smirl, Lisa. 2016. 'Not Welcome at the Holiday Inn': How a Sarajevan Hotel Influenced Geo-Politics. *Journal of Intervention and Statebuilding* 10(1): 32–55.

Smith, Steve. 1996. Positivism and Beyond. In Ken Booth, Steve Smith and Marysia Zalewski (eds) *International Theory: Positivism and Beyond*. Cambridge: Cambridge University Press.

Sylvest, Casper. 2013. Technology and Global Politics: The Modern Experiences of Bertrand Russell and John H. Herz. *International History Review* 35(1): 121–142.

Turner, Stephen. 2003. The Third Science War. *Social Studies of Science* 33(4): 581–611.

Waltz, Kenneth. 1981. The Spread of Nuclear Weapons: More May Be Better. *Adelphi Papers* 171: 1–32.

Wendt, Alexander. 1999. *Social Theory of International Politics*. Cambridge: Cambridge University Press.

White, Lynn H. 1962. *Medieval Technology and Social Change*. Oxford: Clarendon.

Wickham, Chris. 2009. *The Inheritance of Rome: A History of Europe from 400 to 1000*. London: Penguin.

Wight, Colin. 2006. *Agents, Structures and International Relations: Politics as Ontology*. Cambridge: Cambridge University Press.

Winner, Langdon. 1978. *Autonomous Technology: Technics-Out-of-Control as a Theme in Political Thought*. Cambridge, MA: MIT Press.

Wyn Jones, Richard. 1999. *Security, Strategy and Critical Theory*. Boulder, CO: Lynne Rienner.

Zimmern, Alfred. 1928. The Prospects for Democracy. *International Affairs* 7(3): 153–191.

PART I
Theories

2

SOCIAL CONSTRUCTION OF TECHNOLOGY

How objects acquire meaning in society

Mary Manjikian

Ask any analyst to gaze into the future and describe what life will be like in ten or twenty years and, chances are, that analyst will reference technology somewhere in that answer. Some will undoubtedly offer a utopian take on our future – describing a world where individuals are healthier, wealthier, more tightly connected to one another, better informed and more able to communicate, share information and collaborate. To these analysts, the future promises greater equality, greater efficiency, greater speed and greater creativity – all enabled by technologies like three-dimensional printers, ubiquitous computing and advances like virtual reality. Others will undoubtedly offer a much more pessimistic glimpse into our putative future: forecasting the development of a tiered system of information haves and have-nots; a growth in new and better technologies of global surveillance; a system where rights appear to belong to information and those who collect it rather than to individuals, amidst wider projects of ad hoc geoengineering and the global diffusion of advanced weapons and other forms of technologically enabled instability (Smith 2014; Morozov 2011; Manjikian 2015).[1]

What is striking in these two competing visions is that each associates new technologies with particular values, particular ideological stances, and that each group attributes some degree of agency to technology itself. This common-sense notion of technology mirrors, in some respects, the way anarchy in international politics has been viewed as an established and unchanging fact. In 1992, Alexander Wendt famously stated that 'anarchy is what states make of it' in relation to the state system (Wendt 1992; Wendt 1999). Outlining the constructivist school of International Relations (IR) he asserted – against Realist IR theory (cf. Waltz 2010 [1979]) – that the structures of the international system were not so much permanent and unchanging as they were socially created and dynamic. Wendt noted that politicians and experts both had the ability to 'do things with words', in essence using language to create particular state identities, norms and understandings of how the world works, thereby establishing friendships, rivalries and alliances which could be both done and undone through the power of language. Wendt argued that IR theorists had erred in attributing so much causal power to the structure of international system and material factors like the balance of power, ignoring the ways in which individuals and groups exercised agency in creating and maintaining the logic of anarchy. State behaviour towards that system, he argued, had important implications for the properties of the international system itself (Wendt 1999). Wendt's intervention prompted a sustained debate in IR as to whether material factors or ideas, interests or identities were the central motivating causal force in international politics.

As we think about the role of technology in international relations, a similar set of questions emerges: To what degree do technological systems and artefacts, bearing a set of values and use regimes, cause its users to behave in certain ways? And to what degree do users themselves – either individually or collectively – have the ability to shape how new technologies are used and the roles which they will come to play in our lives, in our communities and in the wider international system? The relationship between structure and agency in the politics of technology is central to determining how, if at all, we can shape our possible technological futures.

As Steve Woolgar and Javier Lezaun (2013) note, the traditional formulation put forth by political scientists is that politics is about 'who gets what when and how', as famously stated by Harold Lasswell (1936). According to this formulation, politics is about distribution: Who gets resources and who doesn't get them, and why? While important, the nature of the 'what' that is distributed is often sidelined in political science and international relations, black boxed to focus primarily on Lasswell's questions. Science and Technology Studies (STS) in IR asks us to focus on the 'what': What are the material qualities of the resources that are being distributed and used? Why were the resources created and realized in this way in the first place, rather than in some other way? STS-IR approaches allow us to extend Wendt's project to consider the social construction of technology in global politics.

This chapter will discuss these issues through an engagement with Social Construction of Technology (SCOT) perspectives. In contrast to popular images of technological innovation as the production of brilliant lone innovators, SCOT outlines a complex relationship between designers, interest groups and the wider social environment. We will introduce central SCOT concepts – such as technological closure, **momentum**, path dependency, **reverse salient**, and the first-mover advantage – to outline a middle way between determinism and constructivism. This perspective is not uniform, of course. Another variant of social constructionism, radical constructivism, asserts that a technology's meaning cannot be understood apart from the language or discourse which exists to describe it. We will thereby outline this approach and consider its emphasis on **interpretive flexibility**. The indeterminacy of physical objects for radical constructivists means that different societies and cultures can interpret a technology and its meaning differently, both across time and at the same moment in time. This view of the constraints exercised by the material composition of technological artefacts represents the central divide within SCOT. Finally, we look towards the future, speculating about how SCOT may explain new and emerging technologies and a new environment in which technological innovation is increasingly bottom-up rather than top-down.

Beyond the individual innovator: the Social Construction of Technology

As noted, the characteristics of a tool are not natural or fixed, but rather arise initially as a result of design decisions. The power of the individual designer or innovator to shape society features heavily in our popular imaginations, in the figures of a Thomas Edison, Nikolai Tesla, Steve Jobs or Elon Musk. Designers often have the power to shape who can and cannot use a tool, as well as the conditions under which the tool might be used. Designers thereby, consciously and unconsciously, carry out a policing function helping to establish what constitutes a correct or incorrect use of a tool or technology. In this way, one can argue that 'artefacts have politics' – designers can build their political biases into technological artefacts (Winner 1980). Design decisions have political effects that manifest in a variety of ways. They may limit the groups that are empowered by new technologies. Groups excluded from the use of a new technology might include those of the 'wrong' gender, 'wrong' age group or those with disabilities. For example, a designer might create a piece of farm equipment which is extremely heavy and therefore more likely to be used by men. Or a kitchen designer might create appliances which are 'feminine' in appearance – such as a pink refrigerator. An object may thus come to be associated with a certain social class, a certain set of practices or values or a certain gender either because a designer intentionally decides to create tools which are exclusionary or, less consciously, makes design decisions that reflect the biases which exist within a particular era.

In the United States, a White House Commission formed to look at the problem of gendered toys suggested that fewer women may pursue science and technology careers as adults since they had less access to construction and engineering toys as children. Design decisions of even simple everyday objects, like toys, may be central to sustaining specific forms of life over the long term. Even decisions which affect the price of an item have the effect of setting parameters for who may acquire the technology, since it may not be economically accessible to all who desire to use it.

Those who are excluded may not be considered by designers as relevant actors whose needs are important, and these same individuals may not have the resources to come together to demand changes to the technological specifications once tools are created. Here, for example, we can consider the ongoing debate in the United States about the role of women in military combat. For many years, those who opposed the inclusion of women in combat pointed to physiological differences between men and women, and the physical limitations women might thus encounter in a combat role. Women were told that the equipment they would be asked to carry was too heavy, that the guns were too big and that they would encounter inadequate bathroom facilities in the field. However, in recent years, technological advances have rendered most of these arguments moot. Today, women – and men – can engage in combat using computer-mediated drone strikes, fighting from a desktop at an air base in Nevada; and, in situations where ground troops are used, new types of robots can carry heavy equipment, while wearable exoskeletons can be used to augment an individual's own capabilities to lift and carry objects. In this new environment, one can no longer argue that physical specifications should exclude women from combat.

The problem with focusing on designer intent alone, however, is that it grants too much agency to designers. It allows us to circumvent technological determinism (see Introduction), but at a cost. In particular, it assumes that every decision a designer makes in developing a new technology is made consciously, with an eye towards all of the possible social, economic and political ramifications of these decisions – even when it is doubtful that designers can anticipate all of these ends. And in some instances a designer may be particularly focused on achieving one particular end – such as moving packets of information across the Internet in the most efficient way possible – and may as a result build other values and ethics into a technology along the way, not consciously, but almost accidentally.

SCOT broadens the designer-centric picture of innovation in a number of ways. In their seminal 1984 work, sociologist Trevor Pinch and philosopher Wiebe Bijker presented the foundational account of SCOT, merging ideas from the philosophy of technology with sociological insights gleaned from the Sociology of Scientific Knowledge (SSK) and social theories of power. In contrast to the picture of the heroic and powerful innovator, they placed the design of technological objects within a wider social and historical context. Technological developments are not merely the result of specific decisions enacted by specific individuals or groups, as they often are in popular accounts of innovation, but are part of more general sociological processes in which multiple actors are participants. Designers and manufacturers have particular visions of how a technology will be used in society, who will use it and what it will mean. But, Pinch and Bijker argued, the intentions of designers are entangled with multiple actors and in specific, and complex, historical contexts. Artefacts take on a particular shape as the result of social, political, economic and normative struggles between manufacturers, users, designers and a host of other interested parties.

In contrast to the technological determinism of traditional accounts of technology, Pinch and Bijker argued that, in order to understand how technology is created, one has to break down the division between the social and the technical. SCOT suggests that new technologies are created within a world that is social and technological, using the term 'socio-technical' to capture the deeply integrated and co-constitutive nature of these relations.[2] While engineers physically construct or make an object, interest groups also construct the object – by virtue of the language they use to describe the object, the ways in which it is marketed and sold, and the ways in which it is regulated and understood.

SCOT approaches use a number of concepts and metaphors to capture how technologies are connected to one another and to the social world in which they are constituted and used, referring to a 'network', 'web' or 'system' of technologies (Hughes 1987; Bijker 2010). However, unlike approaches such as Actor-Network Theory (ANT), in SCOT systems or networks are understood to be embedded within contexts that have certain pre-existing parameters and constraints which help shape technologies.[3] At the same time, SCOT does not emphasize which actors will be most important in a given social context prior to empirical investigation, in contrast to the Critical Theory of Technology's stress on the importance of modes of production in defining powerful actors. In a now classic example, Pinch and Bijker (1984) asked readers to consider the debates that occurred when the first bicycle was invented: between manufacturers who sought to maintain bicycling as an elite leisure activity performed by men who engaged in daring races and disenfranchised groups who also clamoured for access to the technology which would provide them with increased mobility, freedom and economic opportunities in society. Victorian ladies pressed for modifications that would allow them to bicycle while wearing skirts.

The bicycle became an instrument of commerce as well, used for making deliveries and ferrying salespeople through a larger territory. The technology did not belong to one group only – due to either facets of the technology or the designer's intent. Instead, the design was modified in response to diverse social pressures, and in the long run the technology of bicycling ended up looking quite different from how it was originally envisioned by its designers and manufacturers. Even today, it may look different in a wealthy society than it does in a less wealthy society, where the bicycle may still serve as a means of conducting economic activities as well as providing the family's only means of transportation.

Ultimately, meaning emerges as the result of negotiations between technological constraints and social groups, which Pinch and Bijker term 'relevant actors', who can only be determined in the course of empirical investigation. They thus refer to a 'co-evolution' which leads to the specification of a particular role for a tool. The function of the bicycle emerged in society through the actions of many individuals and groups until it stabilized through technological closure (Pinch and Bijker 1984: 426–428). Technological closure, the process by which the meaning of a given technology is settled, defined a specific version of the bicycle as acceptable.

For SCOT approaches, the success or failure of a new technology is thus not straightforward. It is possible for a technology to 'fail' if its parameters are far out of step with what society is ready for and willing to accept. In other words, whether or not a technology 'fails' or 'succeeds' is determined by social factors, not the natural form which a given object must take. SCOT thereby embraces the principle of symmetry – the need to explain technological success and failure using the same factors (Bijker et al. 1987: 8). Here, for example, we can consider the failed attempt in 2001 by Dean Kamen to convince individuals to ditch their cars for the Segway a two-wheeled, battery-powered, individual vehicle. Despite a high-profile launch of this product, it failed to find a niche within the transportation market – not because there was anything technologically wrong with it (it 'worked'), but because consumers couldn't figure out what it was or why they needed one (it was not economically successful), and government regulators couldn't figure out how it might be regulated.

The technology, while innovative and different, was not seen as solving a clear problem or providing a solution to an identified need (Sloane 2012). A technology has both a physical and symbolic meaning; the symbolic process of defining the meaning of a new technology and the forms of society it enables (or prevents) is central to SCOT. As we will note, scholars working within a SCOT framework have introduced central concepts such as momentum, reverse salient and first-mover advantage to describe some of the limits to agency imposed by these processes, discussed via the analysis of large technical systems (LTS) and ordinary household objects (Pinch and Bijker 1984; Bijker et al. 1987; in IR, see Herrera 2006; Fritsch 2011; Carr 2012; Sylvest 2013). The relationship between these limits to agency and the scope for interpretive flexibility is discussed in a later section.

Enduring technologies: momentum, path dependence, reverse salients and the first-mover advantage

SCOT analysts have arrived at a number of ways of thinking about how the environment can and does constrain the designer's agency. Technological momentum, reverse salient and first-mover advantage are concepts used to capture the limits to designers' (and users') agency in the deployment of technological objects. In 1969, Thomas Hughes introduced the idea of technological momentum. He argued that a new technology does not develop in isolation, but rather as part of a large technical system which has both technological and social or human components. The technology's evolution is driven by both these forces, with different forces exercising greater influence at different parts of the cycle. He argues that new technologies might initially be the subject of social control – showing how, for example, communities in America were able to organize against the further development of nuclear power due to fears of contamination and risks from reactor leaks (Hughes 1994). However, Hughes argues that, over time, a technology comes to exert influence over the individuals in the system as well:

> The degree of freedom exercised by people in a system ... depends on the maturity and size, or the autonomy of a technological system ... Old systems like old people, tend to become less adaptable but systems do not simply grow frail and fade away. Large systems with high momentum tend to exert a soft determinism on other systems, groups and individuals in society.
>
> *(Hughes 1987: 54–55)*

Hughes, while highlighting the constructedness of technology at one phase of its 'life cycle', also captures its determination of society over time. Technological determinism is not a natural fact, but itself the product of closure produced by human agents.

Technological objects are comprised of many parts. What consumers, for example, might view as a new or improved consumer product (such as a new type of computer, washing machine or automobile) is actually the combination of technological developments in a number of hierarchically arranged sub-systems which come together to form the consumer product as a whole. The development of both individual artefacts and LTS relies upon sub-systems that comprise them. Within SCOT, the military concept of the reverse salient describes the process whereby the constituent parts that enable a larger object may not all develop at the same rate. The different speeds of sub-system development can create reverse salients that can impede the momentum of a system. As a result, technological advances for the device as a whole can be either moved forward or held back by technological limitations or advances within a constituent sub-system.

In looking at the design of video-gaming systems, Dedehayir and Mäkinen (2011) argue that game developers cannot simply design any game they want. Rather, they have to consider the computing speed and power which both they and the gamers will have available to them, and the cost of upgrading these technologies. The history of gaming is replete with examples of games with highly developed concepts and software whose hardware components could not yet execute their code – the 1980s' classic *Dragon's Lair* or the Nintendo Power Glove of the 1990s are classic examples. Game developers are thus limited by what is technologically possible for other elements within their constituent system. When the 'front' of an LTS does not develop evenly, designers may be forced to reconfigure, abandon or redefine the purpose of existing artefacts.

In addition, designers need to consider issues related to interoperability. Consider a programmer's decision to design for the Microsoft rather than the Apple computing environment. Wang et al. (2016) describe the decisions which designers make as occurring within an ecosystem in which certain design practices and limits already exist. In particular, they describe the decision which designers of peripheral technologies had to make beginning in the mid-1990s when it became clear that their technologies (such as cell/mobile phones) could often interface with either an Apple computer system or a Microsoft Windows-based computer system, but not both. The decision to design either for Apple or Microsoft thus locked a company into certain relations with other vendors and into the adoption of certain practices. Again, momentum or path dependence – the tendency for technologies to become locked into certain pathways as the result of earlier decisions made – serves as a constraint on the unfettered creation of new technologies. In this instance, path dependence is the product of market relations at a specific moment in time, not the uneven development of technical sub-systems that characterizes reverse salients. Soft technological determinism is itself a socio-technical product.

Finally, firms may be limited in designing within a particular environment as a result of their decision to enter the field either early or late in the game, enjoying either first-mover advantage or developing a technology after its initial weaknesses have been identified. As Lieberman and Montgomery (1988) point out, those who are the first movers or early entrants to a field can accrue certain advantages over time, from having a significant market share of consumers to helping set the parameters within which later entrants must operate. For example, we can think of the first online bookstore, Amazon.com. Being the first in that market allowed Amazon to condition customers to expect to receive goods in a very quick timeframe. Other bookstores that did not have that same capacity eventually went bankrupt. Amazon also captured a significant share of the market for e-readers, and later entrants to that field struggled to keep up and compete with the Amazon Kindle. As a first mover into the e-reader market, Amazon was able to capture market share quickly and lock in its technology as the preferred format for readers and publishers. As we can see, SCOT provides a mid-range answer to the question of whether society shapes technology or vice versa. SCOT falls between social determinism (which says that society decides what a technology means) and technological determinism (Herrera 2006: 32–34) by stressing that both elements are central to the development of socio-technical systems at different moments in time, due to both 'technical' and social factors.

Discourse and interpretive flexibility: how radical a constructivism?

While SCOT perspectives share a generic approach to the study of technology in society, it is important to note that there are differences within this approach overall. In one camp, technological artefacts are understood to have values built into them, shaping how users encounter the object and how it may be used (Bijker et al. 1987; Herrera 2006). For this approach, which is the most prominent strand of SCOT, objects literally 'have politics' embedded within their material make-up. The materiality of technology exerts pressure on society to act in some ways rather than others.

In the other camp, technological artefacts do not have any meaning coded into their design – their physicality does not direct politics in any specific direction (Woolgar and Grint 1995; cf. Brey 1997). Steve Woolgar and Keith Grint (1995: 291) argue that:

> A thoroughgoing critique of essentialism would insist that values (in this case, politics) are imputed to an artifact in the course of their apprehension, description, and use – which, of course, includes imputations by the historian of science and/or technology.

This radical constructivism stresses that users may invent novel and unique uses for a technology beyond what the designers themselves ever conceptualized, and that the construction of meaning can never be reduced to the materiality of an object. One cannot discern what an object is without considering what it means and how it is understood within a particular context. An object's meaning is enacted or constituted through a number of factors, including the language which may be mobilized to describe the object. Thus, for example, what one individual might term 'wasting time on the internet' might be seen as a valuable activity or enterprise in another context; wasting time is not a property of the Internet (Goldsmith 2016). Included within this process of meaning-making are the scholars of technology themselves, as the above quote makes clear, requiring that students of technology treat their approach to the topic with significant reflexivity.

The 'FinFisher' controversy is a useful example of radical constructivist arguments. In 2015, a British company developed software which could be used to monitor and search internet communications. It sold the software to many government clients, intending that it be used as a weapon in the fight against terrorism. However, it was later revealed that clients like the governments of Belarus and North Korea had purchased the software, not for the purposes of carrying out counter-terrorism measures, but rather as a way of monitoring the communications of their own citizens to make sure that they were not engaged in dissident or anti-state activities. The software thus was not a vehicle for security but rather for repression.

The controversy which developed centres on the designer's intent: should the company have anticipated that the software might be used for this purpose, and should it have taken measures to assure that this did not occur, such as refusing to sell the software to repressive regimes? Despite the difficulties inherent in predicting every way in which a new technology might be used, contemporary policymakers often *do* assume that designers and creators of new technologies are able to anticipate how their products will be used, and that they therefore bear a responsibility for seeing that such technologies are used in a responsible and ethical way. For example, the multilateral Wassenaar Arrangement on Export Controls for Conventional Arms and Dual-Use Goods and Technologies (currently signed by forty-one nations) establishes an export control regime. Manufacturers of technologies are asked to anticipate whether their products, such as a vaccine or industrial chemical, might have military applications, such as the creation of a biological or chemical weapon. Manufacturers are prohibited from trafficking in products which might have such dual uses. Currently, designers of biological and chemical materials are asked to abide by the Wassenaar Arrangement, though in 2015 policymakers attempted, unsuccessfully, to extend the agreement to cover cyber technologies which might be modified to serve as cyber weapons.[4]

A designer could argue that those who used the FinFisher technology for surveillance were not using it correctly, since it was designed not for citizen surveillance but for security monitoring. A radical social constructivist would not accept this argument, but not because the stated intentions of the designer are incorrect. Rather, they would highlight the meaning given to the monitoring software by the end user, in this case North Korea and Belarus. Using this approach, Brey (1997) notes the centrality of interpretive flexibility – the notion that the 'facts' or meaning of a technology, its use and function, can change depending on context. Here we might consider the matter of children's toys and the ways in which, until quite recently, young children 'learned' that Lego building bricks are for boys while toy kitchens are for girls. In this way, the social facts related to the gendering of toys are undergoing a reorientation, as consumers renegotiate the ideology and rules associated with these toys while the shape or colour of the toys remains unchanged. The impact of the claims on how we conceptualize power and responsibility in the politics of technology is profound.

Recently, Woolgar and Lezaun (2013) have extended the radical constructivist stance, arguing that technological artefacts are, like gender, performative. An object becomes something by virtue of how it is enacted, used and described. Like gender performativity, object performativity suggests that an object's 'thingness' is not fixed and that it might vary in meaning due to how it is used, the culture and the time period in which it resides. An object could thus be described according to its physical characteristics, but it might also function as a symbol. For example, Alexander Barder (2015) describes the ways in which barbed wire is both a physical object and a technology for keeping things (like cattle) confined, as well as a symbol which often appears in the popular press in connection with stories about prisons, refugee camps and detention facilities. This simple tool thus also serves as a symbol of confinement and may figure in stories about human rights and those accused. It is thus more than simply a piece of wire with spikes on it, and to describe it as such would be an incomplete rendering of what it is. As Woolgar and Neyland (2014: 324) write:

> Objects do not acquire a particular meaning in, or because of a given context; they cannot be accounted for by reference to the external circumstances of their existence. Rather, objects are brought into being, they are realized in the course of a certain practical activity, and when that happens, they crystallize, provisionally, a particular reality ... They invoke the temporary action of a set of circumstances.

That is, they argue that objects and technologies are ontologically constituted within a particular context. Technologies and objects are all embedded within a particular (political) narrative. Take the mention of a random selection of technological innovations, such as the Dalkon Shield or Agent Orange. Without contextual knowledge the story of these technologies is incomplete. Instead, the reader needs to know that the Dalkon Shield was a form of artificial birth control which was 'dumped' on the developing world when it was determined that it was dangerous for women in the developed world, and that Agent Orange was a deforestation agent used in the Vietnam War which later proved harmful to the soldiers who had served in Vietnam. Here we can also pause to consider the example of two human reproductive technologies – egg donation and gestational surrogacy. It would be too simplistic to merely describe the physical activities which are carried out in creating and using these technologies. Attempts to describe their use as merely medical or scientific leave out the politics of these definitions, not to mention the politics of the actual use of the technology. The technology of international gestational surrogacy in particular is an act which is embedded and intertwined with questions of colonialism (including the power politics of the core and periphery); with questions of economics and the neo-liberal economic system; with questions of religion and culture; and with a discourse about women and bodily autonomy (Scott 2009). To grasp their context-dependent meaning, consider: How would the technology of egg donation and gestational surrogacy be described and understood by a group of actors (or interest groups) as diverse as an impoverished, illiterate woman from a village in India, a Catholic cardinal in Rome and a medical researcher in a Western developed nation? In each case, the technology means something different, is understood differently and, in a very real way, is something different ontologically.

We might also consider the ways in which ordinary household objects – like a pressure cooker and a box cutter – have now come to symbolize the Boston Marathon bombing and the airline attacks on 9/11 respectively, in the American psyche. In each case, the object's original meaning is often buried in the larger political narrative into which the object fits. In American life in general the term 'box cutter' no longer represents a device used by those in the moving industry but a weapon used by a hijacker during a traumatic historical event. The technology is now embedded in a narrative about terrorism, the deaths of civilians and vulnerability. No one in America will ever look at a box cutter in the same way again. In a sense, it would be wrong to describe a box cutter merely as a device used for opening boxes. It is no longer merely that.

Defining technological artefacts occurs across a range of symbolic registers, in high and low culture. It is undertaken by both poets and politicians. Woolgar and Lezaun (2013) point out that governments act to regulate technologies through labelling and classifying them, powerfully defining the meaning publics ascribe to technological artefacts in different circumstances. They describe the ways in which ordinary objects – like water bottles and knitting needles – were reclassified as the result of security measures enacted at airports to deal with terrorism after 9/11. Citizens' relations with their water bottles and knitting needles were altered as they were enlisted in security activities which required policing. They became different things due to the new ways in which they were described and understood.

SCOT, global pluralism, and the fluid meaning of objects

As noted, SCOT helps explain the role which individuals, groups and governments undertake in regulating new and emerging technologies, thus shaping the functions these technologies play in society. Regulation may take the form of specific laws and licensing regimes, as well as the application of social norms and mores to describe how technologies should be used within a particular culture.

Today, we can apply social constructivist explanations to thinking about how the Internet and social media have changed in form and function over time – sometimes in unpredictable and highly idiosyncratic ways. Here, for example, we might consider the ways in which a learning management system (LMS) for online education – like Blackboard, Moodle or Desire 2 Learn – can be utilized within a university or college. Any academic institution purchasing such a platform would have to create classes, enrol students and configure utilities like gradebooks. Nevertheless, depending on location, universities still use the platforms quite differently. Much of the original rhetoric about online education focused on the ways in which these technologies could alter social relations in the university, the university classroom and society. Early adopters spoke of the 'disruptive' potential of online learning, describing a paradigm shift which they argued would inevitably occur within the university environment. The traditional hierarchy between professor and student might vanish, and a more democratic way of learning, thinking and making knowledge would inevitably result, according to these analysts. Indeed, it is likely that the designers of such platforms had these end results in mind. They might have described the 'correct' or intended use of an LMS as one in which individuals and groups came together in a non-hierarchical, unstructured environment where everyone was free to contribute and participate.

However, an online learning environment looks very different depending on the context in which it is deployed. And, in many cases, it does not represent a brand-new environment, but rather reproduces the existing power relations and structures of the world in which it resides. Consider the ways in which education technology has been integrated into both men's and women's universities in Saudi Arabia. Although we might expect educational technology to perform a liberating function, allowing for direct interaction between all genders and social classes, this technology has been harnessed so that it allows the sharing of educational resources only – without violating existing societal and social norms regarding gender and gendered behaviour. For example, instructional technologists in Saudi Arabia have configured synchronous learning systems so that students at a men's university and those at a women's university may share a syllabus and instructor in order to take the same course. However, the LMS used creates only a one-way link between the male professor on the male campus and the female students in a classroom on their campus. This allows the female students to see the male instructor, the audio-visual material he presents and their fellow students. However, those observing from the male classroom – including the instructor – can only hear the female students' voices. They have no visual communication with the students or their classroom (Al Lily 2013). Society thus dictates the 'proper' use of learning management systems and audio-visual technology, although the 'proper' use in Saudi society may be very different from what the Western engineers who designed the technology intended. A 'disruptive' product developed to increase democratization and free conversation may ultimately be used to support segregation, hierarchy and stability.

Similarly, we can consider how different schools in Bangalore, India, have incorporated educational technology into their classrooms. Erik Byker (2014) describes how schools where students are predominantly of a very low socio-economic status incorporate the technology, telling students that it is an important tool in achieving economic status in society. He notes that in classrooms where students have higher socio-economic status, the emphasis may be on mastering a technology which increases ties to the West, without the emphasis on improving socio-economic status.

Thus, the function of a technology and its meaning within society can vary by geographic location, socio-economic location or factors like gender and age. The pluralism of international society disrupts any uniform meaning being attributed to a given object. SCOT argues that a technology does not have a fixed or a universal meaning. As we have seen, access to computer education technology does not have one meaning; nor is there any inherent set of values which are associated with technology itself. Rather, it can be 'read' differently within the different cultural contexts that comprise the international system of states.

Looking towards the future: what role will new technologies play?

The SCOT framework, in its original form, focused on technologies that were mass produced by industry. Until quite recently, traditional manufacturing has been largely centralized, with goods being produced on a mass scale in factories. This centralization allowed corporations significant product and quality control, essential as they license their facilities and pass checks on the quality of workmanship across factory locations. While corporate actors could never entirely control the symbolic meaning users would attach to their products, the system of mass production gave them greater power to set the agenda within which this contest would occur.

Today, by contrast, the growth of technologies like the Internet and three-dimensional printing has enabled goods and services to be created on a small scale in more geographically dispersed areas. This presents new challenges to the abilities of governments and society to monitor and regulate the design and use of artefacts. Rather than wait for industry to decide what type of products to offer based on market research and price signals, individuals can increasingly embrace a do-it-yourself culture. Today, individuals might 'hack' a technology themselves within their own homes. They can source components globally and even manufacture a product within their home, with 3-D printed handguns the most high-profile example. These processes present new sorts of challenges, since it may be less clear who owns a technology, who the inventor actually is or who has the right to license, regulate or use it. Thus, it is useful to consider how social constructivism can be applied as a paradigm to explain future technological developments. In doing so, we can consider two ideas that characterize emerging technologies, particularly in the area of information technology (IT).

First, new technologies are being created through cooperative arrangements, such as the incorporation and use of open source code. Today, technological innovators may share pieces of code which form the building blocks of many new programs used in both the private and government sectors. This code can be modified as it is shared in ways where it is no longer clear who, if anyone, 'owns' the final product since it may actually be the work of multiple designers and creators. In his classic work on computer code and legal regulation, Lawrence Lessig (2006) claims that even the technology of reading is undergoing a fundamental transformation. He describes reading as having been historically a top-down activity in which some individuals manufacture content and others merely utilize it, receiving it from the developers. This is distinct from culture today, which he describes as being 'read-write' in that recipients often talk back to the content, modifying it and reusing it, thereby taking ownership of it. Today's technological culture is sometimes referred to as a 'mashup culture', in which ideas and technologies no longer circulate exclusively in a top-down fashion. Users are also co-creators, hacking existing technologies and finding new and novel uses for products beyond the goals for which they might have been designed (Lee et al. 2011).

Second, if technological innovation today is often open source and non-hierarchical, it is also often decentralized. Technologies like 3-D printers mean that individuals can now manufacture and modify their own tools. This encourages innovation while simultaneously complicating the task of regulation. For this reason, techno-logical innovation today is often characterized as anarchic. Blockchain technology, a new development in computer code which is having significant impacts in the fields of finance, illustrates this well. In 2014, the software world underwent a series of disruptions with the advent of a platform known as Ethereum. Ethereum is a technology which allows for decentralized economic transactions among citi-zens, corporations and states, using virtual currencies like Bitcoin. Using this tech-nology, monetary transactions can take place instantly using peer-to-peer computer networking. A transaction no longer needs to be 'cleared' through a bank, with individuals waiting for transactions to clear. Instead, software allows for the auto-matic execution of contracts through a decentralized ledger which is shared with all of the participants in a network. Blockchain technology – which allows for the creation of a decentralized ledger of transactions which is automatically updated to all nodes on a network (or decentralized autonomous organization, DAO) – has been hailed as the greatest development since the Manhattan Project (Buntix 2016).

As one ponders the implications and use of this new technology, it is easy to identify both opportunities and threats. Proponents of Ethereum and the DAO describe it as having large positive effects on society. They point to the generation of open decentralized ledgers as providing for greater transparency, suggesting that Ethereum could be used to track state finances, thus doing away with corruption. If Ethereum is used for voting and the tracking of campaign contributions, they suggest, it could make rigged elections a thing of the past. Others, however, urge caution. They point to the fact that transactions will be instantaneous, possibly anonymous and decentralized. While Ethereum might be used to crowdsource funding for solution to a problem like global warming, it could just as easily be used to establish an assassination market or to crowd-fund attacks on the servers of unpopular celebrities or political figures (Boase 2013).

As new technologies emerge, it is not clear what agency or body should be responsible for regulating them; nor is it clear whether they can be regulated at all, since innovation is as likely to emerge from the bottom up as it is from the top down. The capacity of states or corporations to impose a uniform socio-technical order may not be equal to the task when the ability to innovate is so diffuse. Legal regulations developed for a mass-production society, in which clear intellectual rights and patent systems defined the authors of innovation, seem increasingly outdated as technological change accelerates. Indeed, this has prompted New Materialist approaches to employ a biological analogy to characterize our contemporary condition, suggesting that tools and technologies can evolve and mutate over time, leading to unpredictable results – in the same way that a biological entity might adapt and change over time. Agency, from this perspective, is significantly more distributed than within classic SCOT approaches. It is at this point that central concepts, such as momentum or closure, may need to be rethought within a changed historical context. Whether or not SCOT – an approach centrally developed around historical analysis of nineteenth- and twentieth-century technologies (Hughes 1987; Herrera 2006) – can adapt to analyse highly distributed systems of innovation remains to be seen.

Conclusion: beyond the material–ideational divide

Tensions remain between conventional and radical constructivist approaches to technology, similar to those expressed in IR theory more generally (Zehfuss 2000). While the initial thrust of SCOT stressed that the material features of technology express definite politics, more radical and reflexive approaches emphasize symbolic meaning and performativity in the use of technology. As this chapter has indicated, for both approaches there is no reason to believe that a technology is inherently peaceful, inherently belligerent, inherently disruptive or inherently stable. Both stress that technological objects develop within systems where designers and regulators have some agency, but where they do not enjoy a monopoly to dictate the ways in which a technology emerges or functions within society. Whether or not material objects really do have politics remains a potentially irresolvable point of contention.

Perspectives from the Social Construction of Technology (SCOT) approach in STS offer significant resources for the analysis of the politics of technology in International Relations. Using SCOT concepts, IR theorists have studied the technological closure, momentum and interpretive flexibility of railways, nuclear weapons, the Internet and the interaction capacity of international systems as a whole (Herrera 2006; Sylvest 2013; Carr 2012; Fritsch 2011). The extension of IR constructivism beyond the embrace of a positivist 'rump materialism' (Wendt 1999) has proven empirically fruitful for the study of world politics. SCOT approaches have been effective in drawing out how moments of **technological determinism** and moments of social construction coexist, appearing at different times in the life cycle of a given technological system and empowering, or disempowering, different users.

Notes

1 For a more optimistic take, see Mayer-Schönberger and Lazer (2007).
2 STS literature also employs 'co-production' to capture this process, with reference to technology but also science more broadly. See Jasanoff (2004).
3 This distinction between SCOT and ANT is captured most clearly in Bloor (1999).
4 See www.wassenaar.org.

References

Al Lily, Abdulrahman. 2013. Social Change and Educational Technologies: By Invitation or Invasion. *Journal of Organizational Transformation and Social Change* 10(1): 42–63.
Barder, Alexander. 2015. Barbed Wire. In Mark Salter (ed.), *Making Things International 2: Catalysts and Reactions*. St. Paul: University of Minnesota Press.
Bijker, Wiebe E. 2010. How is Technology Made? That is the Question! *Cambridge Journal of Economics* 34(1): 63–76.
Bijker, Wiebe E., Thomas P. Hughes and Trevor Pinch. 1987. *The Social Construction of Technological Systems: New Directions in the Sociology and History of Technology*. Cambridge, MA: MIT Press.
Bloor, David. 1999. Anti-Latour. *Studies in the History and Philosophy of Science* 30 (1): 81–112.
Boase, Richard. 2013. Sinister New Site 'Assassination Market' Enables Users to Contribute Bitcoins for Murder of US Officials. *Coindesk.com*, 19 November. Available at: www.coindesk.com/sinister-new-site-assassination-market-enables-users-contribute-bitcoins-m urder-us-officials/. Accessed 23 August 2016.
Brey, Philip. 1997. Social Construction for Philosophers of Technology: A Shopper's Guide. *Techne: Journal of the Society for Philosophy and Technology* 2(3–4): 6–78.
Buntix, J.P. 2016. Ukraine Embraces Ethereum Blockchain for Election Transparency. *NewsBTC*, 12 February. Available at: www.newsbtc.com/2016/02/12/ukraine-embra ces-ethereum-blockchain-for-election-transparency/. Accessed 23 August 2016.
Byker, Erik. 2014. ICT Oriented toward Nyaya: Community Computing in India's Slums. *International Journal of Education and Development using Information and Communication Technology* 10(2): 19–28.
Carr, Madeline. 2012. The Political History of the Internet: A Theoretical Approach to the Implications for US Power. In Sean S. Costigan and Jake Perry (eds) *Cyberspaces and Global Affairs*. Farnham: Ashgate.
Dedehayir, Ozgur and Saku Mäkinen. 2011. Determining Reverse Salient Types and Evolutionary Dynamics of Technology Systems with Performance Disparities. *Technology Analysis and Strategic Management* 23(10): 1093–1112.
Fritsch, Stefan. 2011. Technology and Global Affairs. *International Studies Perspectives* 12(1): 27–45.
Goldsmith, Kenneth. 2016. *Wasting Time on the Internet*. New York: Harper Perennial.
Herrera, Geoffrey. 2006. *Technology and International Transformation: The Railroad, the Atom Bomb, and the Politics of Technological Change*. Albany: State University of New York Press.
Hinton, Peta, Tara Mehrabi and Josef Barla. 2014. New Materialisms/New Colonialisms. Available at: http://newmaterialism.eu. Accessed 26 September 2016.
Hughes, Thomas P. 1969. Technological Momentum in History: Hydrogenation in History 1898–1933. *Past and Present* 44(1): 106–132.
Hughes, Thomas P. 1987. The Evolution of Large Technological Systems. In Wiebe E. Bijker, Thomas P. Hughes and Trevor Pinch (eds) *The Social Construction of Technological Systems: New Directions in the Sociology and History of Technology*. Cambridge, MA: MIT Press.

Hughes, Thomas P. 1994. Technological Momentum. In Merritt Rose Smith and Leo Marx (eds), *Does Technological Drive History? The Dilemma of Technological Determinism*. Cambridge, MA: MIT Press.

Jasanoff, Sheila (ed.). 2004. *States of Knowledge: The Co-Production of Science and Social Order*. London: Routledge.

Lasswell, Harold. 1936. *Politics: Who Gets What, When and How*. New York: Peter Smith.

Lee, Kevin, Nicolas Kaufman and George Buss. 2011. Trust Issues in Web Service Mash-Ups. *First Monday* 16(8). Available at: http://journals.uic.edu/ojs/index.php/fm/article/view/2911/3025. Accessed 27 March 2017.

Lessig, Lawrence. 2006. *Code: and Other Laws of Cyberspace, Version 2.0*. New York: Basic Books.

Lieberman, Marvin and David B. Montgomery. 1988. First-Mover Advantages. *Strategic Management Journal* 9(S1): 41–58.

Manjikian, Mary. 2015. The Magic of Completeness and the Politics of Invisibility: A Feminist Theory of Big Data. Unpublished manuscript presented at International Studies Association. New Orleans, March. Available at: www.academia.edu/11010983/The_Magic_of_Completeness_and_the_Politics_of_Invisibility_A_Feminist_Response_to_Big_Data.

Mayer-Schönberger, Victor and David Lazer. 2007. *Governance and Information Technology: From Electronic Government to Information Government*. Cambridge, MA: MIT Press.

Morozov, Evgeny. 2011. *The Net Delusion: How Not to Liberate the World*. London: Penguin.

Pinch, Trevor J. and Wiebe E. Bijker. 1984. The Social Construction of Facts and Artefacts: Or How the Sociology of Science and the Sociology of Technology Might Benefit Each Other. *Social Studies of Science* 14(3): 399–441.

Scott, Elizabeth. 2009. Surrogacy and the Politics of Commodification. *Law and Contemporary Problems* 72(3): 109–146.

Sloane, Paul. 2012. A Lesson in Innovation: Why Did the Segway Fail? *Innovation Management.se*. Available at: www.innovationmanagement.se/2012/05/02/a-lesson-in-innovation-why-did-the-segway-fail/. Accessed 4 October 2016.

Smith, Aaron. 2014. US Views of Technology and the Future: Science in the Next 50 Years. 17 April, Philadelphia, PA: Pew Research Center on Internet, Science and Technology. Available at www.pewinternet.org/2014/04/17/us-views-of-technology-and-the-future.

Sylvest, Casper. 2013. Technology and Global Politics: The Modern Experiences of Bertrand Russell and John H. Herz. *International History Review* 35(1): 121–142.

Waltz, Kenneth. 2010 [1979]. *Theory of International Politics*. Longrove, IL: Waveland.

Wang, Jens, Jonas Hedman and Virpi Tuunainen. 2016. Path Creation, Path Dependence and Breaking away from the Past: Re-Examining the Case of Nokia. *Journal of Theoretical and Applied Electronic Commerce Research* 11(20): 16–27.

Wendt, Alexander. 1992. Anarchy is What States Make of It: The Social Construction of Power Politics. *International Organization* 46(2): 391–425.

Wendt, Alexander. 1999. *Social Theory of International Politics*. Cambridge: Cambridge University Press.

Winner, Langdon. 1980. Do Artefacts Have Politics? *Daedalus* 109 (1): 121–136.

Woolgar, Steve and Keith Grint. 1995. On Some Failures of Nerve in Constructivist and Feminist Analyses of Technology. *Science, Technology and Human Values* 20(3): 281–310.

Woolgar, Steve and Javier Lezaun. 2013. The Wrong Bin Bag: A Turn to Ontology in Science and Technology Studies? *Social Studies of Science* 43(3): 321–340.

Woolgar, Steve and Daniel Neyland. 2014. *Mundane Governance: Ontology and Accountability*. Oxford: Oxford University Press.

Zehfuss, Maja. 2000. *Constructivism in International Relations: The Politics of Reality*. Cambridge: Cambridge University Press.

3

ACTOR-NETWORK THEORY

Objects and actants, networks and narratives

Christian Bueger and Jan Stockbruegger

At the heart of renewed interest in the role of technology in global politics and the intensifying conversation between the discipline of International Relations (IR) and Science and Technology Studies (STS) is a distinct approach: Actor-Network Theory (hereafter: ANT).[1] ANT is an approach that has been developed in STS from the 1980s as an alternative to studying the making of scientific facts, objects and technologies. ANT is widely known for its unique take on technological objects and the idea to give them equal status to humans. Several overlapping concerns led to the development of the approach. Theoretically it was inspired by semiotics and literature theory, in particular the work of Gabriel Tarde and Michel Serres; but it was also an attempt to critique and advance post-structuralist ideas (Law 2009). In methodological terms ANT was influenced by ethno-methodology and its interest in everyday and practical activities. ANT is an established approach in STS, yet it is one which is continuously under construction and revision in the light of empirical problems. Although ANT is somewhat prominent and often seen as an emblem of STS achievements, one should not equate ANT and STS since, as the other chapters in this volume document, STS is a much richer and diverse field. ANT is best known for its claim to take materiality seriously. But, as our introduction shows, ANT is much more than this. It offers a rich repertoire of concepts and ideas, but also a profound rethinking of how we do scientific analysis.

IR scholars became interested in ANT from the 2000s (Walters 2002; Lidskog and Sundqvist 2002; Bueger and Gadinger 2007). Turning to relational approaches, the concept of practice and international practice theory, and attempts at rethinking materiality, led to a wider interest in ANT. Increasingly ANT is seen as an established approach to the study of the international (Best and Walters 2013; Bueger and Gadinger 2014). Since ANT shares little with conventional notions of 'theory' and has been rightfully called an 'attitude' or 'sensitivity' (Law 2009; Mol 2010; Bruun and Gadsen 2010), there remains however much confusion as to what one can do with ANT. The richness, diversity and complexity of research clustered around ANT prevents presenting it as a coherent approach. For us though, the most promising way of introducing ANT dwells in the rich studies that have been made, understanding the problems they address and the concepts they developed. In consequence, our introduction is based on the reading of a range of classic contributions on ANT which have direct relevance to questions of technology and global politics. It is as much an overview as it is an invitation to read these classics for yourself. Many of the classic ANT studies, especially the ones we introduce, make fantastic and often even entertaining reading.

The chapter is structured in three sections. In the following section we introduce six classic ANT studies of technologies, each giving a particular snippet of what ANT is and how one analyses with it. On the basis of these studies, the next section discusses a range of concepts that have been developed in ANT. We do not suggest that ANT should be reduced to these, but they provide major starting points and inspiration for conducting ANT analyses. Our discussion continues with a review of how ANT has become translated to IR and the study of global governance. In particular, the fields of global environmental governance, international political economy and critical security studies have documented how productive ANT is to studying the international. Moreover, ANT is increasingly located within the turn to international practice theory and recognized as vital to further this approach and adopt it more broadly to study international politics and global governance. We conclude with a number of core points to keep in mind if embarking on an empirical ANT project.

Technological innovation: insights from ANT classics

ANT is very much an 'empirical theory', or a theoretical position that is primarily concerned with empirical questions. Not only does ANT aim at facilitating empirical research, but it has also in fact been developed through empirical work. ANT was basically constructed out of empirical studies that develop concepts. To understand ANT and its conceptual apparatus, we therefore need to read some of the studies by its pioneers and founding fathers, such as John Law, Michel Callon, Bruno Latour and Anne-Marie Mol. This also gives us an idea about how ANT approaches the world empirically; how it develops narratives of politics, power, technology and transformation; and how its concepts try to make sense of complex situations.

John Law's (1987) analysis of Portugal's maritime empire in the fifteenth century is a good starting point. It illustrates ANT's approach to studying technological innovation with regard to the big questions of world politics – that is, the global distribution of power and the making of empires. Law tries to understand how the Portuguese managed to create and maintain an empire. His answer is the invention of new shipping technologies that enabled the Portuguese to sail around the African continent and to eventually dominate trade and politics in the Indian Ocean. High waves, heavy winds and strong currents made the sea journey to the Indian Ocean a dangerous undertaking. Initially, neither the sailing ships nor the skills of the Portuguese were able to cope with this hostile natural environment. The ships sank and did not return.

Three types of innovations were necessary to solve this problem and to master the forces of nature at sea:

- First, the ships had to be redesigned to withstand the harsh weather.
- Second, navigation techniques based on the magnetic compass had to be invented in order to enable seafarers to maintain their course in the absence of clear skies and without seeing the coast.
- Third, the invention of a new sailing method, so-called circle sailing, allowed the Portuguese to cope with and effectively make use of strong winds and currents at sea.

The Portuguese thus eventually managed to master and realign the destructive forces of nature through technological innovation.

Law (1987) describes this process as 'system building'. Heterogeneous materials such as planks and wind, water and navigation skills were assembled, controlled and stabilized in a specific way. They formed relatively durable structures in which competing elements and materials are held together. Law's study thus 'displays the strategies of system-building and, in particular, the heterogeneous and conflicting field of forces within which technological problems are posed and solved' (1987: 252). His study is important because it shows that political power and the production of globality depend on technology. Technological innovations were essential for Portugal's rise. Without those technologies, Portugal could not have established a global maritime empire.

While Law's work on the Portuguese empire sheds light on how durable and stable structures evolve, Michel Callon (1986) is more interested in fragility, disorder and the limits of power. Rather than empires, he studies a local episode of collaboration in St Brieuc Bay in Brittany, on the English Channel coast. It is a story of collaboration between scientists, fishermen and scallops. Yes, scallops! The start of the story is the attempt by scientists to solve the problem of declining scallop stocks in the bay. To do so they wanted to introduce a new type of breeding device. The success of this innovative research project was based on several assumptions: namely that the scallops disappear because they are overfished; that the scallops will use the new breeding devices to ensure their survival; and that the fishermen will support the project because they want to maintain or even increase production. In other words, the scientists had designed a heterogeneous network in which the problems of human and natural actors are interlinked and in which their interests intersect. However, the network of scallop-breeding device, fishermen and scientists turned out to be very fragile. The scallops in particular were unhappy, and refused to use and settle at the new breeding devices. Part of the failure to attract the scallops was that the devices could not withstand the currents in St Brieuc Bay; but the fishermen also undermined the project when they began fishing in areas protected for scallop breeding. The project failed terribly.

Callon's study of the scallops of St Brieuc Bay is an important ANT work for several reasons. He describes the scallops as 'actors' who have the capacity to disrupt, resist and sabotage human practice. Nature and material objects have agency too, Callon argues, and they cannot be controlled and 'domesticated' easily. The study also hints at ANT's distinct approach to power, one shared in many ways with other approaches emerging from STS (cf. Chapters 2, 4 and 5). Power is not simply located in material capabilities; it is also where those capabilities are created, ordered and arranged. Callon thus stresses the central role that knowledge and scientific practices, as in the case of the domestication of scallops, plays in the exercise of power.

A study of more mundane encounters with material agency and power is Bruno Latour's 'Sociology of a Door-Closer'.[2] In the article, Latour demonstrates in mundane detail how door-closer technology structures human practices in everyday encounters. It is a fascinating introduction to how ANT often takes very basic and everyday observations as a starting point for theorization. Latour argues that door-closers are responses to what he calls the 'hole-wall dilemma': 'Walls are a nice invention, but if there were no holes in them, there would be no way to get in or out.' Technology like the door – a 'hole-wall' since it has features of both – is designed to solve this problem. Yet, installing a door leads to a new set of problems. The users of a door often forget to close it. A door that is not closed is like a hole (Johnson 1988: 298–299).

Solving the door-closer problem is thus essential to overcoming the hole-wall dilemma. One solution would be to stick a note on the door asking for it to be closed after use. But it is very likely that door-users would not pay any attention to the note, and that the door would stay open. Another solution would be to employ a porter to close the door. But this is expensive, and one also needs to solve the supervision problem and make sure that the porter is motivated to fulfil this boring task effectively. The third solution to the door-closing problem is a technological one – the installation of a spring mechanism to make the door close automatically. Yet a powerful spring mechanism – to ensure that the door closes – also slams the door so violently 'that you, the visitor, have to be very quick in passing through and that you should not be at someone else's heels; otherwise your nose will get shorter' (Johnson 1988: 301). In other words, the spring mechanism forces humans to adapt and to behave in a certain way.

Latour uses the case of the door-closer to demonstrate that human and non-human practices essentially intersect, and that a distinction between them cannot be maintained. Society would not function without mundane technologies such as the door-closer, which in many ways replace and take over jobs previously performed by humans. Technologies stabilize and enable human practices, but in doing so they also constrain and condition them. The world of Latour is hence one of mundane power struggles. Everyday practices of domination and resistance are manifested in socio-material interactions, like door-stoppers. Indeed, Latour and other ANT researchers have used such mundane examples quite frequently, not only in demystifying technology but also to show that it is often the details that matter.

Latour has however also been interested in 'big' technology. A particular fascinating example is his 1996 book *Aramis, or the Love of Technology*. The book presents a fictionalized reconstruction of a failed innovation in urban transportation. It investigates the so-called Aramis initiative, an attempt to develop a personal rapid transit system to be installed in Paris. It was developed for more than a decade, but was never realized in urban transportation. Latour's book is a milestone in ANT literature, in particular because of the way it focuses on the empirical research process. It is written as a detective story. The reader follows a professor and his assistant as they try to find out what kept Aramis 'alive' for so long, why it eventually 'died' and what or who actually 'killed' it. The two detectives gather evidence and interview officials, project managers and engineers involved in different phases of the project. The two encounter very different and often contradictory explanations of why the project failed. They find 'technological' explanations, such as that Aramis was technologically infeasible and that it did not work in a major transportation system. They also find 'social' explanations, for instance that the government did not support the project or that the wider public had no interest in it. The two protagonists of the book hence struggle to create a consistent picture of the Aramis project, why it was kept alive and what exactly caused its death. They fail to come up with a consistent explanation.

This account is significantly different from previous ANT studies, which gave neat answers to empirical problems. Callon, for instance, had explained the failure of the domestication technology by the resistance of the scallops. By focusing on the empirical research process, however, Latour creates a world that is so complex, chaotic and contradictory that it cannot be grasped and explained in a single narrative. The question of what or who killed Aramis cannot be conclusively answered. In the end, the two researchers therefore conclude that Aramis's death was not inevitable, and that neither technological nor social explanations can be found. Aramis died because the actors involved did not sustain it through further negotiations and adaptations. They did not 'love' it any more; and when they stopped caring about it, Aramis died and ceased to exist. With the book, Latour not only powerfully points to the parallels between the criminal detective and the academic (ANT) researchers; he also undermines the idea that the outcome of research should be concise explanations, judgements or linear narratives.

Issues of direct concern to IR and security studies scholars have also been addressed by classic ANT research. Two of our favourite examples are a co-authored study by Law and Callon (1992) on a defence technology project in the UK and a study of technology transfer for development by Marianne de Laet and Annemarie Mol (2000). In 'The Life and Death of an Aircraft', Law and Callon investigate the development of a new aircraft for the Royal Air Force (RAF). The TSR.2 project, initiated in the late 1950s, was part of a complex political negotiation process in which the aircraft 'represented different things to different actors' (Law and Callon 1992: 25). For the RAF and the Ministry of Defence (MoD), TSR.2 was part of a military strategy to defend Britain and the Western Alliance: the Treasury saw the aircraft as a sufficiently cheap end product; and for the

Ministry of Supply (MoS) it was an industrial policy instrument.[3] This fragile political compromise, which Law and Callon describe as a 'global network', resulted in the construction of local networks of companies and sub-contractors to translate TSR.2 into a concrete aircraft. However, technological problems and political interference complicated this process. Project designers had to reconcile the RAF's demanding specifications with constraints imposed by physical forces and the limits of technological solutions available to them. They also had to deal with political interference and budget constraints by the Treasury. Furthermore, contractors and sub-contractors competed over resources as they tried to promote their technologies in TSR.2.

Political opposition to TSR.2 grew as costs exploded and progress remained slow. Suggestions by the MoD that the aircraft could also be used in a nuclear capacity were criticised by the political Left, which wanted to stop nuclear proliferation, as well as by military experts, who argued that TSR.2 was not designed for that purpose. The first test flight of the TSR.2 aircraft eventually took place in 1964, but the project was cancelled only a year later under a new Labour government that had promised to put an end to expensive 'prestige projects'. Like the Aramis story, Law and Callon give us a fascinating account of the failure of technology in which various actors and interests intersect but can no longer be aligned.

With similar means of investigation, de Laet and Mol provide a remarkable story of success and adaptation. In a case of technological innovation in a non-Western context, they study the working of a water pump in Zimbabwe. The mechanical water-pumping technique was originally invented to support the expanding agricultural sector and industrial development in Europe. The first model of the so-called 'Zimbabwe bush pump' was designed in 1931 to improve farming in what was then the British colony of Southern Rhodesia. Today the bush pump brings water to thousands of rural communities across the country. De Laet and Mol argue that the pump functions as part of a web of socio-material relations. The pump is a multiple object: It is a hydraulic device that provides water; a public health device that enhances community well-being; a participation device that needs a local community to use, build and maintain it; and a national standard and nation-building device that is actively promoted by the Zimbabwean administration. The boundaries of the pump are thus fluid and its size varies. It encompasses families, communities and the entire Zimbabwean nation.

The bush pump works because it is part of multiple relations. It is impossible to say who or what makes it work and guarantees its success. The engineer who invented it, the company that produces it, the community that adapts it and the administration that promotes it – they all 'own' the Zimbabwean bush pump and make it work. The pump is constantly being shaped and reshaped by these multiple 'authors', and its invention and development is thus an ongoing and never-ending process.

Looking at the aircraft study and the bush pump study allows for a comparative perspective on technological innovation across fields. Both technologies have multiple and fluid ontologies. Their respective performances hang together and are closely interrelated; but they are not based on the same logics and they turn the same object into different practical devices. Furthermore, neither the aircraft nor the water pump is controlled and managed by one actor or one interpretation. Yet the aircraft project fails because its different interpretations clash and cannot be reconciled, and because the project cannot control the intersection of local and global networks on which it depends. For the water pump, on the other hand, multiplicity, distributed ownership and lack of control are not problematic at all. Instead, the pump thrives and spreads exactly because no one can control it, because it is so adaptable to multiple environments and situations, and because it can be used in many different ways. This shows that, from an ANT perspective, the success or failure of a new technology is contingent and cannot be predetermined. In-depth empirical investigations are required.

With these six stories we have a good range of examples of how ANT works. Breeding devices, door-stoppers or bush pumps seem very small or even boring objects of study. But, as ANT researchers demonstrate, there is actually a rich and fascinating universe which makes these possible. The breeding device required a rich web of associations, of all sorts of actors, to work, as did the other technologies. Hence what appears unimportant or marginal from the outset is actually crucial and fundamental – the magnetic compass has tremendous importance, even when compared to the Portuguese empire. Through reconstructing these webs of associations and relations ANT provides narratives not only of success, but also of technological failure; and it shows how power is inscribed into these networks. The Aramis story, in particular, has shown us how ANT researchers want to work: they are detectives aiming to reconstruct particular empirical outcomes.

Sensitizing concepts: ANT's vocabulary

ANT has often been criticized for not actually being a 'theory', since it does not offer a coherent system of generalizations which we could adopt or 'test' universally. Indeed, whether or not ANT should be called a 'theory' at all was hotly debated even among its proponents, with Latour (1999) and Callon (1999) preferring to dub it differently. Yet the label ANT was sticky. Instead of renouncing the term 'theory', researchers pointed out that ANT profoundly challenges what we might want to understand by that term (Latour 2005; Mol 2010). Indeed, ANT is a web of conceptual associations in itself, and these have been developed to facilitate empirical enquiry.

The way these concepts work and how they are used in ANT research is hence quite different from many other approaches in the study of global politics. To understand this difference it is helpful to think about the conventional role of concepts in theories. Many IR theories, for instance, start from the assumption that the world consists of 'states' and that the international system is 'anarchic'. 'States' and 'anarchy' are part of a conceptual apparatus that guides and constrains empirical investigations. The task of a researcher is then to study interactions between states under conditions of anarchy. ANT, in contrast, avoids making any a priori assumptions about the world and the entities that exist in it. It does not aim at developing a universal meta-language that can be matched to that world. In ANT there are no fundamental ontological concepts such as 'state' or 'anarchy'. ANT does not aim at explaining the world 'theoretically', in that it does not seek to limit empirical investigations to predefined entities and dynamics such as 'interactions between states under conditions of anarchy'. ANT aims at liberating empirical investigations from such constraints, and it seeks to generate concepts and explanations based on empirical investigations rather than on ontological deliberations. ANT is, as pointed out before, an empirical theory.

This is reflected in ANT's conceptual vocabulary. ANT concepts need to be understood as flexible research tools that facilitate empirical investigation. ANT concepts are vague, ambiguous and overlapping. They do not explain the world, but help to explore and to describe it. The ANT vocabulary draws attention to empirical problems and challenges without suggesting how to solve them. The main function of these concepts is to sensitize. According to Mol (2010: 261, 262), ANT concepts 'help in getting a sense of what is going on, what deserves concern or care, anger or love, or simply attention'. They provide 'modes of engaging with the world', ways 'of asking questions' and 'techniques for turning issues inside out or upside down'. In consequence, ANT has not developed a comprehensive conceptual apparatus. ANT concepts are developed on an empirical basis, and are constantly adopted and further developed through empirical research. To a certain extent, each ANT study needs to develop its own conceptual apparatus to explain and analyse a specific empirical problem, a significant challenge. Existing ANT studies provide a repertoire from where to start. Yet, there is no universal vocabulary fit to capture the manifold practices and processes in the world. If an empirical investigation starts from existing concepts, it also generates new concepts and terms tailor-made to capture its empirical problems. A number of basic concepts in the ANT literature have proved particularly useful for empirical research.

Perhaps one of the most vital concepts is given by the very name ANT – that is, 'Actor-Network'. The term has been as controversial as the notion of theory in ANT, and a range of alternatives were proposed – such as 'assemblage' or 'actant-rhizome' (e.g. Latour 1999). The main motive behind these proposals was to clarify that ANT has little in common with conventional 'network theory' as it became increasingly popular in social science and IR (Gad and Bruun Jensen 2011). Before we explore this difference, let us first discuss the notion of 'Actor-Network'. The basic idea of ANT is that the whole world consists of networks, and that every organization, process or practice can therefore be described in network terms (Latour 1997: 3). Exploring how 'networks' evolve, how 'associations' are stabilized and how 'connections' dissolve is the main task and purpose of an ANT investigation. Also an actor needs to be seen as a network that consists of many other actors. Actor and network always come together – hence the hyphen in the term 'actor-network'. An actor can be taken apart, and its components can be disassembled and reassembled. Agency is distributed within a network or 'collective'. Who or what acts is always an empirical problem that can only be determined by investigating the network though which an effect is being produced.

An actor–network is therefore also more than the sum of its components. It takes on a logic of its own that cannot be reduced to that of its constituting actors and practices. ANT articulates a **relational ontology** since actors and effects are produced through relations within networks.[4] This is the core difference from network theory, which takes the elements (or nodal points) of a network for granted (Gad and Bruun Jensen 2010). For instance, in Law's analysis of Portugal's maritime empire, the sailing technique cannot be reduced to the elements it is made of (planks, water, wind, etc.). The logic of the technique is the way it connects those elements within a durable network. The network vocabulary hence also enables ANT to locate material agency within a network, and to study heterogeneity as a network consisting of material and non-material elements. In the words of Law (1992: 383), 'the social is nothing other than patterned networks of heterogeneous materials, or an effect produced by such a network'. Society, the state, the political – these are all produced by networks.

ANT's understanding of agency is captured in the concept of actant, which is a core concept to grasp materiality. Originating in semiotics, the concept holds that anything potentially has agency, and that there is no difference in the ability of humans, animals, technologies or other non–humans to act. The scallops in St Brieuc Bay, for instance, have agency because they resist association with the breeding devices provided to them. There are hence no intrinsic qualities that make or constitute an action, and agency is neither characterized by reflectivity, the essential or necessary features of an object or entity, nor by intentionality or the logic of teleology. Instead agency is understood as an effect or as the modification of a state of affairs. Agency in that sense is everything that has an impact and makes a difference in the world. What matters is that the scallops undermined the restocking project designed by the scientists. An actant can therefore not act on its own. Agency is realized through networks and in association with other actants. An actant is configured in specific networks through which an effect is being produced.

A network, in other words, gives an actant shape and turns it into a concrete actor. The door–closer technology analysed by Latour, for instance, makes a huge difference in the world. It replaces the work of humans or other non–humans that would be required to close the door in its absence (e.g. a porter). The agency of the door–closer is realized in association with the wall, the hole, the door and its human users. This heterogeneous network configures the door–closer and makes it part of a mundane practice. In the words of Latour (2005: 71), '*anything* that does modify a state of affairs by making a difference is an actor – or, if it has no figuration yet, an actant'.

Barbara Czarniawska (2014: 58) summarizes the core of the actant concept:

> If all the characters are known from the beginning, there is no story to tell; if powerful actors can do what they want, there is nothing more to say. From an ANT perspective one should ask: 'By what route have certain actants become powerful actors and others have not, or how is power constructed?'

The concepts we explore in the following sections are responses to that question: they identify mechanisms of this route to become actors and powerful.

The first concept that is essential is that of **mediator**. Mediators are technologies that do not function as passive objects and that do not simply pass on some effect from one actant to another. Instead, to use the words of Latour (2005: 339), they 'transform, translate, distort, and modify the meaning or the elements they are supposed to carry'. The concept of mediators hence enables investigations into how technologies shape practices and the effects that they help produce. The multiple performances of the Zimbabwe bush pump studied by de Laet and Mol exemplifies this point. As we showed before, the water pump 'performs' the nation, the community, public health and hydraulics. Yet it does not simply carry, reproduce or represent these effects. Instead, it produces them and makes them possible in the first place. There would be no nation without national identification symbols and standards such as the water pump; public health concerns would remain irrelevant without tools, such as the water pump, to address them; there would be not the same community without joint practices and common understandings associated with using and maintaining a water pump; and even hydraulic mechanisms would not exist if they were not enshrined in mundane technologies such as the Zimbabwe bush pump.

As such, the water pump is not a neutral object – it is not a mere tool, but shapes and makes a difference to the effects that it helps produce. The community performed through the water pump varies depending on where the pump is located within a village and how many families use it. A water pump that is located centrally in the middle of a village and that is used by the whole village produces a larger community than a pump at the fringes of a village that provides water to the immediate neighbourhood only. In other words, the water pump is a mediator that produces communities, and that also shapes and configures the community that is produced through it.

A related concept is that of the black box. A black box is a combination of actants – such as a device, system or technology – whose internal workings are hidden and no longer matter for those who use it and the way it is used. A case in point is the door and the door–closing technology analysed by Latour (Johnson 1988). A door is like a hole in the wall that can be opened and closed as desired. This effect is produced through a complex and carefully arranged socio-technological actor-network. It includes hinges, which enables the door to open; the door-closer, which makes sure that the door closes automatically; and door-users who know how to use a door. Yet door-users do not need to know anything about the hinges and the door-closer, and they also do not need to think about how to open the door and how to pass through it. The internal mechanisms of the door and the way it is being used have been successfully 'black boxed'; they have become invisible, and all that remains is the door and the effect it produces – namely that people can pass through it. Black boxing hence transforms a complex object or technology, like a door, into a simple tool that can be used in practice.[5] And, despite its internal complexity, it can be treated as a single unit.

According to Latour (1987: 3), a black box is used 'whenever a piece of machinery or a set of commands is too complex'. However, Latour also shows what happens if a black box fails to produce the desired effect. Problems arise if the door-closer is on strike and refuses to work, or if the door closes too quickly for people to pass through it comfortably. In such moments, the black box of the door is reopened again and all that was hidden inside it – the hinges, the door-closer and the way it is used – reappear and become visible again.

World politics is made up of many black-boxed technologies that produce stable and predictable effects. A case in point are cyber systems, which have become essential in almost all walks of international life, though most people using them have no idea how they actually work. Yet the problem of cyber security has reopened that black box (see Chapter 7; Carr 2012, 2013; DeNardis 2009). It has become obvious that cyber systems are actually rather fragile and vulnerable con-structs, and that they can easily be attacked and dismantled. The cyber security discourse is thus a very technical one in which the inner workings of the cyber black box are being analysed and discussed. Almost every organization or govern-ment nowadays has a cyber security department that tries to keep the cyber black box safe and secure so that the Internet can function as one unit.

The concept of **translation** within ANT describes the quality of relations and associations, capturing the ways in which hybrid networks are formed. The con-cept tries to grasp how different actants which have never interacted before become connected and start to behave as part of a network. In other words, the concept of translation is all about relations. It is a device to study the evolution of new relations, what happens to the actants in that relationship and how they struggle over the shape and content of their relationship. According to Callon (1986: 203), translation is the process 'during which the identity of actors, the possibility of interaction and the margins of manoeuvre are negotiated and delim-ited'. In his study of the scallops of St Brieuc Bay, where he coined the ANT understanding of translation, Callon analysed in detail how three scientists tried to construct and manage the relationship between scallops, the new breeding device, the fishermen and the scientific community.[6]

As we explained before, specific roles were assigned to these actors to make them work together in a specific way. The scallops were supposed to use the new breeding device; the fishermen were meant not to fish in areas designed for scallop breeding; and the scientific community would accept the research findings of the three scien-tists. The network was assumed to rely on a joint interest of all its actors in the survival of the scallops. The three scientists at the centre of the network defined the interests and identities of the network's actors and how they would cooperate. Trying to make the actors interact and work together, however, proved difficult. Not only did the scallops refuse to be enrolled in a relationship with the breeding device, but the fishermen also did not play the role assigned to them by fishing in protected areas. Put differently, the translations designed by the three scientists failed. The interests of the scallops, the breeding device and the fishermen did not align in the end, and the relationships between them remained fragile and ultimately broke apart.

Finally, let us consider the concept of **inscription**, another key term in ANT's relational terminology. It captures the outcome of a successful translation process. The concept of inscription describes a stable relationship between two (heterogeneous) actors in which their roles are clearly defined, their behaviours are attuned to each other and their patterns of interactions are well established. A successful inscription can turn a complex technology, like a door, into a black box that functions like a single unit. The concept of inscriptions is particularly useful to think about how technologies have become part of everyday practices and how they dominate the way that things are done. For instance, in Latour's analysis the door-closer technology is inscribed onto the behaviour of humans and the way that they use and pass through the door (Johnson 1988). The concept of inscription hence also refers to a power relationship in which one actor dominates the behaviour of another. In Latour's study, the door-closer imposes certain restrictions and patterns of actions on the user of the door. The technology determines how much time there is to pass through the door, and it can force people to move very fast.

Yet inscriptions – and this is the trick – also work the other way around. The success of an inscription depends on the performance of the actors and their ability to execute the script of action imposed on them. In our example, the nature of the door-users also imposes certain restrictions and limitations on the door-closer and its ability to determine how the door has to be used. A cat is faster than a human, and could thus be forced to move through the door much quicker. Hence, inscriptions need to be understood as relationships of power that go both ways. The power of the dominant actor is limited and it relies, at least to some degree, on the dominated actor and whether it accepts and is able to execute the script imposed on it. Resistance is an option, power and domination are fragile and inscriptions can fail. The concept of inscription allows us to explore empirically relationships of power between actors and the tension between dominance, resistance and cooperation within a heterogeneous network.

These concepts are examples of the type of vocabulary that ANT develops and draws on to develop empirical narratives. Concepts sensitize us to the empirical material. They tell us what to look out for, but not what we are going to find. Concepts on their own do not provide answers. ANT's vocabulary should always be read together with the empirical stories in which the concept plays a role to describe relations. As Blok and Elgaard Jensen (2011: 111) summarize it, 'no metatheorizing is found here, no grandiose social explanation; and no "pure" human relations that are not already closely interwoven with esoteric details'.

ANT and the practice turn in International Relations

International Relations scholarship has started to play and experiment with ANT concepts and the epistemic style that it encourages. Actor-Network Theory initially became influential in IR through its utility in rethinking the role of science in international politics. The question of how science can or should influence international politics is perhaps as old as the first attempts to set up international organizations. Starting with Henri de Saint-Simon in the eighteenth century, a prominent line of social theory has argued that international relations should be in the hands of science and scientists, rather than those of diplomats and the governments they represent (Mazower 2012: 96). These early technocratic ideas visibly influenced works that became known in IR as 'functionalism', elaborated by David Mitrany in the inter-war period and by Ernst Haas in the post-World War II era (Bueger 2014: 42–43). The functionalist research agenda was concerned about the roles that scientists perform in global governance processes. The prevalent framework since the 1990s was the so-called 'epistemic community' concept, which aimed at identifying scientists as (external) actors influencing national and global governance (Davis Cross 2012).

The role of epistemic communities was discussed primarily via issues of environmental governance, a sphere of global politics where science and technology is particularly visible. ANT was introduced to this debate as an alternative to the epistemic community concept. In particular, Lidskog and Sundqvist (2002) argued that ANT allows us to understand the intersection of science and politics in the creation of transnational environmental regimes. Studying the Convention on Long-Range Transboundary Air Pollution (LRTAP), they illustrate how one of the most effective global environmental regimes during the Cold War was jointly co-produced by scientists and politicians. Lidskog and Sundqvist argue, in a nutshell, that environmental science provided a neutral ground for political cooperation between Cold War adversaries. As they put it, the 'politicians' search for neutral – politically uncontroversial – issues to cooperate on was an important explanatory factor with regard to the scientific character of the regime' (2002: 89). Scientific knowledge has continued to shape the evolution of the LRTAP regime in the following years. Drawing on ANT, Lidskog and Sundqvist describe in particular how, in the 1990s, scientists became crucial in translating the interests of states into the expanding LRTAP regime, enabling them to cooperate in a far-reaching agreement to cut emissions.

ANT categories have also shaped discussion in the subfield of International Political Economy as it turned to the role of everyday political practice in sustaining or challenging global economic networks (Hobson and Seabrooke 2007). Of particular importance in this agenda was the recognition that economists are significant economic actors, since their technological devices, fashions and theories influence economic life significantly (e.g. Callon and Muniesa 2005; MacKenzie et al. 2007). The idea that economics and markets lend themselves to ANT analyses was originally proposed by Callon (1998) and has inspired a growing body of literature that studies processes of 'economization' and the construction of markets. This literature analyses in detail how the theories and concepts of economists are inscribed into market technologies, including 'standards, calculating instruments, metrology and, more generally, material infrastructure in market formation' (Çalışkan and Callon 2009: 384).

Originally discussed mainly in economic sociology, a rich vein of research in International Political Economy has emerged. A recent study by Lasse Henriksen, for instance, investigates changing practices in development finance and how the World Bank helped construct a global market for microfinance. Henriksen (2013: 407) is particularly interested in the 'politics of equipping for calculation'. He shows that the web-based infrastructure of performance indicators, standardization techniques and calculation devices derived from neo-classical economic theory is key to understanding how the global market for microfinance operates. Others show how the effect of economics can lead to market failure. Hall, for instance, argues that 'financial market behaviour is performative rather than reflective', and that the practices leading into the financial crisis were driven by 'the intellectual products of financial economics' (2009: 454, 457). In another study, Kessler (2011) draws on the economization framework to compare and reconnect processes of 'financialization' and 'securitization' in world politics. He points towards the centrality of the notion of risk to highlight 'the emergence of new networks, actors, practices, temporalities and even the very mode in which security and finance are understood and observed.'

Closely linked is the debate on a particular contemporary governance technique, namely that of indicators and statistics. The number of measurement techniques in global politics has skyrocketed in recent years, as 'big data' has allowed the development of a wide range of indicators for a range of international political practices and problems, extending from the measurement of liberty and freedom to indicators of educational achievement, problems of corruption, and general security and social stability (Davis et al. 2012). Indicators and statistics, such as the Fragile States Index (formerly Failed States), are developed by various actors, ranging from international organizations to advocacy organizations, to philanthropic organizations and academics (Bueger and Bethke 2014). ANT is a particularly helpful tool to understand how these technologies work by focusing on how they assemble, develop translations and create powerful actors (Bueger 2014; Porter 2012; Davis et al. 2012).These studies all employ ANT to theorize science as a particular 'technology of governance'. Studies of science as a technology of governance that draw on ANT explore the relations which make these technologies of governance and allow them to govern states and people.

A second set of studies in IR are interested in technology and non-human objects more immediately. In particular, critical security studies have become concerned with ANT to study surveillance technology, new types of warfare or to rethink nuclear politics. Here the interest in ANT is spurred by the attempt to rethink 'materiality' (Aradau 2010; Srnicek et al. 2013). William Walters (2002) was perhaps the first to point to the usefulness of ANT to recover the material side of doing international politics, examining the role of documents in European integration. Since then the US-led global war on terror has spurred the interest of security studies scholars in the role of technology as part of international security networks. Studies of the airport as a particular security space which hosts technologies took inspiration from ANT (Salter 2007; Schouten 2014), while another path of investigation has focused upon warfare and weapons technology. Pouliot (2010), for instance, discusses the role of nuclear warheads in constituting NATO–Russia relations, while others have utilized ANT concepts to develop symmetrical positions of nuclear politics that embrace the ambivalence of nuclear technology (Harrington and Englert 2014).

Within IR there is a growing awareness that ANT is part of what has been called a 'practice turn' (Adler and Pouliot 2011; Bueger and Gadinger 2014). Theories of practice were initially mainly associated with the work of Pierre Bourdieu, within and beyond IR (see Pouliot 2008; Ortner 1984); but it became increasingly clear among IR scholars, social theorists and, indeed, the ANT community that ANT should be seen as part of a general trend towards the study of practice in the social sciences. ANT scholars such as Knorr Cetina (2001) have long understood their work in such a way; others, such as Law (2012), have more recently pointed out that ANT's concept of relation can be seen as more or less equivalent to the notion of practice; and social theorists as well as IR scholars have situated ANT within practice theory discussions (e.g. Schatzki 2002; Nicolini 2013; Gad and Bruun Jensen 2014; Bueger and Gadinger 2014). The importance of recognizing this link should not be underestimated. ANT developed as a programme of research in a specific discipline (STS); yet many of its core ideas, and the epistemic style it embraces in particular, share family resemblance with discussions developed in cultural sociology, feminism, anthropology, history and pragmatist philosophy. To foreground relations, to understand science as a practice, to focus on the mundane and everyday, to consider non-humans as active components, to embrace complexity, hybridity and multiplicity are features shared by practice theorists (Bueger and Gadinger 2014). ANT is not some 'exotic' form of research.[7] It is part of a larger more general trend to rethink (social) science and direct it towards the study of practices and relations. This context implies that there are many other partners in the conversation that ANT is part of. Hence there are also multi-fold connections that can be made if one analyses global politics and aims at rendering ANT studies intelligible to specific disciplines such as IR or political science.

What to do with ANT: in conclusion

ANT can be understood as a social theory which offers a unique take on technology as part of and made in webs of associations (actor-networks). But it is much more than that. ANT is a methodology which encourages us to do science differently. It offers a distinct style of how to produce knowledge about the world by being in that world. ANT wants us to be detectives who go out and explore the world and how humans and non-humans work together. We should take less for granted before we start our research:

- Do not assume that you already know who the actors are.
- Do not start from the assumption that humans and non-humans are essentially different.
- Go explore relations and how actants become actors and powerful.

These are some of the guidelines that ANT equips us with. As a result of these provisos the objectives of doing research change. Our goal is no longer to identify the one coherent explanation or verify and falsify a system of general claims. The aim is to appreciate incoherence, to embrace and to explore multiplicity. An ANT researcher does not want to tell one clean, sanitized narrative, and make the empirics 'fit' your theory. Instead it is to draw on the empirical material, let it speak for itself as far as possible – as Callon or Latour might say: Yes, let the scallops and door-closers speak! It is to reconstruct complexity and incoherence.

But where does one start, if not from theoretical assumptions? If the world is contingent and fluid, what are the empirical starting points? Whether we are investigating how things work in practice or why they fail, the anchor is always a problematic situation – that is, a state that causes problems and in which something is at stake. Rescuing scallops, closing holes in a wall or providing water to local populations – these are all problematic situations. Starting from this problem, ANT gives us an open and flexible vocabulary to record and describe the work by which these problems are made and unmade. It allows us to pursue open, flexible and indeterminate empirical enquiry beyond epistemological and ontological constraints.

All this sounds radical if thought of in philosophical terms. But if one appreciates the narratives that arise out of ANT research, it is actually not. What we get are narratives which are creative, thought-provoking and eye-opening. IR and the study of global politics will benefit from these new types of narratives, about how technology acts and how out of the messiness of international life actors evolve and become powerful because of the associations and relations they are part of.

Notes

1 Research for this chapter benefitted from a grant by the Economic and Social Research Council (ESRC). For comments and suggestions we are grateful to Daniel McCarthy and Peer Schouten.
2 Published under the pseudonym Jim Johnson (1988).
3 The MoS, a government agency created in 1939 to direct supply functions for the British war effort, was defunct by 1959.
4 See Chapter 4 for an alternative rendering of relational ontology.
5 For a related notion, see the discussion of technological closure in Chapters 2 and 7.
6 Callon identifies four steps in the translation process, namely problematization, interessement, enrolment and mobilization. Each of these terms has become part of the ANT vocabulary, and they have been used and further developed widely.
7 Some studies have claimed that ANT is, politically, somewhat conservative (see Fuller 2000).

References

Best, Jaqueline and William Walters (eds). 2013. Forum on 'Actor-Network Theory' and International Relationality: Lost (and Found) in Translation. *International Political Sociology* 7(3): 332–349.
Bueger, Christian. 2014. From Expert Communities to Epistemic Arrangements: Situating Expertise in International Relations. In Maximilian Mayer, Mariana Carpes and Ruth

Knoblich (eds) *International Relations and the Global Politics of Science and Technology*. Wiesbaden: Springer, pp. 39–54.

Bueger, Christian and Felix Bethke. 2014. Actor-Networking the 'Failed State': An Enquiry into the Life of Concepts. *Journal of International Relations and Development* 17(1): 30–60.

Bueger, Christian and Frank Gadinger. 2007. Reassembling and Dissecting: International Relations Practice from a Science Studies Perspective. *International Studies Perspectives* 8(1): 90–110.

Bueger, Christian and Frank Gadinger. 2014. *International Practice Theory: New Perspectives*. Basingstoke: Palgrave Macmillan.

Çalışkan, Koray and Michel Callon. 2009. Economization, Part 1: Shifting Attention from the Economy towards Processes of Economization. *Economy and Society* 38(3): 369–398.

Callon, Michel. 1986. Some Elements of a Sociology of Translation: Domestication of the Scallops and the Fishermen of St Brieuc Bay. In John Law (ed.) *Power, Action and Belief: A New Sociology of Knowledge?* London: Routledge, pp. 196–223.

Callon, Michel. 1986b. The Sociology of an Actor-Network: The Case of the Electric Vehicle. In Michel Callon, John Law and Arie Rip (eds) *Mapping the Dynamics of Science and Technology*. Basingstoke: Macmillan, pp. 19–34.

Callon, Michel (ed.). 1998. *The Laws of the Markets*. Oxford: Blackwell.

Callon, Michel and Fabian Muniesa. 2005. Peripheral Vision: Economic Markets as Calculative Collective Devices. *Organization Studies* 26(8): 1229–1250.

Czarniawska, Barbara. 2014. *Social Science Research: From Field to Desk*. London and Thousand Oaks, CA: SAGE Publications.

Davis, Kevin, Angelina Fisher, Benedict Kingsbury and Sally Engle Merry (eds). 2012. *Governance by Indicators: Global Power through Classification and Rankings*. Oxford: Oxford University Press.

Davis Cross, Mai'a K. 2012. Rethinking Epistemic Communities Twenty Years Later. *Review of International Studies* 39(1): 137–160.

De Laet, Marianne and Annemarie Mol. 2000. The Zimbabwe Bush Pump: Mechanics of a Fluid Technology. *Social Studies of Science* 30(2): 225–263.

Gad, Christopher and Casper Bruun Jensen. 2010. On the Consequences of Post-ANT. *Science, Technology and Human Values* 35(1): 55–80.

Gad, Christopher and Casper Bruun Jensen. 2014. The Promises of Practice. *Sociological Review* 62(4): 698–718.

Hall, Rodney Bruce. 2009. Intersubjective Expectations and Performativity in Global Financial Governance. *International Political Sociology* 3(4): 453–457.

Harrington, Anne and Matthias Englert. 2014. How Much is Enough? The Politics of Technology and Weaponless Nuclear Deterrence. In Macmilian Mayer, Marianna Carpes and Ruth Knoblich (eds) *The Global Politics of Science and Technology, Vol. II*. Wiesbaden: Springer.

Henriksen, Lasse F. 2013. Performativity and the Politics of Equipping for Calculation: Constructing a Global Market for Microfinance. *International Political Sociology* 7(4): 406–425.

Hobson, John M. and Leonard Seabrooke (eds). 2007. *Everyday Politics of the World Economy*. Cambridge: Cambridge University Press.

Johnson, Jim. 1988. Mixing Humans and Nonhumans Together: The Sociology of a Door-Closer. *Social Problems* 35(3): 298–310.

Kessler, Oliver. 2011. Beyond Sectors, Before the World: Finance, Security and Risk. *Security Dialogue* 42(2): 197–215.

Knorr Cetina, Karin. 2001. Objectual Practice. In Theodore R. Schatzki, Karin Knorr Cetina and Eike von Savigny (eds) *The Practice Turn in Contemporary Theory*. London: Routledge, pp. 175–188.

Latour, Bruno. 1987. *Science in Action: How to Follow Scientists and Engineers through Society*. Cambridge, MA: Harvard University Press.

Latour, Bruno. 1999. On Recalling ANT. In John Law and John Hassard (eds) *Actor Network Theory and After*. Oxford: Blackwell, pp. 15–26.

Latour, Bruno. 2005. *Reassembling the Social: An Introduction to Actor-Network Theory*. Oxford/New York: Oxford University Press.

Latour, Bruno and Steven Woolgar. 1979. *Laboratory Life: The Social Construction of Scientific Facts*. Beverly Hills, CA: Sage.

Law, John. 1987. On the Social Explanation of Technical Change: The Case of the Portuguese Maritime Expansion. *Technology and Culture* 28(2): 227–252.

Law, John. 2009. Actor-Network Theory And Material Semiotics. In Bryan S. Turner (ed.) *The New Blackwell Companion to Social Theory*. Oxford: Blackwell, pp. 141–158.

Law, John. 2012. Collateral Realities. In Fernando Dominguez Rubio and Patrick Baert (eds) *The Politics of Knowledge*. Abingdon: Routledge, pp. 156–178.

Law, John and Michel Callon. 1992. The Life and Death of an Aircraft: A Network Analysis of Technical Change. In Wiebe E. Bijker and John Law (eds) *Shaping Technology/Building Society: Studies in Sociotechnical Change*. Cambridge, MA: MIT Press, pp. 21–52.

Lidskog, Rolf and Goran Sundqvist. 2002. The Role of Science in Environmental Regimes: The Case of LRTAP. *European Journal of International Relations* 8(1): 77–100.

Mackenzie, Donald, Fabian Muniesa and Lucia Siu. 2007. *Do Economists Make Markets? On the Performativity of Economics*. Princeton, NJ: Princeton University Press.

Mazower, Mark. 2012. *Governing the World: The History of an Idea*. London: Penguin.

Mol, Annemarie. 2010. Actor-Network Theory: Sensitive Terms and Enduring Tensions. *Kölner Zeitschrift für Soziologie und Sozialpsychologie* 50(1): 253–269.

Nicolini, Davide. 2013. *Practice Theory, Work and Organization*. Oxford: Oxford University Press.

Porter, Tony. 2012. Making Serious Measures: Numerical Indices, Peer Review, and Transnational Actor-Networks. *Journal of International Relations and Development* 15(4): 532–557.

Pouliot, Vincent. 2008. The Logic of Practicality: A Theory of Practice of Security Communities. *International Organization* 62(2): 257–288.

Pouliot, Vincent. 2010. The Materials of Practice: Nuclear Warheads, Rhetorical Commonplaces and Committee Meetings in Russian–Atlantic Relations. *Cooperation and Conflict* 45(3): 1–17.

Salter, Mark B. 2007. Governmentalities of an Airport: Heterotopia and Confession. *International Political Sociology* 1(1): 49–66.

Schatzki, Theodore R. 2002. *The Site of the Social: A Philosophical Account of the Constitution of Social Life and Change*. University Park: Pennsylvania State University Press.

Schouten, Peer. 2014. Security as Controversy: Reassembling Security at Amsterdam Airport. *Security Dialogue* 45(1): 23–42.

Srnicek, Nick, Maria Fotou and Edmund Arghand. 2013. Introduction: Materialism and World Politics. *Millennium: Journal of International Studies* 41(3): 397.

Walters, William. 2002. The Power of Inscription: Beyond Social Construction and Deconstruction in European Integration Studies. *Millennium: Journal of International Studies* 31(1): 83–108.

Waltz, Kenneth N. 1979. *Theory of International Politics*. New York: McGraw-Hill.

4

CRITICAL THEORY OF TECHNOLOGY

Design, domination and uneven development

Daniel R. McCarthy

Critical Theory approaches to International Relations (IR) are well established in the field, forming a rich strand of theoretically sophisticated and politically engaged scholarship.[1] They highlight the often problematic nature of core theoretical assumptions in IR, asking that we enquire into the constitution of the key concepts that underpin the discipline. As a project, Critical Theory is both sociological and normative. Rather than take the world as it is and attempt to smooth its functioning, Critical Theory seeks to de-naturalize commonly held theoretical assumptions about the world and our knowledge of it in order to outline possibilities for progressive social change. Its empirical accounts investigate how the features of global politics, such as anarchy or nationalism, came into being historically. Historical sensitivity allows Critical Theory to draw out features of international politics that can change, and empirically identifies the resources within world politics that will allow for change in an emancipatory direction. This approach has been fruitful across a range of issue areas, from security studies and international political economy to global environmental politics and normative and ethical theorizing (Booth 2004; Morton 2007; Eckersley 2012; Linklater 1998).

Curiously, however, for an approach with roots in Marxist historical materialism, Critical Theory in IR has, in general, tended not to pay sustained attention to the place of technology or the non-human in global politics. It has, of course, elaborated on the material, social and historical conditions that generate specific political processes under analysis, such as the conditions that enabled the rise of American hegemony after World War Two (Rupert 1995; Van der Pijl 1984). But, beyond a few examples, it has not really sought to outline how materiality matters or how technology is designed, developed and disseminated globally within structures of social power and domination (Wyn Jones 1999; Peoples 2010; McCarthy 2015). Despite this lack of attention, Critical Theory presents a promising way to grapple with the complex global politics of technology. In contrast to other approaches to the politics of technology in International Relations, Critical IR Theory combines sustained attention to the political economy of global capitalism with a focus on the complex dynamics of cultural power that derive from enduring structural inequalities. It links normative critique and sociological analysis in order to realize deeper forms of democracy and equality in international politics.

While this project is incipient in IR, it has wider roots and contemporary resonances. In keeping with the general flowering of Critical Theory since the turn of the twenty-first century, a diverse range of scholarship taking its cues from Marxism and Critical Theory has emerged in the humanities and social sciences beyond IR to theorize and analyse the politics of non-human objects. The conceptualization of 'prosumerism' and modern digital capitalism (Dyer-Witherford 1999, 2015; Fuchs 2014), the reappropriation Bolshevik thought for application in the Anthropocene (Wark 2014) and the development of an 'accelerationist' critique of neoliberal society (Srnicek and Williams 2015) nestle alongside more traditional philosophical projects (Feenberg 1996, 2002; Lynch and Fuhrman 1991; Wendling 2009), forming a diverse range of work. These theoretical developments have reached beyond their initial formulation – largely within the fields of Media and Communications Studies, the Philosophy of Technology and Science and Technology Studies (STS) – into IR since 2000. The Critical Theory of Technology in IR thereby represents a synthesis of critical social theory, Marxist historical sociology and Critical IR Theory. IR scholarship has extended these approaches by considering the role that 'the International' plays in constituting the politics of technological design and use, outlining how this all-important element of 'lateral' causality (Rosenberg 2006) shapes, and is shaped by, objects and artefacts.

This chapter will discuss these themes as follows. First, it will lay out the central elements of Marx's intellectual project as it relates to technology, as these ideas are the foundation for later Critical Theory approaches. This sustained ground-clearing is important given the occasional misrepresentation of this work in the wider literature. Second, it will outline the technological determinism of the Second International[2] and the problematic treatment of non-human objects in Western Marxism, with a specific focus on the Critical Theory of the Frankfurt School. Third, it will note the important break with this legacy developed by Andrew Feenberg. This section will introduce the important concepts of technological **ambivalence** and **bias** to flesh out an approach to thinking about technology from a Critical Theory perspective. Finally, it will lay out a more sociologically concrete approach to studying technology from a Critical IR Theory perspective, focusing in finer detail than Feenberg on the role of the state and the uneven and combined development of international society in technological politics.

Marx and Engels on technology and the forces of production

> The hand-mill gives you society with the feudal lord, the steam engine gives you society with the industrial capitalist.
>
> *(Marx 1847)*

These oft-quoted lines from Karl Marx's *The Poverty of Philosophy* may not immediately suggest that Marxist historical materialism is a promising approach for the study of technology in global politics. They lend themselves to a theory of history that is technologically determinist, and Marxism has often been interpreted as a crudely **materialist** theory of history in which societies inevitably proceed through preordained stages of technological development on their way to a fully realized communist future (Rigby 1998: 7–16). Yet, at the same time, the ambiguity in Marx's work has also provided the building blocks for a more sophisticated account of the politics of technology. A brief account of Marx's intellectual project will help outline the central elements of Marx's thought that persist in contemporary Critical Theory accounts of technology.

The intellectual horizon for Marx's project was initially set by G.W.F. Hegel, whose system of philosophy dominated German intellectual life in the decades either side of his death in 1831. For Hegel, human history was explained by the progressive realization of Spirit in the world. Spirit objectifies itself in the world, analogous, perhaps, to an artist objectifying their ideas or emotions in a painting. The material world is the vehicle through which Spirit expresses itself and comes to know its own nature (Taylor 1977: 91–92). What the world is, at any given moment in time, is required by Spirit moving through the stages of its self-realization. The details of this picture are, of course, far more complex (and challenging) than this brief summation suggests (see Taylor 1977; Beiser 2005). The central point is that Hegel posited an **idealist** theory of historical development.

This understanding of historical change was potentially quite conservative in its implications, suggesting that the world is as it is out of natural necessity. Marx took up Ludwig Feuerbach's critique of Hegel – Feuerbach had argued that Hegel's Spirit was merely the mistaken attribution of human powers to a higher entity – and radically extended it from its focus on religion to an examination of political economy and the practical material actions of human beings in the world (Marx 1975 [1845]; Marx and Engels 1998 [1845]). Marx and Friedrich Engels asserted that ideas about the world were embedded in specific social and political contexts that changed over time. If one wanted political change, they argued, it was not enough to change the way people think about the world – the material conditions of human societies had to be altered as well. Marx and Engels' polemical arguments against German idealism have led to claims that they ignored the role of ideas in history in favour of a simple brute materialism, but this is mistaken. Historical materialism was not a rejection of the importance of ideas as a moving force in history, as the question of the causal priority of ideas or materiality was not of particular interest to Marx, despite later ideas to the contrary (Schmidt 2014 [1971]; Eagleton 2011: 128–159). It was, rather, an attempt to note that social and political change, even when motivated by changed ideas, had to be practically enacted, and that this practice was limited by certain material conditions.

Marx combined Hegel's **dialectics** with a historical approach to political economy in order to analyse capitalist modernity. The starting point for this project was human embodiment in the natural world. At the most basic level of our existence, human beings must eat and must have shelter and clothing. Marx placed the production of material subsistence at the core of his social theory, locating humans within nature, as we have specific natural bodily capacities that exist as the 'first fact' of all human history, and as capable of changing nature (and ourselves) as we remake the world through production (Marx and Engels 1998 [1845]: 37, 38–51; Fracchia 2005). Human communities shape how biological capacities are used or not used by different people. Using these capacities, human societies have organized themselves in a wide range of ways throughout history, from hunter-gatherer societies to nomadic pastoral groups to modern industrial capitalist states, each with their distinctive definitions of human needs and each with a unique relationship to nature. Technological artefacts are part of this metabolism with nature, extending our natural physical capacities in ways that transform us and nature at the same time.

Marx locates these material practices within broader social structures, stressing enduring structural features of social order that shape technological development in a way often occluded in STS (Klein and Kleinman 2002; Feenberg 2002: 27–32; Feenberg 2010: 130). For our purposes, it is sufficient to demarcate social structures by the social property relations that dominate in a given historical period. Robert Brenner (1976: 31) defines social property relations as 'the inherently conflictive relations of property – always guaranteed directly or indirectly, in the last analysis, by force – by which an unpaid-for part of the product is extracted from the direct producers by a class of non-producers'.[3] Social property relations structure the nature of class struggles within a society. To simplify complex class relations for heuristic value (cf. Marx 1977 [1852]; Wright 2014), modern capitalist societies are largely defined by the relationship between capitalists who own the means by which commodities are produced and who take the profit from the sale of these commodities, and labourers, who sell their ability to work to capitalists and receive a wage in return. Marx understood capital and labour as having opposed interests, leading to conflict between them.

Neither social structures nor individual roles in these structures are static in this historically sensitive approach. Marx employed a relational ontology, often called a philosophy of 'internal relations', asserting that the character of an object or person is determined by their relationship to other persons or actors within a larger social structure (Ollman 1976). A capitalist is not a capitalist based on owning objects that have the quality of being capital; we **fetishize** objects when we fail to recognize the social processes that define the meaning of land, lathes or laptops. A capitalist is a capitalist by virtue of their relationship to labourers; labour and capital are mutually constitutive. This relational perspective views capitalism and its internal relations as a totality, in contrast to other relational ontologies, such as Actor-Network Theory, which explicitly reject this approach to social theory (Law 2004; on totality see Jay 1984). Over time, these relations will inevitably undergo some form of change – this is, after all, a *historical* materialism – resulting in new social forms and new sets of property relations.

Capitalism is distinguished from other forms of social organization, such as feudalism or ancient slave-based societies, by its technological dynamism. Marx

(1976 [1867]) noted that capitalist social property relations pressure market-actors to innovate. Capitalists must successfully compete against other capitalists in the marketplace in order to stay in business; as a result, capital is incentivized to continually revolutionize the **forces of production** (Brenner 1986; Braverman 1974). This is historically unique. Two important social dynamics result from these structural pressures on social actors. First, continuous improvements in technology allow for the replacement of workers at an ever-growing rate. Anyone living through our contemporary era in the developed West – in which unemployment due to technological innovation is a topic of concern for academics, politicians, and society at large – can readily grasp this course of development (Srnicek and Williams 2015). More workers competing for fewer jobs means lower wages for workers and higher profits for capital – technological innovation has an impact on how wealth is distributed in society. Second, ownership of the means of production is understood by Marx and subsequent Marxists to grant capital significant social control over labour in the workplace. This process has often been understood as a drive to deskill labour in order to weaken the power of labour over production, preventing highly skilled workers from gaining significant bargaining power due to their irreplaceable skills while also reducing costs (e.g. Braverman 1974; Kristal 2013).

Capitalist power was, for Marx, more than simply the ability to gain advantage in the class struggle through the labour process. Marx outlines a deeply normative critique of how the bodies of workers under capitalism are deformed and contorted, shaped in accordance with the needs of capital rather than the human needs of the worker for work that enables human flourishing. Marx (1976 [1867]: 481–482) argues that capitalism:

> converts the worker into a crippled monstrosity by furthering his particular skills as in a forcing-house, through the suppression of a whole world of productive drives and inclinations … the individual himself is divided up, and transformed into the automatic motor of a detail operation … which presents man as a mere fragment of his own body.

The division of labour 'brands the manufacturing worker as the property of capital' (Marx 1976 [1867]: 482). For Marx, the alienation of human creative powers was central to the ethical critique of capitalism (Wendling 2009). Only when workers could control their work lives would this be overcome. Similar injunctions inform Critical Theory of Technology in its drive to democratize technological development (see Chapter 10).

At the same time, however, these claims raise serious questions about the agency of historical actors to alter socio-technical practices and institutions that sustain domination. Marx often emphasizes the ability of human beings to create technological objects and make their world. This is evident in stress placed on the capacity of capitalists to structure the labour process, noted above. At other moments, however, Marx articulated a strong technologically determinist picture of historical causation. In the famous 1859 'Preface to a Critique of Political Economy' – a passage often viewed as the singular statement capturing Marx's theory of history, Marx writes:

> At a certain stage of their development, the material productive forces of society come in conflict with the existing relations of production, or – what is but a legal expression of the same thing – with the property relations within which they have been at work hitherto. From forms of development of the productive forces these relations turn into their fetters. Then begins an epoch of social revolution.
>
> *(quoted in Cohen 1978: n.p.)*

Here, Marx suggests that as the forces of production develop, they come into conflict with the existing **relations of production**. This contradiction between advanced technological forms and a set of economic relationships that hold back the development of new technologies – for example, industrial technology and the feudal economic relations of the *ancien régime* – creates a crisis, and this crisis must be resolved to enable the further development of technology. The forces of production have, in this passage, a developmental dynamic of their own, over and above the actions of human agents. Reading this passage as foundational, G.A. Cohen argued in a classic (if flawed) book that Marx's theory of history was technologically determinist – it was the self-propelling character of technological development that led to social change. This approach, also called 'productive force determinism', has often served as a short-hand for Marxist views of technology as a whole (Heilbroner 1967; Rigby 1998: 17–174; Bimber 1990).

The history of Marxist thought about technology features competing characterizations of these passages (Cohen 1978; Harvey 2006: 98–99; Ollman 1976). These exegetical arguments reflect, in one measure, the deeply problematic status accorded to Marx's arguments as a source of legitimacy and authority within Marxist scholarship, but they also reflect genuine attempts to grapple with the dilemmas of technological determinism in a serious and sustained way. We will now trace the development of these arguments in the twentieth century, focusing on the theorization of technology within Western Marxism.

Technological artefacts: instruments of liberation or structures of domination?

At the turn of the twentieth century the reception of Marx's thought was primarily through the popularization of his work by theorists heavily influenced by positivism and largely ignorant of the Hegelian heritage of Marx's thought. Thus Karl Kautsky – chief theoretician of the largest socialist party in the world, the German Social Democrats (SPD) – outlined a picture of Marxism in which the forces of production, conceptualized as heavy machinery, were seen to have a natural development dynamic. The forces of production were, for Kautsky, entirely determining of social development; this sidelined any role for human agency in the creation of social and political outcomes. The political impact of this technological determinism was all too evident to Kautsky's many socialist critics – it pushed towards political quietism and even apathy (Gouldner 1980: 86). Yet, despite this weakness, Kautsky's general theoretical perspective was largely shared by the leading lights of the Second International, endorsed by the 'Father of Russian Marxism', Georgi Plekhanov, and central to the reformist political theory of social democrats.

In the aftermath of the First World War and the Bolshevik overthrow of Tsarism the technologically deterministic picture of human history seemed to have been decisively refuted in practice. Vladimir Lenin and the Bolsheviks had seized power in the most technologically and economically backward state in Europe, contrary to theoretical expectations of Marxist technological determinists (Trotsky 1932). In the most technologically advanced states – Britain, Germany and the United States – socialist revolutions did not occur. Facing a situation in which the working classes were not turning to Marxism, and were instead being drawn into the orbit of far-right fascist ideologies in Italy and Germany, Marxist theorists in the West faced the task of explaining how this had come to pass. The resulting theoretical outpouring greatly expanded the remit and depth of Marxist theory. Studies of cultural politics and the renewed development of ideology-critique emerged among a range of scholars to explain the dilemma of a non-revolutionary working class and to reconsider the appropriate aims of Marxist political practice within the firm earthworks of Western capitalism.

However, despite the dynamic expansion of Marxist thought, Western Marxism – as the body of critical thought developed in Western Europe during this time came to be known (Anderson 1976) – accepted rather than challenged the deterministic understanding of technology inherited from the theorists of the Second International. The three key thinkers of this first wave of Western Marxism – Georg Lukács, Karl Korsch and Antonio Gramsci – did not discuss the politics of technology in any depth (cf. Lukács 1967 [1923]; Korsch 1970 [1923]; Gramsci 1971). Rather, Lukács, Korsch, Gramsci and the diverse group of scholars based at the Institute for Social Research (IFS) in Frankfurt – the 'Frankfurt School' – focused their attention on developing critiques of positivist epistemology and methodology. Western Marxists directed sustained attention to the socially and historically embedded character of knowledge, yet did not, to any significant degree, extend this analysis to scientific knowledge or technological development. Indeed, Max Horkheimer, director of the IFS, outlined in his classic essay 'Traditional and Critical Theory' two distinct sets of knowledge practices, one appropriate for the natural world and one appropriate for human society (Horkheimer 1992 [1937]). Horkheimer had an optimistic view of technological progress at this time. As Richard Wyn Jones notes of this essay, 'Horkheimer equates technological progress with progress itself in that it improved prospects for human emancipation – understood in terms of the rational, planned domination of nature' (Wyn Jones 1999: 84; Wiggershaus 1995: 48–49, 118–122). Critical Theory, as the Frankfurt School project came to be known, relied on a distinction between nature and culture in its foundational statement. In its first manifestation, Western Marxism accepted a definition of science and technology as separate and distinct from the social order in its creation and use, assuming technological development as historically progressive.

The industrialized slaughter of soldiers and civilians during the Second World War far surpassed the horrors of the First. In this atmosphere, any sparks of optimism in the Frankfurt School faded. Their approach to society generally, and technological progress in particular, embraced a darker and far more pessimistic view of the possibility of human emancipation. A substantial normative re-evaluation of technological change occurred, with Theodor Adorno and Horkheimer's *Dialectic of Enlightenment* (1997 [1947]) exemplifying this shift. Grafting together Weber's characterization of modernity as the increasing dominance of instrumental rationality with technologically determinist Marxism, Horkheimer and Adorno now portrayed technology as a source of oppression. In this account, modern industrial society has extended instrumental rationality to all areas of human life, in contrast to pre-modern forms of social life; Adorno and Horkheimer argued that the human pursuit of mastery over nature, expressed in science and technology, necessarily involves a totalizing domination over other humans (Jarvis 1998: 27; Feenberg 2002: 111).

This represented a serious challenge to the general Marxist political project, which had viewed technological progress as central to providing the material foundations for socialism. Simon Jarvis effectively summarizes Adorno and Horkheimer's stance: 'Power over nature, the real advance of human freedom, is paid for with impotent subjection to the social divisions and domination which grant that power' (Jarvis 1998: 27). If the technological change required for socialism undermined social and political freedom in the process of its creation, the entire political project of the Left seemed caught within an impenetrable impasse.

The solutions offered to this apparent impasse by the second generation of Frankfurt School theorists similarly rested upon acceptance of the basic division between the technological and the social. While political resignation was the preferred option for Horkheimer, even theorists who viewed the resumption of the critical project of Enlightenment as a live option only did so by arguing that technological rationality must be sequestered from other human social practices. Thus the drive to quarantine the technological is foundational to Jürgen Habermas's reconstruction of Critical Theory as a theory of communicative action and discourse ethics (McCarthy 1978: 22–24; Feenberg 1996; Habermas 1971a, 1971b: 301–317). For Habermas, we cannot overcome the threats to human freedom represented by technological reason, but we can limit them. The dominance of instrumental rationality in social life is a product of the inappropriate extension of technical values into spheres where they do not belong (Bimber 1990: 337). Adorno, Horkheimer and Habermas asserted that the inappropriate extension of instrumental rationality was the product of capitalist social relations. Habermas, like Horkheimer and Adorno, thereby retains a historicist approach to technology at one level while relying, at another, on technological essentialism.

The implications of this approach are not, then, the political quietism of the Second International, but they are also not supportive of a more thoroughgoing revolution of science and technology itself. Perhaps informed by the fear of Lysenkoism (Lewontin and Levins 1976), Habermas does not advocate a new science for a new politics.[4] Granting technology its own sphere, he wishes to retain its positive gains and restrain its negative implications. In our era, in which the claims of the scientific community are regularly attacked by a flock of ill-informed sceptics, religious fanatics and conspiracy theorists on issues ranging from vaccination to evolution to climate change, the desire to shield science and technological design from public input may appear to have some merit.

Beyond the impasse: Feenberg's Critical Theory of Technology

Despite the resources provided by Marx and Critical Theory – such as its focus on material practices, unequal power relations, its attentiveness to the place of technology in history, and its sensitivity to historical change – moving beyond the impasse of determinism in Critical Theory was not a straightforward project. Among the first generation of the Frankfurt School, it was the work of Herbert Marcuse (1964, 1968) that did most to prompt an interrogation of Critical Theory approaches to technology. Unlike Habermas, who argued that instrumental rationality was just one form of rationality among others and could thereby be isolated, Marcuse criticized Weber's characterization of instrumental rationality as such (Feenberg 1996; Marcuse 1968: 201–226). Marcuse argued that definitions of rationality and 'efficiency' could not be understood outside their historical context. Even efficiency, 'defined formally as the ratio of inputs to outputs', should not be understood a-historically:

> [Within] the notion of efficiency, one must decide what kinds of things are possible inputs and outputs, who can offer and who acquire them and on what terms, what counts as waste and hazards, and so on. These are all socially specific, and so, therefore, is the concept of efficiency in any actual application.
>
> *(Feenberg 1996: 51)*

Making the concept of efficiency and rationality more concrete allows us to develop historically and contextually specific accounts of technological development. However, Marcuse, for all the strengths of his work, never fully developed these insights. This fell to Andrew Feenberg, the foremost inspiration for the Critical Theory of Technology in IR, who undertook this task through a reconsideration of technological determinist elements in Critical Theory. Marxists and Critical Theorists had tended to favour either the instrumentalist or essentialist side of the question of technology; by contrast, Feenberg sought to transcend this division while retaining the insights of each position.

Rather than simply argue that the nature–society divide is false, Feenberg reconceptualizes the nature of technology and technological rationality, accepting some facets of both the instrumentalist and essentialist forms of determinism (see Introduction). Feenberg thereby argues, in contrast to the Marxism of the Second International, that technological artefacts are not simply tools. They cannot be turned to any purpose. Instead, a given form of technological object determines how users can employ that object for a specific purpose. Objects are biased as a product of their design, created to achieve some aims and not others (Feenberg 2002: 80–82). The material form of technical artefacts literally expresses these aims, beyond the meaning we may give them at a specific moment in time. Biased technological objects aid in the reproduction of social systems through their path dependency; once created, a technological institution tends to aid in the reproduction of a specific form of life. Hegemony, the blend of coercion and consent that allows some social groups to dominate others (Gramsci 1971; Thomas 2009), is supported and partially constituted through the material objects created by dominant social actors (McCarthy 2015). Accepting this element of determinism, Feenberg acknowledges that technological objects shape human society.

This concession to essentialism is not full-blooded, however. While technological objects carry a bias, this bias is never entirely secured due to them ambivalence of non-human objects. While complex technological institutions may have very high levels of bias, their future developments can never be fully determined, and they are necessarily composed of less complex parts. These two aspects of ambivalence recapture aspects of instrumentalism and, with it, human agency to change our socio-technical orders. Ambivalence keeps the door open for progressive social change, stressing that the parts of a given technological object can be rearranged to realize new social purposes. For example, nuclear weapons have a strong bias; it is very difficult to see any bright future in which they are central to global society. However, one of their key parts, the gyroscope, is nevertheless highly ambivalent. As part of the targeting system of a nuclear Intercontinental Ballistic Missile (ICBM), gyroscopes partially constitute objects with highly determined purposes (Mackenzie 1990). Yet they can be removed from these weapons to construct entirely different technological objects with quite different purposes, as found in the use of gyroscopes in the Mars Rover or the Hubble Space Telescope, or in commercial aircraft. The gyroscope can be part of highly determined objects, yet its ambivalence, as a relatively simple object, allows it to be used for all sorts of purposes. Objects like nuclear weapons or aircraft are comprised of parts that can be rearranged to achieve different social purposes. This ambivalence at the lower levels of a technological object presents the opportunity to rework material objects into a different form.

Similarly, Feenberg (2002: 53) stresses that it is possible to build socialism on the basis of capitalist technologies: 'technology can be reshaped as machines developed under capitalism are employed to produce a new generation of machines adapted to socialist purposes. Class power determines which of the ambivalent potentialities of the heritage will be realized'. While an already existing large technical system may support the social relations of the status quo, Feenberg suggests that their ambivalent future development allows for the realization of alternative political possibilities. Ambivalence underscores the exercise of human agency in the process of technological design, and allows Feenberg's Critical Theory of Technology to avoid the pessimistic vision of modern industrial society laid out by Horkheimer and Adorno.

In hindsight, the theoretical resolution of this problem appears deceptively simple, encapsulated in the concise formula describing technology as 'biased but ambivalent'. However, central problems in Critical Theory, present in social theory more broadly (Latour 1993; Jasanoff 2004), needed to be overcome. The main challenge was rooted in Marxist theory's resolutely realist approach to the philosophy of science. Once technological objects are viewed as socially constructed it can seem that we are questioning the mind-independence of the world, anathema for most historical materialist approaches. If technological knowledge is merely the product of power relations, then material contexts can be moulded in any way we would like. This is clearly not the case. Asserting that it is denies the validity of any of our knowledge claims, opening the door to relativism and irrationalism.

As a result of this potential problem, many Marxists and Critical Theorists have resisted this intellectual move (cf. Turner 2003). Alan Sokal, author of the (in)famous 'Sokal Hoax' paper published in *Social Text* in 1996 at the height of the 'Science Wars', stressed the emancipatory motivation behind his attack on postmodern theory: 'I confess that I'm an unabashed Old Leftist who never quite understood how deconstruction was supposed to help the working class' (Sokal 1997: 93). Sokal argued that the reality of quantum mechanics was not affected by its social context, and that the computer science and related technological innovations based on these mechanics were not subject to social construction, even as social context determined what scientific questions may be asked. Addressing this concern yet still arguing for the context-specific determination of technology has thereby operated as a central challenge for the Critical Theory of Technology.

Feenberg responded to this challenge as follows. First, he argued, in conjunction with related strands of Marxist and Critical Theory, that recognition of the constructedness of technological objects does not alter the ontological distinction between nature and society (Feenberg 2002: 27–35; Schmidt 2014 [1971]; Smith 1984). Humans and non-human animals and objects are different types of things and should not be treated as equivalent in our analyses. This is an important point, as breaking down the distinction between the natural and the social would seem to be at the heart of the project of Science and Technology Studies and a central reason for its introduction into International Relations. Yet, as Dick Pels (1996) has argued from a non-Marxist perspective, treating different objects as ontologically symmetrical introduces false equivalences and minimizes very real differences in the capacities that different actors can mobilize in the social world (Vandenberghe 2002; Wendling 2009: 63–65). Human beings do not create the capacity of copper to conduct electricity or the inability of wood to do so; laptops do not write literature or chapters of textbooks, even if suggesting they do can be a useful rhetorical flourish.

In this respect, and in contrast to Actor-Network Theory and aspects of New Materialist and Posthumanist STS-IR, the Critical Theory of Technology remains resolutely – perhaps unfashionably – **humanist** (Feenberg 2002: 34). Human beings, as animals, are ultimately a part of nature, yet our capacity to reflect upon our nature and create technological objects also sets us 'apart from' nature. Socially produced explanations of nature do change over time – the shift from flat-earth thinking is the clearest example (Kuhn 1970 [1962]) – and remain open to contestation, but these explanations do not create the earth or its place in the solar system. Feenberg (2002: 37) is quite explicit on his endorsement of modern scientific practice, noting that 'this approach does not involve an ontological challenge to modern science'.

A second major challenge is the shift away from functionalist explanations of technological change. Marxist and Critical Theory approaches in IR, for example, tend to assume that capitalist social property relations are entirely determining of which technologies are created in the global political economy (Cox 1987: 21, 315; cf. McCarthy 2011). This assumes that a singular socio-technical solution exists to solve problems of profitability for capital, ignoring other aspects of social and political life that inflect technological design and development, such as norms and culture. Crucially, Feenberg integrates the broadened agenda of Critical Theory, in which culture features as a significant object of study, with a focus on the historically specific rationalities of capitalist technological development (Feenberg 2002: 135–139). In other words, capitalism may pressure actors to develop technologies that allow them to compete in the market; but there is significant scope for agency in determining how this will occur and what set of cultural values will be embedded within technological institutions. This includes distinct cultural values around gender, race, class and nationality. Thus, even as class sits as the central cleavage defining the politics of technology, other terrains of social struggle around the subjugation of women and minorities inform the politics of technology.

Socialist feminist approaches to **technoscience**, for example, stress how capitalist structural pressures intersect with ideas about gender and hierarchical gender positions. This occurs both for technologies of production – the classical focus of Marxist critique – and in the commodities that are produced for consumers. Cockburn and Ormond's classic study of the design of the microwave oven in the United Kingdom highlights the gendered nature of the technology's creation (see also Wajcman 2010). Microwave ovens, conceptualized as a female technology due to their associations with cooking and housework in general, were designed by male engineers, with only marginal input from female workers employed in a test kitchen. Ovens were designed 'largely in ignorance of domestic realities'; Dorothy, a home economist working for the 'Electro' company, noted that they were 'designed by men, for a man, without taking into consideration the woman and her cooking' (Cockburn and Ormond 1993: 78–79). The high value placed on technological gadgetry by male engineers sat in contrast to the functionality of the object as defined by female end users. Gendered norms work their way in technological objects in conjunction with the profit motive. Structural power positions, defined by social property relations, allow some dominant social actors to direct and design technological development in line with their non-economic cultural values.

Culture shapes technological development more broadly. Cultural practices can unite groups in society with seemingly opposed economic interests, such as capital and labour, into highly cohesive political movements and parties; discourses around nationhood or race are often important in this respect (Morton 2007: 95–98). The symbolic politics of technology are also at play in this process. Popular cultural products – Hollywood films, commercial television, genre fiction and so forth – inform our visions of possible technological futures in complex ways. Cultural products help to define socio-technical imaginaries and 'common-sense' views of technology (Peoples 2010: 44, 53–58, 254–265; Jasanoff and Kim 2015). Creating dominant political coalitions is a complex process that relies upon creating appealing cultural visions of society, and socio-technical imaginaries feature prominently in this role.

Conceptualizing technological institutions as 'biased but ambivalent' pushes the Critical Theory of Technology away from the deterministic pictures of both classical and Western Marxism. In turn, it requires that our study of technological objects – their design, development and diffusion – is embedded within a historicized account of innovation. Technology, stripped of its universal character, receives its bias from social actors in concrete historical circumstances. For Feenberg, and the Critical Theory of Technology in general, these concrete historical circumstances are defined by specific social property relations. This approach recaptures central elements of Marx's original project, particularly its historicism, its focus on concrete material practices and its relational ontology. Feenberg points towards a narrative of historical development quite distinct from the first generation of Frankfurt School theorists, allowing for a more fine-grained appreciation of technological development within a complex, differentiated and multilinear modernity.

Technology, the state, and uneven and combined development

Feenberg's approach reconstruction of Critical Theory's approach to technology forms an excellent starting point from which to elaborate a more fine-grained and sociologically detailed account of how technology operates in global politics. In order to do this, the schematic presentation of capitalism outlined above has to be filled in. We will now briefly note the central role played by the state in organizing technological development in the modern capitalist societies, before outlining how the uneven and combined development that characterizes the International adds an element of 'lateral' causality. This undermines the idea that technological development is the product of political and social relations bounded by the nation-state, foregrounding the international dimensions of the politics of technology. A brief discussion of changes in global car manufacturing technologies over the course of the twentieth century will help illustrate these concepts.

While the structural relationship between capital and labour is the central dynamic of modern political economy, political institutions mediate how these relations are expressed, with the state acting to secure the conditions necessary for capitalist reproduction in the long term. The role of the state is central to the politics of technology. States support private property rights by providing laws that underpin them, combined with the means necessary to back up these laws in the form of the judiciary, police, army and other correctional bodies. As Ellen Meiksins Wood has argued (1995: 30):

> Absolute private property, the contractual relation that binds producer to appropriator, the process of commodity exchange – all these requires the legal forms, the coercive apparatus, the policing functions of the state. Historically, too, the state has been essential to the process of expropriation that is the basis of capitalism. In all these senses, despite their differentiation, the economic sphere rests firmly on the political.

The right to direct the process of technological development held by the owners of private property is guaranteed by the state. State power is central in constituting the structural power of capitalists in the politics of technology.

While states provide the legal and coercive foundation of social property relations, they also undertake a wider range of tasks that maintain specific material politics. These occur in an indirect and mediated fashion. States, to the degree that they are able, support the basic activities that underpin research and development in contemporary societies. Publicly financed research and development, whether undertaken in national laboratories or the university system, is one of the central building blocks of innovation systems (Nelson 1993; Chen and Kenney 2007). Systems of innovation, both national and transnational, provide the underpinnings for commercialized innovation by corporations. Corporate actors will not undertake this innovation as basic research often does not provide a clear path to profit or an easily recognized return on investment. States are present at the birth of almost all of the most innovative products of contemporary global politics, from the Internet to the iPhone.

A state, of course, exists within a system of states. The presence of multiple political communities shapes the politics of technology in manifold ways, which recent IR scholarship on uneven and combined development in world politics allows us to draw out (Rosenberg 2006; Anievas 2014).[5] Briefly, political communities develop economically and technologically at different rates – they develop unevenly. As advanced technological objects are created, they spread throughout the international system, compelled by security competition, emulation and coercion, among other processes. Once social norms, political institutions and technological objects diffuse, they combine within 'backward' states to create new social forms.[6] The classic example is Tsarist Russia prior to the Russian Revolution, in which the most advanced elements of capitalist social relations and forces of production combined with authoritarian political institutions and vast numbers of peasants involved in subsistence-level farming, creating a state that did not resemble any classical picture of a modern capitalist society (Trotsky 1932). Combination creates multiple paths of sociological development, undermining claims that modernity is a singular process through which all states must pass.

In addition to these developmental dynamics, uneven and combined development foregrounds the significance of inter-societal comparison in global politics. This comparative dimension of world politics should not be underestimated. Technology is often a central point of comparison between national communities, imbuing national cultures with a sense of superiority or inferiority as a result (Adas 1989; Edgerton 2009; cf. Trotsky 1932). Nationalism, as one articulation of inter-state comparison, can be expressed by championing technological achievements like washing machines and refrigerators, as Richard Nixon and Nikita Khrushchev demonstrated during the Cold War. Encounters between the technologically sophisticated and the relatively backward have been central to the politics of modernity, engendering a complex dynamic of resistance and appropriation across the globe, from Japan's Meiji Restoration to Germany's course of authoritarian state-led development, to more recent examples in South and East Asia (Allinson and Anievas 2009; Anievas 2014; Gray 2011). Hierarchy in international politics is constituted by different technological capacities *and* their associated symbolic values. Inter-societal technological comparison, conducted in moral, aesthetic and political terms, is internal to the course of social development and finds its manifestation in material objects. While emulation is important, fear of domination by technologically more advanced states also places pressure upon 'backward' states to adopt the latest technologies. The scope to reject new technologies is thereby circumscribed by inter-state security competition.

At the same time, security competition directly involves the state in technological development, as the client and consumer of military technologies. Foreign policy officials set out strategic visions that guide the process of technological development and, again, can have substantial systemic impact as weapons diffuse throughout the system. For example, Britain's strategic imperative to control the world's oceans as part of its grand strategy in the late nineteenth and early twentieth century was instrumental in driving forward a series of changes in naval technologies to meet this aim, including its most high-profile symbol, the battleship HMS *Dreadnought* (Horowitz 2010: 138–145). As Horowitz notes, 'The battlefleet innovation shifted the speed of interactions along with expectations of the timing and outcome of battles, which had spillover into broader strategic planning' (2010: 152). Fears of being penned in on the Continent saw German policy-makers respond with a programme of battleship development in kind, with this arms racing contributing to wider tensions pre-World War I (Horowitz 2010: 15). State officials do not tell designers precisely how to create weapons systems, but they set the agenda within which weapons development occurs. Similarly, diplomatic interactions produce the state in its socio-technical manifestations, as negotiations over climate change targets or arms control, for instance, impact the power of domestic actors and the kinds of technologies that these actors can create. It is important for our purposes to note that no generic strategic rationale existed to which Britain or Germany conformed. Rather, their foreign policies were the product of the specific domestic balance of class forces in each of their respective states (Anievas 2014). Class struggle between capital and labour and between capitalists in different states shaped the development of these military technologies.

An extended example, looking at the global political economy of the automotive industry, will be helpful in drawing together the pieces of the Critical Theory of Technology in IR.[7] In the early part of the twentieth century, American car manufacturers, led by Henry Ford, introduced production methods and technologies designed to be more efficient by cutting labour costs and increasing productivity. These included the moving assembly line made famous in Charlie Chaplin's *Modern Times* (1936), but also the manufacture of interchangeable parts, engine milling and single-purpose machine tools (Tolliday 1998: 58; Hounshell 1984: 221–222). The Fordist production regime exemplified mass-production techniques, reducing production costs and, thus, the cost of cars to consumers. Its initial incarnation allowed Ford to lower the cost of its famous Model T from $823 in 1908 to only $290 in 1926, a reduction of 65 per cent (Maxton and Wormald 1995: 68–69, quoted in Paterson 2007: 96; Dassbach 1994: 493–499). This mass-production approach was a deeply rooted expression of American culture (Gramsci 1971: 279–318; Rupert 1995: 60–62).

Fordism relied on technologies of mass production and their associated social relations, present in the United States but absent in Europe, where car production was still viewed as a craft industry (Dassbach 1994: 495–498). Workers and managers in France, Germany, Italy and Britain fought back against the imposition of Fordism by their domestic manufacturers due to a belief that mass production was detrimental to quality (Dassbach 1994: 497). The specific Fordist socio-technical order, with its division of the mental labour of technological design from the manual labour of car construction, clashed with European interests and values. In the 1930s, as European countries hiked tariffs on car imports to protect their markets from cheaper American imports, American manufacturers shifted production to Europe itself. Rather than attempt to alter ingrained cultural values and preferences in order to implement American-style mass production, US manufacturers were assimilated into European ways of working, with an attendant reconfiguration of their production processes and the commodities they produced (Dassbach 1994: 507). The political response to American first-mover advantage – tariffs – blunted the threat to Europe's domestic industry, with the partial adoption of Fordist production methods in a reconfigured European auto industry representing an acceptable form of socio-technical order on the Continent.

A similar process took place in the auto industry from the 1970s to the 1990s. After World War II, Japan, in keeping with its post-Meiji Restoration form of state-led development, embarked upon state-sponsored industrial development policies (Hall 2004: 84–85). This included infant-industry protection to ensure that Japanese domestic car manufacturers would not have to compete with their American rivals (Dassbach 1994: 499). After a period of catch-up, Japanese automakers developed new socio-technical orders – on the basis of existing American technologies – that would disrupt the global car industry. In a series of technological innovations, engineers at Toyota developed the 'just-in-time' or lean production method of car making. Taiichi Ohno, the Toyota engineer central to this process, noted of Western production systems that:

> [T]hey had two logical flaws. First, he reasoned that producing components in large batches resulted in large inventories, which took up costly capital and warehouse space and resulted in a high number of defects. The second flaw was the inability to accommodate consumer preferences for product diversity.
>
> *(Holweg 2007: 422)*

Toyota sought to reorient production to both allow for greater variation in vehicle configuration and to cut back on warehousing costs. It did so via lean production methods that also introduced greater flexibility into employment relations in the auto industry. Japanese workplace culture has been viewed as significant in the shaping of this socio-technical settlement:

> Critics point to the fundamental imbalance of power which underlies the Japanese production regime: the early postwar destruction of independent unionism in the Japanese auto industry and the subsequent use of company unions and work groups as a means to motivate workers and to limit and channel their participation in ways which serve the interests of the firm; the relentless intensification of work which results from the deliberate managerial strategy of continually stressing the entire production system through systematic understaffing and the elimination of buffer stocks; incentive pay linked to individual and group performance, and individual advancement based upon managerial valuation rather than seniority; and the ideology of identification with the work team, the plant, and the firm.
>
> *(Rupert 1995: 183)*

The ability of Toyota to save costs on car production combined with the flexibility to easily produce a diversity of cars more attractive to consumers. Strong US domestic worker militancy in the 1960s and 1970s had limited the ability of the Big Three – General Motors (GM), Ford and Chrysler – to speed up production and cut costs, bringing less expensive Japanese imports an increased market share in the United States (Gartman 2004: 185–187; Panitch and Gindin 2011: 207). This sparked a nationalist response by the American auto industry. 'Buy American' became the slogan of the day on television, billboards and in newspapers. This was the symbolic expression of car import limitations on Japanese vehicles that were put in place by legislators. However, as Japanese companies shifted to producing cars in the United States to skirt these limitations, American manufacturers were forced to reconfigure the socio-technical order that underpinned their success. Lean production subsequently diffused throughout the American auto industry in the 1980s and 1990s.

At the micro level, lean production created greater control over the labour process on the shop floor for US car makers. An absence of surplus inventory means that automotive workers are placed under significant time pressures in a way that can be easily monitored (Herod 2000: 523; Rupert 1995: 182–183; Babson 1997). Structurally, lean production allowed for the introduction of greater labour market flexibility in the auto industry, as workers could be employed on a flexible basis according to alternating periods of high and low demand, lowering base wage rates. Yet lean production was not implemented in the United States entirely smoothly. The capital–labour bargain in the American auto industry did not permit the forms of incentive-based pay and team-based production methods of Toyota in Japan to be replicated at GM in Detroit. Even as the Big Three emulated the Japanese model, they were required to modify the implementation of lean production in the face of worker resistance, both on the shopfloor and by the United Auto Workers (UAW) union. Only a larger series of crises in the North American auto industry in the early 2000s, culminating in the 2008 auto bailouts, finally broke the back of labour in the American and Canadian car sectors (Siemiatycki 2011).

In this brief example, all of the analytical elements of a Critical IR Theory perspective on the global politics of technology are in play. The structural pressures of global markets pressed car manufacturers to invest in high levels of technological innovation, and then to realize profits on the basis of these sunk costs. This favoured the development of technologies that created high levels of efficiency in the production process, with 'efficiency' defined in terms of profit rates. Uneven development, both globally and within the auto industry itself, meant that some car manufacturers – with particular national cultural values[8] – had the power to create socio-technical orders that reflected these values. Workers attempted to contest the definitions of technical efficiency and rationality on offer, and were at times successful in promoting alternatives. Technological institutions were biased towards the increased exploitation of labour, but this bias was shaped by the national context of their initial emergence; for Fordism, this was the United States and its mass-production ethos, while in Japan lean production relied on its specific set of values around workplace cultures.

As these socio-technical orders diffuse, the pressure first movers place upon laggards leads these orders to be emulated, rejected or reconfigured (if they can afford it). European, Japanese and American corporations all emulated aspects of the leading forms of socio-technical car production at various times. At the same time, a measure of ambivalence in Fordist production technologies allowed European automakers to reconfigure these technological institutions in line with their different social and political context. Similarly, in the relationship between the Japanese and American auto industries, Japanese car manufacturers were able to build upon a technological base initially set by Fordism. The subsequent development of lean production by Toyota granted Japanese car companies significant advantages in the marketplace, which forced both a legislative and cultural response by an American state acting to ensure the continued existence of the Big Three. As it became clear that Japanese car makers would simply shift production to the US to avoid import limits, the Big Three were forced to engage in technical restructuring. Yet the balance of power between capital and labour was different in the American context, limiting the duplication of the fully fledged system of lean production as it existed in Japan. Domestic class struggle, whether in Europe in the 1920s or the US in the 1980s, reshaped the socio-technical form of car production that had diffused throughout the global political economy.

The Critical Theory of Technology in IR provides an account of the politics of technology in which sensitivity to historical context and the specific trajectories of individual technological artefacts and systems combines with a macro-sociological account of modernity. As with Critical IR Theory in general, it avoids the a-historicism and state-centrism of much mainstream IR theory. It emphasizes how specific power struggles over the precise configuration of technology, conducted between classes and states, enables and sustains social hierarchies – not simply hierarchies between states – in global politics. It also points towards a normative critique of these global practices. This critique has not been significantly developed yet (but see Chapter 10), although the intellectual means to do so are certainly present in the Critical Theory of IR more broadly.

Conclusion: the ambivalent futures of the Critical Theory of Technology in IR

Critical Theory has long engaged with the question of technology. From its roots in Marx through its development in the twentieth century to the present, the materialism of Critical Theory and its central emphasis on political economy has required that its proponents grapple with the objects and artefacts that structure our lives. Fundamentally historical in its orientation, Critical Theory directs our attention to the ongoing process by which technologies are produced through complex structural power relations and the pressures these systems exert. It focuses our attention on how these power relations allow some actors to embed their norms and values within technological institutions; at the same time, of course, it highlights the potential to change these objects through social struggle and the expansion of democratic governance. How we extend our bodily capacities, how we define them, who directs this process and who carries out these directions is shaped by the structural asymmetries of power and their ideological supports that exist at a given period in time – but times change.

None of this is to suggest that the Critical Theory of Technology in IR provides a complete picture of the global politics of technology. Tensions between the precise balance of structure and agency in accounts of technological politics remain, particularly with regard to the role of capitalism and culture as the drivers of technological change. To date, this approach to STS-IR has focused on large technical systems such as ballistic missiles or the Internet, with a relative neglect of the kind of technologies – like the microwave oven – that shape our societies in myriad small ways. There has also been a relative neglect of the wider dimensions of ideology that shape socio-technical orders. While political cultures have prominently featured in Critical Theory, the manifestations of popular culture that inform our dreams and nightmares about technology on a daily basis, in their global dimensions, remain to be studied. This is fertile ground for future research, with Marxist cultural materialism a promising conversation partner for co-productionist approaches and the literature on post-colonial technoscience in STS (Jameson 2005; Jasanoff and Kim 2015). Questions of the politics of technological expertise remain to be thoroughly engaged from an STS-IR viewpoint; here dialogue with recent developments in international law seems promising (Kennedy 2016). Finally, the normative theorization of global socio-technical democratic futures represents a promising avenue of study. The Critical Theory of Technology in IR exhibits significant potential to deepen our understanding of technology in world politics, but it is a potential yet to be realized on a broad scale.

Notes

1 Please note that Critical Theory in IR is used here to denote a range of approaches broadly inspired by Western Marxism, e.g. by the work of Antonio Gramsci, the Frankfurt School and classical Marxism. See Cox (1981), Linklater (1998) and Rosenberg (2006) for examples. When critical theory is not capitalized it refers to a much broader range of theory in IR, such as approaches primarily inspired by poststructuralism.
2 The Second International Workingmen's Association (1889–1916) was a transnational organization of socialist and labour parties.
3 Teschke (2003: 7) notes that these class relations are fixed by political institutions, with this fixity created by sociological rules and norms, their legal manifestations, and the means of violence that underpin them. Thus, while classes are the central actors within Marxist social theory, their actions are not narrowly economic. See, more broadly, Wood (1995), Eagleton (2011: 107–127) and Jameson (2005).
4 Trofim Lysenko was a Soviet geneticist whose views on genetic evolution were shaped by Stalin's orthodox dialectical materialism.
5 Please note that these approaches do not investigate technological politics in depth.
6 Neither of the terms 'advanced' or 'backward' should be taken to imply any normative judgement.
7 Due to space constraints it is not possible to outline the full socio-technical manifestation of automobility as a large technical system. For an outstanding treatment, albeit one not explicitly drawing on STS, see Paterson (2007).
8 The impact of national culture on the design process remains today, even as the car industry has shifted into a more disaggregated form of commodity chain production – R&D facilities still tend to be based within the 'home' states of specific corporations and reflect the cultural values of their location.

References

Adas, Michael. 1989. *Machines as the Measure of Men: Science, Technology, and Ideologies of Western Dominance*. Ithaca, NY: Cornell University Press.

Adorno, Theodor W. and Max Horkheimer. 1997 [1947]. *Dialectic of Enlightenment*. London: Verso.

Allinson, Jamie C. and Alexander Anievas. 2009. The Uses and Misuses of Uneven and Combined Development: An Anatomy of a Concept. *Cambridge Review of International Affairs* 22(1): 47–67.

Anderson, Perry. 1976. *Considerations on Western Marxism*. London: Verso.

Anievas, Alexander. 2014. *Capital, the State, and War: Class Conflict and Geopolitics in the Thirty Years' Crisis, 1914–1945*. Ann Arbor: University of Michigan Press.

Babson, Steve (ed.). 1995. *Lean Work: Empowerment and Exploitation in the Global Auto Industry*. Detroit, MI: Wayne State University Press.

Beiser, Frederick. 2005. *Hegel*. London: Routledge.

Bimber, Bruce. 1990. Karl Marx and the Three Faces of Technological Determinism. *Social Studies of Science* 20(2): 333–351.

Booth, Ken (ed.). 2004. *Critical Security Studies and World Politics*. Boulder, CO: Lynne Rienner.

Braverman, Harry. 1974. *Labour and Monopoly Capital*. New York: Monthly Review Press.

Brenner, Robert. 1976. Agrarian Class Structure and Economic Development in Pre-Industrial Europe. *Past and Present* 70: 30–75.

Brenner, Robert. 1986. The Social Basis of Economic Development. In John Roemer (ed.), *Analytical Marxism*. Cambridge: Cambridge University Press, pp. 23–53.

Chen, Kun and Martin Kenney. 2007. Universities/Research Institutes and Regional Innovation Systems: The Cases of Beijing and Shenzhen. *World Development* 35(6): 1056–1074.

Cockburn, Cynthia and Susan Ormond. 1993. *Gender and Technology in the Making*. London: SAGE.

Cohen, G.A. 1978. *Karl Marx's Theory of History: A Defence*. New York: Oxford University Press.

Cox, Robert W. 1981. Social Forces, States and World Orders: Beyond International Relations Theory. *Millennium: Journal of International Studies* 10(2): 126–155.

Cox, Robert W. 1987. *Power, Production and World Order: Social Forces in the Making of History*. New York: Columbia University Press.

Dassbach, Carl H.A. 1994. The Social Organization of Production, Competitive Advantage and Foreign Investment: American Automobile Companies in the 1920s and Japanese Automobile Companies in the 1980s. *Review of International Political Economy* 1(3): 489–517.

Dyer-Witherford, Nick. 1999. *Cyber-Marx: Cycles and Circuits of Struggle in High-Technology Capitalism*. Chicago, IL: University of Illinois Press.

Dyer-Witherford, Nick. 2015. *Cyber-Proletariat: Global Labour in the Digital Vortex*. Cambridge: Pluto Press.

Eagleton, Terry. 2011. *Why Marx Was Right*. New Haven, CT: Yale University Press.

Eckersley, Robyn. 2012. Moving Forward in the Climate Negotiations: Multilateralism or Minilateralism? *Global Environmental Politics* 12(2): 24–42.

Edgerton, David. 1999. From Innovation to Use: Ten Eclectic Theses on the Historiography of Technology. *History and Technology* 16(2): 111–136.

Feenberg, Andrew. 1996. Marcuse or Habermas: Two Critiques of Technology. *Inquiry* 39(1): 45–70.

Feenberg, Andrew. 2002. *Transforming Technology: A Critical Theory Revisited*. Oxford: Oxford University Press.

Feenberg, Andrew. 2010. *Between Reason and Experience: Essays in Technology and Modernity*. Cambridge, MA: MIT Press.

Fracchia, Joseph. 2005. Beyond the Human-Nature Debate: Human Corporeal Organisation as the 'First Fact' of Historical Materialism. *Historical Materialism: Research in Critical Marxist Theory* 13(1): 33–62.

Fuchs, Christian. 2014. *Digital Labour and Karl Marx*. London: Routledge.

Gartman, David. 2004. Three Ages of the Automobile: The Cultural Logics of the Car. *Theory, Culture and Society* 21(4–5): 169–195.

Gouldner, Alvin W. 1980. *The Two Marxisms: Contradictions and Anomalies in the Development of Theory*. London: Macmillan.

Gramsci, Antonio. 1971. *Selections from the Prison Notebooks*. London: Lawrence & Wishart.

Gray, Kevin. 2011. The Social and Geopolitical Origins of State Transformation: The Case of South Korea. *New Political Economy* 16(3): 303–322.

Habermas, Jurgen. 1971a. *Towards a Rational Society*. London: Heinemann.

Habermas, Jurgen. 1971b. *Knowledge and Human Interests*. Boston, MA: Beacon Press.

Hall, Derek. 2004. Japanese Spirit, Western Economics: The Continuing Salience of Economic Nationalism in Japan. *New Political Economy* 9(1): 79–99.

Harvey, David. 2006. *The Limits to Capital*. London: Verso.

Heilbroner, Robert L. 1967. Do Machines Make History? *Technology and Culture* 8(3): 335–345.

Herod, Andrew. 2000. Implications of Just-in-Time Production for Union Strategy: Lessons from the 1998 General Motors–United Auto Workers Dispute. *Annals of the Association of American Geographers* 90(3): 521–547.

Holweg, Matthias. 2007. The Genealogy of Lean Production. *Journal of Operations Management* 25(2): 420–437.

Horkheimer, Max. 1992 [1937]. Traditional and Critical Theory. In *Critical Theory: Selected Essays*. New York: Continuum.

Horowitz, Michael C. 2010. *The Diffusion of Military Power: Causes and Consequences for International Politics*. Princeton, NJ: Princeton University Press.

Hounshell, David. 1984. *From the American System to Mass Production, 1800–1932*. Baltimore, MD: Johns Hopkins University Press.

Jameson, Frederic. 2005. *Archaeologies of the Future: The Desire Called Utopia and Other Science Fictions*. London: Verso.

Jarvis, Simon. 1998. *Adorno: A Critical Introduction*. London: Routledge.

Jasanoff, Sheila (ed.). 2004. *States of Knowledge: The Co-Production of Science and Social Order*. London: Routledge.

Jasanoff, Sheila and Sang-Hyun Kim (eds). 2015. *Dreamscapes of Modernity: Sociotechnical Imaginaries and the Fabrication of Power*. Chicago, IL: University of Chicago Press.

Jay, Martin. 1984. *Marxism and Totality: Adventures of a Concept*. Berkeley: University of California Press.

Kennedy, David. 2016. *A World of Struggle: How Power, Law and Expertise Shape Global Political Economy*. Princeton, NJ: Princeton University Press.

Klein, Hans K. and Daniel Lee Kleinman. 2002. The Social Construction of Technology: Structural Considerations. *Science, Technology and Human Values* 27(1): 28–52.

Korsch, Karl. 1970 [1923]. *Marxism and Philosophy*. London: New Left Books.

Kristal, Tali. 2013. The Capitalist Machine: Computerization, Workers' Power, and the Decline in Labor's Share within U.S. Industries. *American Sociological Review* 78(3): 361–389.

Kuhn, Thomas S. 1970 [1962]. *The Structure of Scientific Revolutions*, 2nd edition. Chicago, IL: University of Chicago Press.

Latour, Bruno. 1993. *We Have Never Been Modern*. Cambridge, MA: Harvard University Press.

Law, John. 2004. And If the Global Were Small and Noncoherent? Method, Complexity, and the Baroque. *Environment and Planning D* 22(1): 13–26.

Lewontin, Richard and Richard Levins. 1976. The Problem of Lysenkoism. In Hilary Rose and Steven Rose (eds) *The Radicalisation of Science: Ideology of/in the Natural Sciences*. London: Macmillan, pp. 32–64.

Linklater, Andrew. 1998. *The Transformation of Political Community*. Cambridge: Polity.

Lukacs, Georg. 1967 [1923]. *History and Class Consciousness*. London: Merlin.

Lynch, William T. and Ellsworth R. Fuhrman. 1991. Recovering and Expanding the Normative: Marx and the New Sociology of Scientific Knowledge. *Science, Technology and Human Values* 16(2): 233–248.

Mackenzie, Donald. 1990. *Inventing Accuracy: A Historical Sociology of Nuclear Missile Guidance.* Cambridge, MA: MIT Press.

Marcuse, Herbert. 1964. *One-Dimensional Man: Studies in the Ideology of Advanced Industrial Society.* New York: Beacon.

Marcuse, Herbert. 1968. *Negations: Essays in Critical Theory.* London: Penguin.

Marx, Karl. 1975 [1845]. *Early Writings.* London: Penguin.

Marx, Karl. 1955 [1847]. *The Poverty of Philosophy.* New York: Progress.

Marx, Karl. 1977 [1852]. *The Eighteenth Brumaire of Louis Bonaparte.* Moscow: Progress.

Marx, Karl. 1976 [1867]. *Capital: A Critique of Political Economy, Volume I.* London: Penguin.

Marx, Karl and Friedrich Engels. 1998 [1845]. *The German Ideology.* New York: Prometheus Books.

McCarthy, Daniel R. 2011. The Meaning of Materiality: Reconsidering the Materialism of Gramscian IR. *Review of International Studies* 37(3): 1215–1234.

McCarthy, Daniel R. 2015. *Power, Information Technology, and International Relations Theory: The Power and Politics of US Foreign Policy and the Internet.* Basingstoke: Palgrave Macmillan.

McCarthy, Thomas. 1978. *The Critical Theory of Jürgen Habermas.* Cambridge, MA: MIT Press.

Morton, Adam David. 2007. *Unravelling Gramsci: Hegemony and Passive Revolution in the Global Economy.* London: Pluto Press.

Nelson, Richard R. (ed.). 1993. *National Innovation Systems: A Comparative Analysis.* Oxford: Oxford University Press.

Ollman, Bertell. 1976. *Alienation: Marx's Conception of Man in Capitalist Society,* 2nd edition. Cambridge: Cambridge University Press.

Panitch, Leo and Sam Gindin. 2011. *The Making of Global Capitalism: The Political Economy of American Empire.* London: Verso.

Paterson, Matthew. 2007. *Automobile Politics: Ecology and Cultural Political Economy.* Cambridge: Cambridge University Press.

Pels, Dick. 1996. The Politics of Symmetry. *Social Studies of Science* 26(2): 277–304.

Peoples, Columba. 2010. *Justifying Ballistic Missile Defence: Technology, Security and Culture.* Cambridge: Cambridge University Press.

Rigby, S.H. 1998. *Marxism and History: A Critical Introduction,* 2nd edition. Manchester: Manchester University Press.

Rosenberg, Justin. 2006. Why is There No International Historical Sociology? *European Journal of International Relations* 12(3): 307–340.

Rupert, Mark. 1995. *Producing Hegemony: The Politics of Mass Production and American Global Power.* Cambridge: Cambridge University Press.

Schmidt, Alfred. 2014 [1971]. *The Concept of Nature in Marx.* London: Verso.

Siemiatycki, Elliot. 2011. Forced to Concede: Permanent Restructuring and Labour's Place in the North American Auto Industry. *Antipode* 44(2): 453–473.

Smith, Neil. 1984. *Uneven Development: Nature, Capital and the Production of Space.* Oxford: Blackwell.

Sokal, Alan D. 1997. Transgressing the Boundaries: An Afterword. *Dissent* 43(4): 93–99.

Srnicek, Nick and Alex Williams. 2015. *Inventing the Future: Postcapitalism and a World without Work.* London: Verso.

Taylor, Charles. 1977. *Hegel.* Cambridge: Cambridge University Press.

Teschke, Benno. 2003. *The Myth of 1648.* London: Verso.

Thomas, Peter D. 2009. *The Gramscian Moment: Philosophy, Hegemony and Marxism*. Leiden: Brill.

Tolliday, Steven. 1998. The Diffusion and Transformation of Fordism: Britain and Japan Compared. In Robert Boyer, Elsie Charron, Ulrich Jurgens and Steven Tolliday (eds) *Between Imitation and Innovation: The Transfer and Hybridization of Productive Models in the International Automobile Industry*. Oxford: Oxford University Press, pp. 57–96.

Trotsky, Leon. 1932. *The History of the Russian Revolution*. Chicago, IL: Haymarket Books.

Turner, Stephen. 2003. The Third Science War. *Social Studies of Science* 33(4): 581–611.

Van der Pijl, Kees. 1984. *The Making of an Atlantic Ruling Class*. London: Verso.

Vandenberghe, Frederic. 2002. Reconstructing Humants: A Humanist Critique of Actant-Network Theory. *Theory, Culture and Society* 19(5–6): 51–67.

Wajcman, Judy. 2010. Feminist Theories of Technology. *Cambridge Journal of Economics* 34(1): 143–152.

Wark, Mackenzie. 2014. *Molecular Red: Theory for the Anthropocene*. London: Verso.

Wendling, Amy E. 2009. *Karl Marx on Technology and Alienation*. London: Routledge.

Wiggershaus, Rolf. 1995. *The Frankfurt School: Its History, Theories, and Political Significance*. Cambridge, MA: MIT Press.

Wood, Ellen Meiksins. 1995. *Democracy against Capitalism: Renewing Historical Materialism*. Cambridge: Cambridge University Press.

Wright, Erik Olin. 2014. *Understanding Class*. London: Verso.

Wyn Jones, Richard. 1999. *Security, Strategy and Critical Theory*. Boulder, CO: Lynne Rienner.

5

NEW MATERIALISM AND POSTHUMANISM

Bodies, brains, and complex causality

Nick Srnicek

Across a wide variety of fields, the past decade has seen a proliferation of interest and ideas around materialism, technology and the embodied nature of our social lives.[1] Grouped under the moniker of 'new materialisms', speculative realism, **posthumanism** or object-oriented philosophy, these investigations have charted new paths in social and political thought and made significant inroads into transforming established academic fields. Within International Relations (IR), these new materialisms can broadly be distinguished from what might be described as the old materialisms: approaches such as geopolitical theories, historical materialism, and the rump or naïve materialism of social constructivism. For the first, in its paradigmatic – which is to say, least nuanced – form, geography is determinative of international relations (cf. Gray 2004; Ashworth 2013). Empires rise and fall on the basis of shifting interplays between the environment and technology, and ideas have only a superficial force.[2] For historical materialism, in its simplest form, economic struggles are determinative of history. Modes of production, defined by the nature of productive technologies, lay out the basis for class struggle, and history is transformed according to a set process. Meanwhile, the rump materialism of social constructivism simply continues the naïve philosophical realism of a 'common-sense' attitude to the nature of the world.[3] Things simply are as they appear, and a solid objective reality exists outside of us. The questions and problems that Immanuel Kant formulated against such brute empiricism are ignored, and reality becomes aligned with our intuitions about it. In all of these old materialist approaches, there is a strict and clear division between the social world and the natural world. The latter may impinge on the social world, but it does so in a more or less deterministic way, while matter itself operates mechanistically.

By contrast, the new materialisms offer a different image of matter. While diverging on a number of issues, the new materialist turn can arguably be said to find expression in a few common elements.[4] In the first place, they all engage, to varying degrees, with natural science research. Whether it is complexity science, biology, or neuroscience, each shows a healthy respect for the study of the physical world and attempts to incorporate findings from these sciences into our understanding of the social world. In addition, in different ways they all seek to overcome the division between humans and nature, mind and body. In traditional social theory and in the dominant approaches to International Relations, society and nature are mutually exclusive realms, with often deterministic relationships between them. By contrast, the new materialisms reject the **anthropocentric** assumptions of much classical IR theory, and recognise the importance of non-human elements that enter into the constitution of social life. Perhaps most significantly, they seek to overcome the traditional division between humans and non-humans without falling into a reductionist account which would see all social phenomena as stemming from physical phenomena, as found, for example, in attempts to describe human warfare as rooted in evolutionary drives for genetic survival (see Gat 2006).

The consequences of these shifts in philosophical foundations ramify across the study of world politics. The new materialisms involve a displacement of several classical disciplinary focal points. Some move attention away from purely social phenomena and towards the natural world; others emphasise becoming, perpetual change and contingency, and the production of novelty over the standard emphasis on order and stability; and some shift the focus away from abstractions like the state and towards the concrete realities of lived bodies. In any case, these new materialisms present an important challenge to the habitual patterns of thought in IR. In particular, as we will see, they bring about a shift in epistemology, in ethical visions of global politics, and to the kinds of causal stories we might tell.

Why have these ideas emerged in recent years? Here, we might ask after the conditions – both historical and conceptual – which have given rise to these new materialisms. On a purely philosophical level, they have no doubt emerged from a sense that the famed linguistic turn of the twentieth century had exhausted itself. From early twentieth-century reflections on how language attaches to the world to the 1970s' pinnacle of deconstructive analysis of texts, language had been of pre-eminent importance and focus for much of the century. But among many younger scholars, there was often a sense that a focus solely on textual issues in philosophy and social theory had reached its critical limits. The methods of critical deconstruction – so often used to highlight the contingent nature of social oppressions by deconstructing supposedly natural categories of race, gender or sexuality – had sedimented into a new common sense and became applied indiscriminately across the humanities. There was a desire and search, therefore, for new critical methods. Equally, there has been a subterranean concern for more materialist analysis than the poststructuralist canon, exemplified by the work of Jacques Derrida, Jean-François Lyotard and Jean Baudrillard, typically allowed. The work of the philosopher Gilles Deleuze, in particular, seemed to offer a framework that went deeper than his contemporaries'.[5] Beyond the linguistic surface of our lived realities, Deleuze sought out the material and non-human ground out of which experience emerged. Beneath the play of concepts and words, Deleuze pursued a materialist becoming which could explain the generation of relatively stable linguistic and conceptual formations. This other tradition of poststructuralist thought has been central to the revival of materialism in recent years. The Deleuzian notion of **assemblages** has been widely adopted and adapted by various scholars (Sassen, 2008), and, alongside Spinoza, Whitehead and Bergson, he remains among the most cited authors in new materialist scholarship. Debates internal to the tradition of continental philosophy have thereby generated new ways of thinking about social life and its materialist constitution.

Yet intellectual concerns are never separate from historical changes, and the new materialisms are no exception. In an age where climate change threatens masses of humanity, where technology is drastically changing our societies, and where economic crisis permeates everyday life, it is unsurprising to see a renewed attention to the materialist aspects of our world. It is impossible to believe that the social world is somehow cleanly demarcated from the natural world. Instead, the two spheres are intensely implicated in each other, and this has demanded new concepts and theories in order to understand the contemporary situation. The critical tools forged in poststructuralism, postmodernism and deconstruction have all served their purpose – but many feel they have faltered in the face of new political problems. It is in this historical context that a turn to the new materialisms makes eminent sense.

This chapter will examine and reflect upon a variety of different new materialisms in an effort to show their contributions to the study of International Relations. In contrast to sociologically oriented approaches surveyed elsewhere in this volume, new materialist scholarship prompts reflection on our ethical orientations to the world without prescribing precise methods of analysis. In the first section, I will discuss the recent emphasis on bodies within global politics, particularly as inflected through feminist concerns. The next section will examine **neuropolitical** ideas, and how their ontology transforms IR's traditional ideas of epistemology and identity. The third section looks at posthumanism and how it alters concepts of agency, structure, and epistemology. Finally, the conclusion will reflect back on some of the broad new materialist themes and outline the limits of these approaches. In particular, I will argue that the drive to blur the lines between humans and non-humans is problematic for a critically oriented IR theory, while the loose reliance on scientific metaphors often obscures more than it reveals.

The body in IR

Traditionally, bodies have been set outside the scope of IR theorising. What has been deemed of primary importance are (theoretically abstracted) of states and their interactions. In fact, reading most IR, one could be forgiven for thinking it was a disembodied virtual world – absent of friction, flesh, desire or death. For mainstream IR, violence is an entirely disembodied phenomenon, something carried out by rational minds on inert and unimportant bodies. In war, bodies count simply as statistics, while in game theory, bodies are completely discarded from the formal analysis of war, replaced by algebraic symbols. Yet, by taking the body into account, we can begin to reveal the ways in which bodies shape and are shaped by violence, the ways in which they become gendered and racialised, and the effects this has on world politics (Wilcox 2015: 3). As numerous scholars have noted, it is odd that a field which is defined, in the last instance, by reflections on violence against bodies nevertheless rarely takes the body as a site of inquiry. Indeed, as Lauren Wilcox has argued, IR tends to assume the body as an individual and pre-existing material entity upon which 'real' politics is played. The body itself does not enter the political space, but merely acts as a background condition for sovereign subjects (Wilcox 2015: 17; Edkins and Pin-Fat 2005; Shinko 2010). Bodies, in other words, are incidental to traditional IR.

By contrast, feminist theorists have long been attentive to the importance of the body in politics – both the ways in which women's bodies have constrained and limited full entrance into the political sphere and the ways in which society encodes norms and rigid identities onto those same bodies (Enloe 1989; Daigle 2015; Shepherd 2014). The history of women is the history of the ways in which their bodies have been the basis for an entire series of oppressions. Feminists have therefore been at the forefront of analysing and highlighting the ways in which the body plays into politics. By rejecting the image of an inert body, this work has raised important questions about the constitution and unnaturalness of particular bodily formations. Why are women ascribed certain roles in society on the basis of their physical nature? How are women marked off and segregated from certain positions by virtue of their appearance? And how have the powerful deployed the tropes of biological division in order to maintain their power? These sorts of questions, in turn, continue a long line of de-essentialising gestures within feminist thought (Butler 2011). Drawing upon Judith Butler's work on normative violence, Wilcox has recently placed the body firmly in the lens of IR theorising. Here, 'normative violence' refers to the ways in which particular norms shape what bodies should be in society, what lives matter in politics, and what bodies are grievable in war (Wilcox 2015: 9; Butler, 2010).[6] Why is it, for instance, that we grieve over particular bodies while passing others by with complacency? How is it that these divisions between bodies are socially constructed to become a natural and unquestioned reaction? The positioning and elaboration of particular bodies into these categories is what grounds the violence that has been the traditional object of study for IR. In this sense, bodies are foundational to IR.

But this also means that bodies are objects of politics – not merely as entities to be saved against sovereign violence, but more fundamentally as entities to be known and managed through what Michel Foucault (2009) called '**biopolitical**' mechanisms. For Foucault, whereas *sovereign* power operated by controlling who died (through executions or war), *biopolitical* power operates by controlling who lives and how. Think, for example, of the multitude of regulations and rules that are designed for public health. These are oriented towards maintaining, quite literally, a healthy body politic. The regulation of the population is a key concern of international politics, and bodies are therefore constructed through various security and health measures – as illustrated, for example, in the 'securitisation' of HIV/ AIDS in the interests of national security (Elbe 2005; McInnes and Rushton 2012). Reproduction of the species becomes a concern of government, interventions are made into bodily formations, and certain lives become demarcated according to whether they should live or die. At the extreme, bodies become rendered as objects upon which any manner of state violence can be perpetrated: torture, forced feeding, solitary confinement, drone strikes and so on. The turn towards the body helps us recognise the ways in which these actions are made possible in the first place.

One example of the implication between bodies and politics is particularly relevant to IR: the relationship between war, the military and bodies (Protevi 2013; Sylvester 2012). As the philosopher John Protevi makes eminently clear, human bodies are not naturally predisposed to the demands of modern warfare. Numerous studies have shown that humans in war have avoided shooting to kill, and even shooting at all in many cases (Protevi 2013: 60; Grossman 1996). Soldiers must be trained, modified, adapted and shaped into machines for killing (we can see here the importance of biopolitical power and its regulation of bodies). In particular, soldiers must be trained to avoid conscious judgement in order to kill: they must dissociate themselves from their own actions in order to achieve the goals of the state. In a sense, this means they must relinquish some of their agency – or, perhaps more accurately, they must delegate agency to a non-conscious aspect of their body. This is similar to what happens when we are playing a sport or a musical instrument. In such cases, instinct takes over and conscious self-reflection actually gets in the way. And, as anyone who does these actions will tell you, it is a lengthy process of training and practice which enables the body to take over and the conscious mind to step aside. This is the entire point of military training – a procedure which integrates bodies, politics and war into the military formations that IR takes as a primary object of inquiry.

As Protevi notes, this training has to weave its way between two tasks: to incite the non-conscious agency that enables effective killing in war, but also to turn it off when needed (e.g. when on base or in a civilian area). The two tasks are in tension with each other, and highly sophisticated procedures have been developed to try to grapple with these contradictory tendencies. Two methods in particular shape soldiers into the prime zone between a rage that enables killing and a calm that enables sober reflection. In reflex training, for instance, soldiers' muscle memory is trained in order to instinctually respond to figures of the enemy. Silhouettes of the enemy are presented in firing ranges, and an entire battery of racial slurs is deployed to turn the enemy into an inhuman other. As Protevi writes (2013: 66), 'contemporary military training cuts subjectivity out of the loop so that most soldiers' bodies are able to *temporarily* withstand the act of killing'. With more recent digital technologies, training deploys more nuanced means to achieve its goals. Simulators take away the reality of violence while also allowing for more discrimination between civilians and enemies. Meanwhile, real-time team-based communication distributes responsibility along group lines rather than individual lines (Protevi 2013: 68), making it easier to dispel the worries about guilt. The problem of turning bodies into soldiers becomes ever more fine-tuned with such technologies, and we can begin to see here the importance of attending to how bodies are constructed in international relations and how they shape politics. This discussion of the body in war leads us into the next section: a fully fledged attempt at theorising the mutual entanglement of nature and society.

Neuropolitics and knowledge politics

In one of the more theoretically elaborated versions of this approach, William Connolly seeks to demonstrate the ways in which the brain and **affects** enter into politics, and vice versa. This is a form of what he calls 'neuropolitics'. Essential here is a focus on a 'micropolitics' below the levels of legislation, deliberation, and policy, but underpinning them (Connolly 2002: 21). This is the level of embodiment – the waves of affects and bodily coordination that set the ground for intelligible discourse, and that murmur beneath the formal qualities of politics. It is the level of emotion, gut instinct, and barely conscious feelings, all formulated within the brain. While we may not be conscious of these elements, they nevertheless shape and direct our intuitions, our beliefs and our desires. In other words, this level forms a basis for much of what has traditionally been the focus of political theory and IR.

We might place Connolly's work productively alongside social constructivism to highlight its distinctiveness. Where the latter emphasises the linguistic means through which identity is built, the former highlights the construction of affect, desire and emotion that underpins our visceral senses of identity. Identity is not just something in our head; it is something that we *feel*. Identity, for many of us, is encoded on our bodies – gendered and racialised. And identity is something that comes to be embedded in our brains in the form of instinctual reactions. Perhaps the most important insight here is that adopting a neuropolitics perspective gives us an explanation for why identities are so sticky and significant to people. Why, despite all the pressures that may be mobilised against them (up to, and including, the threat of death in some cases), do people still hold onto particular identities? Or what enables suicide bombers to kill themselves on the basis of their religious or political identity?

Traditional explanations have been offered in attempts to outline the 'rationality' of these gestures, but these explanations feel woefully inadequate. Self-interested calculation is unable to explain these phenomena. And while social constructivist accounts have been useful for highlighting how identities and interests are built up through social interaction, they have been equally insufficient at explaining the power and force of identity. For many, identity has simply been something that people are socialised into through ideas, and that perhaps guides preferences. But neuropolitics gives identity its affective charge which we all, in our everyday life, know exists. The visceral reactions against threats to a national identity or religious identity are something that often occurs before rational and self-conscious thought even appears on the scene. The incorporation of neuropolitics into IR can therefore help make sense of the limits of discursive deliberation and the stickiness of identities and values. It can assist in cross-cultural engagement and added depth to the constructivist accounts of identity.

This level of affective flows also reveals a general truth of the world for Connolly: that it is a world in flux, and that the world of ideas and the world of bodies are continually intermingling. In a particularly clear articulation of a basic new materialist tenet, he writes about the task of moving beyond traditional divisions between nature and culture:

> 'Nature' and 'culture', on my reading, are not defined by categorical differences between the material and the immaterial, or between that which is highly predictable and that which is unpredictable, or between that which is simple and that which is complex, or between that which lacks a history and that which is not, or between that which lacks a capacity for discrimination and that which expresses such a capacity.
>
> *(Connolly 2002: 63)*

Drawing upon Nietzschean and Deleuzian ideas, Connolly argues that the world is not comprised of similarities and identities, but rather differences and flows (Connolly 2002: 50–79). The stability of the world that we experience every day is itself simply a matter of flows slowing down to a level where they appear more stable than they are. Think, for instance, of our climate and the historically peculiar stability which it has seen over the past 10,000 years, and which has enabled humanity to thrive. For all intents and purposes, our climate appears as a nearly eternal and stable system. But of course today we know that is not the case, as climate change threatens to upset the delicate balance and introduce a rapid series of climatic changes. For Connolly, this is the general nature of the world – flows of materials at different speeds which self-organise into relatively stable entities (bodies, subjectivities, communities, states, international systems).

Given this ontology, there are a number of ramifications on epistemology and our understanding of the limits of knowledge. Perhaps most important is the question of where uncertainty and unpredictability lie: are they due to limited human cognition or intrinsic features of the world? If the former holds, the positivist assumption of universal laws of society or nature that apply in all times and places may still be sustainable, even if we remain only partly capable of articulating them. Universal laws would actually exist in the world, even if our minds only ever partially approximate them. But if uncertainty is a feature of the world itself, however, the belief in universal laws and theories based around them would obscure a world in flux. We would have to give up on positivistic assumptions and rethink what knowledge means. It is, unsurprisingly, the latter position that Connolly argues for. Humanity, in his account, is capable of encountering the world of differences – and, through the layering of similarities, is able to partially grasp events and transform them into knowledge. But the world inevitably upsets our stable categories and laws. As a result, the traditional demand for truth is downplayed (though not rejected) by Connolly, and a different ethical stance to the world is instead articulated. In a world of becoming, absolute truth becomes impossible, and it is necessary to continually revise knowledge as the world changes.

This does not mean that the search for knowledge should be abandoned; but it does place strict philosophical limits on the stability of knowledge. Rather than a demand for absolute truth, the ontology of becoming emphasises that the world is constantly in flux. As such, this ontology requires cultivating a particular set of ethical stances towards the world – ones that are at odds with the sort of dominating impulse behind much knowledge creation. For Connolly, the priority of becoming over **being** demands an attentiveness towards the fleeting creativity of the world that escapes established categories. The goal is to be alert to those movements which inaugurate something new into the world, rather than forcing them into pre-established ideas. Likewise, for political theorists such as Jane Bennett (2010), the new materialisms demand building a sensibility of respect for the non-human elements of our world – for their fragility and agency.

However, these positions remain problematic insofar as they apparently seek to reduce politics down to ethics – the implicit idea behind these positions being that if people freely adopted a different ethical stance towards the world, then structural power would dissipate and we could solve major problems like climate change or the crises of neo-liberalism. But this is to greatly underestimate the weight of those problems, and to greatly overestimate the capacity of ethical stances to change the world. While Connolly may be right that we need to rethink what 'knowledge' means, it does not follow that ethics is an adequate substitute for collective politics.

Posthumanism versus anthropocentrism

We turn now to a different strand of new materialisms – what has been called the 'posthuman turn'. We take as an exemplar of this position the work of Erika Cudworth and Stephen Hobden, who have sought to surpass the anthropocentric limits of traditional IR theory.[7] Common to the other new materialisms, Cudworth and Hobden's project attempts to overcome what they see as the gap between humanity and nature in traditional social theory. For them, such a division embeds a mistaken anthropocentrism into the heart of our theories – one which leads to a misguided normative belief in the possibility of liberating ourselves from attachments to nature (Cudworth and Hobden 2011: 2; Youatt 2014; Chandler 2015). But, unlike many of the other new materialisms, in Cudworth and Hobden's approach there remain important distinctions between human and non-human systems: human systems have more potential for self-organisation; human individuals have the capacity for self-reflection and intentional action; and the reliance on signification through language introduces a whole host of abilities that are absent from non-human systems. In their own words, 'rather than seeing a separation between the human and the non-human, [their approach] sees the human world as embedded within the natural world' (Cudworth and Hobden 2011: 48–49). The posthuman turn gives up on the belief that our theories must centre on humanity, but it does not mean giving up on the unique qualities of humanity.

To escape any anthropocentric presumption, Cudworth and Hobden advocate an approach based upon complex systems theory, which enables social systems to be conceived as nested within a natural world, and which overcomes the limits of thinking in terms of linear relations between elements (where an increase in one cause leads to an equal increase in one effect). Complex systems, by definition, are systems which involve non-linearities, sensitivity to initial conditions, and strict limits to predictability. For example, in a linear system, if 1 ton of steel produces two cars, 2 tons of steel will produce four cars. In a non-linear system, an increase in inputs may create effects that are entirely unpredictable in linear terms – an increase in global temperatures of 2–3 degrees may have vastly different impacts than an increase of 1–2 degrees.

Set against classic IR theories about the international system, the complexity view makes a number of advances: it rejects the static nature of realist theories of structure; it overcomes the singular logic of both realist and neo-Marxist accounts; and it surpasses the linear logic which relates the behaviour of agents directly to structures (Cudworth and Hobden 2011: 52–63). By contrast, a complex systems approach sees structures as plural (invoking political, economic, social, and natural structures); as creative and open to emergence; and as intrinsically dynamic (though also open to periods of relative stability). It helps give an explanatory framework that can encompass significant changes in the world order (e.g. from feudalism to capitalism), and that can help articulate how certain unexpected elements can emerge (e.g. the breakdown of the Soviet Union or the rise of non-state terrorism). Moreover, it is a framework which begins to include the dynamics of the natural world as one key element of world politics, rather than as a static background condition for geopolitics. Particularly important is the fact that complexity theory sees systems as nested within each other, mutually shaping and altering outcomes. It is not, in other words, that there is a natural world and a separate social world. Rather, the two mutually overlap, even if there are some distinct elements to each.

One of these distinct aspects is agency – the capacity to act, rather than merely react. Indeed, common to many of the new materialisms is a rethinking of what agency means; though, as we will see, this is often done in a questionable way. Within traditional IR, the agent–structure debate has been prominent in recent years thanks to the work of Alexander Wendt (1987), where he sought to incorporate insights from sociology into IR. Today, the question of agency has been receiving renewed attention, with Diana Coole's work epitomising this trend. For her and the new materialists more broadly, agency is decentred away from its traditional locus in the human, and instead distributed among a variety of non-human forces.[8] The logic behind this dispersal is quite straightforward: in classical materialisms, matter was deemed inert and mechanical, while humanity was considered to have agency and act in the world. For the new materialisms, this traditional distinction breaks down, and some of that agency gets reinscribed within a lively form of matter (Coole 2013: 456). This ranges, depending on the theorist, from the inclusion of animals and organic matter in the world of agency, to a full-blown dispersal of agency to even inorganic materials (Latour, 2005; Bennett 2010).

For Coole, it takes a more modest form, with some elements of the organic world being included but an entire ontology of agency being rejected. Here, agency is characterised by three qualities (Coole 2013: 458–461). First, there is perception, through which an agent interacts with the world – changing the environment as it is changed by the world. Second, there is a minimal element of reflexivity which enables an actor to change course in light of a change in the environment. This need not entail the sorts of rational reflexivity characteristic of human agents, but reflexivity forms a sort of pre-conscious basis for it. Third, human agency includes responsibility – particularly for the environment and our entanglement in the natural world. Agency demands care-taking for this material basis of humanity, at the very least as a life-support system for our species.

But whether one follows Coole in maintaining some unique aspects of human agency or others in distributing agency across the non-human realm, the redistribution of agency carried out by the new materialisms leads to a greater focus on the micro-ways through which the grand ideas of traditional agency, intentionality and rationality are constructed. In other words, it is not an outright denial of traditional accounts of agency, but instead new materialism is an account that stresses the genealogy of these traditional figures. Much like Connolly's work on neuropolitics and the submerged level of affect, this is an account that seeks out the non-agential basis of agency.

The new materialisms in general – and complex systems-based approaches in particular – also entail shifts in our understanding of epistemology and the nature of the academic discipline of IR. As the philosopher of science Sandra Mitchell has argued, complexity calls for an entirely new epistemology (2009: 13). In the first place, it involves a rejection of reductionist accounts. While IR has often avoided the simplest version of this (for example, a reduction of system behaviour to state behaviour), it nevertheless often partakes in a formally similar reduction by reducing state behaviour to systemic behaviour. The neorealist account is the clearest version of this, but similar forms exist in a multitude of IR theories (Waltz 2010). With complexity, however, comes a type of emergence that is irreducible to a different level. Epistemology must therefore acknowledge the plural and multiple levels which are causally responsible for a given phenomenon. Quite simply, reductionist projects must be rejected as inadequate (though not outright wrong). Equally, complexity requires that we escape from the idea of universal laws and the presuppositions guiding positivist thought. While there has been a broad post-positivist turn in IR, this has often been under the rubric of more hermeneutical and philosophical approaches (Smith et al. 1996).

By contrast, complexity suggests a way to move beyond positivistic accounts of universal laws and instead integrate causality into a more sophisticated framework. There is a recognition of the effects of context here, as well as the intractability of the 'open' systems of the real world, as opposed to the 'closed' systems of experiments and theoretical models. Whereas the latter creates an artificial environment in order to uncover regularities, the everyday world is instead characterised by a vast set of interacting events which escape any closed system. Epistemology must therefore admit a complex notion of causality (rather than rejecting it). A final related effect is that knowledge becomes a dynamic and flexible body of partial claims, rather than an attempt to determine absolute truths. We must not mistake our current theories for a disembodied and decontextualised piece of knowledge, but instead should be aware of how they reflect our own interests, social conditions, and finite cognitive abilities. Particularly in the social sciences, new phenomena will inevitably emerge which require new theories and new concepts in order to render them intelligible. A complexity approach therefore offers an alternative to both the positivist mainstream and the critical post-positivist turn.

Novelty for the sake of novelty? Problems in the new materialisms

I want to turn now to elaborate a few criticisms of the new materialisms in IR. In particular, I want to focus on the problems that emerge in the attempt to overcome divisions between nature and culture, mind and body. Out of this project, there is both a problematic elision of salient distinctions between the two and an insufficient elaboration of metaphorical terminology. These points do not apply equally to all the new materialisms covered in this chapter; but they do highlight tensions within the project that should be avoided if new materialist scholarship is to fulfil its aims of reconfiguring our view of IR and social theory.

The first notable problem arises from the attempt to overcome the division between society and nature (or some proxy for that division). The tendency is to focus on the ways in which nature and culture enter into a zone of indistinction, but in the work of some authors this can end up negating *any* difference between human and non-human elements. It is important to remember that a distinction need not entail a division; the entire process of knowledge production involves making meaningful distinctions. Yet in some of the new materialist work this task is largely sidelined.

This reaches its apex in Actor-Network Theory (ANT), in which everything is an actor and any meaningful sense of agency is lost. The sociologist Bruno Latour – increasingly cited in IR – is emblematic of this problem. In his work, agency is simply the capacity to make a difference. The idea of a deliberative and reflective agent – the traditional idea of human agency – is evaporated into a proliferation of what Latour calls 'actants'. This leads to a complete rejection of the unique qualities of human agency in an effort to bridge the gap between humans and non-humans, but it does so in a way which erases the peculiar qualities of humanity. Particularly in the field of world politics, intentional and deliberative action is a key

factor in understanding and interpreting events. An ontology that erases the differences between humans and non-humans risks becoming unable to comprehend
the machinations of world politics. Jane Bennett, who often draws on Latour's
work, recognises these risks, and tends to pull back from Latour's more radical redescription of agents, but without clear criteria for doing so beyond her inclinations
(Bennett 2010: 104).

Blurring the distinctions between the human and non-human remains a persistent risk in all the new materialisms. This indistinction is problematic for a number
of reasons, not least because it seems to ignore the various unique qualities of
humanity. Here, we will focus on two related problems that stem from this indistinction: a misunderstanding of both agency and causality. On the one hand, the
understanding of agency often collapses into something vague secured only by
hunch or habit. A more thoroughgoing attempt to elaborate a clear distinction
between human and non-human agency, and how the former emerges from the
latter, may present a possible solution to this dilemma but undermine claims of
new materialism to its newness. The careful negotiation of this tension remains a
central challenge for new materialist scholarship.

This leads to the second major problem, which is that causality often gets either
forgotten or simply re-described in the new materialisms. Throughout this work,
one of the commonly drawn distinctions is between a mechanistic and dead vision
of matter and a vitalist and living image of matter (Bennett 2010). The former is
ascribed to the old materialism, whereas the new materialism is about a matter that
is creative and self-organising. This distinction makes sense, and there is undoubtedly a long line of mechanistic philosophy that did ascribe such a role to matter.
The problem is that the new image of matter – a self-organising and in-flux
image – is entirely contained within a scientific image of reality based upon causality. In
other words, there is no need to bring in ideas of 'life' or 'vitalism' or an amorphous
idea of 'energy' in order to understand the self-organising processes of matter.

These ideas both emerge from the natural sciences and are inscribed within their
naturalist and causally centred discourses.[9] The supposed agency of objects often
seems little more than a rhetorical flourish for complex causality – that is, not
something outside the natural sciences, but instead something entirely immanent to
that field. There may be good sociological reasons for a strategic exaggeration of
matter's agency, but a sober reading has to face up to the fact that much of this is
inscribable within more traditional ideas of cause and effect. Complexity theory is
particularly useful here insofar as it demolishes any idea of a simple linear causality.
This latter idea of causality, undoubtedly, is what many of the new materialists are
struggling to separate themselves from. But there are greatly updated visions of
causality that could also be drawn upon.[10] If IR is interested in seeking the causes
of things, scholars should be clear about different kinds of causality, rather than
reducing them to an amorphous idea of vital matter.

These problems perhaps lie in a deeper issue with many of the new materialisms:
an overreliance on metaphorical uses of scientific ideas. At what level is the discussion of neuropolitics and complexity science pitched? It is not a literal, scientific

level, at least within the philosophically oriented approaches surveyed here – for all their drawing upon scientific literature, new materialisms resolutely avoid anything approximating a natural science methodology.[11] Rather, the new materialisms invoke science on a more metaphorical and suggestive level. While we can all agree that metaphor is necessary for thought, this does not negate the responsibility to move beyond the metaphorical stage. A few examples can perhaps clarify this claim.

One increasingly popular approach has been to use the materialist notion of assemblages pioneered by Deleuze and Félix Guattari. However, in the assemblage theory approach, one of the key problems remains a tendency to repeat the terms created by Deleuze and Guattari, and to apply them superficially on top of already existing research – a sort of blind application of ideas to any and all empirical material. But empirical content is rarely changed in this relationship, and assemblage theory risks becoming simply a redescription of already existing processes. It is perhaps poetically more seductive, but analytically no more useful. A similar problem besets much of new materialisms, where rhetorical embellishments obscure the details of the processes being examined. Images of the sedimentation of cultural habits into bodily forms have a visual appeal to them, but leave aside what the primary claim about sedimentation actually means in this context. When these ideas are substantiated in more depth, they again appear to re-describe research from fields such as neuroscience and cognitive science.

For example, many new materialisms rely on terms taken from fields like complexity science. Yet, in those fields, these terms have highly technical and often mathematised meanings. Under new materialism, the general idea is appropriated and unmoored from its technical meaning and reappropriated in a new field. Now, there is nothing inherently wrong with this manoeuvre, and it can serve productive functions when done properly. But too often, in the new materialisms, these terms are left at a metaphorical level and not given a new rigorous meaning. Discussions of neuroscience tip into non sequiturs on politics and culture. What, for example, is the equivalent of a tipping point, or a moment of relative equilibrium in a society? We certainly have intuitive ideas about tipping points or equilibrium, but reliance on intuition is a poor model for science – and, moreover, seems to simply re-describe common sense into more scientific phrases. Likewise, what does it mean to say that the world operates at different speeds? How are different speeds compared and measured?

Again, there is some intuitive sense to these claims, but any attempt to *use* them seems bound to result in wildly disparate meanings. That may foster creativity, but it hardly fosters a meaningful ontology or basis for knowledge. In the end, the function of many of these terms in the discourse of new materialisms seems to be as a suggestive metaphor rather than as a conceptual discrimination of a particular phenomenon. Useful for turning our attention towards these processes, they are less successful at building a new theory capable of offering insight into concrete processes of politics. This is a major failing of the new materialist project to date. These analytical shortcomings threaten to undermine the larger new materialist ethical project of redescription and reimagination of bodies and brains in global politics.

Conclusion

In the end, the new materialisms offer an invigorating new entry into IR, and provide a number of essential insights and productive avenues for further research. The new focus on bodies and the ways in which they function as a militarised, racialised and gendered locus of power is an important advance against the immaterial world of traditional IR. Likewise, neuropolitics gives us an important addition to understanding how identity operates and how conflicts can emerge on the basis of them. And complexity theory importantly revises some outdated ideas of knowledge, causality and agency. The problems with the new materialisms largely arise when they step into more metaphysical speculations on the general nature of the social world. Here, these approaches risk effacing important distinctions and becoming parasitical on more concrete empirical work. Yet while there remain philosophical problems with these programmes, they nevertheless provide an indispensable set of resources for thinking about the materiality of world politics today, and they are an important corrective to traditional accounts of matter in IR.

Notes

1 For an overview of the philosophical developments, see Coole and Frost (2010), Dolphijn and Tuin (2012), and Bryant et al. (2011).
2 For a contemporary updating of geopolitical materialism, see Deudney (2007).
3 While rump materialism is first set out in his earlier work, Alexander Wendt has more recently revised his position on the nature of materialism (see Wendt 2015).
4 For an alternative, complementary analysis of new materialism, see Connolly (2013: 399–403).
5 While this is not the place to discuss it, in certain moments, even Jacques Derrida seems to approach Deleuze's position – claiming, for instance, that *différance* received its positive formulation in Deleuze's non-conceptual difference.
6 The resonance with the recent #BlackLivesMatter protests should be obvious. Within the US, black lives typically do not count as meaningful lives, as they are subject to police brutality that routinely goes unpunished.
7 Beyond International Relations, see Haraway (1990) and Braidotti (2014). For a popular, and pessimistic, account, see Fukuyama (2002).
8 See the discussion of Actor-Network Theory in Chapter 3.
9 To be sure, there is a good case to be made that Gilles Deleuze gave a philosophical voice to these ideas prior to science. See, in particular, Deleuze (1994) and DeLanda (2002).
10 For a sophisticated take on causality within IR, see Kurki (2008).
11 There are approaches to neuropolitics in IR that are scientific in orientation, applying the latest neuroscience directly to social explanation (see Holmes 2013).

References

Ashworth, Lucian M. 2013. Mapping a New World: Geography and the Interwar Study of International Relations. *International Studies Quarterly* 57(1): 138–149.
Bennett, Jane. 2010. *Vibrant Matter: A Political Ecology of Things.* Durham, NC: Duke University Press.
Braidotti, Rosi. 2013. *The Posthuman.* Cambridge: Polity.

Bryant, Levi, Nick Srnicek and Graham Harman (eds). 2011. *The Speculative Turn: Continental Materialism and Realism*. Melbourne: re.press.

Butler, Judith. 2011. *Bodies That Matter: On the Discursive Limits of Sex*. New York: Routledge.

Butler, Judith. 2010. *Frames of War: When is Life Grievable?* London: Verso.

Chandler, David. 2015. A World without Causation: Big Data and the Coming of Age of Posthumanism. *Millennium: Journal of International Politics* 43(3): 833–851.

Connolly, William. 2013. The 'New Materialism' and the Fragility of Things. *Millennium: Journal of International Studies* 41(3): 399–412.

Connolly, William. 2002. *Neuropolitics: Thinking, Culture, Speed*. Minneapolis: University of Minnesota Press.

Coole, Diana. 2013. Agentic Capacities and Capacious Historical Materialism: Thinking with New Materialisms in the Political Sciences. *Millennium: Journal of International Studies* 41(3): 451–469.

Coole, Diana and Sam Frost (eds). 2010. *New Materialisms: Ontology, Agency, and Politics*. Durham, NC: Duke University Press.

Cudworth, Erica and Stephen Hobden. 2011. *Posthuman International Relations: Complexity, Ecologism and Global Politics*. London: Zed Books.

Daigle, Megan D. 2015. *From Cuba with Love: Sex and Money in the Twenty-First Century*. Berkeley: University of California Press.

DeLanda, Manuel. 2002. *Intensive Science and Virtual Philosophy*. New York: Continuum.

Deleuze, Gilles. 1994. *Difference and Repetition*. New York: Columbia University Press.

Deudney, Daniel. 2007. *Bounding Power: Republican Security Theory from the Polis to the Global Village*. Princeton, NJ: Princeton University Press.

Dolphijn, Rick and Iris van der Tuin. 2012. *New Materialism: Interviews and Cartographies*. Ann Arbor, MI: Open Humanities Press.

Edkins, Jenny and Veronique Pin-Fat. 2005. Through the Wire: Relations of Power and Relations of Violence. *Millennium: Journal of International Studies* 34(1): 1–24.

Elbe, Stefan. 2005. AIDS, Security, Biopolitics. *International Relations* 19(4): 403–419.

Enloe, Cynthia. 1989. *Bananas, Beaches and Bases: Making Feminist Sense of International Relations*. Berkeley: University of California Press.

Foucault, Michel. 2009. *Security, Territory, Population: Lectures at the Collège de France 1977–1978*. Basingstoke: Palgrave Macmillan.

Fukuyama, Francis. 2002. *Our Posthuman Future: Consequences of the Biotechnology Revolution*. New York: Picador.

Gat, Azar. 2006. *War in Human Civilization*. Oxford: Oxford University Press.

Gray, Colin S. 2004. In Defence of the Heartland: Sir Halford Mackinder and His Critics 100 Years On. *Contemporary Strategy* 23(1): 9–25.

Grossman, David. 1996. *On Killing: The Psychological Cost of Learning to Kill in War and Society*. New York: Back Bay Books.

Haraway, Donna. 1990. *Simians, Cyborgs, and Women: The Reinvention of Nature*. London: Routledge.

Holmes, Marcus. 2013. The Force of Face-to-Face Diplomacy: Mirror Neurons and the Problem of Intentions. *International Studies Quarterly* 67(4): 829–861.

Kurki, Milja. 2008. *Causation in International Relations: Reclaiming Causal Analysis*. Cambridge: Cambridge University Press.

Latour, Bruno. 2005. *Reassembling the Social: An Introduction to Actor-Network Theory*. New York: Oxford University Press.

McInnes, Colin and Simon Rushton. 2012. HIV/AIDS and Securitization Theory. *European Journal of International Relations* 19(1): 115–138.

Mitchell, Sandra. 2009. *Unsimple Truths: Science, Complexity, and Policy*. Chicago, IL: University of Chicago Press.

Protevi, John. 2013. *Life, War, Earth: Deleuze and the Sciences*. Minneapolis: University of Minnesota Press.

Sassen, Saskia. 2008. *Territory, Authority, Rights: From Medieval to Global Assemblages*. Princeton, NJ: Princeton University Press.

Shepherd, Laura J. 2014. Sex or Gender? Bodies in World Politics and Why Gender Matters. In Laura J. Shepherd (ed.) *Gender Matters in Global Politics: A Feminist Introduction to International Relations*, 2nd edition. London: Routledge, pp. 24–25.

Shinko, Rosemary. 2010. Ethics after Liberalism: Why (Autonomous) Bodies Matter. *Millennium: Journal of International Studies* 38(3): 723–745.

Smith, Steve, Ken Booth and Marysia Zalewski (eds). 1996. *International Theory: Positivism and Beyond*. Cambridge: Cambridge University Press.

Sylvester, Christine. 2012. War Experiences/War Practices/War Theory. *Millennium: Journal of International Studies* 40(3): 483–503.

Waltz, Kenneth. 2010. *Theory of International Politics*. Long Grove, IL: Waveland Press.

Wendt, Alexander. 2015. *Quantum Mind and Social Science: Unifying Physical and Social Ontology*. Cambridge: Cambridge University Press.

Wendt, Alexander. 1987. The Agent-Structure Problem in International Relations Theory. *International Organization* 41(3): 335–370.

Wilcox, Lauren B. 2015. *Bodies of Violence: Theorizing Embodied Subjects in International Relations*. Oxford: Oxford University Press.

Youatt, Rafi. 2014. Interspecies Relations, International Relations: Rethinking Anthropocentric Politics. *Millennium: Journal of International Studies* 43(1): 207–223.

PART II
Illustrations

6

NUCLEAR TECHNOAESTHETICS

Sensory politics from Trinity to the virtual bomb in Los Alamos

Joseph P. Masco[1]

A striking feature of nuclear weapons science – as a science – is that its experimental form would seem to have been most powerfully determined by non-scientists. From the 1963 Atmospheric Test Ban Treaty through the 1992 Underground Test Moratorium, the experimental regimes open to nuclear weapons scientists have been predominately defined by international treaties and governments' nuclear policies rather than by experts within the laboratory. In the post–Cold War period, this means that American nuclear weapons scientists cannot conduct what would appear to be the most basic experiment in their profession: namely, detonating a nuclear device. Moreover, the stated goal of post–Cold War nuclear weapons science is not to produce an explosive technology per se, but rather to provide the technological infrastructure for a nuclear deterrent – a means of preventing a particular species of war. Thus, at Los Alamos National Laboratory (LANL), the center of U.S. nuclear weapons science, scientists today self-consciously devote their careers to engineering the bomb so that it will never actually be used *as a bomb*. Caught between the competing demands of a shifting experimental foundation, state secrecy and the increasingly symbolic role nuclear weapons have come to play in (inter)national politics, the reality of the bomb as both a machine and a weapon of mass destruction for all but its most direct victims has become difficult to locate in post–Cold War America. Outside the national laboratories, U.S. nuclear weapons have come to exist primarily as political constructs.

In Los Alamos, the post–Cold War order has consequently presented a unique set of technoscientific challenges. Since weapons scientists trained after the 1992 test moratorium may never actually conduct or witness a nuclear detonation, it is important to ask: what constitutes the continuing intellectual appeal of nuclear weapons science *as a science*? To answer this question we need to critically engage the **technoaesthetics** of the bomb – the evaluative aesthetic categories embedded in the expert practices of weapons scientists. Weapons scientists have negotiated the bomb at the level of sensory experience since 1945, and technoaesthetics largely determine the politics of this enterprise within the **epistemic cultures** of the laboratory. Technoaesthetics are also important because they are the non-classified everyday modes of interacting with nuclear technologies, forms of perception and practice that unify divergent groups of physicists, chemists, engineers, and computer specialists as nuclear weapons scientists. In Los Alamos, it is in the realm of technoaesthetics that both the meaning of the bomb and the pleasures of conducting nuclear weapons science are constituted and expressed.

This chapter explores how the reconfigured experimental regime of the post-Cold War period has altered how Los Alamos scientists experience the bomb as a technology, changing the terms of our collective nuclear future. By examining the epistemic spaces where scientific bodies and nuclear devices actually interact – through pleasure – we can see the complicated world of nuclear weapons science as both an ideological and a technoscientific practice. The shifting experimental regimes open to Los Alamos weapons scientists have, over time, worked to position the U.S. nuclear arsenal within the laboratory as an increasingly aesthetic–intellectual project, one that is both normalized and depoliticized.

Turning from the explicit ideology of weapons science to an analysis of the technoaesthetic production of the bomb within the laboratory itself, this chapter identifies three distinct experimental regimes: First, how weapons scientists experienced the bomb – at the level of sense perception – during the era of above-ground nuclear testing (1945–1962). Second, how the move to underground nuclear testing (1963–1992) reconfigured sensory access to the exploding bomb, both abstracting its destructive potential and encouraging an intellectual engagement with complexity. Finally, how the post-Cold War experimental program known as 'science-based stockpile stewardship' (1995–present), which relies on an increasingly virtual bomb, systematically confuses bodies and machines in such a way as to transform the experience of nuclear science from a military reality to one of potentially infinite technoaesthetic pleasure. The structural achievement of post-Cold War nuclear science in Los Alamos is to have reinvented the bomb – at precisely the moment when America's nuclear project and the laboratory's future seemed most uncertain – as an unending techno-national project that is simultaneously fragile, essential, and beautiful.

The bomb's future

Time – in terms of both endings and possible futures – has been a defining concern within the U.S. nuclear complex from the very start of the Manhattan Project. Time is also a primary domain for the expression of the technoaesthetics, and thus the meaning, of nuclear weapons science. Indeed, an intellectual genealogy of Los Alamos weapons science reveals an ongoing conceptual fixation on the futurology of the bomb. On October 16, 1945, his last day as director of what was known during World War II simply as 'Site Y', J. Robert Oppenheimer gave a farewell speech to his Los Alamos colleagues in which he was troubled by the apparent success of the Manhattan Project, telling the first generation of nuclear weapons scientists:

> If atomic bombs are to be added as new weapons to the arsenals of a warring world, or to the arsenals of nations preparing for war, then the time will come when mankind will curse the names of Los Alamos and Hiroshima. The peoples of this world must unite or they will perish. This war that has ravaged so much of the earth, has written these words. The atomic bomb has spelled them out for all men to understand. Other men have spoken them, in other times, of other wars, of other weapons. They have not prevailed. There are some, misled by a false sense of human history, who would that they will not prevail today. It is not for us to believe that. By our works we are committed, committed to a world united, before this common peril, in law, and in humanity.
>
> *(quoted in Hawkins 1983: 260–261)*

The time will come when mankind will curse the names of Los Alamos and Hiroshima. In this presentation, time has all but run out for America, and the very availability of a future hinges on a new kind of international order devoted to controlling atomic weaponry, for what Oppenheimer proposes here is nothing less than a race against a future arms race, as he attempts to mobilize nuclear fear to energize a new kind of international order.

Oppenheimer's depiction of a nuclear state of emergency is more attenuated, but still a defining logic in the official statements of Norris Bradbury, who was the second director of 'Los Alamos Scientific Laboratory' from 1945 to 1970. Looking back on his tenure as director in a 1970 talk entitled 'Los Alamos: the first 25 years', Bradbury reviewed the history of Los Alamos while presenting a slightly longer view of the nuclear future:

> No one makes nuclear weapons or bombs of any sort with any desire to use them. There is no pleasure in using them. In fact, one makes them with a profound desire never to have to use them, never to want to use them, never to find a need to use them. The whole project of the nuclear weapons business has been to put itself out of business. Strange business to be in but it's a fact. And yet, if you asked me in 1945, would we still be making bombs 25 years later, I would have said I don't think so. By that time the major powers would have seen some common sense. But we're still at it. And we have lots of partners in the race. What do you want to give me? Another 25 years, 50 years, 100 years, a thousand years, will we still be making atomic bombs? I simply don't know. I must admit to some personal discouragement; I didn't think it would last this long, but it has.
>
> *(Bradbury 1980: 164–165)*

The whole project of the nuclear weapons business has been to put itself out of business. Here, the job of Los Alamos weapons scientists has become to put themselves out of business by building ever-better nuclear weapons, so perfectly destructive as to insure that warfare is simply removed as an international option for solving conflict. Nuclear weapons are presented as merely a temporary solution to international fear, an unpleasant one that has already gone on too long, contaminating the present with its longevity. For both Oppenheimer and Bradbury the stated goal for weapons scientists is to end the military nuclear age they worked so tirelessly to create, to ultimately deny a future to nuclear weapons science in order to produce a more stable world. Bradbury's depiction of the nuclear arms race as a temporary solution to the international crisis was an important conceptual statement in Cold War Los Alamos, one that encouraged scientists to invest in weapons of mass destruction as a means of achieving peace in the short term. It ultimately enabled scientists to intellectually mobilize the destructive power of the hydrogen bomb as a peaceful, even non-violent project. This notion of 'buying time' for politicians to diffuse potential conflicts through nuclear deterrence was the dominant ideology at the laboratory throughout the Cold War, and remains an often evoked, core understanding among weapons scientists at Los Alamos to this day.

Los Alamos nuclear weapons scientists, however, 'bought time' in ever-smaller units from 1945 to 1992. The nuclear attacks on Hiroshima and Nagasaki took weeks to plan and days to execute by American forces, but by the mid-1960s the nuclear triad of always on alert bombers, intercontinental missiles, and nuclear submarines (all carrying warheads designed at Los Alamos) meant that nuclear war could begin with less than a 15-minute window of warning, and could exceed the total explosive power of World War II in less than two hours of actual nuclear conflict. Thus, if securing 'time' was the objective of the Cold War weapons program, Los Alamos weapons scientists pursued this goal through a complicated logic of technological determinism, in which the future was increasingly foreshortened in the name of producing a present-oriented space for political action. As explicitly a temporal project, the technoscience of nuclear deterrence simultaneously collapsed global space so efficiently during the Cold War that living on the brink of nuclear conflict quickly became naturalized as the very foundation of national security.

Studies by the Strategic Air Command (SAC) in 1960, for example, concluded that with a 10-minute warning of Soviet attack only 14 percent of U.S. nuclear-equipped planes could be airborne, but with a 14-minute warning 66 percent of U.S. bombers would be in the air (Richelson 1999: 20). Four minutes, thus, separated the possibility of a successful Soviet first strike against the U.S. from the establishment of a U.S. nuclear deterrent. Nuclear weapons were at the center of a nationalist cosmology in which Los Alamos scientists sought to regulate a world of minute-to-minute threat through military technologies. Nuclear weapons science in Los Alamos also constantly refined the immediacy of that threat. By steadily improving the size, weight, explosive power, and versatility of nuclear devices throughout the Cold War, Los Alamos scientists were not merely advancing a technical understanding of nuclear explosives, but were intimately involved in a technologically mediated form of international relations. Seconds and minutes were not just the temporal horizon before the start of a nuclear war; they were the conceptual space of a new global economy of risk and communication in which multiple redundant nuclear weapons systems (of bombers, missiles, and submarines) were deployed and constantly refined in hopes of producing a degree of certainty in international affairs.

After a half century of accelerated development in nuclear weapons technologies on these terms, new design work formally stopped at Los Alamos at 3:04pm on September 23, 1992 with 'Divider,' a 20-kiloton device that was the last U.S. underground nuclear test of the 1990s. On the 50th anniversaries of the atomic bombing of Hiroshima and Nagasaki, Siegfried Hecker (then director of Los Alamos), addressed the nuclear future of the laboratory for employees, writing in its internal bulletin:

> In spite of grave political differences, nuclear weapons deterred the super-powers from global war. Over 80 million of the 100 million war-related deaths of this century occurred in its first half. I believe the devastation and the psychological impact of Hiroshima and Nagasaki, combined with the realiza-tion of the even greater destructive power of modern nuclear arsenals, drove deterrence diplomacy and bought us time … Let's keep the horrid images of Hiroshima and Nagasaki in front of us as a stark reminder of what we must learn to avoid. Let's turn our attention to dealing with the current nuclear dangers to the benefit of all of mankind so that at the 100th anniversary people can look back and say that the Manhattan Project turned out all right.
>
> (Hecker 1995: n.p.)

So that people can say the Manhattan Project turned out all right. Here the military nuclear age is no longer explicitly marked as a regrettable or temporary situation, but has become a positively valued achievement, one enabled by a remarkable accounting maneuver: by tallying up the wartime dead before and after the invention of the atomic bomb, Hecker argues that Los Alamos weapons scientists have saved lit-erally millions of lives, having purchased a series of short-term futures (through the logics of deterrence) with each new Los Alamos-designed weapons system. For Hecker, nuclear weapons are no longer just a short-term fix to the international crisis – with a focus on minutes and hours – but are a longer-term structure in the world system. Indeed, nuclear weapons now explicitly have a future for the first time, as Hecker imagines Los Alamos celebrating its 100th birthday in 2042 still devoted to ending the global nuclear danger – a project that was already on Oppenheimer's mind in 1945 and on Bradbury's in 1970.

In a highly influential June 2000 essay entitled 'Nuclear Weapons in the Twenty-First Century,' Stephen Younger (then the Associate Director of Nuclear Weapons Programs at Los Alamos) argues for a fundamental rethinking of the use value of nuclear weapons for the new century. Identifying nuclear weapons as the 'ultimate' defence of the nation, Younger asks what kind of nuclear forces the U.S. will need in the year 2020. He notes that advances in precision-guided weapons could reduce the U.S. reliance on some nuclear weapons while underscoring that the threat of 'national annihilation' remains the supreme deterrent against all kinds of state aggression. Concluding that 'it is almost impossible to conceive of technological and political developments that would enable the United States to meets its defense needs in 2020 without nuclear weapons', Younger articulates a number of new uses for nuclear weapons – from 'mini-nukes' (explosives under 1 kiloton) to 'earth-penetrator' weapons (for attacking buried structures), to a new type of robust warhead (based on the Hiroshima bomb) that could be built and deployed without underground nuclear testing (Younger 2000). Younger works here to reenergize the official nuclear imaginary, offering new targets, new technologies, and an updated but still foundational U.S. reliance on weapons of mass destruction. Unlike Oppenheimer, Bradbury, and Hecker, Younger presents the nuclear future here not as an unfortunate necessity whose time will eventually come, but rather as an expanding technoscientific project and a fundamental aspect of American power.

The transition from Oppenheimer's 'nuclear state of emergency' to Younger's 'endless art form' marks not only a shift in the rhetorical debate about our collective nuclear future; it also signals more fundamental changes in how nuclear weapons science is conducted in the post-Cold War order, for if the epistemic cultures of the Cold War nuclear program provided a cognitive orientation for weapons scientists – a cosmology linking military technoscience and global politics – the end of the Soviet Union and of underground nuclear testing eliminated two central elements in that conceptual circuit: the arms race and its accompanying experimental regimes.

How weapons scientists negotiated the resulting technological and ideological changes in post-Cold War Los Alamos constitutes the conceptual center of the American commitment to nuclear weapons in the twenty-first century, for if the temporal discourse of the bomb has shifted in fundamental ways since the end of the Cold War, so too has the tactile experience of nuclear weapons work for scientists. As we shall see, an increasing abstraction of the bomb within the experimental regimes of U.S. weapons science makes it difficult for Los Alamos scientists to ever experience the explosive totality of the nuclear weapons they have designed and now maintain. The bomb is becoming increasingly beautiful in Los Alamos, not because it explodes but because it can be rendered in ways that are aesthetically pleasing to weapons scientists and that articulate an expanding view of the nuclear future.

The above-ground testing regime (1945–1962): on tactility and the nuclear sublime

> I firmly believe that if every five years the world's major political leaders were required to witness the in-air detonation of a multi-megaton warhead, progress on meaningful arms control measures would be speeded up appreciably.
>
> *(Agnew 1983: 71)*

In his study of American spectacular technologies, David Nye (1994) argues that nuclear weapons are so terrifying that they cannot be experienced through an aesthetic of the **sublime** (see Kant 1986; Burke 1993). For Nye, the visual power of the Brooklyn Bridge or the *Apollo 11* Moon mission fuses an experience of the sublime with a national consciousness for all spectators, creating a feeling of pride in American technology and a collective notion of uplift. The bomb, on the other hand, has no such positive dimension, as 'to anyone who contemplates them, nuclear weapons can only be a permanent, invisible terror that offers no moral enlightenment' (Nye 1994: 253). Los Alamos scientists, however, have banked their careers on a diametrically opposed proposition: namely, that nuclear weapons are so powerful that they fundamentally reshape human consciousness in ways that can enable global security and peace. Harold Agnew, director of Los Alamos Scientific Laboratory from 1970 to 1979, for example, has argued that the visual power of a multi-megaton explosion is transformative for all viewers (1983: 71). In calling for regular public demonstrations of the power of the thermonuclear bomb, Agnew explicitly deploys a notion of the nuclear sublime to foster international enlightenment in the form of disarmament (Ferguson 1984).

But if human consciousness can be so thoroughly transformed by a physical experience of the exploding bomb, as Agnew argues, this also identifies a basic cognitive problem produced by the move to underground nuclear testing during the Cold War. Put simply, since no American has witnessed an atomic explosion without the use of prosthetic senses (computer screens and seismic monitors) since the signing of the 1963 Atmospheric Test Ban Treaty, who now has full cognitive access to the technology? And if, as Agnew suggests, the conceptual power of a nuclear weapon is fundamentally linked to a direct human sensory experience of the explosion, how has the shifting experimental regime of nuclear weapons science transformed the meaning of the technology within the laboratory?

For the first Los Alamos scientists, the first nuclear detonation on July 16, 1945 (codenamed 'Trinity') was not merely an intellectual accomplishment but an overwhelming physical event. I.I. Rabi, for example, recoiled from the power of the flash, describing it as:

> the brightest light I have ever seen or that I think anyone has ever seen. It blasted; it pounced; it bored its way right through you. It was a vision which was seen with more than the eye. It was seen to last forever.
>
> *(quoted in Rhodes 1986: 672)*

Experiencing the first nuclear explosions as something that 'pounced' and 'bored' through the human body, for Rabi the millisecond ushering in a new world of nuclear physics was terrifying. In first-hand descriptions the sight, the sound, and the heat of the first nuclear explosion – all part of the objective of the experiment – nonetheless still terrify, making the weapons scientist's body the most important register of the power of the bomb. Though protected by goggles, barriers, and miles of buffer zone, the Trinity explosion not only overwhelmed senses but also physically assaulted scientists: Enrico Fermi was so physically shaken by the explosion that he was unable to drive his car afterward; and Robert Serber, who looked directly at the blast without eye protection, was flash-blinded for 30 seconds. In this first nuclear explosion, the weapons scientist's body was the primary register of the explosion, the physicality of blast effects – light, sound, shockwave, and heat – all assaulting human senses and demonstrating the fragility of the human body when confronted by the power of the bomb.

Consider, for example, how Los Alamos weapons scientist Ted Taylor describes seeing his first atomic explosion in the spring of 1951 on Enewetak Atoll during Operation Greenhouse:

> It was all extremely exciting, including many hours of floating in the lagoon with snorkel and face mask, watching countless numbers and varieties of tropical fish so close that one often touched them. The countdown started close to dawn ... 1 minute ... thirty seconds (put on your dark goggles) ... fifteen ... four, three, two, one: instant light, almost blinding through the goggles, and the heat that persisted for a time that seemed interminable. I was sure I was getting instant sunburn, and the back of my neck felt hot from the heat reflected off the beach house behind us. Goggles came off after a few seconds. The fireball was still glowing like a setting sun over a clear horizon, a purple and brown cloud rising so fast that in less than a minute we had to crane our necks to see the top. I had forgotten about the shock wave, a surprisingly sharp, loud crack that broke several martini glasses on the shelf on the beach house bar. The sight was beautiful at first, in an awesome way, then turned ugly and seemed threatening as the gray-brown cloud spread and began drifting towards us. I tried hard to shake off the feelings of exhilaration, and think about the deeper meanings of all this, without success. It was just plain thrilling.
>
> (Taylor 2001)

It was just plain thrilling. Here the pattern of pleasure is constantly interrupted by the threat of the bomb – the instant sunburn that disrupts the visual display, the shockwave that travels 15 miles to break glasses – but still ends in aesthetic pleasure. Taylor remembers lying down on the beach to relax and ponder the event, but his contemplative moment was interrupted by a peculiar cloud overhead raining down bits and pieces of metal. The circuit of pleasure here – the beauty of the mushroom cloud and the intellectual achievement of the blast – is constantly interrupted by physical danger. The weapons scientist's body was ultimately exposed to the reality of the bomb as an explosive device and to radioactive fallout as an airborne threat.

By the 1950s, Los Alamos scientists (post-Hiroshima and Nagasaki and in the midst of a Cold War arms race) were directly confronted with the military implications of their experiments. Consider the Apple II shot on May 5, 1955, which was part of Operation Teapot conducted at the Nevada Test Site. For Los Alamos scientists the primary task of the Teapot series was to work on miniaturizing nuclear warheads while simultaneously enhancing the explosive yield – to extract more destructive energy from a smaller machine. But while their research was focused on how to 'boost' the nuclear yield by introducing a mixture of deuterium-tritium gas into the hollow core of a plutonium sphere during the implosion process, the Apple II detonation was also the center of a U.S. nuclear war fighting program. Los Alamos scientists conducted an elaborate set of experiments to test the radiation and blast effects of the explosion on machines, on human mannequins distributed around the test area, and on animals. Simultaneously, the U.S. military conducted 'Exercise Desert Rock VI'. Intended to acclimatize troops to an atomic battlefield and develop nuclear war fighting tactics, 1,000 troops, 89 armoured vehicles, and 19 helicopters participated in the exercise, which constituted an armoured assault on ground zero (U.S. DOD 1955). The Apple II detonation was also the center-piece of Operation Cue, a civil defense exercise designed to measure how a 'typi-cal' American community would look after a nuclear attack. An elaborately rendered town was built on the test site, consisting of a fire station, a school, a radio station, a library, and a dozen homes in the current building styles. Resi-dences were populated with mannequins dressed in brand-new clothing and posed with domestic theatricality – at the dinner table, cowering in the basement, or watching television (like the national TV audience).

The Apple II device was, thus, at the center of a schizophrenic space in which the same Los Alamos physics experiment was simultaneously a U.S. nuclear strike against an imagined enemy and a U.S. nuclear attack on an American suburb. The bullets in army machine guns may have been blanks, but the bomb detonated with a force of 29 kilotons (twice that which destroyed Hiroshima); and the troops, pilots, civilian observers, and neighboring communities were all subjects of a real radiological experiment in the form of exposure to atmospheric fallout (Miller 1986: 237; see also Gallagher 1993; Hacker 1994: 164–169). As physics experiment, nuclear attack, civil defense exercise, national spectacle, and theatrical display of resolve for the Soviets, the Apple II explosion cannot be reduced to simply the goal of producing either a nuclear deterrent or a specific nuclear device: Los Alamos technology was used here to enact a nuclear event in which Americans were conceived simultaneously as military aggressors and victims. The complexity of this kind of national spectacle grounded the experimental work of weapons scientists in both Cold War politics and nuclear fear. In other words, the above-ground testing regime was devoted not only to the basic science of producing atomic, and then thermonuclear, explosions, but also to researching precisely how nuclear explosions traumatize the material structures of everyday life as well as the human body (see Glasstone and Dolan 1977).

In response to the accruing health and environmental problems of atmospheric nuclear testing, a U.S.–Soviet test moratorium from 1958 to 1961 led to the Partial Test Ban Treaty in 1963, which banned all nuclear explosions in the atmosphere, underwater, and in outer space. Today, Los Alamos scientists remember the Partial Test Ban Treaty – the first international effort to restrain weapons science – as both a public health measure and as a means of shielding nuclear tests from Soviet observation. However, the move to underground testing contained more than simply the nuclear device; it also redefined how Los Alamos scientists could experience the power of a nuclear explosion, fundamentally changing the **technoaesthetic** potential, and thus the politics, of the bomb.

The underground test regime (1963–1992): embracing complexity, fetishizing production

The consolidation of nuclear testing at the Nevada Test Site after 1963 regularized nuclear weapons science with a more stable experimental form. During the underground test regime, seven formal stages in the development of a new weapon were institutionalized – conception, feasibility, design, development, manufacturing, deployment, and retirement – placing Los Alamos weapons scientists on both a carefully modulated calendar and at the center of a vast industrial machine (U.S. DOE 1984). Los Alamos weapons scientists trained during the underground test regime consequently experienced the Cold War as a relentless series of nuclear warhead design and test deadlines. Multiple weapons systems were under production simultaneously, and were designed with the understanding that they would be replaced by a next-generation system within 15–20 years. The resulting pace of U.S. nuclear weapons research was impressive: The United States conducted 1,054 nuclear detonations from July of 1945 to September of 1992. This averages out to roughly two tests per month over the 46 years between the first nuclear explosion, 'Trinity' (July 16, 1945) and the last, 'Divider' (September 28, 1992) (NRDC 1998). For Los Alamos scientists the nuclear age remains perfectly tangible – visible in machine form – with each nuclear test part of a technological genealogy of design concepts dating back to the very first nuclear explosion.

From a scientific point of view, the challenge of underground testing was how to both contain the explosion and make it visible to machine sensors, to safely extract technical data from an underground space in the midst of the most extreme pressures and temperatures imaginable (see OTA 1989). As one Los Alamos weapons scientist trained during the underground regime described it:

> It is possibly like astrophysics. It is in a regime that is inaccessible to you: high temperature, high density. You can't put [detectors] in the [device] because it will affect the performance. You learn something from radiochemistry because of the neutrons that come out of it; you put radiochemical detectors in the ground after the shot – and they were in where the action was – and that's the nearest you get to seeing how it actually behaves. So the difficulty [of underground testing] comes from the inaccessibility of the regime, for all those reasons.

The difficulty comes from the inaccessibility of the regime. Here we see the change in experimental regimes registered at the level of sensory perception, for the challenge of underground testing is revealed to be not the effort to protect the human body from the effects of the explosion, but rather to make the exploding bomb visible to human senses. However, the 'visibility' of the exploding bomb has fundamentally changed. No longer is a primary aspect of weapons science to investigate the effects of the bomb on everyday objects – an experimental project which made each above-ground test also explicitly a nuclear war fighting exercise. Instead, underground testing left weapons scientists to work on the internal complexities of the nuclear explosion itself; that is, Los Alamos scientists became more narrowly focused on the physics of the detonation and the robustness of the machine, rather than on the effects of the bomb, substantially consolidating the experimental project while displacing the consequences of global nuclear war.

The shift from above-ground (1945–1962) to underground testing (1963–1992) not only regularized nuclear production; it also fundamentally changed the technoaesthetic experience of conducting weapons science. Underground testing rendered the exploding bomb all but invisible, also eliminating the immediate threat to the body of the scientist. When Los Alamos weapons scientists trained during the underground test regime talk about nuclear weapons they tend not to put forward their own sensory experience of the explosion (as did the previous generation of weapons scientists), but rather the intellectual complexity of the detonation as a set of physical processes. For this generation, the intellectual pleasures of weapons science derive from investigating events that take place at millions and billions of degrees of heat, at millions of pounds of pressure, which releases incredible energy in billionths of a second.

During above-ground testing, part of the cognitive understanding of the 'test' was the sheer visceral power of the explosion, which necessitated goggles, protective barriers, escape routes, and miles of distance to protect scientists from the results of their experiments. The restriction of weapons science to underground testing at the Nevada Test Site after 1963 allowed permanent control rooms to be established in which weapons scientists no longer watched the detonation itself, but rather data presented on video screens and seismic monitors for confirmation of a successful test. The explosion became almost totally mediated by technology. New prosthetic senses provided ever more precise and immediate information about the implosion as an experiment, while insulating scientists from a direct physical perception of the blast and radiation effects. Consequently, a sensory appreciation of the power of the exploding bomb was increasingly displaced in favor of mechanical measurement. Some weapons scientists, for example, would rank their tests among recent naturally occurring earthquakes, while others would take a ceremonial visit to the crater produced by the exploding bomb to gain an appreciation of its scale (see Bailey 1995: 76; Gusterson 1996a: 138).

After 1963, weapons scientists would not know the yield of the explosion until days later, after radiochemical analysis of soil samples revealed the power of the event. This yield calculation was highly fetishized within the nuclear program, as the final number was important to military planners who might someday use the device. However, what could be appreciated at a glance in the above-ground test regime (the scale of destruction) was in the underground regime a subject of retrospective reconstruction. Weapons scientists focused on the complexity of the explosion; but the answer it produced was simply a number, not a visceral understanding of the destructive power of the bomb in relation to the human body.

Consequently, while an above-ground explosion was always an exciting spectacle and marked event for weapons scientists, an underground detonation could be boring. The most exciting period, from the scientists' point of view, was in the build-up to the experiment deadline (Wolff 1984; Wolff 1988). The intellectual excitement was also in the period after the test, when the data was in hand (sometimes days later). The sensory experience of an underground detonation (a monthly occurrence from 1963 to 1992) was the most predictable and normalized aspect of the experience. Thus, the underground test regime not only contained the radioactive effects of the bomb to the Nevada Test Site while shielding U.S. nuclear science from Soviet eyes, it also worked over time to make nuclear explosions routine.

For Los Alamos weapons scientists, the technoaesthetic reinvention of the bomb during the underground test regime was enhanced by two factors: 1) new arms control treaties and 2) the commitment to designing an increasingly 'safe' nuclear arsenal. In 1970, the U.S. signed on the Nuclear Nonproliferation Treaty, pledging to eliminate its nuclear arsenal at the earliest opportunity. By the mid-1970s weapons scientists were 'perfecting' military technologies that were never experimentally tested in the ways they would actually be used during a nuclear conflict. The technoscientific production of 'certainty' which had characterized the goal of Los Alamos weapons science since the Trinity Test has, over time, thus developed an increasingly virtual dimension: first, because nuclear devices could not be tested in the way they would actually be used after 1963; second, as Galison (1996) has shown, the increasing sophistication of computer simulation techniques encouraged theorists within the weapons program to confuse how their mathematical model of the bomb performed with the actual machine. In other words, the experimental proof of nuclear testing – the detonation that registered for a global audience the power of American nuclear technology – became only a partial demonstration of that power after the mid-1970s.

Changes in the experimental regime of Cold War nuclear weapons science have produced profound changes in the epistemic culture of the laboratory, most readily visible in the technoaesthetics of weapons science. The underground regime allowed the process of conducting weapons research to be increasingly abstracted from the military reality of the technology. The difference between testing the explosive power of the bomb on a model American community in the midst of a nuclear war fighting exercise in 1955 and engineering a 'safe and reliable' nuclear device through underground testing in 1975 is conceptually important, and reveals a deep domestication of the technology by the end of the Cold War. This cognitive shift is not readily apparent in the discourse of nuclear policy, which has always positioned the bomb as a tool of international relations, but is immediately visible in the technoaesthetic evolution of weapons science. Experienced through prosthetic senses, the bomb produced by underground testing became a philosophical project increasingly linked not to mass destruction or war but to complexity, safety, and deterrence within the laboratory, allowing new generations of scientists increasingly to invest in nuclear weapons as a patriotic intellectual enterprise to produce machines that could only prevent conflict.

The Soviet nuclear threat always provided a counter to this ideological construction of the bomb within the laboratory, threatening discourses of deterrence and pure science with the possibility of a real war. The post–Cold War period is consequently the only time in which Los Alamos weapons science has not been justified in relation to an arms race. In post–Cold War Los Alamos, each nuclear device has been purified of its destructive potential, as the experimental regime extends the aesthetic project of nuclear weapons science in new ways, eliminating not only the human body but also the nuclear explosion from the space of the experiment, allowing weapons scientists potentially endless technoscientific pleasure. In other words, the bomb has been reinvented in Los Alamos in ways that free its aesthetic possibility from its destructive potential, finally allowing the bomb to cease being a bomb at all.

The Science-Based Stockpile Stewardship regime (1995–2010): on virtual bombs and prosthetic senses

In Los Alamos, the post–Cold War period began not with the end of the Soviet Union but with the cessation of underground nuclear testing and nuclear weapon design work in 1992 – an experimental regime and conceptual project that had defined generations of weapons scientists. The Clinton Administration's subsequent support for a Comprehensive Test Ban Treaty (signed in 1996, but voted down by the Senate in 1999) committed the weapons laboratories to maintaining the existing U.S. nuclear arsenal, as well as their nuclear weapons expertise, without conducting nuclear detonations. The new experimental regime devoted to this task in Los Alamos was dubbed 'Science-Based Stockpile Stewardship' (SBSS), an effort to maintain the Cold War U.S. nuclear arsenal through a combination of subcritical and non-nuclear explosive testing, a fleet of new experimental facilities, archiving Cold War experimental data, and modeling the combined insights on state-of-the-art computer simulations. SBSS was conceived in 1995 as a 15-year project with a projected cost of $4.5 billion a year – making it significantly more expensive than the Cold War project of nuclear weapons design and testing it replaced. As an experimental regime, SBSS is not only an effort to maintain U.S. nuclear weapons under a test ban, but also a programmatic effort to reconstitute the pleasure of conducting weapons science for nuclear experts confronting a radically changed mission. As we shall see, SBSS fundamentally alters the material form of Los Alamos weapons science, promoting a different concept of the bomb while reconfiguring sensory access to its destructive potential.

A deputy director of nuclear weapons technologies at Los Alamos offered this concise explanation of the consequences of the shift from underground nuclear testing to the 'science-based' model for maintaining the U.S. nuclear arsenal (Smith 1995):

> For 50 years the Nuclear Weapons Program relied on nuclear testing, complemented by large-scale production, to guarantee a safe and reliable stockpile. New weapons were designed, tested, and manufactured on a regular basis. If the surveillance program discovered a defect, its significance could be established by nuclear testing. If the defect was serious, it could be repaired by the

production complex. Even if the defect was not significant, the weapon was likely to be replaced by a more modern system in only a few years. As the stockpile ages far beyond its anticipated life, we can expect a variety of defects which will break the symmetries which were used in the design process. This means that weapons gerontology is far more challenging than designing new weapons. We are sometimes accused by anti-nuclear activists of wanting [new] facilities ... in order to design new weapons. My answer is that we know how to design new weapons. But we do not know how to certify the safety, reliability and performance of weapons as they age. Thus the SBSS challenge can be stated quite simply: 'since we can't test them, we will have to understand them at a fundamental level.'

Weapons gerontology is far more challenging than designing new weapons. Weapons scientists have become gerontologists, involved in studying how nuclear weapons age. If the Cold War program speeded up time through constant production, the immediate post-Cold War project became, to prevent nothing less than ageing itself, a kind of technological cryogenics, to be thawed in case of future nuclear emergency. However, the inability to stop time completely in Los Alamos – to keep bodies and machines safely on ice – promoted 'aging' as the major threat to U.S. national security after the Cold War. The arms race may be on hold in post-Cold War Los Alamos, but a new race against time is at the center of the laboratory's nuclear mission, a programmatic effort to endlessly defer a future of aged, and perhaps derelict, U.S. nuclear machines.

The vulnerable body, carefully scripted out of the Cold War experimental regime of underground testing, has also returned to the discourse of Los Alamos scientists. But the body in question is not the human body threatened by the exploding bomb; it is the bomb itself as fragile body, exposed to the elements, aging, and increasingly infirm. Within this post-Cold War program of weapons gerontology, nuclear weapons have 'birth defects,' require 'care and feeding,' 'get sick' and 'go to the hospital,' get regular 'checkups,' 'retire,' and have 'autopsies.' Individual weapons systems are now undergoing formal 'life extension' projects, new regimens of surveillance, and component replacement to extend the viability of the oldest weapons in the U.S. nuclear arsenal past their planned deployment. This use of productive bodily metaphors for supremely destructive technologies, which runs throughout the U.S. nuclear project, has always been part of the larger cognitive process of domesticating nuclear technology and giving machines a 'life course' – literally translating nuclear weapon time into human time.

A strategic confusion of bodies and machines is a common technoaesthetic technique for internally controlling the meaning of laboratory work (see Knorr Cetina 1999; Traweek 1988). Within the nuclear complex, however, there is an added political consequence from confusing the animate and the inanimate, and deploying highly gendered categories for massively destructive technologies. Cohn (1987) has demonstrated that the expert discourse of defense intellectuals grants military machines and not people agency, making it linguistically impossible to represent the victims of military technology. And Gusterson has shown, in his study of Lawrence Livermore National Laboratory, that when weapons scientists use birth metaphors to describe the bomb they are deploying 'the connotative power of words to produce − and be produced by − a cosmological world where nuclear weapons tests symbolize not despair, destruction, and death but hope, renewal, and life' (1996b: 145). But while a combination of technoaesthetic discourse and successful experiments are the keys to producing a 'community' of experts, it is also important to underscore what is evacuated from the project of nuclear weapons science by these techniques, and to recognize its historical transformation in the post–Cold War period.

When Edward Teller announced the first successful detonation of a thermonuclear device in 1952 by cabling his Los Alamos colleagues the phrase 'It's a boy' (see Ott 1999), he was not only linguistically transforming the most devastating force yet achieved into a purely productive event, he was deploying an image of the human body to enable the complete evacuation of people and the environment from the space of the experiment. But if the Cold War discourse produced an image of the bomb as invulnerable body (the 'boy' that can vaporize islands faster than a 'shake of a lamb's tail'), the post–Cold War discourse has reversed the conceptual circuit of this logic, offering a image of the masculine bomb-body as senior citizen, so aged and weak as to be unable to perform. No longer the 'baby boy,' the bomb is now structurally positioned at the end of its life course, as the 'old man,' struggling against the progression of time and failing faculties. What is important for our purposes here is not the technical accuracy or political strategy of deploying this allegorical form to communicate the challenges of SBSS within the laboratory. Rather, by attending to the technoaesthetic production of the bomb we can see an important transformation in the everyday logics of laboratory life, as weapons scientists have become more directly concerned with protecting the vulnerable weapon of mass destruction from a catastrophic future than the human body.

Indeed, under SBSS, a sensory engagement with the bomb produces not fear of the explosion, but rather increasing concern about the viability of the machine as an embodied aesthetic form. The cornerstone of SBSS is a surveillance regime devoted to identifying how time and the elements are influencing each device in America's nuclear arsenal. Every year, eleven warheads from each of the nine deployed U.S. weapons systems are pulled from submarines, missile silos, bombers, and weapons storage and subjected to component by component inspection and testing (U.S. DOE 1998, 1999). Nuclear weapons have 6,000–7,000 parts, and each part of each weapon under SBSS has a specific inspection program devoted to it (see Medalia 1998, 1994). The Cold War world of weapons science has been reduced for some weapons scientists to an unending surveillance of aging machines. While this might seem a simple progression from the nuclear sublime to the nuclear banal, the logics behind the SBSS program are more complicated than they first appear.

The formal goal of SBSS is to understand how aging effects on any single component might alter safety and performance over decades of storage. But given the extreme pressures, velocities, and temperatures operating within a nuclear implosion/explosion, this effort to model the bomb also promises a new and more nuanced understanding of how a variety of materials behave in extreme conditions. The SBSS program promises weapons scientists the opportunity to replace nuclear production with, what a former head of the Los Alamos weapons program has called, the 'holy grail of nuclear weapons theory' (Hopkins 2000); namely, a 'first principles' understanding of nuclear processes. As an experimental regime, the intellectual appeal of SBSS is that weapons scientists can pursue the kinds of questions that would allow a totally scaleable understanding of what happens inside a thermonuclear blast, a generalized model applicable to all weapons systems. Since a first principles understanding of nuclear weapons is not necessary for producing a nuclear arsenal (as the Cold War arms race demonstrated), the decision to pursue the 'equations of state' for U.S. nuclear weapons is an explicit effort to make nuclear weapons science compelling to scientists, to re-energize their nuclear imaginary in the absence of nuclear detonations and the arms race.

Uncertainty about the ageing bomb-body has been mobilized, in other words, to turn each U.S. nuclear weapon into a potentially endless universe of basic questions about material science. One weapons scientist captures the depoliticized understanding of this task:

> I read things in the newspaper: The activists say, 'We know everything we need to know about weapons'; I've seen members of the senate stand up and say, 'We can just model it on the computer' – and I just want to tear my hair out. No! It's just factually wrong. We don't understand everything there is to know about basic properties.

We don't understand everything about basic properties. Each new experimental regime in Los Alamos has produced not only new kinds of knowledge but also a new concept of the bomb. Moreover, a 'first principles' understanding of nuclear technology produces a deep understanding of how, for example, plutonium behaves over time and under extreme conditions. There is no need to worry about the human body in this experimental regime, as there are only non-nuclear detonations occurring in Nevada, which are constituted as basic experiments in exotic material science. The nuclear weapon produced by SBSS is one that primarily exists in component parts, each framed by a discourse of uncertainty about ageing; and the military value of each nuclear device is produced not by an explosion, but through a high-tech inspection.

In the post-Cold War period, certainty comes not from an explosion but from a process of 'certification' – a yearly report from the directors of the national laboratories stating that they see no reason why the U.S. nuclear arsenal would not function as planned during a nuclear war. While experimental 'certainty' and 'certification' may be different experimental and political concepts, we should remember that through the second half of the Cold War the U.S. was routinely deploying weapons that had not been tested in the ways in which they would actually be used in a nuclear war, and the nuclear device that destroyed the city of

Hiroshima in 1945 was never tested prior to its military use. Thus, the current pursuit of a 'first principles' understanding of nuclear weapons marks a significant change in the technoaesthetic construction of the bomb. Put simply, within the post–Cold War order the bomb is being evaluated not on its ability to be perfectly destructive, but rather on the perfectibility of its form, pointing towards an essentialist understanding of technology and the non-human world deeply rooted in the Western philosophical tradition.

Nuclear weapons science has always been a compartmentalized experimental project in the United States, in which the rules of state secrecy as well as the division of expertise among theorists, physicists, chemists, and engineers has divided the bomb into a series of discrete experimental projects. The detonation of a nuclear device during the Cold War was thus a coordination of a vast array of scientific experiments distributed throughout the laboratory, which together constituted the technology as both a military machine and the material form of Mutual(ly) Assured Destruction (MAD). In the absence of the arms race, as well as any material trace of the destructive power of the bomb, the SBSS focus on 'first principles' fragments the bomb into a series of basic science questions that have no direct connection to the military reality of nuclear weapons. In post–Cold War Los Alamos, the bomb is consequently many things, but rarely a weapon of mass destruction. In post–Cold War Los Alamos, nuclear weapons are frequently compared to a garaged automobile, often an ambulance that might not be able to start if one needed to race to the hospital in ten or twenty years.

An SBSS exhibit in the Bradbury Science Museum, which is the primary public space at Los Alamos National Laboratory, pushes this technoaesthetic project further, suggesting that a nuclear weapon is like a 911 emergency call. The exhibit asks visitors to:

> Pretend that this phone is going to be used by your local 911-emergency operator. Can you test it and verify that it will work whenever it is needed? There is one important rule. You are not allowed to make or receive a call to test it.

The exhibit then invites visitors to check the dial tone, to press the keys and listen to the key tones, as well as test the ringer. It then asks: 'Are you confident that this phone will work if needed for an emergency,' and gives visitors a chance to vote on whether the phone could successfully complete a 911 call or not. To dramatize the technical problem of how to maintain nuclear weapons without actually detonating them, we see here an attempt to normalize the destructive power of the U.S. nuclear arsenal not as the instrument that threatens the human body, but rather as an institutional emergency response that attends to physical trauma – as ambulance, fire truck, or police action. Weapons gerontology thus promotes an image of the aging bomb as body to mobilize a new kind of nuclear fear: fear not of the bomb that explodes, but of the bomb that cannot.

Without the 'truth test' of the nuclear detonation to evaluate theoretical results, some senior Los Alamos scientists do not believe that future weapons scientists will have the right experimental expertise to properly evaluate U.S. nuclear weapons. Hardly a stable form, SBSS is simultaneously portrayed in Los Alamos as either a highly challenging means of perfecting nuclear technology or as simply an economy of appearances, a discrepancy that could be mobilized as a rationale for a return to U.S. underground nuclear testing in the near future.

It is important to recognize, however, that the theory, the instrumentation, and the experimental method of Los Alamos weapons science have changed in the post-Cold War era (see Galison 1997). SBSS assumes that one can test the components and processes in a nuclear weapon separately, and assemble a picture of the military performance of the device from the collected data. The Cold War program was focused on the detonation of the actual weapons system, with success judged by how accurately weapons scientists were able to predict and reproduce the explosive yield. The instrumentation of nuclear weapons science is no longer a combination of the nuclear device, test sensors, and radiochemistry, but is rather a series of discrete hydrodynamic test facilities, non-nuclear material science studies, and computer simulations. And finally, the experiment is no longer an earthshaking rumble in the Nevada Desert registered on seismographs around the world, but is now a virtual nuclear explosion simulated on the world's fastest computers located in air-conditioned buildings at Los Alamos, Lawrence Livermore, and Sandia National Laboratories.

In Los Alamos, the pleasures of nuclear science have always been at odds with the destructive potential of the military machine. The experimental trajectory of Cold War weapons science, as we have seen, diminished sensory access to the destructive power of the bomb with the move to underground testing, which encouraged a technoscientific focus on the internal characteristics of the explosion rather than its material effects. The post-Cold War regime of SBSS has taken this conceptual mediation of the enterprise one step further by eliminating nuclear detonations altogether while reinvesting in weapons science on a new scale. The three-dimensional simulation of the thermonuclear explosion is presented in the form of a movie, which is displayed in state-of-the-art 'visualization centers' in Los Alamos. In these new SBSS facilities, scientists are positioned at the center of an 'immersive theater,' and oriented towards a 'Power Wall,' the largest and most detailed projection screens on the planet. Standing in front of the 16 by 8 foot Power Wall, scientists are physically dwarfed by the microscopic processes that make up a simulated nuclear explosion, which are rendered in full color and projected on a massive scale. The goal of this project in Los Alamos is to provide a microsecond by microsecond portrait of the densities, pressures, velocities, and turbulence that make up a nuclear implosion/explosion, and to be able to track all of these processes in three dimensions with perfect resolution. The first major achievement of the post-Cold War virtual laboratory is, thus, to have repositioned a nuclear explosion at the center of Los Alamos weapons science. However, this nuclear detonation is experienced not through vulnerable human senses that need to be protected from the blast, but rather through prosthetic devices that enable the body to interact with the simulated explosion within the safety of a secured room. The half-century progression from protective goggles (necessary to prevent flash-blindness during an above-ground event) to virtual-reality gloves and goggles (needed to interact with the nuclear simulation) is the most significant evolution in the material form of Los Alamos weapons science, as this new experimental regime evacuates the destructive bomb entirely through a compelling new form of virtual embodiment.

SBSS ultimately promotes the possibility of a new kind of intimacy between scientists and the exploding bomb, allowing us to chart a logical conclusion to the multigenerational bomb-as-body concept in Los Alamos. If the fifteen-year project of SBSS is successful, Los Alamos weapons scientists will be able to evaluate and account for the significant 'gerontological' issues in the nuclear stockpile, as well as design new weapons in virtual reality with confidence that the systems would work if actually built and detonated. The technical knowledge drawn from a half century of U.S. nuclear testing, as well as the advanced material science and computational achievements of SBSS, will be archived in permanent form – securing the technoscientific legacy of the Manhattan Project. Moreover, the next generation supercomputers in combination with next generation 3-D virtual reality technologies will complete the ongoing revolution in the body–bomb relationship for weapons scientists. Future weapons scientists will no longer interact with their experimental data via computer screens, which maintain a separation between the physical body of the scientist and the bomb as technoscientific project. Instead, the next-generation visualization center will place scientists at the center of a highly sophisticated virtual space. In the near future, Los Alamos scientists will track specific particles, velocities, pressures, and flows through new, technologically mediated, but nonetheless felt senses – and they will do so not from office chairs and via a computer screens, but from *inside* the nuclear explosion.

The weapons laboratory of the early twenty-first century will ultimately allow weapons scientists to walk inside a virtual hydrogen bomb, and experience the most destructive force imaginable through physical senses that are not vaporized by the assault of the explosion, but rather tuned to the aesthetic properties of the simulation. The promise of SBSS is, thus, not only to perfect and indefinitely maintain nuclear weapons technologies through non-nuclear testing, but also to resolve the multigenerational technoaesthetic confusion of bodies and machines in Los Alamos by creating a conceptual space in which weapons scientists and weapons of mass destruction can comfortably coexist – at the very moment of detonation. The bomb's new body is increasingly that of the weapons scientists themselves, as the intellectual pleasure of nuclear weapons science and a tactile sensory experience of the exploding bomb, are being merged through a massively engineered technoaesthetic spectacle in virtual reality. The intimacy of this conceptual project – the desire to physically interact with a thermonuclear explosion in all its nanosecond and atomic detail – eliminates fear of the exploding bomb altogether in favor of a phantasmagoria. This flooding of the senses with virtual images of a detonating nuclear device reinvents the bomb as a purely creative project. Purified of its military reality, the bomb that will ultimately be produced by SBSS is no longer geriatric or living on borrowed time: it will have an expanding future horizon, making weapons science no longer a temporary political solution to the global crisis, but an aesthetic project capable of existing finally on its own terms. The pleasures of nuclear weapons science are being reinvented in post–Cold War Los Alamos through new experimental facilities that promise to free nuclear science from the politics of the bomb. However, this is a high-tech mystification, as the destructive reality of nuclear arsenals persists, despite, and in the future because of, this aestheticization of laboratory science.

Conclusion: of bombs and bodies in the plutonium economy

In post–Cold War Los Alamos the technoaesthetic production of the U.S. nuclear arsenal is internally structured by a complicated dual deployment of time and the human body. Consider the following critique, spontaneously offered to me by a senior weapons scientist concerning public ideas about nuclear weapons. Non-weapons scientists usually describe nuclear weapons as 'apocalyptic' – as the end of time – he said. But if you look at the damage produced by a 1 megaton warhead detonated at maximum yield height over New York City it would incinerate everything within a 1-mile radius on the island and severely damage a much larger area – but parts of Queens, Brooklyn, and New Jersey would still be there; thus, he said, it would be devastating but decidedly not apocalyptic. Moreover, he noted that a full-scale nuclear war would not be the end of everything. Instead he offered an image of nuclear war as a kind of time travel, stating that a full-scale nuclear exchange would return the United States to 'roughly the year 1860,' 'You'd lose the power grid,' he offered, 'but there would still be blacksmithing technology for making horseshoes and the like.'

In this presentation, all human achievement is collapsed through the bomb into a specific notion of temporal-technological progress. Consequently, after a nuclear war, techno-time would simply start over again at the 1860 level and the U.S. would build itself out of the ashes by producing new machines. In fact, within this concept, time might actually be speeded up after a nuclear war because this would be the second time around for the Industrial Revolution. In this case, destruction is not ignored – indeed, it is precisely measured; but it is defined in terms of the presence or absence of technology. The effect of radioactive fallout on people, animals, or the environment is understated, which allows the meaning of nuclear war to be fixed in the realm of a specific notion of temporal technological progress (that is, through a focus on the horseshoes and not the horse).

The black humor in this narrative, characteristic of Los Alamos weapons science, is complicated in that it not only measures the destructive radius of the bomb on a U.S. city, but also mobilizes an implicit image of an invulnerable scientific body, one that would be left to rebuild New York after the blast.

If, as we have just seen, the bomb can be interpreted as enabling a form of time travel, illustrating a complicated understanding of where bodies and military nuclear technologies interact, this weapons scientist's story also points to a cognitive rupture experienced at Los Alamos by the end of the Cold War, for if time itself is measured in terms of a specific narrative of techno-military progress within the laboratory, the break-up of the Soviet Union in 1991 and the accompanying U.S. moratorium on underground nuclear testing in 1992 would seem to have denied weapons scientists the possibility of a nuclear future on these very terms. The end of the Cold War thus challenged the cosmology supporting nuclear weapons science at Los Alamos while fundamentally changing its experimental form.

The question SBSS ultimately poses is not how to maintain nuclear weapons as a technology – as machines – but how to maintain a conceptual understanding of what it means to detonate a nuclear device. Each experimental regime from 1945 to 2001 has, in fact, produced a different articulation of the bomb, diminishing cognitive access to the destructive power of nuclear weapons in favor of an aesthetic-intellectual form. Over time, when the bomb is closer to a perfected technoaesthetic form – lovingly rendered in virtual reality by scientists who are generations removed from those who last experienced the heat, shockwave, and atmospheric effects of a nuclear detonation – Los Alamos scientists will certainly know much more about how a thermonuclear device operates than they did during the 1950s' era of nuclear testing in the Pacific. But who can argue that a computer simulation will offer the same level of conceptual understanding as did those above-ground detonations, where the destructive power of nuclear explosions was experienced not only as intellectually powerful but also as brutally, terrifyingly destructive? This slippage between the virtual and the real, which started with the first efforts to mathematically model nuclear explosions immediately after World War II in Los Alamos and continued through the Cold War testing regimes (Galison 1996), threatens now to become the ascendant aspect of weapons science in the twenty-first century and the ultimate institutional compensation for the terror of the nuclear sublime.

This is not to suggest that U.S. nuclear devices capable of exploding with massive destructive force will not be deployed around the globe or to argue for a return to underground nuclear testing; it is rather to point out that the expertise necessary to maintain those machines is in danger of being separated from an understanding of the consequences of using the technology. An experience of the nuclear sublime provoked by an above-ground nuclear detonation involved a moment of terror that was ultimately resolved for scientists through an intellectual compensation, allowing the project of nuclear weapons science to continue. SBSS, as an experimental regime, blocks access to any visceral understanding of the power of the U.S. nuclear arsenal, replacing it with sophisticated material science questions and a virtual spectacle, which together offer only complexity and aesthetic pleasure. The beauty of nuclear weapons science in Los Alamos has always been one of its most dangerous elements, allowing an aestheticization of scientific knowledge to circumvent the political import of engineering weapons of mass destruction. In his 1936 critique of the Italian Futurists' beautification of war and the machine body, Walter Benjamin argued that the movement revealed a 'sense perception that has been changed by technology' and a European society on the eve of World War II whose 'self-alienation has reached such a degree that it can experience its own destruction as an aesthetic pleasure of the first order' (Benjamin 1969: 242). The bomb is America's response to forces unleashed at that historical moment, and the post–Cold War transformation of each U.S. nuclear device from a weapon of mass destruction into an opportunity for exotic material science and cutting-edge computer simulation advances the aestheticization of politics through a reconfigured sense perception to a new order for a new century. It is vital to recover the politics that SBSS works to erase, even as the future of the bomb in Los Alamos becomes no longer that of a bomb, but rather of America's technoaesthetic spectacle *par excellence*.

Note

1 This chapter is a revised version of Joseph Masco (2004) "Nuclear technoaesthetics: Sensory politics from trinity to the virtual bomb in Los Alamos", *American Ethnologist* 31 (3): 349–373. Permission from the American Anthropological Association to reprint this revised version is gratefully acknowledged.

References

Agnew, Harold. 1983. Vintage Agnew. *Los Alamos Science* 7: 71.

Bailey, Janet. 1995. *The Good Servant: Making Peace with the Bomb at Los Alamos*. New York: Simon & Schuster.

Benjamin, Walter. 1969. The Work of Art in the Age of Mechanical Reproduction. In Walter Benjamin, *Illuminations*. New York: Schocken.

Bradbury, Norris. 1980. Los Alamos: The First 25 Years. In Lawrence Badash, Joseph O. Hirschfelder and Herbert P. Broida (eds) *Reminiscences of Los Alamos 1943–1945*. Boston, MA: Reidel, pp. 161–175.

Burke, Edmund. 1993. A Philosophical Enquiry into the Origin of Our Ideas of the Sublime and Beautiful. In Ian Harris (ed.) *Pre-Revolutionary Writings*. Cambridge: Cambridge University Press.

Cohn, Carol. 1987. Sex and Death in the Rational World of Defense Intellectuals. *Signs* 12(4): 687–718.

Ferguson, Francis. 1984. The Nuclear Sublime. *Diacritics* 14(2): 4–10.

Galison, Peter. 1997. *Image and Logics: A Material Culture of Microphysics*. Chicago, IL: University of Chicago Press.

Galison, Peter. 1996. Computer Simulations and the Trading Zone. In Peter Galison and David J. Stump (eds) *The Disunity of Science: Boundaries, Context and Power*. Stanford, CA: Stanford University Press.

Gallagher, Carole. 1993. *American Ground Zero: The Secret Nuclear War*. Cambridge, MA: MIT Press.

Glasstone, Samuel and Philip J. Dolan (eds). 1977. *The Effects of Nuclear Weapons*, 3rd edition. Washington, DC: U.S. Department of Defense and U.S. Department of Energy.

Gusterson, Hugh. 1996a. *Nuclear Rites: A Weapons Laboratory at the End of the Cold War.* Berkeley: University of California Press.

Gusterson, Hugh. 1996b. Nuclear Weapons Testing: Scientific Experiment as Political Ritual. In Laura Nader (ed.) *Naked Science: Anthropological Inquiry and Boundaries, Power, and Knowledge.* New York: Routledge.

Hacker, Barton. 1994. *Elements of Controversy: The Atomic Energy Commission and Radiation Safety in Nuclear Weapons Testing, 1947–1974.* Berkeley: University of California Press.

Hawkins, David. 1983. *Project Y: The Los Alamos Story.* Los Angeles, CA: Tomash.

Hecker, Sig. 1995. Reflections on Hiroshima and Nagasaki. *Los Alamos National Laboratory Newsbulletin,* 4 August.

Hopkins, John C. 2000. Nuclear Stockpile Stewardship. Sumner Associates Inc. Available at: https://web.archive.org/web/20090310184556/http://www.sumnerassociates.com/stockp ile.html. Accessed 9 October 2016.

Kant, Immanuel. 1986. Analytic of the Sublime. In Ernst Behler (ed.) *Philosophical Writings.* New York: Continuum.

Knorr Cetina, Karin. 1999. *Epistemic Cultures: How the Sciences Make Knowledge.* Cambridge, MA: Harvard University Press.

LANL. 1988. *The Los Alamos Nuclear Test Program: Field Test Operations.* Los Alamos, NM: Los Alamos National Laboratory.

Medalia, Jonathan. 1998. *Nuclear Weapons Production Capability Issues.* Washington, DC: Library of Congress Congressional Research Service.

Medalia, Jonathan. 1994. *Nuclear Weapons Stockpile Stewardship: The Role of Livermore and Los Alamos National Laboratories.* Washington, DC: Library of CongressCongressional Research Service.

Miller, Richard L. 1986. *Under the Cloud: The Decades of Nuclear Testing.* New York: Free Press.

Natural Resources Defense Council (NRDC). 1998. NRDC Nuclear Notebook: Known Nuclear Tests Worldwide, 1945–1998. *Bulletin of the Atomic Scientists* 54(6): 65–67.

Nye, David E. 1994. *American Technological Sublime.* Cambridge, MA: MIT Press.

Office of Technology Assessment (OTA). 1989. *The Containment of Underground Nuclear Explosion.* Washington, DC: U.S. Government Printing Office.

Ott, Thomas. 1999. *Race for the Superbomb.* Boston, MA: Public Broadcasting Service (PBS) Home Video.

Rhodes, Richard. 1986. *The Making of the Atomic Bomb.* New York: Simon & Schuster.

Richelson, Jeffrey T. 1999. *America's Space Sentinels: DSP Satellites and National Security.* Kansas City: University of Kansas Press.

Smith, Jas Mercer. 1995. The SBSS Challenge. *Weapons Insider* 2(4): 1–4.

Traweek, Sharon. 1988. *Beamtimes and Lifetimes: The World of High Energy Physicists.* Cambridge, MA: Harvard University Press.

U.S. Department of Defense (DOD). 1955. *Shot Apple 2: A Test of the TEAPOT Series.* Washington, DC: Defense Nuclear Agency.

U.S. Department of Energy (DOE). 1999. *Stockpile Stewardship Plan: Executive Overview, Fiscal year 2000.* Washington, DC: DOE Office of Defense Programs.

U.S. Department of Energy (DOE). 1998. *Stockpile Stewardship Plan: Second Annual Update (FY 1999).* Washington, DC: DOE Office of Defense Programs.

U.S. Department of Energey (DOE). 1984. *Nuclear Weapons Planning and Acquisitions.* Albuquerque: DOE Albuquerque Operations Office.

Wolff, Walter P. 1984. *A Typical Los Alamos National Laboratory Underground Nuclear Test.* Los Alamos, NM: Los Alamos National Laboratory.

Younger, Stephen. 2000. *Nuclear Weapons in the Twenty-First Century.* Los Alamos, NM: Los Alamos National Laboratory.

7

THE GLOBAL POLITICS OF INTERNET GOVERNANCE

A case study in closure and technological design

Monroe Price

The Internet, as we have come to know it as a series of institutional, mechanical and human interactions, has elements of revolution and disruption with widespread political and social consequences. This chapter is about the ongoing contest in international society to characterize the Internet as a specific kind of technology, the contest to gain some consensus as to what functions it should play and not play, how it should be conceived and how regulated. How it revolutionizes, what is disrupted and how collectively do governments and publics come to understand these impacts – all of this is in play. This is a story of how the concept of newness is wielded – as a shield to protect developments or as a sword to foil misadventure. Notwithstanding its quasi-military origins, the Internet has often, perhaps predominantly, been presented as an instrument for the free flow of information, an instrument in the global battle for democracy and a driving force in the politics of globalization. But we know that this image is subject to complex shaping – an issue of controversy and contention among states, not the expression of a natural essence.

This chapter will add to discussions of how governments, corporations, publics struggle to define what the Internet is, what it may become, how it is thought to emerge, how some sort of consensus can emerge and make policy choices in this issue area easier to make and to evaluate. A narrative – a set of stories – about the Internet gets told over and again in international politics. Various mechanisms are employed to encase that narrative and make it a useful reality, to the advantage of some actors over others. In the politics of Internet governance the ability to create a strong picture of what the Internet is and could be is central.

Each new technology is surrounded by particular dramas that surround issues of definition. Companies, countries, civil society all vie to characterize novel technological phenomenon, often to suit existing political realities. During these moments of significant technological change there is the struggle for settlement, for assurance that a particular way of perceiving the technology becomes the surviving, possibly dominant one. As Daniel McCarthy has argued, societies come to conceptualize systems not through 'a given technological rationality', but rather as the outcome of a politically contested process in which past and future technological projects are framed in competing ways (see McCarthy 2011: 90; Feenberg 1991; Pinch and Bijker 1987: 37–39; Bijker 1995). The effectiveness of technological innovations is dependent, in part, on a socially constructed vision of political and social order. Those for whom this process of definition is meaningful – often entities I have placed under the umbrella of strategic communicators (Price 2015) – seek to obtain deep and long-term support for their particular mode of thinking about the technology.

McCarthy (2011: 90), drawing on both the Social Construction of Technology (SCOT) approach and the Critical Theory of Technology developed by Andrew Feenberg, outlines the concept of technological **closure** as the moment when 'a design process works to define a particular technological artifact as natural, as an accepted part of the social environment'. The objective – and a solid and important one – for most Western democracies has been to see the Internet in its full democratic plumage. Closure occurs if that characterization 'no longer strikes its users as interesting or novel'. The idea of the Internet as naturally furthering good governance, citizen involvement and accompanying economic growth would become taken for granted; and it is this very quality – the taken-for-grantedness – that is a significant source of its power.

Current virulent debates about the Internet and its governance present an opportunity to illustrate this theoretical approach.[1] These debates, at one level, are how to come to closure – or how to make an attempt at closure more questionable. There are competitors for closure. Technological closure could be a generalized understanding and acceptance of some set of propositions by those who advocate a 'free and open Internet'. But these advocates vie with those whose emphasize a desire that Internet usage be monitored, perhaps filtered and controlled, for reasons of national sovereignty, or who envisage that cyberwar or some other dire set of circumstances might break out, and that therefore modes of control must be put into place (see, for example, Clarke 2010; cf. Rid 2013). Few doubt that states will find, even in a verdantly open Internet, reasons for regulation. What is at stake in the contest for closure is the general *gestalt*, the overall structure of an Internet environment that contains formidable questions of architecture, purpose and aspiration. I explore these issues by looking first at general connections between closure and the politics of Internet governance, before turning to skirmishes (or more) between China and the United States to gain the upper hand in the struggles. I end with what I call 'domestication' of the implications of this process, partly as a consequence of the Snowden revelations. Drawing on methodological insights of SCOT, I focus on controversial cases to highlight the politics of technological design at work (Pinch and Bijker 1987: 19–21, 34; Bijker 1995).

Closure, legitimacy and Internet governance

Closure matters. If a free and open Internet is taken as the dominant understanding of how the Internet should function in international society, then the outliers or violators of the to-be-accepted norm can be more easily identified – along lines of censorship and control and, possibly, violations of privacy. Alliances are formed to render and reinforce this as a dominant characterization. But we know this process of closure is highly contested. China, Russia, Iran and others have substantially competing models of what the Internet is and should be. Indeed, societies, including those in the West, are trying both to understand and to persuade the international community what iteration, what idea, what complex relationship to government and business should characterize the Internet and other new media technologies.

The Internet governance debate, carpeted in neutral-sounding terms, involves competing architectures of information policy contained in sets of words and concepts. Within these arguments rival tropes are repeatedly invoked to justify one approach or another. Competing entities – states, but also corporations, non-governmental organizations (NGOs), academics and activists – seek to steer the debate. Each group seeks to produce an enveloping and comforting account of the technology and its role in society that is strategically relevant to its interests and that supports a particular governing approach.

Seeking technological closure for new modes of communicating is a familiar sport. It was a long process, over centuries, for a nuanced understanding of freedom of expression to evolve that was specific to a print society, one featuring primarily newspapers and books (Curtis 2000; Habermas 1989). And even then that consensus had regional and otherwise limited circumscription – these were not universally held norms. The last half of the twentieth century saw efforts to settle ideas and institutions for the electronic media and their relation to freedom of expression (Hamelink 1994). These were decisions often cabined in specific language relating to the scarce availability of the radio spectrum or the power of television images on children. A consensus on these matters was hard to achieve, and struggles over the role of public service media or depictions of sexual activity and violence are still prevalent throughout the international system. The codification of norms around freedom of expression for international society – expressed, for example, in Article 19 of the International Covenant on Civil and Political Rights (ICCPR) and Article 10 of the European Convention on Human Rights (ECHR) – were efforts, episodically successful, to reach international consensus on approaches to transfrontier communications. The requisite consensus on the governance of new information technologies, including social media and the Internet, is not yet at hand.

The search for closure is epitomized by the way the U.S. State Department and the White House, together with like-minded states, have sought to make 'Internet freedom' the conclusive narrative of a global Internet. Hardly alone, and building on the extraordinary success of the technology's advances, these government officials emphasize how a minimally encumbered Internet can be the (imagined) fulfilment of hopes for free expression, human rights and democracy. Creating and establishing that hopeful narrative of legitimacy, a legitimacy purportedly embedded in the norms of the international community, has been a long-term effort requiring the work not only of government and civil society but also of transnational companies like Google, as well as academics and other actors. In this multistakeholder world, engaging diverse parties is essential. This is certainly less true in authoritarian societies; but even there, efforts to convince and build support among a range of actors is not wholly absent.

For technological closure to occur, background ideas and ideals must be organized and sustained to assure the proper cultural and symbolic understandings. Gaining and sustaining acceptance of a narrative requires fixing and reinforcing a norm, institutionalizing a set of ways of thinking about ensuring freedom of expression that subsequently are expressed by the hard and soft architectures of the Internet. It is in those circumstances where the benefits of legitimacy are conferred, with a coherent goal – 'the stabilization of an artifact and the "disappearance" of problems' (Price 2015: 2; Pinch and Bijker 1987). This condition only occurs (as McCarthy and others suggest) when relevant social groups see important definitional issues as being more or less resolved. This may happen either through definitions that impact the design of a technology or by redefining the problem which an existing technology may be said to solve. When closure occurs, additional institutions may more likely fall into line and act according to the desired standard – technological closure affects legal, social and political institutions in which a technological artefact is embedded. There is a kind of halo effect that results. For instance, judges, where there is the occasion for reviewing legal disputes over telecommunications, will more easily confirm a line of action that conforms to an existing picture of the Internet.

Controlling the high ground of legitimacy and acceptedness softens the circumstances in which broad doctrine can be easily circumscribed. Closure could make it more likely that large companies would be absolved of intermediary liability – wide legal responsibility for the content of material carried on their platforms – and it could emphasize how limited exceptions might be for rights to receive and impart information. Closure might help resolve difficult questions over jurisdiction, traditionally viewed as one of the central issues of Internet law and governance (Goldsmith and Wu 2006). General settlement around the Internet Freedom agenda almost automatically incorporates a broader set of overarching attitudes towards global Internet governance, including an enlarged role for civil society and a more limited role for agreements among states – a set of structures identified in Internet governance parlance as multi-stakeholder governance (see Carr 2015; Mueller 2010).

The contest to shape closure is epitomized by complementary international campaigns and clashing conceptions for Internet design as articulated by the United States and by China in the period around 2010. Both countries had, and have, a great deal at stake domestically in terms of the evolution of Internet system design, and both sought to project their views onto an international stage. Two statements about the campaign for closure (one from the United States, one from China) are useful to explore these questions of design: a 2010 speech by then U.S. Secretary of State Hillary Clinton and a China-originated Internet White Paper issued not long afterwards. These are presented as visions of what future generations of the Internet should look like, but they are also presented as visions about the international society that the Internet would create or reinforce. This competition is illustrative of a modern phenomenon: those advocating change in communications policy, both nationally and globally, have enmeshed their conceptions in various techno-logical, social and political categories to improve the chances that these policies will be adopted. They have sought to 'hard-wire' their ideas of speech and society into evolving digital infrastructures. Both documents are also formulated to be read in an international context, to gain support from influential institutional audiences.

The U.S. 'Internet Freedom' strategy

In January 2010, Secretary of State Clinton delivered a much-acclaimed speech called 'Remarks on Internet Freedom' at a temple of free speech, the Newseum in Washington, DC. As an exercise in narrative framing, the talk was a dramatic effort to define proper structuring of the Internet in a global setting. The speech threw down a gauntlet: 'Both the American people and nations that censor the Internet should understand that our government is committed to helping promote Internet freedom,' and this requires that the U.S. government fight for a global policy consistent with these views (Clinton 2010; cf. Thierer and Crews 2003).[2] Left somewhat vague was what Internet freedom would actually mean in terms of system implementation. In 2006, the Bush Administration had already established a Global Internet Freedom Task Force (GIFT). The Clinton State Department, renaming GIFT as the NetFreedom Task Force, provided an upgraded bureaucratic framework to make the Internet – and U.S. policy concerning it – a priority in bilateral and multilateral discussions and to develop grant programmes, policy initiatives and other steps to further that goal.

The Secretary's Newseum presentation provided the earmarks of a 'new information' enthusiasm, celebrating the glories of the technology:

> The spread of information networks is forming a new nervous system for our planet. [...] Now, in many respects, information has never been so free. There are more ways to spread more ideas to more people than at any moment in history. And even in authoritarian countries, information networks are helping people discover new facts and making governments more accountable.

The speech contained the normal duality of benefits and dangers, the litany of grounds for concern (including child pornography and national security and opti-mism). Grounds for exporting a specific form of architecture were clearly articulated.

Secretary Clinton's argument depended on a tree of logic in which U.S. interests are served by an increase in democratic values in states throughout the world. Drawing on democratic peace theory, U.S. policy officials hold that a world that is more dependably democratic is more stable, possibly more prosperous and less likely to lead to conflict with other democracies (Smith 2007; Doyle 1983). Related to this is the belief that openness to information, and press freedom more specifically, is linked with democracy, as a system of information diffusion that empowers individuals leads to greater accountability and improves or enhances the demand side for democratic governance. 'Internet freedom' is, at least in part, shorthand for a series of policies concerning the Internet that would advance these democratic values and expedite more democratic political outcomes. It entails a commitment to an 'enabling environment,' one that asserts the rule of law and may in fact respect it (Price and Krug 2000).

A second strategy for an 'Internet freedom' agenda – not necessarily inconsistent with this first one – is an economic one, with at least two branches that implicitly favour U.S. economic output. First, an 'Internet freedom' agenda may be an umbrella for expanded demand for approaches and products developed by American suppliers (or transnational companies with strong U.S. and Western ties). An 'Internet freedom' rationale encourages a system for the diffusion of information that is highly consistent with a freer market in goods and services – a market that is also beneficial to a liberalized economy. For example, as satellite services transformed modes of supplying information, they created broad new markets both for video programmes and for consumer goods advertised or promoted on the new channels of distribution. This was a market in which American entertainment providers had an historic advantage. The same, of course, is potentially true for the Internet and American corporations such as Google, Facebook, Amazon and Twitter. In this sense, an 'Internet freedom' agenda is also an agenda for a robust transnational economy in which the United States considers it has a stake.

Clearly, Secretary Clinton's speech was playing on the anxiety that a great opportunity for free expression would be lost if the United States, in concert with others, was not vigilant. The Internet provided the long-hoped-for chance of a liberating technology, one that had the potential to increase education, serve as the basis for stronger citizenship and advance democratic values. And 'freedom' is, itself, perhaps the core U.S. foreign policy narrative or brand (or has been most consistently in recent decades). 'Internet freedom' in this sense implies some vindication for American approaches, American aspirations. 'Internet freedom' as an idea exports both a legal structure and a culture of expression that, at least on the surface, favours American foreign policy aims. It implies the structuring of a competitive environment for entry and reception in which U.S. interests have historically done well. And the alternative – more closed Internet systems – can be seen as encouraging an environment where counter-narratives have privileged if not exclusive access (Mackinnon 2012).

How does one make such a vision, incomplete and aspirational as it is, operational? Clinton's speech created the prospect of a new design element, a potential international 'right to connect'. This is a high-minded right that sought to bring rhetorical grandeur to the proposal and use entitlement discourse to ground a policy approach. Creating a 'right' is an example of deploying international norms as a persuasive underpinning for a strategic outcome. By creating a movement towards a 'right to connect' (or an obligation to ensure a 'freedom to connect') – in other words, a right to communicate[3] – the U.S. government would establish a public and external framework in which steps towards the Internet freedom structure would be seen as almost mandatory.

At the heart of the U.S. position seemed to be this architectural point, which was immediately subject to multiple interpretations: 'We stand for a single Internet where all of humanity has equal access to knowledge and ideas.' Combining the 'single Internet' idea with the 'right to connect' provided the basis for a legal model whereby the Internet should not be splintered into many national Internets, each with its own rules of entry and separate regulatory frameworks reflecting differences among national publics. What was desired was 'One Internet' with overwhelming access, regardless of territoriality. Setting out a vision and encapsulating it in a pithy term is an important element of rhetorical strategy. Narratives of technological closure often require the exclusion of complex details – details that might detract from the appeal of the more clearly stated idea. As we shall see, it is this feature, the idea of 'One Internet', that pits the U.S. position directly in contrast with that of China.

In terms of strategy, the Clinton speech was the public launch of a global campaign aimed at building an international consensus for the vision. By June 2010, Kenneth Corbin – reporting on a speech by then State Department communications guru Alec Ross – could write that the 'Department had made Internet censorship a key pillar of its foreign policy and now factors the issue into its diplomatic relations with every other nation' (Corbin 2010). Ross argued that:

> Internet freedom has gone from being something that's a piece of what could at best be called a piece of foreign policy arcanum – a little thing that a handful of people work on – to something becoming increasingly central in our foreign policy.
>
> *(Corbin 2010)*

The field of engagement was wide, but troublesome:

> 2009 was the worst year in history in terms of Internet freedom ... There are now literally dozens of countries with less-than-stellar internet freedom records. And it's increasingly the case that governments view the Internet as less something built on a single end-user-to-end-user principle than something that can be sort of built to spec, that looks and feels and works more like an intranet than an Internet.
>
> *(Corbin 2010)*

A strategy must be attentive to its many parts and create what counts as an accep-table agenda. An 'Internet freedom' strategy requires further policy development on standards – for controls, for pricing, for content – and on the legal enabling environment on which an open Internet depends. For instance, the liability rules imposed on Internet Service Providers (ISPs) or other intermediaries, the dis-couragement of licensing at any level, the repeal of laws concerning criminal libel, and so forth are all elements that need to be addressed. Governments constantly seek to have platforms like Facebook and Twitter monitored and policed, often at the specific behest of the authorities. And bloggers are threatened with being treated like the media, subject to licensing and imposition of standards. These are the tools and techniques that can hobble the prospect of 'openness', and are always areas that require attention. 'Openness' itself is defined and applied in a highly specific manner. There are areas in which the U.S. government had policies inconsistent with what it was recommending abroad, issues where it was not necessarily beyond criticism for its own melding of restrictive and open efforts. These include issues concerning cyberwar and cybersecurity[4] and the demanding debate over protection of intellectual property (IP) on the Internet.[5]

A public conversation in February 2011 between then Assistant Secretary of State Michael Posner and Leslie Harris of the Center for Democracy and Tech-nology dealt candidly with inconsistencies and challenges in fostering a coherent strategy (Posner and Harris 2011). The United States recognized that it needed to think about issues of jurisdiction and power. Would there be universal standards of Internet governance, and how would they be enforced? Who would referee this world? Here there is the classic political question: who decides? Where should authority to make these decisions lie? In the conversation, Harris said, 'We have to figure out some kind of global governance bodies that don't force us into a race to the bottom.' Here was another area, Harris stated, where an American vision might collide with other visions:

> There are some calls around the world for governance bodies, like the UN, where we would be negotiating what works on the internet or what ought to work with countries who have very, very different values ... I'm hoping that in the first instance, that we can reach agreement with other democratic gov-ernments on what we believe the right policy principles are, so that we can start demonstrating the way that the Internet should be governed cross borders. But the questions of who should manage the Internet in a global environment is the thorniest and the biggest challenge.
>
> *(Posner and Harris 2011)*

Posner, too, recited 'a range of anxieties about throwing this issue and many others into the United Nations'. He subsequently outlined the US position on these issues:

> We believe in the United Nations; it has a lot of important roles to play. But we have great trepidation that if this became a UN-sponsored initiative, all of

the most – all of the governments that have the greatest interest in regulating and controlling content and protecting against dissident speech in their own countries would be very loud voices.

(Posner and Harris 2011)

This forwarding of an American architectural strategy for the next-generation Internet has to be seen in the context of the formative U.S. role – the early history of the Internet and the role of national security institutions in shaping its foundations (Zittrain 2008; Abbate 2000; Townes 2012). The Internet is a creature of various U.S. international communication strategies in the past, and the 'Internet freedom' narrative is primarily a way to try to sustain influence on Internet governance and architecture through a rearticulation of goals. A new historical moment, and the need to develop a new constituency for Internet regulations, requires a repackaging and, to some extent, a conceptual redesign. Ultimately, a close examination of this process is required to show what role 'Internet freedom' plays: is it an end in itself? Or is it a means of achieving a variety of other objectives, acting, for example, as an inducement for trade, or as a way to enlarge Western influence globally? One can ask whether the strategy of promoting 'Internet freedom' helps preserve U.S. management or influence over key narratives that shape both the politics of Internet governance and, more broadly, the dominant understandings of civil liberties, human rights and democracy in international society.

Elements of the bureaucratic embodiment of the U.S. strategy are useful to note. In addition to making the condemnation of online censorship a plank of its diplomatic work, the State Department established monitoring and reporting mechanisms to produce a more reliable picture – as in its annual Human Rights Reports (U.S. Department of State 2015; McCarthy 2015: 110, 117–120) or the largely U.S. government-funded Freedom House Reports on Internet Freedom (Freedom House 2016). The Department accentuated its support of grassroots efforts advocating for Internet freedom or expressing dissident views in blogs and other online forums. It offered funding for research and study into how groups in repressive societies use the Internet and how Internet opportunities can be extended; and, most directly, provided funding for the production and distribution of circumvention software to avoid filtering in societies deemed unfree.[6] It encouraged the Global Network Initiative (GNI), an entity for companies to come together with NGOs to further social responsibility objectives (Department of State 2011).[7]

Many Internets for many states? The China Internet White Paper

Beginning again with the premise that large-scale strategic players seek to seal their visions into favourable technological infrastructures, China's architectural approach to the Internet can be contrasted with that of the United States. Viewed together, what seemed to be emerging was a global competition over influence on infrastructure. The China Internet White Paper (PRC 2010), released in June 2010, is more impersonal compared with the U.S. position as declared by Secretary Clinton (with its receptions, banners and idealistic bell-ringing), a product more of a bureaucracy than of a single campaigning figure and a tradition of advocacy.[8] The White Paper was a product of careful deliberation: polished and clearly manicured. Given the timing, it seemed to be a response to the American initiative. Like the American position, it was ultimately addressed to an international audience, and oriented towards building a competing international consensus.

China's argument in the White Paper, its distinct selling point, was based on a position attractive to many governments. China stressed the important – indeed necessary – role of the state and the deep significance of national sovereignty as a means of asserting rules and imposing obligations. The White Paper mentions both enlarging the field of expression and emphasizing industrial policy (the way in which the Internet expands and is an engine of economic growth), but more significantly emphasizes the latter. For China, the appropriate architecture of the Internet is not measured mainly by its 'openness' but rather by the extent of its harmonious integration into existing society, its reach and its widespread use. For China, as outlined in the White Paper, the country's record with respect to the Internet is one of pride and achievement.

According to the document, the Chinese Internet, far from being an example of repression, stands as an example of expanded opportunities for citizenship and economic growth. The White Paper heralds China's comparative Internet accomplishments and denotes the volume of citizen use. It celebrates industrial policy. It highlights the achievement of goals in the country's successive Five-Year Plans. Here, then, is the essence of China's advocacy of its model: 'To build, utilize and administer the Internet well is an issue that concerns national economic prosperity and development, state security and social harmony, state sovereignty and dignity, and the basic interests of the people' (PRC 2010). To this end, administration and management, not autonomous free market growth, are the key to making the Internet successful in society. Administration and management are the antidotes to anxiety. They are what allow China simultaneously to create growth while maintaining some control over the national narrative.

From the perspective of China, this set of goals and achievements demonstrates why national legal regulation is warranted, indeed central:

> The Chinese government has from the outset abided by law-based administration of the Internet, and endeavored to create a healthy and harmonious Internet environment, and build an Internet that is more reliable, useful and conducive to economic and social development ... China advocates the rational use of technology to curb dissemination of illegal information online. Based on the characteristics of the Internet and considering the actual requirements of effective administering of the Internet, it advocates the exertion of technical means, in line with relevant laws and regulations and with reference to common international practices, to prevent and curb the harmful effects of illegal information on state security, public interests and minors.
>
> (PRC 2010)

This formulation was written, obviously, to appeal to other states. It establishes a bias with which many other states, and their leaders, might concur:

> Within Chinese territory the Internet is under the jurisdiction of Chinese sovereignty. Internet sovereignty of China should be respected and protected. Citizens of the People's Republic of China and foreign citizens, legal persons and other organizations within Chinese territory have the right and freedom to use the Internet; at the same time, they must obey the laws and regulations of China and conscientiously protect Internet security.
>
> *(PRC 2010)*

It is not only in this idea of the exercise of sovereignty that the China-originated design for the Internet differs from the 'One Internet' aspiration articulated by the U.S. Department of State, although that is a significant distinction. What is common between the two countries is their desire to maintain their own initiative, to lead and to influence in the shaping of Internet policy. Each sees the evolution of Internet policy as linked to basic theories of the role of the state and issues of leadership in global matters. The U.S. position embraces the elements of Article 19 of the Universal Declaration of Human Rights that promise the right to receive information regardless of frontiers and advocate universal principles for free expression within borders. This position, as interpreted by many of its champions, discourages sovereign states from filtering or eliminating speech that comes from outside one's borders.[9] The assertion of sovereignty in the White Paper leans towards recognition of other interests and values; indeed, this conventional (if often caricatured) understanding of Westphalian sovereignty is used to advocate that governance decisions should be made in state-led forums and international organizations.[10] The tendency of the United States to disfavour the United Nations as a decision-maker in setting these standards has already been mentioned; in contrast, the Chinese White Paper calls for 'the establishment of an authoritative and just international Internet administration organization under the UN framework through democratic procedures on a worldwide scale.' As the White Paper says:

> China holds that the role of the UN should be given full scope in international Internet administration. China supports the establishment of an authoritative and just international Internet administration organization under the UN system through democratic procedures on a worldwide scale. The fundamental resources of the Internet are vitally connected to the development and security of the Internet industry. China maintains that all countries have equal rights in participating in the administration of the fundamental international resources of the Internet, and a multilateral and transparent allocation system should be established on the basis of the current management mode, so as to allocate those resources in a rational way and to promote the balanced development of the global Internet industry.
>
> *(PRC 2010)*

The debate over Internet policy is, in many ways, a conflict between different visions of sovereignty as much as different visions of freedom of expression. Governments may, however, distinguish their views of sovereignty depending on the issue involved. A state may be more protective of its boundaries when addressing a domestic audience than when it is seeking influence abroad; and it may have a different view of sovereignty on immigration issues than on Internet policy. The debate also raises other questions: Is global democracy characterized by the participation of states as national representatives, or should a 'new global sphere' be the prerogative of individuals and a transnational civil society as well? The place of China as a postcolonial state and the role of sovereignty as protection from remembered imperial depredations in the decolonizing world are significantly related elements in this conflict of visions.

There will be serious and continuous jousting as the United States and China and their allies find opportunities for continued engagement. Laura DeNardis treats this question in her work *The Global War for Internet Governance* (2014). In 2012, the site for contestation was the World Conference on International Communication (WCIT) in Dubai, held to review existing international telecommunications regulations. The United States saw the debates leading up to the WCIT as a threatening shift in Internet governance away from institutions such as the Internet Corporation for Assigned Names and Numbers (ICANN) – the entity that governs Internet names and numbers[11] – that are technical, engineer dominated and were designed under nominal U.S. management.

The apprehension was that governance would tilt away from a multi-stakeholder approach towards increasing intervention from the International Telecommunications Union (ITU) or other state-centric international organizations. The final document published by the ITU included an aspiration that 'all governments should have an equal role and responsibility for international internet governance' (WCIT 2012), but this seemingly anodyne language was portrayed as masking a potential attack on existing arrangements favourable to the United States. In that context, even proposals for change that could have been interpreted as constructive were warily received. A provision, for example, on regulating spam was seen as a Trojan Horse for a broader system of content controls for the Internet. Seemingly simple and uncontroversial 'technical' solutions thereby took on a deeply political character.

This exercise in competitive large technical system> (LTS) design has outcroppings in contexts other than the Internet, as both the United States and China are interested in encouraging adoption of their view in different forums for wider geopolitical and trade purposes. One such strategy of the Chinese government, and its associated companies, has been to enhance their direct involvement in the telecommunication and media markets in Africa, Ethiopia being a prime example. The Chinese government has also provided significant support to state broadcasters in selected countries, such as Kenya and Zambia. Finally, China has worked to expand the reach and content of its international broadcasters, including China Central Television (CCTV) and China Radio International (CRI).

The emphasis on technology and system design is supplemented by other efforts to bolster the Chinese presence. In a study of how China's media- and telecom-related policies in Africa compare to those of the United States and Europe, Oxford's Programme in Comparative Media Law and Policy (PCMLP) tracked how in recent years China has rapidly become an important player in the media sector (not just the Internet) in many African countries:

> [I]ts economic success and the growth of media players and users within China have quietly promoted an example of how the media can be deployed within the larger political and economic strategies of developing states, moving beyond the democratization paradigm promoted in the West.
>
> *(Gagliardone et al. 2010: 1)*

The Oxford study argued that heavy investment in media and information and communication technologies 'can go hand-in-hand with a tight control over them, posing a lesser challenge to local governments and to political stability' (Gagliardone et al. 2010: 1). As the report concludes:

> Chinese actors prefer to frame their activities in the media sector as forms of collaboration and exchange, aimed at encouraging mutual understanding, at strengthening diplomatic and economic ties, and at counterbalancing the negative reporting of both China and Africa in Western media.
>
> *(Gagliardone et al. 2010: 2)*

Versions of these competing ideas of the Internet and the wider information technology environment continue to be marketed by the two powers. At the Organisation for Economic Co-operation and Development, the future of the Internet has been framed in terms of innovation and the capacity to drive economic growth (OECD 2011; cf. Ermert 2011). The White House issued an International Strategy for Cyberspace, designed to 'build an international environment that ensures global networks are open to new innovations, interoperable the world over, secure enough to support people's work, and reliable enough to earn their trust'. It notes that U.S. federal policy would 'encourage an environment in which norms of responsible behavior guide states' actions, sustain partnerships, and support the rule of law' (Schmidt 2011). Google has invested in supporting the U.S. position, including in the publication of its Transparency Report, which tracks government requests for removal of data or for user data.

It is hardly adequate to describe the clash over the future of the Internet as one that is a duel between the United States and China. The world is neither composed of a single superpower nor is it bipolar. Other models and approaches to system architecture exist. Iran seeks to implement a 'halal Internet', structured to conform to a particular view of national and religious morals and Shari'a jurisprudence. This would constitute a severe and comprehensive architecture of management, a strong version of what, in earlier Internet days, was called a 'walled garden' approach. In Russia there are a range of sophisticated means of structuring the Internet, as Alexey Sidorenko and others have noted (Sidorenko 2010, 2011; Asmolov 2015). Deibert and Rohozinski (2010), for instance, emphasize the 'Russianness' of the 'Runet'.[12] They point out that, unlike much of the Internet – which remains dominated by English and dependent on popular applications and services that are provided by U.S.-based companies such as Google, Yahoo and Facebook – the Runet is a self-contained linguistic and cultural environment with well-developed and highly popular search engines, web portals, social network sites and free email services. As Sidorenko highlights, increasing government activity makes the Internet environment not only 'more Russian' but also more state affiliated. The new initiatives, such as the Cyrillic domain, contribute not only to further the Russianness of the Runet, but also implement a higher level of state influence. Second, only platforms and software that are supported by the government are used in the educational system. Consequently, they become part of the socialization process for the new generations of 'digital natives'. An emerging multipolar international system is shaping the technology of the Internet and its users, and vice versa.

States and non-state actors scramble, in shifting alliances, to outline competing visions of the Internet and its potential futures, drawing on existing narratives and governance institutions to do so. The result are pictures of information distribution that support technological closure. But the pursuit of closure is rarely a smooth process; disruptions and crises play havoc with the best-laid plans of strategic actors. These disruptions can be economic, climatological or the consequence of other major surprises. The revelations by Edward Snowden of patterns of U.S. surveillance are a prime example of such disruption.

Disruptions and the Snowden factor

Closure can be fragile. In 2013, depictions of massive global surveillance by the United States and its National Security Agency (NSA) became a serious factor undermining closure. By then, the open Internet or Internet freedom narrative was ascendant, but had not yet been perfectly and globally accepted as the 'natural' and settled narrative. Much progress had been made in that direction, at least in the minds of its proponents. The freedom of expression narrative had become the widely accepted, perhaps default, account of what an Internet should be, with every new measure (such as those involving domain names, net neutrality, filtering, transparency and privacy) evaluated in terms of conformity to that prevailing narrative.

Revelations of broad internal and extraterritorial surveillance produced a momentary check on progress in establishing Internet freedom as the established norm. The inference arising from accounts of the NSA's activities (an inference long suggested yet never realized so powerfully) was that the new technologies, even while advancing freedom of expression goals, could also be an instrument for subverting the very same objectives. Persistent surveillance, made possible by the structure of the Internet, could be seen as potentially undermining rights to receive and impart information. The global 'One Internet' concept was, in some way, hoist by its own petard. Advocates had built much of the argument for a specific design of the Internet on the normative value of human rights in the struggle against alternative conceptions of the new technology. The Internet had been engineered for the free flow of information; that was its bias.

Now, cruelly, the arguments for 'One Internet' and seamlessness could be turned against its dedicated supporters. Approaches that were hailed as 'technologies of freedom' became tarred, at least for the moment, as engines of surveillance. International trust as a foundation for thousands of public and private arrangements was eroded, and the potential for technological closure around the Internet freedom narrative declined, although there were rapid efforts at repair. Too great were the questions at stake for the narrative setback to be conclusive. Yet Internet governance became subject to the unsettled status of greater re-examination. Complex international events, propelled forward by a generic sense of national insecurity that came to dominate the United States post-9/11, thereby generated surveillance practices that ultimately undermined their own conditions of emergence. Here we see the broad ramifications of international relations on the Internet infrastructure succinctly encapsulated.

These events also demonstrated how much international discourse and strategic communication is based on a suspension of disbelief (in this case the willingness to take for granted the benign face of the new technologies and the collective wish for the opiate quality of closure). The surveillance disclosures impaired what might have continued as virtually unquestioning support for relatively unquestioned innovation. In the aftermath of the Snowden revelations, words that signified one thing before the disclosures had somewhat different implications after. Altruism, industrial optimism and concepts of freedom all became recrystallized or remixed, affected by the shifting waves of public information and ensuing debate.

In the ensuing vacuum created by the crisis, Brazil sought to assume a mantle of leadership. At the UN and in speeches at home, President Dilma Rousseff offered her own vision of the Internet. She sponsored Net Mundial, a global conclave designed to pursue technological closure by gathering a huge group of global proponents and simultaneously endorsing a Marco Civil, a Brazilian landmark law that would incorporate an Internet Governance Bill of Rights. In the process – given the Snowden disclosures – there were modifications to the preexisting options for closure. One suggested element, for example, included in versions of the Marco Civil, required foreign-based Internet companies to maintain in data centres inside Brazil. This step, called 'data localization', was consequential in that these foreign companies could be more easily governed by Brazilian privacy (and presumably other) laws (see Powers and Jablonski 2015: 180–202). Asserting sovereignty in this way, as Brazil proposed, would trigger an alternate narrative pathway to closure, one that was attractive for many states opposed, often for troubling reasons, to the 'One Internet' umbrella of ideas. Yet this approach was, and is, clearly distinct from the Chinese or Russian alternatives.

After Snowden, sovereignty became a greater component in the collection of tropes surrounding closure. Asserting sovereignty is hardly novel, but what was striking was the context in which sovereignty was more aggressively asserted – a world of data transmission, servers and complex software codes. Much of the history of media regulation is composed of relinquishing and reasserting sovereignty over technologies that have transnational potential. This was true of radio, of television and of satellite. And its force, the force of state power, becomes a greater element in the global struggle for technological closure. We can think of this as 'domestication': quite complex and sometimes desperate efforts to take what would be a disruptive technology and, essentially, make it perform, to the extent possible, according to the norms that bound information delivery structures that preceded it, often seeking to regulate its impact within extant political borders. Domestication defeats innovation, but it can serve the needs of those in power; the domestication of the railway in nineteenth-century Europe provides a potent example. Domestication does not need to be complete. There is always some level of uncontrollable change. A government seeking to domesticate new media entrants often singles out preferred beneficiaries who receive the advantages of new technologies while denying them to the populous as a whole. It may merely slow adoption, but otherwise be sensitive to the demands of the public.

How does domestication take place? Domestication can take place by bilateral agreement. A long-ago agreement between Mexico and the United States is a relatively minor example, in which each country arranged to place transmitters so they would have minimal impact on the spectrum allocation of the other (the effort was not wholly successful).[13] Domestication takes place by international treaty, for example through the ITU, which has its rules concerning purposeful 'spillover' or transmitted cross-border projection of a broadcast signal. Domestication takes place through informal pressures, one state upon another, or pressure by a state against a lessor of transponder space on a satellite. It proceeds by seeking to create technological borders, as in the proposed Intranet in Iran.

There are many other examples of a full-court press, in forums around the world, to instil what should become generally agreed approaches to the Internet, a hoped-for closure. The United States helped initiate a Freedom Online Coalition of like-minded states who stood together to assert basic principles.[14] A distinguished Global Commission on Internet Governance was established with the comforting website, ourinternet.org. Civil society, through such mechanisms as the Internet Governance Forum (IGF) and other offshoots of the UN World Summit on the Information Society (WSIS), engage with states, corporations and international governmental organizations (IGOs) to influence the outcome. Cyberwar and cybersecurity issues loom as a trumping aspect of debate, and have the potential of disturbing consensus. Twin processes of narrative universalization, as in the U.S. or China's vision for a global Internet, confront the politics of domestication through these issues. Their resolution remains some way off.

Conclusion: strategic narratives, closure and Internet foreign policies

Technological closure, as discussed here, is a complex integration of the technological and the discursive. The future of the Internet will be a function of how design and innovation integrate with complex political realities. Indeed, the word 'Internet' itself begins to show signs of age as new technologies, new visions, create possibilities of new architectures for information delivery. As the examples from China and the United States demonstrate, the consequences are sufficiently significant that intense competition over policy outcomes will continue as comprehensive strategic architectures struggle and are received globally.

I have focused on China and the United States because of their deep investments in fashioning the outcome of these debates. But other states – in Europe, Latin America, the Middle East, Europe, Asia and Africa – will continue to gain entry into this debate and find issues that are significant to them as part of their strategies of communication. There is, as a consequence, the need for continuing research and questioning about these developments. Consider the world as encompassing many 'foreign policies of Internet policy':

- How do such foreign policies interact?
- What efforts are there by the major competitors to influence the Internet policy of 'swing states'? For example, how does Brazil – as suggested earlier – build coalitions for various approaches to closure?
- What is the relationship between domestic policies and global outreach?
- Do states seek to assure global policies that protect their more local initiatives or, in some cases, can they and must they tolerate and encourage global norms that vary from their current practices?
- What are the myriad legal, social and political ways in which the pursuit of closure, and resistance of such pursuits, are manifested?

The shaping of Internet policy is, then, an example of the complexities of gaining technological closure. The process of building and extending information technologies has been one of the great stories of the twentieth and twenty-first centuries. How to establish a convincing narrative of its purpose and structure has been the ongoing companion of the modes of engineering and formation of policy. This chapter has been about closure with respect to a particular technology, but other examples of closure disclose different genealogies and consequences. As the technologies of information evolve, so too will patterns of shaping their social construction; and so, too, will the interaction between the technology and its construction.

Notes

1 This approach differs from McCarthy's in focusing on interest groups, not classes – it is closer to SCOT in this respect.
2 For a critique of the prevailing Internet freedom rhetoric, see Morozov (2011).

3   The 'right to communicate' was first articulated in the 1960s by Jean d'Arcy (1969). See also Fisher (1982). More recently, McIver et al. (2003) have discussed the right in the context of the Internet.

4   Indeed, the rise of externally directed rhetoric on Internet freedom in the U.S. has more or less coincided with a rise of internally directed concerns about cybersecurity and the need for additional protection and surveillance measures. See, for instance, the comments of former National Security Agency (NSA) director Mike McConnell (2010).

5   This was the case with the Preventing Real Online Threats to Economic Creativity and Theft of Intellectual Property Act (PIPA) and the Stop Online Piracy Act (SOPA) controversies in 2011 and 2012. See, for instance, Lemley et al. (2011) This debate explicitly aligned with similar struggles over perceived inconsistencies in 'Internet freedom' over the international Anti-Counterfeiting Trade Agreement (ACTA). See Jolly (2012).

6   This U.S. approach to fostering 'Internet freedom' has contributed to a competitive market for resources among activists and resistance movements. See, for instance, Bob (2005).

7   Established in 2008, GNI 'is modeled on previous voluntary efforts aimed at eradicating sweatshops in the apparel industry and stopping corruption in the oil, natural gas and mining industry. As with those efforts at self-regulation, this one came at a time when Internet companies were seeking to polish their image and potentially ward off legislation' (Kopytoff 2011). Google, Yahoo! and Microsoft were charter corporate participants. On the international political economy of the Internet more broadly, see Powers and Jablonski (2015).

8   See the excellent analysis by Rebecca MacKinnon (2010) and, more broadly, MacKinnon (2012).

9   On filtering and censorship practices, including discussion of the technical aspects of filtering, see Deibert et al. (2008, 2010, 2011).

10 On September 29, 2011, Wang Chen, head of China's State Council Information Office (SCIO), spoke in the UK at the Fourth UK–China Internet Roundtable. During his opening remarks, Wang noted the importance of 'sovereign jurisdictions' over the Internet in various countries, and urged his counterparts to refrain from using 'freedom' to seek 'network hegemony'. See *China Daily* (2011).

11 This refers to the process whereby Internet addresses match specific IP numbers on the network, a register of which is kept by the Domain Name Registry. Thus, www.example.com will resolve to 123.456.789 as an IP address.

12 This term is widely used within and outside Russia to denote the Russian-language Internet (both inside and outside the country) as well as the Internet in Russia.

13 Agreement Concerning Frequency Modulation Broadcasting in the 87.5 to 108 MHz Band, November 9, 1972.

14 www.freedomonlinecoalition.com.

References

Abbate, Janet. 2000. *Inventing the Internet*. Cambridge, MA: MIT Press.

Asmolov, Gregory. 2015. Welcoming the Dragon: The Role of Public Opinion in Russian Internet Regulation. Internet Policy Observatory, Annenberg Centre for Global Communication Studies, University of Pennsylvania. www.global.asc.upenn.edu/publications/welcoming-the-dragon-the-role-of-public-opinion-in-russian-internet-regulation/. Accessed 29 September 2016.

Bijker, Wiebe E. 1995. *Of Bicycles, Bakelites and Bulbs: Towards a Theory of Sociotechnical Change*. Cambridge, MA: MIT Press.

Bijker, Wiebe E., Thomas P. Hughes and Trevor Pinch. 1987. *The Social Construction of Technological Systems: New Directions in the Sociology and History of Technology*. Cambridge, MA: MIT Press.

Carr, Madeline. 2015. Power Plays in Global Internet Governance. *Millennium: Journal of International Studies* 43(2): 640–659.

China Daily. 2011. The Fourth UK-China Internet Roundtable. *Chinadaily.com.cn*. www.china daily.com.cn/china/2011-09/29/content_13821444.htm. Accessed 28 September 2016.

Clarke, Richard A. 2010. *Cyber War: The Next Threat to National Security and What to Do about It*. New York: HarperCollins.

Clinton, Hillary. 2010. Remarks on Internet Freedom. Newseum, Washington D.C., 21 July. www.state.gov/secretary/20092013clinton/rm/2010/01/135519.htm. Accessed 28 September 2016.

Corbin, Kenneth. 2010. Net Censorship Central to U.S. Foreign Policy. *Datamation*June 11. www.datamation.com/entdev/article.php/3887326/Net-Censorship-Central-to-US-For eign-Policy.htm. Accessed 29 September 2016.

Curtis, Michael Kent. 2000. *Free Speech, 'The People's Darling Privilege': Struggles for Freedom of Expression in American History*. Durham, NC: Duke University Press.

D'Arcy, Jean. 1969. Direct Broadcast Satellites and the Right to Communicate. *EBU Review* 118: 14–18.

Deibert, Ronald J., John Palfrey, Rafael Rohozinski and Jonathan Zittrain (eds). 2008. *Access Denied: The Practice and Policy of Global Internet Filtering*. Cambridge, MA: MIT Press.

Deibert, Ronald J., John Palfrey, Rafael Rohozinski and Jonathan Zittrain (eds). 2010. *Access Controlled: The Shaping of Power, Rights and Rule in Cyberspace*. Cambridge, MA: MIT Press.

Deibert, Ronald J., John Palfrey, Rafael Rohozinski and Jonathan Zittrain (eds). 2011. *Access Contested: Security, Identify and Resistance in Asian Cyberspace*. Cambridge, MA: MIT Press.

DeNardis, Laura. 2014. *The Global War for Internet Governance*. New Haven, CT: Yale University Press.

Doyle, Michael. 1983. Kant, Liberal Legacies, and Foreign Affairs. *Philosophy and Public Affairs* 12(3): 205–235.

Ermert, Monika. 2011. OCED Faces Concerns over Its Internet Policy Principles. *Intellectual Property Watch*, 28 June. www.ip-watch.org/2011/06/28/oecd-faces-concerns-over-its-internet-policy-principles/. Accessed 28 September 2016.

Feenberg, Andrew. 1991. *Critical Theory of Technology*. Oxford: Oxford University Press.

Freedom House. 2016. Freedom House Reports. https://freedomhouse.org/reports. Accessed 28 September 2016.

Gagliardone, Iginio, Nicole Stremlau and Maria Repnikova. 2010. *China in Africa: A New Approach to Media Development?* Report published by the Programme in Comparative Media Law and Policy (PCMLP), University of Oxford.

Habermas, Jurgen. 1989. *The Structural Transformation of the Public Sphere*. Cambridge: Polity.

Hamelink, Cees J. 1994. *The Politics of World Communication*. London: Sage.

Kopytoff, Vernon G. 2011. Sites Like Twitter Absent from Free Speech Pact. *New York Times*, 6 March. www.nytimes.com/2011/03/07/technology/07rights.html. Accessed 29 September 2016.

Lemley, Mark A., David S. Levine and David G. Post. 2011. Don't Break the Internet. *Stanford Law Review Online* 64: 34–38.

Mackinnon, Rebecca. 2012. *Consent of the Networked: The Worldwide Struggle for Internet Freedom*. New York: Basic Books.

McCarthy, Daniel R. 2011. Open Networks and the Open Door: American Foreign Policy and the Narration of the Internet. *Foreign Policy Analysis* 7(1): 89–111.

McCarthy, Daniel R. 2015. *Power, Information Technology and International Relations Theory: The Power and Politics of US Foreign Policy and the Internet*. Basingstoke: Palgrave Macmillan.

McIver Jr, William, William F. Birdsall and Merrilee Rasmussen. 2003. The Internet and the Right to Communicate. *First Monday* 8(12). http://firstmonday.org/issues/issue8_12/m civer/index.html.

Morozov, Evgeny. 2011. *The Net Delusion: The Dark Side of Internet Freedom*. New York: Public Affairs.

Mueller, Milton. 2010. *Networks and States: The Global Politics of Internet Governance*. Cambridge, MA: MIT Press.

OECD. 2011. OECD Council Recommendations on Principles for Internet Policy Making. www.oecd.org/internet/ieconomy/49258588.pdf. Accessed 28 September 2016.

People's Republic of China (PRC). 2010. The Internet in China. www.china.org.cn/gov ernment/whitepaper/node_7093508.htm. Accessed 28 September 2016.

Pinch, Trevor J. and Wiebe E. Bijker. 1987. The Social Construction of Facts and Artifacts: Or How the Sociology of Science and the Sociology of Technology Might Benefit Each Other. In Wiebe E. Bijker, Thomas P. Hughes and Trevor Pinch (eds) *The Social Construction of Technological Systems: New Directions in the Sociology and History of Technology*. Cambridge, MA: MIT Press, pp. 11–44.

Posner, Michael and Leslie Harris. 2011. Conversations with America: The State Department's Internet Freedom Strategy. Washington D.C. 18 February. www.state.gov.j/drl/rls/rm/157089.htm. Accessed 28 September 2016.

Powers, Shawn M. and Michael Jablonski. 2015. *The Real Cyberwar: The Political Economy of Internet Freedom*. Chicago, IL: University of Illinois Press.

Price, Monroe. 2015. *Free Expression, Globalism, and the New Strategic Communication*. Cambridge: Cambridge University Press.

Price, Monroe and Peter Krug. 2000. The Enabling Environment for Free and Independent Media. Cardozo Law School Public Law Research Paper No. 27. http://papers.ssrn.com/sol3/papers.cfm?abstract_id=245494. Accessed 28 September 2016.

Rid, Thomas. 2013. *Cyber War Will Not Take Place*. Oxford: Oxford University Press.

Schmidt, Howard. 2011. Launching the U.S. International Strategy for Cyberspace. www. humanrights.gov/dyn/launching-the-u.s.-international-strategy-for-cyberspace.

Sidorenko, Alexey. 2010. Quick Overview of Russian Blogosphere in 2009–2010. Global Voices GV Citizen Media SummitMay 13. https://globalvoices.org/2010/05/13/quick-overview-of-russian-blogosphere-in-2009-2010/. Accessed 28 September 2016.

Sidorenko, Alexey. 2011. Russian Digital Dualism: Changing Security, Manipulative State. *Russie.Nei Visions* 63. www.ifri.org/en/publications/enotes/russieneivisions/russian-digita l-dualism-changing-society-manipulative-state. Accessed 28 September 2016.

Smith, Tony. 2007. *A Pact with the Devil: Washington's Bid for World Supremacy and the Betrayal of the American Promise*. London: Routledge.

Thierer, Adam and C.W.CrewsJr. (eds). 2003. *Who Rules the Net? Internet Governance and Jurisdiction*. Washington, DC: Cato Institute.

Townes, Miles. 2012. The Spread of TCP/IP: How the Internet Became the Internet. *Millennium: Journal of International Affairs* 41(1): 43–64.

United States Department of State. 2015. Country Reports on Human Rights 2015. www. state.gov/j/drl/rls/hrrpt/humanrightsreport/index.htm#wrapper. Accessed 28 September 2016.

World Conference on International Communications. 2012. Final Acts of the World Conference on International Communications (WCIT-12). www.itu.int/pub/S-CON F-WCIT-2012/en. Accessed 28 September 2016.

Zittrain, Jonathan. 2008. *The Future of the Internet and How to Stop It*. New Haven, CT: Yale University Press.

8

INFRASTRUCTURES OF THE GLOBAL ECONOMY

The shipping container as a political artefact

Alejandro Colás

Smoothness is the preferred texture of the global economy. Advocates of capitalist globalisation from Henry Luce to Thomas Friedman have celebrated the 'flat', 'seamless', 'lean' features of a world dominated by cheap commodities traded freely across vast oceans acting as humanity's 'great highway' (as American naval historian Alfred Thayer Mahan would have it). Global markets, we are told, have created deep and distant interconnections between continents, extending commercial and communication networks across the planet which in turn reinforce and intensify international integration and interdependence. Goods are produced just-in-time, foodstuffs are available all year round, warehouses disappear, commodities incessantly circulate, societies prosper while products become cheaper – even seasons can be cheated, as Northern consumers spend Christmas on a tropical beach.

The shipping container is perhaps the most emblematic representation of this fluid, globalised space of free trade and unfettered mobility. The twenty-foot equivalent unit (TEU) steel or aluminium box is not only responsible for transporting the vast majority of the world's non-bulk goods ('ninety per cent of everything' in Rose George's catchy 2013 title), it is also an intermodal freight technology premised on universal standards so beloved of liberal internationalists across the centuries.

This chapter aims to look beyond the surface appearance of the container's corrugated exterior and step inside the box, so to speak, rummaging through the complex socio-economic and political processes that allowed the shipping container to become such a ubiquitous feature of the contemporary world economy. Far from being merely the brainchild of entrepreneurial ingenuity responding to a gap in the market, or the result of a natural tendency for firms to seek cost-effectiveness and global economies of scale, the TEU was in fact the outcome of a fraught and protracted bureaucratic process, propelled less by global market forces than by war abroad, political lobbying at home and class antagonisms in local waterfronts.

International organisations – with their norms, values, regulations and technical committees – played a signal role in these developments by universalising and standardising the container as a global cargo technology.

In what follows I therefore analyse the shipping container as a political artefact – a box which is not simply a neutral, cost-cutting technology taking things from one place to another, but rather a powerful force of world politics with its own distinctive spatial effects, sociological impact and (geo)political dimensions (Herrera 2006). Contrary to the prevailing conception of the shipping container as a technology that smoothes economic transactions across borders, thereby deepening international interdependence, I emphasise below the points of friction (Tsing 2005; Cresswell 2014) that accompany the 'social life' (Appadurai 1988) of containers – moments and places where the 'striated' spaces of national jurisdictions, state and international bureaucracies, logistical infrastructures and class politics also act as key protagonists, slowing down yet also facilitating transnational mobility. As we shall see, this is emphatically not an argument against the efficacy of the shipping container as a technology that can accelerate and cheapen the global circulation of commodities, but instead an insistence on the political structures that underwrite and regulate the seemingly faster, low-cost movement of goods and people across the world.

Such an approach carries with it some ontological assumptions about the nature of matter, technology and objects which, in summary form, assumes a metabolic relationship between human labour and non-human things. This dialectic between what Neil Smith (1984) – drawing on Hegel and Lukács – called a 'first' (given) and a 'second' (produced) nature allows us to interpret the shipping container *simultaneously* as a product of historically specific social relations and as a material force affecting those very social relations in all their political, juridical, spatial and economic expressions. The chapter will try to illustrate this dialectical interface between human activity and technological objects, and its insertion into world politics, by first offering a brief account of the shipping container as a freight technology, and then identifying various ways in which it has impacted upon the socio-economic and geopolitical dynamics of contemporary world politics.

The container as a political artefact

Humans have used closed receptacles (including boxes) to move things since time immemorial. The shipping container as we know it today is a very specific historical form of the box as an object that can store and transfer materials: 'Standardization and arrangement into a logistical network of transport optimization', Alexander Klose suggests, 'allowed boxes to become containers: Containers in containers' (2015: 152). Thus 'the container' (itself an English word that has been universalised) arguably has three distinctive properties: it is universal, it is standard and it needs to be moved mechanically (Chilcote 1988; Martin 2013). These material qualities premised on internationally agreed measurements and procedures are, however, the product of socio–economic and political power relations. Against the prevailing 'instrumentalist' approach identified in this book's Introduction – which might interpret the evolution of the shipping container as a linear, cumulative consequence of experiments and innovations leading inexorably to the standard TEU – the account offered here understands the container as a 'socially constructed' object: it certainly has some definite material properties (volume, strength, weight and so forth) but these are rendered meaningful only in and through systematic social interaction.

The official story of the shipping container starts on 26 April 1956 when the *Ideal-X*, a converted World War II tanker, was loaded with fifty-eight metal boxes hauled from trucks stationed on the piers of Port Newark, New Jersey, and five days later offloaded them onto trucks waiting landside at the port of Houston, Texas (Cudahy 2006a, 2006b; Ferguson 2008; Levinson 2006; Stewart-Robinson, 2014). Two years later a similar journey was undertaken to and from Puerto Rico, and by the spring of 1966 the first transatlantic crossing of a container ship carried 236 metal boxes from Port Elizabeth, Newark to Rotterdam and Bremen in Europe (Bonacich and Wilson 2008; Klose 2015). Malcom McLean, a trucking company owner from North Carolina, was the man behind these maiden voyages of the shipping container. Frustrated by the increasing congestion on post-war US highways and the delays occasioned by the conventional break-bulk 'stuffing and stripping' (manual loading and unloading of cargo) that still dominated America's waterfronts in the 1950s, McLean began to explore the possibilities of rolling truck trailers straight onto and off ships, and successfully commissioned a company engineer to design a container that could be detached from trucks and directly stacked onto vessels. By the end of that decade McLean's company, now aptly renamed Sea-Land Service, had taken ownership of half a dozen reconverted containerships capable of handling hundreds of intermodal company containers. 'I don't have vessels', he is reported to have boasted, 'I have seagoing trucks!' (Klose 2015: 3). Together with the other big players (Matson, Mediterranean Shipping Company, Hapag-Lloyd), Sea-Land Service expanded the container industry exponentially during the 1970s and 1980s, with the World Shipping Council currently estimating a worldwide fleet of over 35 million containers, as opposed to a mere 6.5 million TEUs in 1990.[1] It is thus easy to see how the shipping container is often celebrated as the major driver of globalisation – as an invention 'that made the world smaller and the world economy bigger' in Marc Levinson's (2006) phrase, thereby illustrating how technological innovation transforms world politics.

This conventional – and crudely abridged – account of the birth and growth of the container is however partial and problematic in at least two ways that are germane to the concerns of this book. The first relates to the antecedents of the container. Beyond the antiquarian interest in the evolution of the metal box, the existence of intermodal container prototypes in Europe a good twenty-five years before McLean's own model triumphed begs the question why it took so long for the container to become the dominant form of international cargo transport. As Alexander Klose (2015) documents, the shift from rail to road transport after World

War I had occasioned in Europe and elsewhere the search for an integrated solution to freight transfer between these two modes of transport. The so-called *Cassa Mobile* or 'movable chest' (also known in its German form as *Der Behälter* or in French as the *cadre*), which could be detached from and attached to both truck and train, was presented in 1928 as one option, and was subsequently championed by the Bureau International des Containers, a Paris-based international organisation founded in 1933 to promote intermodal transport. On the other side of the Atlantic a new company called Seatrain Lines launched two steamships in 1932 capable of transporting rail carriages in their holds. 'The type of vessel used by the Seatrain Lines, Inc.', a promotional article advised at the time, 'is a step in the direction of conforming ship transportation to the best and most economical practices on land' (cited in Klose 2015: 44).

A large part of the reason for this lag in the adoption of intermodal technology lies in the second absence to the conventional narratives, namely the critical role of coordination among public and private institutions – not just firms – in the universalisation of the shipping container. Levinson (2006) delivers an excellent summary of this tortuous process, which started in the late 1950s with several US government agencies (most prominently the Maritime Administration, Marad), the largest American carriers (principally Pan-Atlantic and Matson) and private sector organisations (the American Standards Association) thrashing out common standards for both container size and construction. The process was plagued by competing government priorities, inter-firm and inter-sector rivalry and engineers disputing the optimal specifications for the standard universal box. It was further compounded once the International Organization for Standardization (ISO) was tasked in 1961 with setting international guidelines on containers. If agreeing standards in the USA had proved difficult enough, the convergence of the ISO's then 37 member states on a common set of rules to facilitate intermodal transport across states appeared nigh on impossible.

This proved to be exactly the case, as seemingly technical discussions over the design of container corner fittings acquired all kinds of legal, economic and political significance related to patent rights, the costs of refitting thousands of containers to one or the other type of hauling device, or the benefits of various government subsidies. The final full draft of the ISO's freight container standards was eventually released in 1970, concluding a convoluted, decade-long exercise which, despite the different interests pulling in all directions, allowed for working compromises to be reached, in turn opening the way for the 'logistics revolution' that followed in subsequent years.

The involvement of public and private institutions, both national and international, proved to be essential in the capital investment necessary for handling containers. Like most technological innovations, the shipping container required ancillary transformations in port facilities and industrial relations to buttress the promise of seamless transit to and from truck, train and ship. In the USA alone, diverse port authorities forged earlier in the twentieth century to manage commercial hubs like those of New York or Oakland were reinvented in the 1960s as container ports (Doig 2001). Indeed, the state-of-the-art wharfs at Port Elizabeth, New Jersey which launched the career of the modern container were built by the Port Authority of New York and New Jersey (PANYNJ), in large measure to reinvigorate that bi-state metropolitan region through a political act of displacement: from the break-bulk wharfs of lower Manhattan and Brooklyn to the mechanised container ports of New Jersey (Levinson 2006). Far from being a purely economic or pragmatic decision driven by market forces, the relocation of manufacturing and processing from New York City to its hinterlands was the outcome of specific decisions taken by a named political authority, the PANYNJ. The container was on this account not just a passive product of inevitable economic change or a technological driver of such transformation: it embodied the political agency aimed at re-orienting and re-scaling the New York–New Jersey region from a national manufacturing centre into a global commercial and transport hub.

Very similar stories could be told of most other contemporary container ports from Los Angeles-Long Beach to Busan. Whether reinventions of historical harbours like Rotterdam or Singapore, or entirely new creations like Shenzhen or Dubai, ports have been relocated from urban waterfronts into what Allan Sekula and Noël Burch (2011) labelled the 'Forgotten Space' – vast 'port-based logistics clusters' in metropolitan hinterlands, managed by public–private partnerships and operated by a dwindling workforce that has been dwarfed by the automation of cargo handling. Deborah Cowen (2014) has recently examined the geographical reconfiguration of such spaces through transnational logistics 'gateways' and 'corridors' which usually have a container port as a terminus (see also Chen 2005 for the east Asian experience). Consortia such as the Asia-Pacific Gateway and Corridor Initiative or the Maputo Corridor Logistics Initiative combine the public legislative and fiscal authority of states with the private capital and resources of corporations to generate intermodal 'freeways' aimed at lubricating and accelerating the flow of goods across borders. Tellingly, one of the most recent of such projects – the Mekong Corridor promoted by the Association of Southeast Asian Nations (ASEAN) – returns the shipping container to a foundational moment in its history, when Sea-Land Services was awarded a US$70 million contract by the Pentagon to supply US forces in Vietnam with foodstuffs and military materiel via their fleet of containerships (Levinson 2006). The tight interconnection between the (geo)political and (geo)economic dimensions to the container's 'social life' thus become readily apparent – a theme to which I now turn when considering the insertion of this freight technology into world politics.

World politics in the container

The potted history of the shipping container offered above clearly supports Geoffrey Herrera's contention that 'It is rare for especially significant technologies to develop and spread entirely within a single national context' (Herrera 2006: 38). This is particularly true of a cargo technology which from the very outset has displayed a global projection as one of its core properties – that is, the ambition to transcend national barriers. Yet the shipping container's interaction with 'the international' is not merely a circumstantial question of technological diffusion or its contribution to the reproduction of systemic hierarchies and inequalities in world politics, important as these two socio-technical effects are. Like other modern modes of transport and communication, the shipping container emerged from and into a world that was fragmented geopolitically into discrete national jurisdictions yet (in its Western hemisphere at least) deeply integrated through capitalist social relations. It surfaced as both a problem and a solution to the tensions between a world organised politically along territorial lines of sovereignty and driven economically by flows of capitalist circulation. To adapt Andrew Feenberg's notion (2002), the container was the product of a historically specific capitalist 'technical code' – a configuration of technical rules, institutions and ideas that offers solutions to problems associated with specific interests or values – and which, I argue here, had intrinsically international characteristics. Specifically, the intermodal box was the combined progeny of military logistics, the neo-liberal recalibration of the relationship between states and markets (or private and public power) and the universalisation of international regimes – all of which are intimately connected to the reproduction of world politics since 1945.

If we take first the military science of logistics, Marc Levinson's research once again provides indispensable and compelling evidence to back up his claim that containerisation 'came of age' as it 'resolved' the 'logistical mess' which the USA had escalated itself into in Vietnam by the mid-1960s (Levinson 2006: 171). Faced with the task of supplying hundreds of thousands of American military personnel in a distant, foreign and underdeveloped land, the US Navy's Military Sea Transport Service contracted seven Sea-Land vessels in early 1967, which twelve months later were carrying over 1,300 containers a month from American west coast ports to south Vietnam. Once Subic Bay (Philippines), Hawaii and several Japanese stopovers were added to the crossing, close to 40 per cent of non-petroleum military cargo shipped in the Pacific was containerised by 1968 (Levinson 2006: 182). Perhaps unsurprisingly, as US troops sank themselves deeper into the Vietnam quagmire, Sea-Land's military contracts rose spectacularly: between 1967 and 1973 McLean's firm secured US$450 million worth of Department of Defense tenders, amounting some years to 30 per cent of the company's annual sales (Levinson 2006: 184).

A conventional account of the container's efficiency would go something like this: The friction of port-side corruption,[2] labour resistance, poor planning and non-existent infrastructure that had caused Washington the proverbial 'logistical nightmare' in 1965 was 'smoothed' and 'resolved' through the containerisation of logistical supply to Vietnam by the end of that decade. In adopting the shipping container as the dominant cargo technology, the public–private partnership between the Pentagon and Sea-Land Services had delivered an integrated solution to a seemingly intractable supply problem for the American war effort in Vietnam.

A more critical reading of this resolution of the Pentagon's logistical crisis in Vietnam, however, might underline the centrality of friction to the appearance of world politics in the container's social life. For a start, there is no more acutely international expression of the conflict and antagonism attached to globalisation than war itself: the shipping container may have 'solved' a logistical problem for the Pentagon in Vietnam, but it also exacerbated the arguably bigger problem for combatants of getting killed through organised violence. War, as is well known, is a handmaiden for many a new technology and, in that sense, McLean's intermodal container was inherently international and partisan. Moreover, insofar as the shipping container acted as a vital component of American escalation in Vietnam, it behaved like other technologies of colonial warfare – as an instrument of domination, a vehicle reinforcing international hierarchies.

More prosaically, the shipping container's success as a logistical solution in Vietnam was premised on the deep and sustained intervention in the country's port infrastructure and labour relations. The nation's largest natural harbour at Cam Ranh Bay was effectively requisitioned by General Westmoreland's newly created 'First Logistical Command' in 1965, as a special barge, appropriately named DeLong Pier, was towed from South Carolina across the Panama Canal, eventually to be drilled into Cam Ranh harbour, thereby becoming the basis for Vietnam's first container port. During subsequent months South Korean welders, cranes and sewage plants imported from the Philippines, American chassis and trucks, as well as local labour, all contributed to the production of a new space – not just geographically, but also socio-politically. In Levinson's characteristically direct formulation:

> The port at Cam Ranh Bay would ease those problems [of corruption, delays, labour resistance] by being entirely a U.S.-run operation, free of Vietnamese corruption and inefficiency. Some top U.S. policymakers even envisioned a model community surrounded by industrial parks and residential subdivisions instead of the usual bars and brothels.
>
> *(Levinson 2006: 174)*

Robert S. McNamara and his aides are likely to have been among those 'top US policymakers' as the then Defense Secretary had taken an intense and direct interest in the development of US military and logistical infrastructure in Vietnam (Levinson 2006). Indeed, McNamara was representative of the 'best and the brightest' (Halberstam 1972) technocrats recruited from the private sector and academia into the top echelons of the Kennedy and Johnson administrations, bringing to the art of government the 'hard' data analysis, statistical calculation and 'scientific' management techniques they had honed as captains of industry (Adas 2006: 281–336). As the Johnson Administration Americanised the Indochina War, McNamara created an Office for Systems Analysis with the aim of performing 'cost–benefit analyses for tasks as diverse as weapons procurement, streamlining the defence bureaucracy, and responding to the volatile situation in Vietnam' (Adas 2006: 294). Together with his fellow 'whiz-kids', W.W. Rostow, Dean Rusk and McGeorge Bundy, Johnson's Defense Secretary deployed in Vietnam what in another context

Timothy Mitchell (2002: 15) has labelled the 'rule of experts': '[a] politics of techno-science, which claimed to bring the expertise of modern engineering, technology and social science to improve the defects of nature, to transform peasant agriculture, to repair the ills of society, to fix the economy'. It was to this audience of technocrats and experts that McLean and his associates would have pitched the original idea of breaking the Vietnamese logistical gridlock with containerisation. In this, they would have had the support of the US Ambassador to Vietnam, Henry Cabot Lodge Jr, who in a true expression of the rule of experts asserted during the debates over US escalation that: 'We have great seaports in Vietnam. We don't need to fight on the roads. We have the sea ... We don't have to spend all our time in the jungles' (Adas 2006: 293).

We can see, then, that world politics was implicated with the shipping container from the very beginning, and that the launch of this new technology, far from plain sailing, was full of socio-economic friction and geopolitical turbulence expressed not just through war in Vietnam, but also in the bureaucratic tensions and disputes within the US Administration over the strategic commitment to containerisation. The protagonism of public–private partnerships in this venture also signals the centrality of a bourgeoning neo-liberal ideology and institutional frameworks in facilitating the universalisation of the TEU as a freight technology – for the physical and legal-regulatory infrastructure, together with the all-important contracts that made the steel box commercially viable, were largely funded by taxpayers. In quintessentially neo-liberal form, the public authority of the state was constantly deployed to create markets for private providers.

The proliferation of semi-autonomous port authorities across the world has been one manifestation of this trend, as competition for custom from shipping operators led to massive capital investments in automated cranes, berthing facilities and truck yards by governments and regional authorities across the globe. Chilcote (1988: 132) usefully charts this transformation as a shift from a 'traditional breakbulk strategy, "go where the cargo is" ... to a new pattern of "cargo following the containership"'. This reduced port calls of any given containership, concentrating port infrastructure around a smaller number of regional hubs and, importantly, tightening the logistical interconnection between sea and land to nodes that offered not just sophisticated container-handling facilities, but also extensive road and railway infrastructure. The ultimate expression of such smoothing of commodity circulation are 'zones' (and their enlarged versions, gateways and corridors explored earlier); 'extrastatecraft' spaces that, in Keller Easterling's pithy formulation 'thrive on a cocktail of exemptions' (2005: 114; see also Bach 2011; Chen 1995; Easterling 2014 and McCalla 1990). From *maquiladoras* to export-processing zones, free-port areas to special economic zones, 'These cross-national zones are not simply open networks, but, rather, special instruments in a complex game of filling quotas, circumventing labour restrictions, and finding favourable logistics' (Easterling 2005: 114).

Assorted international, regional, national and non-governmental agencies have since the 1970s been facilitating and arbitrating this 'complex game'. From 1966, the United Nations Industrial Development Organization (UNIDO) provided 'technical assistance' to countries seeking to establish zones, while the military dictatorships and one-party states of East Asia during that same decade pioneered and 'turbocharged' the Zone as a motor of so-called 'developmental states' across the world (Chen 1995; Easterling 2014; Ong 2006; Woo-Cummings 1999). In advanced capitalist economies too, investment in regional container-port hubs was accompanied by the re-regulation of national rail, road and shipping industries during the 1980s and 1990s aimed at enhancing market competition in these sectors. In the USA alone, a raft of legislation – from the 1980 Staggers Act (liberalising rail freight) and its accompanying Motor Carrier Act (which deregulated domestic truck haulage) to the 1998 Ocean Shipping Reform Act which favoured shippers in rate negotiations – radically transformed American intermodal transport, among other things by facilitating the development of a cross-continental 'miniland bridge' between the east and west coasts of the USA (Belzer 2006; Bonacich and Wilson 2008; Chilcote 1988; Hall 2009).

In sum, the essential capital infrastructure that (literally) paved the way for the global expansion of containerisation was in effect delivered and underwritten by public authorities at various geographical scales which, through technical advice and legislation or government funding and economic statecraft, allowed private enterprise in container shipping to flourish. To adapt a phrase that succinctly defines neo-liberalism, the strong state had generated a free-flowing economy (Gamble 1994).

Little of this would, however, have been possible without the final and perhaps most important and explicitly international contribution to the worldwide proliferation of the shipping container, namely standardisation. Pretty much since the advent of the 'second' industrial revolution in the mid-ninettenth century, international agreements on the standardisation of measures, management techniques and procedures have been at the forefront of the integration in global transport and communication networks. Standardisation has served an obviously functional role in encouraging the circulation of goods and people across national boundaries. But from the outset it also had a pronounced political dimension in the association of such flows with greater peace, prosperity and cooperation among states and peoples. Internationalism – especially in its liberal incarnation – is the shorthand term for this process and principle of global convergence directed by increasing international collaboration on seemingly technical matters relating to the dimensions of objects or the quality of products.

Craig N. Murphy's definitive study on 'global governance since 1850' (Murphy 2004) is still the best guide to the intense process of international standardisation that accompanied global industrial change (see also Mazower, 2012 and Iriye, 2004). Murphy charts the rise of dozens of 'international public unions' from the period of German unification to the start of World War I (followed subsequently by the specialised agencies of the League of Nations and the United Nations system) which came to regulate areas of international intercourse ranging from telegraphy and postal systems (through the 1865 International Telegraphic Union and the 1874 Universal Postal Union) to public hygiene and mapping (1907 International Office of Public Hygiene and the 1909 Central Bureau for the International Map) – with the precursor to the ISO (the International Electro-technical Commission) founded in London in 1906. Murphy identifies two main tasks in the proliferation of these early international organisations: 'creating and securing markets for industrial goods' and 'manag[ing] potential conflicts with organized social forces [effectively, workers] which might oppose the further extension of the industrial system' (Murphy 2004: 34). Since then, such international organisations have 'helped to create international markets in industrial goods by linking *communication and transportation* infrastructure, protecting *intellectual property* and reducing legal and economic barriers to *trade*' (ibid.: 2, italics in original).

The growth of international organisations – both inter-state and non- or quasi-governmental – is thus a central component to the shipping container's prehistory: without the international regimes (and indeed the 'epistemic communities') that buttressed the work of agencies like the ISO, it is unlikely McLean's box would have been universalised. In this sense, as liberal internationalists from Immanuel Kant to David Mitrany have advocated, international cooperation has been critical in fostering technical innovation and global mobility and communication. Yet it would be naïve to interpret this functional integration as a disinterested outcome of applying a liberal pragmatism to international affairs. As Murphy and many other IR theorists inspired by Antonio Gramsci have underlined, the liberal inter-nationalist 'common sense' of universalisation and standardisation was in fact a geographically uneven and politically hierarchical process, where leadership or 'hegemony' by certain states and social forces delivered deeply unequal dividends across the world. The shipping container, we have thus far seen, was the result of numerous public institutions acting at several geographical scales shaping and directing market forces towards certain technological solutions for international cargo transport. As the next section aims to demonstrate, this contribution of world politics to the birth of the shipping container was reciprocated through the latter's impact upon world politics since the 1970s.

The container in world politics

There is an immediate, empiricist way of gauging the influence of the container on world politics, which is to register the phenomenal growth of global trade since the mid-1960s (both in absolute terms and relative to GDP) and chart the eastward shift of the world's economic activity, with the leading container hubs over-whelmingly concentrated along the Pacific rim, and the top five container ports (in terms of TEUs handled) sited in East Asia (Dicken 2011: 424). 'The container', Levinson asserts, 'made shipping cheap, and by doing so changed the shape of the world economy' (2006: 2). The logistics revolution of the 1970s, in which the container played such an important role, facilitated a new international division of labour where transnational commodity chains delivered the just-in-time produc-tion and assemblage of goods across different low-cost geographical locations

(Bernes 2013). Flexibility, mobility, speed and connectivity are some of the key-words that accompanied the rise of the shipping container as the dominant mechanism for long-distance cargo transport. With it has come the global reloca-tion of manufacturing from the North and West to the East and South, and an economic 'tertiarisation' in the reverse direction: the hinterlands of former 'ware-houses of the world' like Hong Kong, Shanghai or Singapore have now become the 'workshops of the world', while the erstwhile warehouses of London's dock-lands have become penthouses for global investors – many of them from Hong Kong, Shanghai and Singapore.

Talk of the shipping container's 'role', 'protagonism', 'impact', 'force', 'vitality' and 'behaviour' in the preceding paragraphs might suggest the steel box be con-sidered as a form of 'vibrant matter' (Bennett 2010) – a more-than-human actant linked to all sorts of networks that generate different kinds of (often unintended) effects and affects upon world politics (Latour 1987; Coole and Frost 2010). As has been argued thus far, there is certainly much mileage in conceiving of the shipping container as a political artefact – an object whose design carries with it what East-erling (2014: 72) has labelled a 'disposition': 'a tendency, activity, faculty, or property in either beings or objects – a propensity within a context'. Specifically, the three key attributes of the container identified earlier – its universality, standard features and automobility – convey a particular disposition, expressing the 'ambivalent' (as opposed to 'neutral') nature of technology whereby certain socially and politically determined technical codes 'invisibly sediment values and interests in rules and procedures, devices and artifacts that routinize the pursuit of power and advantage by a dominant hegemony' (Feenberg 2002: 15). The shipping container is on this account *both* an inanimate box defined by certain internationally agreed technical specifications aimed at accelerating international trade *and* a powerful tool in reproducing and intensifying capitalist power relations through its distinctive design.

Critically, it is its very abstraction as an equivalent unit, complying with universal standards that are globally compatible; its modular character as a structure that can carry anything from rubber ducks to trafficked persons, and be transformed any-where into a retail outlet or a housing unit, that gives the shipping container especially powerful properties. In this it shares with the capitalist commodity form the distinctive attribute of simultaneously appearing as thing-like (with defi-nitive material attributes) and socially constructed (the product of historically specific socio-economic and political power relations). The container is in this regard another example of capitalist reification, concealing in its very universal, abstract and emptiable confines the intense socio-economic and (geo)political conflict and antagonism that accompany its apparently seamless circulation across the world. The metal box thus expresses a clearly identifiable 'disposition'; but crucially, as Easterling reminds us, this unfolds 'within a context' – namely neo-liberal capitalism.

In what remains of this chapter I want to challenge a purely empiricist rendition of the impact of the shipping container on world politics, and return instead to the points of friction that attend to the circulation of TEUs. For all the unquestionably powerful (if uneven) impact of containerisation on the economic geography of the world, what is arguably of equal significance for world politics are the tensions and contradictions thrown up in the process of handling the millions of boxes that daily reproduce the global economy. Here the Zone, as introduced earlier in the chapter, once more becomes an especially intense locus of the overarching tension between a world politically organised into distinctive sovereign jurisdictions yet dominated by an economic system that tends towards the transnational flow of value through the global market. Somewhat polemically, I propose that there is a deeper material quality to the intermodal container which makes it an especially 'tensile' artefact in world politics, namely its capacity to traverse land and sea. The fact that McLean's pioneering firm was called Sea-Land Services is an irresistible foil in exploring the contradictions and combinations between capital flows associated with the 'freeways' of the High Seas on the one hand and the jurisdictional hierarchies and 'spatial fixes' that, on the other hand, accompany state sovereignty on land. More concretely, following the trajectory of the shipping container reveals a number of ways in which the sea–land distinction structures key dynamics of world politics linked to political economy, security and global governance.

The intermodal shipping container is a foundational technology of neo-liberal capitalism. This assertion implies a dialectical understanding of the causal connections between a specific artefact and its social use: while the container is plainly not by itself responsible for the advent of the neo-liberal era, it does play a vital role in the systematic reproduction of neo-liberal social forms, thereby acquiring distinctive causal powers. The proliferation since the 1970s of Special Economic Zones (SEZs, in all their diverse manifestations) is the most prominent expression of such powers as, without the universalisation of this freight technology, it is difficult to conceive of 'zoning' as a distinct tendency of neo-liberal capitalism.

There are currently an estimated 4,300 SEZs spread across three out of every four countries in the world (*The Economist* 2015). Xiangming Chen (1995) identified four main historical phases in the evolution of SEZs, from the late-medieval and early-modern free ports and colonial entrepôts to the Export Processing Zones of the 1970s and 1980s, through to today's cross-national enterprise corridors and gateways (see also McCalla 1990 and Orenstein 2011). The geographical spread of the Zone has been accompanied by its functional mutation from mere trading station or custom-bonded warehouse to the full-blown 'open coastal belts' like those stretching across the Pearl River Delta region in China, which encompass manufacturing, processing and services. It is no coincidence that the exponential growth in the number of TEUs and SEZs took place during the era of neo-liberal globalisation: the main features of the Zone – minimal taxation, export-led industrialisation, light-touch regulation, labour-law relaxation, foreign capital incentivisation – actualised in a delimited location the neo-liberal utopia of 'free-market' economics. Inscribed in its very geographical denomination, 'zoning' involves suspending national laws and regulations in a specifically demarcated area inside the nation – it effectively creates a permanent space of exception within the confines of a given jurisdiction, or what Jonathan Bach (2011: 115) has neatly described as 'The double bordering function of differentiation and integration'.

Historically, the Zone's unique location has been one of its functional qualities, with a premium placed on 'a high degree of accessibility' (McCalla 1990). Although there are multiple instances of inland (and even landlocked) Zones – from the duty-free Principality of Andorra to gaming spots in Native American Reservations – the vast majority of SEZs have developed around coastlines. One important reason for this, I suggest, is that the world's oceans have indeed become 'freeways' for global trade – spaces which come closest to the neo-liberal utopia of a 'liquid modernity' defined by horizontal flows, constant circulation and unencumbered mobility. From this perspective, littoral Zones readily become liminal locations where maritime freedoms combine with terrestrial hierarchies to produce the archetypal neo-liberal polity: a hybrid space of 'variegated' or 'graduated' sovereignty characterised by a 'logic of exception [that] fragments human territoriality in the interests of forging specific, variable, and contingent connections to global circuits' (Ong 2006: 19). In traversing mechanically across land and sea, the intermodal shipping container in turn acts as an eminently neo-liberal object – a freight technology which, being 'neither fish nor fowl' (or both), is able to continuously and ubiquitously reproduce the circulation of commodities, the lifeblood of global capitalism. The amphibious character of the container therefore carries with it a disposition towards flattening space and compressing time.

For all the metaphorical talk in IR of state sovereignty as a 'container' that seals territories and populations (Agnew 1994), the actual, living shipping container in fact does something far more complex: it contributes to the fragmentation of state sovereignty at the same time as it facilitates the integration of vast populations and natural resources into the global economy. Although designed as a mechanism for 'cargomobility' (Birchnell et al. 2015), the TEU also generates a distinctively neo-liberal governance framework that constantly combines hierarchy and freedom: stringent control over workers with the most liberal of regimes for footloose capital; sharp jurisdictional delimitations aimed at fomenting horizontal cross-border trade and communication; high-tech, top-value, export-oriented products manufactured by low-skilled, under-paid, feminised labour form the rural interior. By the start of the twenty-first century, Jonathan Bach has argued, the 'modular' Zone of the 1970s and 1980s as 'primarily used for low-skill, low wage export processing that, like tent camps, can be set up and moved with minimal effort to follow low wages and tax rates' has given way to the contemporary 'Ex-City' as a form of Zone 'premised on infrastructure and transformative of the national economy, focus[ing] on a range of objectives from diversifying a regional economic base to supporting the development of small and medium enterprises, information processing, or off-shore banking, insurance and securities' (Bach 2011: 104). An Ex-City like Shenzhen or Dubai is thus an expansive Zone (both geographically and demographically) that 'fashions urban space out of the mix of exports, excess, exception and exhibition … external to older urban areas, extroverted as it performs its function as nodes of exporter, investment, and modernity, exotic in its lure of modern life' (ibid.: 116).

Neo-liberal fantasists present Ex-Cities as smooth, gleaming surfaces which can be mirrored and reflected back across the planet to create a world after their own image: 'create two, three, many Dubais!' they seem to proclaim.[3] Like the shipping container which connects it to the outside world, the Ex-City Zone is conceived as a neutral, placeless, functional space offering universal, standard services geared towards generating profit. It recognises no qualitative traces of its own activity – either 'upstream' or 'downstream' of the supply chain – in terms of (geo)political, environmental or socio-economic effects of its status as a SEZ, promoting instead the quantitative features of an exceptionally concentrated productivity, competition and efficiency. Yet, as Bach indicates, the Ex-City – like other urban forms – necessarily creates its own shadows: environmental degradation, community displacement, social marginalisation, political corruption and criminality. Rather than absorbing illegal immigrants, processing pollution or accepting political activism within the body politic, the Ex-City externalises these 'toxins', expelling and excluding them beyond the confines of the Zone. Such 'double bordering' – forging a 'city within the city', or in the Chinese case, 'one country, two systems' – is symptomatic of a neo-liberal order insofar as it naturalises the distinction between state and market, urban and rural, the norm and the exception, 'mainland' and 'offshore' while actively obscuring the concerted political effort to coordinate and combine these binaries.

This dialectic of 'differentiation and integration', which both the shipping container and the Zone in their own way reproduce, is perhaps most recognisable in the (geo)political underpinnings of China's SEZs. As Aihwa Ong (2006) has persuasively argued, the variegated sovereignty that sustains China's Open Coastal Belt is as much the outcome of so-called economic globalisation as it is of Beijing's diplomacy of reunification. Since the advent of Deng Xiaoping's economic reforms in the early 1980s, SEZs have attracted overseas Chinese investors, bridging the 'political archipelago' of Taiwan, Macao and Hong Kong with their counterparts on the coastal mainland. Economic integration, it is expected, will soon lead to national reunification. Such intense flows of services, people, expertise, finance and capital also lend regional forums like ASEAN greater political substance beyond the formal diplomatic relations, as informal economic networks generate a *de facto* regional integration. Of course this is exactly what liberal internationalists predict and advocate: formal political agreement follows functional cooperation. Yet, as we have seen here, the opposite is in many ways the case. The conditions for deeper regional integration (or indeed Chinese national reunification) were afforded by the spatial and political *differentiation* between Zone and Nation, through the sovereign creation of the exception.

This is one way of critically interpreting the shipping container as a political artefact, not simply as an agent of ceaseless circulation but also as an object that – like all that moves – generates friction in the shape of the graduated sovereignty and jurisdictional differentiation explored above. Another arena where this paradoxical (some might insist, dialectical) relationship between a freight technology that supposedly smoothes space yet also deeply 'striates' the world lies in the security concerns that, especially since 9/11, have exercised law-enforcement and counter-terrorism agencies around the world, for the 'cocktail of exemptions' that characterises most containerport terminals and SEZs can prove explosive: thousands of standardised boxes, the contents of which are in the main unknown, land daily onshore from distant, often dangerous overseas locations. They are swiftly handled in anonymous, automated 'edgelands' – far enough from city centres to avoid congestion, but sufficiently close to supply them with all kinds of goods, as well as 'bads': narcotics, weapons, toxic materials, counterfeit products. What if global jihadists manage to smuggle a nuclear device into a shipping container destined for the Port of Los Angeles? More plausibly, how resilient would a metropolis like London or Tokyo be to a sustained disruption of the just-in-time supply chains that feed those capitals?

These are the sorts of scenario that have increasingly preoccupied port authorities and border agencies internationally, and which Deborah Cowen (2014) argues have over the past decade transformed the borderline into a 'seam-space' across many states. Instead of a clearly defined contiguous delimitation between an 'inside' and 'outside', the border has, for Cowen (2010), been rendered as a liminal space 'in between' national territories, but also one that blurs military and civilian threats or criminal and terrorist risks. The US has been at the forefront of programmes like the 2002 Container Security Initiative, which placed American Customs and Border Patrol in the world's major containerports to inspect US-bound cargo; or the accompanying Customs Trade Partnership Against Terrorism (C-TPAT), which requires private providers to security-proof their own supply chains (Cowen, 2010). Washington has spurred on international organisations such as the UN's International Marine Organization to promote an International Ship and Port-Facility (ISPS) code which serves as a 'standardized, consistent framework for managing risk' in an estimated 22,000 ports across the 148 contracting states (IMO 2012).

In sum, the familiar challenge for modern states of securing their homeland while maximising the transnational flow of commodities has found partial resolution above and beyond the state, both through institutions of global governance and in public–private initiatives tasked with managing the risk and security of integrated logistics systems. As we have seen above, specifically neo-liberal mechanisms of governance, regulation and zoning have emerged over the past few decades in response to this challenge, with maritime ports and coastal areas presenting an especially acute problem in reconciling mobility and control. The innocuous shipping container, I have argued, has been both cause and consequence of this distinctively modern dilemma of movement and stability, as much as it has been both a product and agent of world politics. The main reason for this unique contribution to modern international relations lies in the shipping container's standardised and mechanised universality, which has made it into such an omnipresent – and powerful – feature of neo-liberal globalisations.

Conclusion: conduits of governance and exploitation

As the Introduction to this volume demonstrates, the recognition that technological artefacts are 'socially constructed' is today uncontroversial among most critical
social scientists. The more challenging question becomes, to paraphrase Robert W.
Cox's famous dictum: socially constructed by whom, and for what purpose?
Focusing on the container, one of the technological icons of globalisation, this
chapter has suggested the answer is: by the already powerful, so that they can sustain their privilege. The TEU as we know it today was the product of global
American hegemony in the postwar period: it was designed, developed and distributed across the world by a range of local, national and multilateral organisations – both public and private – with the aim of integrating the global capitalist
economy. Yet, like American hegemony itself, the universal character of the shipping container allowed for both integration and differentiation in the world economy, particularly in the form of competition among capitalist states. From the
1970s onwards, it was Washington's East Asian 'protectorates' in South Korea,
Japan and Taiwan, and then subsequently mainland China, that appropriated the
universal qualities of the container to build their own economic challenges to the
American hegemon.

A purely instrumentalist interpretation of this technological diffusion would
emphasise the modular features of the container: it is such a successful freight
technology precisely because it carries anything anywhere and can be used for
multiple purposes. It is, on this interpretation, simply a storage and transport
mechanism devoid of normative content. The account offered in this chapter has,
in contrast, underlined the very political attributes of the container, for, embedded
in the metal box's standard, universal and mechanised design, are some of the
central values of capitalist reproduction: commensurability, equivalence, circulation, efficiency, accumulation, internationalism. Naturally, this does not preclude
the use of containers for purposes other than capitalist accumulation (emergency
relief, provisional shelter, a play-space); but it does imply that a post-capitalist
society would likely transform the social power and significance of the shipping
container when catering for democratically agreed human needs by, for instance,
de-scaling international trade and reorienting production from consumer to social
goods, or by re-balancing domestic markets against export-oriented growth strategies (see the interesting contributions by Toscano 2011 and Bernes 2013 on the
communal 'reconfiguring' or 'repurposing' of logistical infrastructure).

These, however are mere speculations. The historical tide has evidently gone in
the other direction, with the shipping container playing a vanguard role, as we saw
above, in the proliferation of neo-liberal spaces and policies across the world. Here,
the TEU operates as an actor-network which draws various (transnational) socio-
technical processes into an assemblage of human and more-than-human 'actants'.
As Christian Bueger and Jan Stockbruegger suggest in Chapter 3 of this volume,
these networks of power in turn generate unintended and unpredictable effects
resulting from their disparate but interrelated material properties. A cognate of

Actor-Network Theory (ANT), the body of work that has come under the label of 'new' or 'vibrant' materialism, also rejects the distinction between the social and the natural, and is deeply sceptical about clear causal hierarchies in either of these domains. The world on this view is far messier, complex and de-centred than a historical materialist emphasis on class relations would allow for.

This chapter has aimed to illustrate the overlap between these different expressions of materialism, deploying an historical-geographical materialism that acknowledges the emergent powers, vital forces and circulating affect of persons, things and matter, yet also emphasises the causal hierarchies and asymmetrical relations that issue from such interactions. Complex processes like zoning or the logistics revolution are not merely contingent, but are punctuated by structural transformations (like the collapse of the Bretton Woods system, the 'long downturn' of the 1970s and the concomitant rise of neo-liberalism) and governed by unequal power relations among different social and natural agents. Sophisticated feedback loops certainly deliver accidental and unexpected effects, but these are always conditioned by powerful interests and forces, principally driven by the capitalist valorisation of nature. Contingency after all presupposes a structure. In the analysis of the shipping container offered here, the neo-liberal 'disposition' of the TEU as a technology that in very concrete (not just metaphorical) ways has allowed the 'offshoring' of terrestrial authority (or in Bernes's phrase (2013), the emergence of 'hydraulic capitalism') cannot simply be read as an effect of globalising networks, but must instead be seen as both cause and consequence of a very specific historical period – the neo-liberal turn in global capitalism. Thus, the elision of unequal distribution of power and capabilities in the world and the historical particularity of this predicament under a global capitalist system present two major stumbling blocks in any quest to reconcile historical and the 'new', critical materialisms or Actor-Network Theory. In the end, this chapter has argued, the shipping container is such a powerful technology in world politics because it acts as a conduit not just of commodities, but also for neo-liberal forms of governance and exploitation.

Notes

1 www.worldshipping.org/about-the-industry/containers/global-container-fleet. Date accessed 14 July 2015.
2 'The savagery of European conquest, the competitive passions of colonial botany, the resistance strategies of peasants, the confusion of war and technoscience, the struggle over industrial goals and hierarchies … It is these vicissitudes that I am calling friction' (Tsing 2005: 6).
3 With apologies to Ernesto 'Che' Guevara, but see Davis and Monk (2008).

References

Adas, Michael. 2006. *Dominance by Design: Technological Imperatives and America's Civilizing Mission*. Cambridge, MA: Harvard University Press.

Agnew, John. 1994. The Territorial Trap: The Geographical Assumptions of International Relations Theory. *Review of International Political Economy* 1(1): 53–80.

Appadurai, Arjun. 1988. *The Social Life of Things: Commodities in Cultural Perspective*. Cambridge: Cambridge University Press.

Bach, Jonathan. 2011. Modernity and the Urban Imagination in Economic Zones. *Theory, Culture & Society* 28(5): 98–122.

Belzer, Michael H. 2006. *Sweatshops on Wheels: Winners and Losers in Trucking Deregulation*. Oxford: Oxford University Press.

Bennett, Jane. 2010. *Vibrant Matter: A Political Ecology of Things*. Durham, NC: Duke University Press.

Bernes, Jasper. 2013. Logistics, Counterlogistics, and the Communist Prospect. *Endnotes* 3: 172–120. http://endnotes.org.uk/en/jasper-bernes-logistics-counterlogistics-and-thecommunist-prospect. Accessed 16 September 2016.

Birtchnell, Thomas, Satya Savitzky and John Urry (eds). 2015. *Cargomobilities: Moving Materials in a Global Age*. London: Routledge.

Bonacich, Edna and Jake B. Wilson. 2008. *Getting the Goods: Ports, Labor and the Logistics Revolution*. Ithaca, NY: Cornell University Press.

Chen, Xiangming. 1995. The Evolution of Free Economic Zones and the Recent Development of Cross-National Growth Zones. *International Journal of Urban and Regional Research* 19(4): 595–620.

Chen, Xiangming. 2005. *As Borders Bend: Transnational Spaces on the Pacific Rim*. Lanham, MD: Rowman & Littlefield.

Chilcote, Paul W. 1988. The Containerization Story: Meeting the Competition in Trade. In Marc J. Hershman (ed.) *Urban Ports and Harbour Management*. London: Taylor & Francis, pp. 125–145.

Coole, Diana and Samantha Frost (eds), 2010. *New Materialisms: Ontology, Agency, and Politics*. Durham, NC: Duke University Press.

Cowen, Deborah. 2010. A Geography of Logistics: Market Authority and the Security of Supply Chains. *Annals of the Association of American Geographers* 100(3): 1–21.

Cowen, Deborah. 2014. *The Deadly Life of Logistics: Mapping Violence in Global Trade*. Minneapolis: University of Minnesota Press, 2014.

Cresswell, Tim. 2014. Friction. In Peter Adey, David Bissell, Kevin Hannam, Peter Merriman and Mimi Sheller (eds) *The Routledge Handbook of Mobilities*. London: Routledge, pp. 107–115.

Cudahy, Brian J. 2006a. The Containership Revolution: Malcom McLean's 1956 Innovation Goes Global. Transportation Research Board of the U.S. National Academies of Science. www.worldshipping.org/pdf/container_ship_revolution.pdf. Accessed 16 September 2016.

Cudahy, Brian J. 2006b. *Box Boats: How Container Ships Changed the World*. New York: Fordham University Press.

Davis, Mike and Daniel Bertrand Monk (eds). 2008. *Evil Paradises: Dreamworlds of Neoliberalism*. New York: New Press.

Doig, Jameson W. 2001. *Empire on the Hudson: Entrepreneurial Vision and Political Power at the Port of New York Authority*. New York: Columbia University Press.

Easterling, Keller. 2005. *Enduring Innocence: Global Architecture and Its Political Masquerades*. Cambridge, MA: MIT Press.

Easterling, Keller. 2014. *Extrastatecraft: The Power of Infrastructure Space*. London: Verso.

Feenberg, Andrew. 2002. *Transforming Technology: A Critical Theory Revisited*. Oxford: Oxford University Press.

Ferguson, James. 2008. The First Container Ship Sets Sail, April 26 1956. *Financial Times*, 30 August. www.ft.com/cms/s/0/cb3a3194-762a-11dd-99ce0000779fd18c.html#axzz3fl nMjrPd. Accessed 10 August 2015.

Gamble, Andrew. 1994. *The Strong State and the Free Economy: The Politics of Thatcherism*, 2nd edition. Basingstoke: Palgrave Macmillan.

George, Rose. 2013. *Ninety Percent of Everything: Inside Shipping, the Invisible Industry That Puts Clothes on Your Back, Gas in Your Car, and Food on Your Plate*. New York: Metropolitan Books.

Halberstam, David. 1969. *The Best and the Brightest*. New York: Random House.

Hall, Peter V. 2009. Container Ports: Local Benefits and Transportation Worker Earnings. *GeoJournal* 74(1): 67–83.

Herrera, Geoffrey L. 2006. *Technology and International Transformation: The Railroad, the Atom Bomb, and the Politics of Technological Change*. New York: State University of New York Press.

International Maritime Organization. 2012. *The International Ship and Port Facility Security Code (ISPS Code)*. London: IMO Publications. www.imo.org/en/OurWork/security/ instruments/pages/ispscode.aspx. Accessed 11 August 2015.

Iriye, Akira. 2004. *Global Community: The Role of International Organizations in the Making of the Contemporary World*. Berkeley: University of California Press.

Latour, Bruno. 1987. *Science in Action: How to Follow Scientists and Engineers in Society*. Milton Keynes: Open University Press.

Levinson, Marc. 2006. *The Box: How the Shipping Container Made the World Smaller and the World Economy Bigger*. Princeton, NJ: Princeton University Press.

Martin, Craig. 2013. Shipping Container Mobilities, Seamless Compatibility, and the Global Surface of Logistics Integration. *Environment and Planning A* 45(5): 1021–1036.

Mazower, Mark. 2012. *Governing the World: The History of an Idea*. London: Allen Lane.

McCalla, Robert J. 1990. The Geographical Spread of Free Zones Associated with Ports. *GeoForum* 21(1): 121–134.

Mitchell, Timothy. 2002. *Rule of Experts: Egypt, Techno-Politics, Modernity*. Princeton, NJ: Princeton University Press.

Murphy, Craig N. 2004. *International Organization and Industrial Change: Global Governance since 1850*. Cambridge: Polity Press.

Ong, Aihwa. 2006. *Neoliberalism as the Exception: Mutations in Citizenship and Sovereignty*. Durham, NC: Duke University Press.

Orenstein, Dara. 2011. Foreign-Trade Zones and the Cultural Logic of Frictionless Production. *Radical History Review* 109: 36–61.

Sekula, Allan and Noël Burch 2011. The Forgotten Space. *New Left Review* 69 (May–June).

Smith, Neil. 1984. *Uneven Development: Nature, Capital and the Production of Space*. Oxford: Blackwell.

Stewart-Robinson, Tristain. 2014. Shipping Containers: 60 Years in the Box. *Tomorrow*, 24 August. http://tomorrow.is/features/shipping-containers-60-yearsbox/#.Vd3jwn0rMrd. Accessed 16 September 2016.

The Economist. 2015. Special Economic Zones; Not So Special. 14 April. www.economist. com/news/leaders/21647615-world-awash-free-tradezones-and-their-offshoots-many-are -not-worth-effort-not Accessed 10 August 2015.

Toscano, Alberto. 2011. Logistics and Opposition. *Mute Magazine* 3(2). www.metamute. org/editorial/articles/logistics-and-opposition#. Accessed 16 September 2016.

Tsing, Lowenhuapt A. 2005. *Friction: An Ethnography of Global Connection*. Princeton, NJ: Princeton University Press.

Woo-Cummings, Meridith (ed.). 1999. *The Developmental State*. Ithaca, NY: Cornell University Press.

9

A REVOLUTION IN MILITARY AFFAIRS?

Changing technologies and changing practices of warfare

Antoine Bousquet

Throughout the 1990s and early 2000s, the American military establishment feverishly debated the notion of a coming 'revolution in military affairs' (RMA), understood as an imminent transformation in the conduct of warfare brought about by new technologies such as precision-guided munitions and information and telecommunication technologies. Its most vocal proponents (Cohen 1996; Owens 2001) predicted a new era of military superiority for the United States if it grasped this epochal opportunity and modernised its armed forces accordingly. The performance of a putatively information-age military in the wars of the twenty-first century has however proven to be much less auspicious, particularly where it has involved confrontation with diffuse and resilient armed insurgencies. Excitable discussions of a revolution in military affairs and an associated military doctrine of network-centric warfare (Cebrowski and Gartska 1998) have accordingly become much more muted in recent years. Yet simultaneously the new figure of the drone aircraft, a weapons system drawing upon RMA technologies, has become the object of insistent debate and frequently seen as heralding the dawn of a new era of robotic warfare (Singer 2009).

That there exists an intimate link between technology and warfare is a claim that can hardly be disputed. Such a relationship is all the more salient when we consider a twentieth century in which was realised an unprecedented mobilisation of industrialised societies for the purpose of waging armed conflict, not least with regard to their scientific and engineering resources. From these efforts have followed the global deployment of motorised forces on land, at sea and in the air, the development of the atomic bomb and the harnessing of the electromagnetic spectrum for light-speed telecommunications and a dramatic extension of perception beyond the natural bounds of the human organism. On the basis of this potent relationship, many commentators have come to the view that technology is *the* central determinant of military power, and that one can trace major transformations in the practices of warfare to the emergence of key technological innovations. Already in the 1950s, the historian Michael Roberts contended that the introduction of portable firearms had induced a radical change in military tactics and strategy in the sixteenth century (and thereby occasioned the rise of the modern state), bequeathing the very term 'military revolution' that has since gained common currency (Roberts 1967).

As seductive and compelling as such accounts of the primary causative power of technology may appear, they typically rest on simplistic and selective treatments of the historical record, as several of Roberts's professional colleagues have been keen to underline (Rogers 1995; Black 2008). At a more fundamental level, such perspectives are vitiated by impoverished understandings of technology and the nature of technical change. As reviewers of Geoffrey Parker's (1988) expanded version of Roberts's original thesis put it, technology is all too often treated 'as a "black box", a primary *explanans* whose nature is itself inexplicable' (Hall and De Vries 1990: 506). The import of such debates is not restricted to the arbitration of historiographical controversies, since the ways in which we conceptualise technology and its relation to the conduct of war is essential to any assessment of a contemporary RMA and its possible geopolitical ramifications, and beyond it of the relation between technology and conflict more generally.

This chapter will argue for the necessity of a series of theoretical and methodological moves for the development of a richer comprehension of the role of technology in war. In the first instance, the chapter will propose a conceptual framework that can overcome the limitations of approaches to the RMA that treat technology and society as two distinct domains, putting the analysis of technology and war on a stronger intellectual footing by drawing upon a theory of assemblages that does not insist on such a rigid delineation of technology and society. Having done so, it will outline and seek to problematise three common conceptions of military technology found in both popular and academic accounts of warfare. Finally, the chapter will argue that while technological developments are significantly impacting contemporary military practice – if rarely with the clear, unambiguous effects hoped by their keenest proponents – the RMA can only be adequately grasped by reference to the wider sociotechnical milieu in which they are taking place.

Opening up the black box of the war machine

If we are to overcome the limitations of many existing accounts of technology in war, it is essential to lay a strong theoretical and methodological foundation upon which original analyses can be built. Drawing upon the perspective outlined in the first half of this volume, an essential first step must be an obstinate commitment to resist any firm delineation between society and technology according to which one can simply be read from the other, as in various brands of technological determinism or social constructivism. Following Bruno Latour (1999: 214), it must be resolutely affirmed that 'we are sociotechnical animals and each human interaction is sociotechnical'.

To this end, the present chapter proposes to deploy a theory of assemblages as first elaborated in the work of Gilles Deleuze and Félix Guattari and which recently has been garnering increasing attention in the social sciences, including International Relations (DeLanda 2006; Marcus and Saka 2006; Acuto and Curtis 2014; Bachmann et al. 2014). The concept of the assemblage – a close cousin to ANT's 'networks' – refers to any collection of heterogeneous elements that can be said to display some form of consistency and regularity while remaining open to transformative change through the addition or subtraction of elements or the reorganisation of the relations between those elements. Thus, concrete assemblages can be seen to cut across the various ideational and material domains that are usually analytically delineated, thereby eschewing the search for causal determinisms between them to privilege the systemic interactions and co-dependencies that constitute such assemblages.

Assemblage theory is applicable across all areas of social and political life. Regarding its implications for our understanding of technology, Deleuze and Guattari (2003: 397) argue that:

> the principle behind all technology is to demonstrate that a technical element remains abstract, entirely undetermined, as long as one does not relate it to an assemblage it presupposes. It is the machine that is primary in relation to the technical element: not the technical machine, itself a collection of elements, but the social or collective machine, the machinic assemblage that determines what is a technical assemblage at a given moment, what is its usage, extension, comprehension, etc.[1]

The above passage makes clear that a technical object is always inserted into broader assemblages that determine its mode of production, the value attributed to it, its distribution in the social field and its employment, none of which are intrinsic features of the object. While technical objects are typically designed and refined with particular uses in mind, these uses are never exhausted by the intentionality of their creators, and objects are always liable to being repurposed as they enter into different assemblages. A simple example would be that of a machete which can just as well be employed for chopping the branches of a tree as for the hacking of human limbs. Such a dual use might perhaps be dismissed as banal given the understood purpose of machetes for the action of *cutting*, but more surprising and unforeseen appropriations can also occur. For example, a passenger aircraft normally inserted in a transport assemblage whose function is to carry goods and bodies from one point to another along repeatable paths takes on a radically different character when wielded as a missile hurled against a building. Strictly identical technical objects can therefore dramatically alter their meaning and effectivity in the world when detached from the assemblages that conferred to them their original usages and meanings.

Of course, the technical object is also an assemblage in its own right, composed of heterogeneous parts and specific functional relations between these parts that we must also be attentive to since they exert their own influence on the wider field of social assemblages. A comprehensive understanding of a technical object therefore also requires that its history and genesis be grasped so as to draw out the co-evolution of its parts. Successful technical objects typically undergo a process whereby early designs in which each constitutive internal element serves a single purpose in a linear causal chain progressively develops into more internally coherent schemes in which their parts take on several functions that mutually support the operation of one another and enter into multiple relations of reciprocal causality. As they do so, the forms of technical objects tend to stabilise, and their designs can remain fixed for extended periods of time.[2]

This point can be illustrated with reference to the development of firearms. The muzzle-loaded musket widely adopted by the European armies of the eighteenth century employed a flintlock mechanism in which a hammer holding a piece of flint strikes the steel of the flash pan and produces a spark, igniting the priming powder which in turn triggers the detonation of the main gunpowder load and causes the weapon to discharge.[3] After each shot, the operator of the musket would then have to reload the weapon from the muzzle end with gunpowder, bullet and wadding, prime the flash pan with some more gunpowder and cock the hammer of the flintlock before taking aim again. In this primitive incarnation, each element of the firearm served a simple purpose in a linear chain, with human intervention required to restore the technical object to a functional condition and address all the changes in the state of the object that are by-products of its operation and prevent its immediate reuse.

The flintlock mechanism was eventually replaced by the percussion cap in the mid-nineteenth century, paving the way for the modern breech-loaded cartridge in which bullet, gunpowder and primer are all combined within a single metallic casing. Starting with the invention of the Maxim gun in 1884, firearm technology then saw the development of semi-automatic or fully automatic designs that use the recoil or a portion of the gases propelling the bullet from the barrel to automatically eject the spent cartridge, load a new cartridge into the breech and ready the weapon for a new discharge, these operations all performed virtually simultaneously. Although a wide range of semi-automatic and automatic weapons exist, these basic principles of firearm operation have remained practically unchanged for a hundred years, suggesting a high degree of optimisation in the harnessing of the physical laws governing the functioning of such devices.

It is generally in this state of internal coherence that the technical object is at its most versatile and flexible in its applications, requiring limited intervention into its workings by its users, and able to operate relatively autonomously from other technical objects. Such a technical object can therefore be much more easily detached from any given assemblage and reintegrated into a new one than is the case with an unstable technical object still in the midst of its evolutionary genesis, more heavily dependent on the mesh of sociotechnical relations that sustain it, and correspondingly exigent in terms of the conditions necessary for its successful operation. To take examples at the two ends of that spectrum, one could contrast the versatility, ease of use and widespread diffusion of the AK–47 Kalashnikov rifle (more on which below) with the F–35 fighter jet and its long list of costly operational requirements – including bespoke runways, software integration and specialist training.

When tracking the emergence and evolution of technical objects, it is also important to recognise the extent to which these have become increasingly intertwined with specific understandings of the natural world and its physical properties. Modern technology is intimately tied to the emergence of a scientific worldview pursuing a systematic empirical interrogation of nature from which are derived mathematical laws and regularities that permit the elaboration and optimisation of the contraptions that rely on them. Conversely, technical artefacts allow for the isolation of natural forces necessary for their scientific study. If we are to better understand the workings of technology in our contemporary societies, it is therefore incumbent upon us to trace the articulation of scientific ideas and discourses, materiality of technique and social practice that might best be referred to as technoscience (Pickering 1995; Ihde and Selinger 2003). Indeed, it is to this very nexus that we must attend when assessing claims of an overarching revolution in military affairs and determining the roles that the information technologies cherished by RMA enthusiasts actually play in the wars of the twenty-first century. For now, however, we must attend to three problematic conceptions that abound within existing accounts of the role of technology in war, but which we can now begin to unpick with the help of the conceptual framework just outlined.

Three shortcomings in discussions of technology and war

The first of the common problems affecting discursive treatments of technology in war is the *disproportionate attention paid to weaponry*. Such bias is easy enough to account for by the intimate relation of weapons to the sharp-end activity of war and the particular fascination that firearms, jet aircraft or nuclear bombs seem to exert on the public at large. However, it is no less misleading for it, all the more as we consider increasingly industrialised and technologically intensive armed forces. For one, the focus on eye-catching weaponry generally results in a neglect of other technologies, some of which may at first appear quite mundane but which can credibly be said to have played as important a role as any weapon system in the development of warfare. One might for instance think of the technology of food canning, and legitimately query whether the vast static fronts of the First World War could have been sustained for so long without the means for the preservation and transport of inexpensive high-calorie nutrition. Another example can be found in the discovery of penicillin, whose anti-bacterial properties saved countless lives and limbs of injured soldiers at risk of infection, restoring many of them to duty and thereby sustaining combat power.[4]

A further problem with a narrow focus on weaponry is that it overlooks the crucial role of logistics in supplying fighting units with the materiel (such as food, fuel, ammunition or medical equipment) they could not operate without.[5]

Logistics has long constituted a major part of military operations but has only become more complex and indispensable as armies have become more technologically sophisticated. Indeed, it has been widely observed that the level of resources or personnel allocated to support roles relative to the actual combat forces they enable (the so-called 'tooth-to-tail ratio') has steadily increased over time such that the former now outnumber the latter by a scale of as much as ten to one in the most advanced militaries.

A fundamental but often occluded truth comes to the fore when we relax the primacy generally accorded to weaponry in accounts of technology in war, and allow for a consideration of the role of other technical innovations and a tracing of the larger logistical chains in which any given technology is inserted. That is to say, no technical object exists in isolation of the wider sociotechnical systems within which it is produced, distributed, sustained and put to use. Such dependencies are in fact typically all the more dense and fragile the more functionally integrated technical objects are with each other. Accounts that isolate particular technical objects from these dependencies in order to attribute to them a primary causative role are accordingly vulnerable not only to charges of arbitrariness but also of resting on a simplistic understanding of both social and technical change.

Indeed, an even more fundamental problem lies in the persistent technological determinism that subtends so many discussions of technology within military affairs. Although such a stance is rarely explicitly theorised or defended, major developments in the conduct of war, along with success and failure in particular military exchanges, are routinely and uncritically attributed to certain key technologies. As prominent a military strategist as J.F.C. Fuller thus does not hesitate to assert that 'tools, or weapons, if only the right ones can be discovered, form 99 per cent of victory' (Fuller 1998: 31). All too often, technologies are treated as *dei ex machina* that seemingly appear from nowhere and induce major transformations in the conditions of war. In such accounts, changes in tactics and organisational arrangements are frequently understood as merely subsequent adjustments to a new technological reality. Where social and cultural variables are considered, they are generally restricted to assessing the extent to which military institutions, so often decried for their supposedly innate conservatism, are able to adapt to this new landscape of war. Thus we find Phillips (2002: 40) bemoaning the fact that his fellow military historians are 'obsessed with technology as the primary determinate of causation within their discipline'.

The limitations of technologically determinist accounts are perhaps best illustrated by reference to a specific example, and here the medieval historian Lynn White and his so-called 'stirrup thesis' can provide a useful case study to think through the issues at stake. In a collection of essays on medieval technology, White (1962) famously develops the claim that the emergence of the feudal order can be traced back to the introduction of the stirrup in horse-riding. White's starting point is that the new technology transformed the practice of war by permitting the effective use of the lance in a charge (since the impact of such a charge would no longer unseat the rider), thereby making the horseman the new dominant unit on the European battlefield in what could retrospectively be construed as a revolution in military affairs. Society consequently turned to the production of mounted knights, whose elevated cost in terms of equipment and training entailed the formation of a class of largely autonomous landed warriors. From this, White claimed, had sprung the feudal period and the different cultural forms that characterised it, such as those associated with ideas of chivalry.

White's arguments generated a great deal of controversy among medieval historians, and his chronology was subsequently heavily criticised; but, for our purposes, it is the more general charge of technological determinism laid at White's feet that interests us most. It is true that the precise origin of the stirrup is not known, and its identification is further complicated by the fact that design and function evolved substantially from earlier single mounting aids to paired riding stirrups connected to a saddle. Reliable representations of horse riders equipped with stirrups can nevertheless be dated back to China in the first centuries of the Common Era and there is some evidence that the earliest forms can be traced as far back as the Assyrians in 850 BCE. What is known with greater certainty is that the stirrup was introduced to Europe by the Avars around CE 600 as they were pushed westwards under pressure from the Turks, eventually leading to a growing European adoption in the eighth and ninth centuries. Crucial to the present discussion of technological determinism is the glaring fact that the stirrup was widely available and put to use in the practice of warfare in many different parts of the world, yet only in Europe did it become associated with feudal forms of social organisation.[6]

Albert Dien (1986) has notably shown how the earlier introduction of the stirrup in China, and the concomitant rise of cavalry, was not accompanied by feudalism there because of the greater strength and reach of the imperial state. Whereas in Europe it was necessary to parcel political authority down to regional levels in order to procure the required mounted units, the advanced Chinese bureaucracy was able to administer the central recruitment of military resources without extensive delegations of power to middlemen. In their discussion of technology, Deleuze and Guattari also explicitly cite White, acknowledging that the stirrup did constitute a novel type of weapon system through a closer binding of man and horse, but simultaneously resisting the attribution of any causal pre-eminence to the technical object since the forms and usage of this new assemblage varied according to the broader social milieu in which it was inserted. They tell us that:

> The stirrup occasioned a new figure of the man–horse assemblage, entailing a new type of lance and new weapons, and this man–horse–stirrup constellation is itself variable, and different effects depending on whether it is bound up with the general conditions of nomadism, or later readapted to the sedentary conditions of feudalism.

> *(Deleuze and Guattari 2003: 399)*

The stirrup did indeed allow for the formation of a novel and effective combat system in cavalry, but this effectiveness was only relative to the other contemporary means of war, and the forms of its manifestation were multiple. So while European societies produced mounted knights who would conduct charges for shock effect, Asian nomads privileged mounted archery, using the stirrup to stabilise their aim (Hildinger 2001). Thus the cases of both the Chinese and the nomadic appropriations of the stirrup underline that it is only under the specific conditions of European sedentary societies that it can be said to have participated in the development of feudalism.

We should therefore resist the seductive resort to technological developments as the unique, or even principal, causal force from which we can directly derive changes in social arrangements. As we have seen with the stirrup, we cannot draw any simple line from the introduction of a technical object to a particular way of fighting, let alone to wider socio-economic transformations. This is not to say that the specificities of individual technologies are irrelevant or that we can satisfy ourselves with the adoption of the view that technology is merely the second-order emanation of social forces or human intentionality. Such a move would be tantamount to merely lurching from one explanatory pole to another when in fact it is the strict dichotomy between technology and society that must itself be brought into question.

The last shortcoming in both popular and academic accounts of technology and war that we must consider is the tendency to *focus on the latest technical developments* involving contraptions reliant on the most recent scientific discoveries and feats of engineering. The eagerness with which the RMA and drones have been seized upon and invested with portentous significance for the future of war is exemplary of such a bias. Material objects thought of as cruder and less 'advanced' in terms of their sophistication and functional complexity are thereby frequently neglected, even where their present impact in the world is considerably greater.

An emphatic example of such a military technology is the AK-47 assault rifle, most commonly known as the Kalashnikov after its Russian inventor. First produced in 1947 and adopted as standard equipment by the Soviet armed forces and most of its Warsaw Pact allies during the Cold War, the Kalashnikov is arguably the most influential weapon active in armed conflicts across the globe (Chivers 2010). Available for less than $100 in some parts of the world, the AK-47 may lack the accuracy or power of later rifle models but retains enduring appeal for its ruggedness, reliability and ease of use and maintenance. The weapon of choice of the insurgent, revolutionary, terrorist and organised criminal, as well as still in widespread use by state militaries, the Kalashnikov has acquired a rare iconic status – represented prominently on the national flag of Mozambique, the coat of arms of Zimbabwe and East Timor, and the banners of such armed groups as Hezbollah and the Iranian Revolutionary Guard. In its multiple variants and imitations, it accounts for no less than 20 per cent of the estimated 500 million firearms in circulation around the world today. As such, the AK-47 is far and away the most deadly weapon system around, killing more every year than all existing tanks, aircraft and ships combined.

The humble but lethal Kalashnikov draws our attention to the fact that the notion of technology covers not merely the so-called cutting-edge of technique (often referred to by the nebulous term 'high-tech'), but rather the much wider gamut of material objects through which human collectives are assembled and interact with both the natural world and each other. Since a new technology is typically expensive to procure, consequently scarce, prone to malfunction and reliant on specially trained producers and users, the initial reach of its direct influence is likely to be limited. Generally speaking, the full social impact of a technology is therefore only truly felt at the point of widespread adoption, if it occurs at all.[7] Such an adoption is itself liable to be determined as much, if not more so, by considerations of cost, reliability and ease of use and maintenance than by its performance in ideal conditions.

An equally illuminating case study is provided by the improvised explosive device (IED), a non-standardised bomb assembled from available materials that has become a particularly prized weapon in the arsenal of insurgent groups opposing more conventional armed forces. In the recent wars in Iraq and Afghanistan, IEDs are estimated to have caused around two-thirds of coalition casualties, prompting the Pentagon to expend billions on combating a device produced for as little as $30.[8] The particularity of the IED as a technical object is that all its incarnations share in common certain key functional components of trigger, detonating fuse, explosive charge and container; but these elements instantiate themselves in each case from a vast array of disparate objects cobbled together and repurposed by the artisan bomb-maker. Explosive charges range from artillery shells and military- or industry-grade high explosives to homemade explosives concocted from fertilisers and household chemicals, while the mechanisms available to either automatically or remotely trigger the detonation include timers, infrared heat sensors, pressure plates, wires and the radio signals emitted by garage door-openers or mobile phones. The IED is thus a highly polymorphous technical object, its endless mutations further spurred by the countermeasures deployed against it. Among the most ingenious of developments, we find the removal of any metallic components liable to be picked up by detectors or the adoption of trigger sensors tuned to the very radio frequencies emitted by coalition devices for jamming earlier instances of radio-controlled IEDs.

The IED, in its accelerated and highly improvised manifestation, illustrates a more general mutability of the technical object that co-evolves alongside the wider socio-cultural ensembles within which it is inserted. It furthermore underlines the open-ended functionality of technical objects such that they can always be repurposed and recombined to produce new ensembles beyond the intentions of their original designers. Armed conflict is undoubtedly a particularly potent accelerant for technological evolution, concentrating minds and resources and subject to an intense dynamic of action–reaction between belligerents that singularly spurs innovation. It is therefore not surprising that so many influential technological developments of the last 100 years can be traced back to military efforts, from nuclear energy and the computer to rocketry and satellite geo-positioning. In fact, it is precisely this intimate relation between war and technoscientific innovation that underlies the claims of an epochal revolution in military affairs that became ever more insistent at the turn of the twenty-first century, and which we can now submit to critical scrutiny.

Technoscientific war in the 'information age'

The question of whether a revolution in military affairs is afoot is one that cannot be addressed through the fine-grained analysis of specific technical objects proposed above, since it pertains to a very broad thesis of a transformation in the technological basis of war. To the extent that a common technological genus can be identified to the trends encompassed under the label of the RMA, this putative upheaval in the conduct of armed conflict is being attributed to the proliferation of information and communication technologies. From the outset, it must be affirmed that such a general grouping covers so wide an array of concrete technical objects that any claims of predictable effects, above all the assurance of military and geopolitical primacy, should be treated with circumspection.

An analogy can be drawn with the advent of military aviation, surely one of the most significant developments of the last century in opening up a whole new spatial dimension to warfighting (Adey 2010; Van Creveld 2011). While contingent on the application of the internal combustion engine to heavier-than-air aircraft, no simple line can be drawn from the appearance of powered flight to the definite military uses that have been shaped as much by political decisions, doctrinal statements, bureaucratic institutions and tactical schemes as by the available state of aviation technology. Indeed, the various development paths taken by aircraft have been heavily influenced by their intended purposes, even if not strictly beholden to them. A plethora of fixed-wing and rotary-wing designs have been produced to fulfil such diverse roles as ground support, air-to-air combat, aerial bombardment, troop transport, reconnaissance and surveillance or command and control, all of which have been further integrated into wider tactical and strategic schemes such as blitzkrieg, strategic bombing and air mobility. If mastery of the air is therefore manifestly a major component of military power today, the operational uses to which it has been put are manifold and necessarily related to the conduct of war in its other dimensions. Furthermore, it must be acknowledged that the exercise of airpower has failed to reliably deliver the decisive outcomes its most fervent proponents have imagined for it (Hippler 2013; Pape 1996).

Information and communication technology has similarly (and often in combination with airpower) been embraced in some quarters as a panacea, fuelling enraptured visions of omniscience and omnipotence on the battlefield. Already in 1969, General William Westmoreland, head of American military operations in Vietnam, could prophesise the arrival within a decade of the 'automated battlefield' in which 'an integrated area control system that exploits the advanced technology of communications, sensors, fire direction, and the required automatic data processing' would allow 'enemy forces [to] be located, tracked, and targeted almost instantaneously' with 'first round kill probabilities approaching certainty' (West-moreland 1969). Towards the end of the 1970s, spurred by Soviet discussions of a 'military-technical revolution', elements of the Pentagon led by the influential strategist Andrew Marshall began to theorise technologically driven changes in the character of warfare that would come to be referred to as the revolution in military affairs (Krepinevich 2002). By the nineties and the emboldening success of the First Gulf War, the notion of an RMA had diffused widely, prompting giddy declarations that new technologies were on the verge of granting military commanders 'an omniscient view of the battlefield in real time, by day and night, and in all weather conditions' and allow for the delivery of 'the coup de grace in a single blow' (Owens 2001: 14). We can recognise here the insistent recurrence of what Paul Virilio (1994: 70) has referred to as 'the will to see all, to know all, at every instant, everywhere, the will to universalised illumination: a scientific version of the eye of God which would forever rule out the surprise, the accident, the irruption of the unforeseen'.

As suggested by Virilio, such dreams of power may be ancient but their modern incarnation is to be understood by reference to a contemporary scientific world-view, and in particular to an informational episteme that has been recasting our understanding of nature, society and human subjectivity as processes of informational exchange. Although prior antecedents can be traced (Mindell 2003), the crucible of this worldview most clearly lies in the Second World War in which the first computers were assembled and the modern foundations of the information sciences were laid (Galison 1994; Hayles 1999).

Receiving further impetus from the intense superpower rivalry of the Cold War that saw computation and networking technologies increasingly deployed throughout the military (Edwards 1997; Bousquet 2008a), this informational paradigm has firmly established itself as the technoscientific regime of our time. Notions of the rise of an information society qualitatively distinct from its pre-decessors have accordingly become common currency within both popular and academic discourse (Bell 1973; Toffler 1980; Hardt and Negri 2000) with Manuel Castells's pronouncement (2000: 500) that 'networks constitute the new social morphology of our societies' succinctly expressing the contemporary credo.

The American military enthusiastically embraced this view in the 1990s, produc-ing a doctrine of 'network-centric warfare' (NCW) that purported to achieve 'information superiority' and 'full spectrum dominance' (Alberts et al. 2002). Taking inspiration from the non-linear sciences of chaos and complexity, this latest version of the RMA argued for a decentralisation of command that would grant the various constituents of the armed forces a capability for self-organisation and unparalleled operational flexibility (Bousquet 2008b; Bousquet 2009). By the onset of the War on Terror, US Secretary of Defense Donald Rumsfeld (2001, 2002) was keenly promoting an agenda of 'transformation' requiring a 'leap into the information age' and the establishment of a new 'set of interconnections' that would allow small, nimble forces to outperform more numerous non-networked opponents.

Yet the translation from grandiose rhetoric to prosaic reality proved itself to be considerably more challenging. Initial successes in Afghanistan and Iraq at the turn of the century gave way to protracted and indecisive campaigns in which much of the supposed technological superiority of Western militaries was negated by determined insurgencies that made use of commercially available technologies such as mobile phones and the Internet to organise, but never relied on them exclusively (Shachtman 2007). The aura of network-centric warfare dimmed accordingly, its terminology quietly dropped in the latter half of the 2000s (Guha 2016).[9]

This is not to say that information and communication technologies are not significantly altering the landscape of armed conflict, or even that elements of the RMA vision have not been realised. The present ability to survey the battlespace and persistently track entities within it is truly unprecedented. The precision with which munitions can be delivered to any point of the globe to devastating effect is increasing all the time.[10] The digitisation and networking of armed forces is continuing apace, driving both automation and an increasingly tight cybernetic integration of humans and machines (Coker 2013; Holmqvist 2013; Wilcox 2015). All these developments are significant and certainly merit thorough analysis, but the claims of military superiority and strategic pre-eminence attached to them remain to date unsubstantiated.

The RMA is not best understood, however, as a thesis on the future development of war whose validity is to be assessed. For the reasons outlined above, it is too broad and general a thesis to withstand any sustained probing, and we are better served by a more careful and detailed analysis of specific sociotechnical systems. Information and communication technologies are contributing to altering the ways in which wars are being fought; but these changes remain too variegated and uncertain for them to be encapsulated under a single movement, let alone one that can be conveniently steered to the benefit of a single party, particularly when such technologies are so widely accessible and relatively inexpensive.

We can, however, benefit from an appreciation of the ideological function that talk of an RMA serves within wider socio-cultural imperatives. In this respect, Jeremy Black's assessment remains particularly insightful:

> Belief in the RMA [is] symptomatic of a set of cultural and political assumptions that tell us more about modern Western society than they do about any objective assessment of military options [...] The RMA acts as a nexus for a range of developments and beliefs, including an unwillingness to accept conscription, a very low threshold for casualties, an assertion of Western superiority, and the ideology of machinism.
>
> *(Black 2003: 97)*

In other words, technology is seen as the means by which the United States and its allies can continue to exert military influence globally while avoiding both the human casualties and compulsory enlistment such a policy might otherwise entail and which have become deeply unpopular with their populations since the

Vietnam War. Indeed, Western policy-makers have become increasingly sensitive to both the wider public's reduced tolerance of casualties (the so-called 'body-bag syndrome') and the resistance that mandatory conscription would likely encounter today. In this regard, the recent turn to drones for the prosecution of the Global War on Terror is merely the latest expression of the aspiration to a technicist fix for this bind, appearing to provide yet another means to 'project power without projecting vulnerability' (Chamayou 2015: 12).[11]

This ideological investment in the power of technological contraptions to resolve the inherent tensions within the geopolitical designs outlined above may well be precisely that which condemns the RMA and its avatars to repeated failures to live up to their inflated promises. The more Western states attempt to pursue 'riskless wars' (Shaw 2005) through the application of technology, the more they render themselves susceptible to, and indeed invite, the strategic response of their adversaries to make conflict as costly in human lives as possible, including for the civilian populations these states purport to secure. In the words of General Stanley McChrystal, former Commander of Coalition forces in Afghanistan:

> To the United States, a drone strike seems to have very little risk and very little pain. At the receiving end, it feels like war. Americans have got to under-stand that. If we were to use our technological capabilities carelessly [...] then we should not be upset when someone responds with their equivalent, which is a suicide bomb in Central Park, because that's what they can respond with.
>
> *(Rose 2013: 7)*

War is a clash of wills, Clausewitz wrote almost 200 years ago (1976: 13). To expect wars to be fought only on the terms dictated by a single side is quite simply to wish away the agency of such an opposing will. There is little to suggest that any technology is likely to fulfil such a yearning any time soon, however much faith in this vision satisfies the ideological requirements of Western societies.

Conclusion: assemblages of the war machine

More so than in any other sphere of social existence, the brute physicality of war confronts us with the pervasive role that material objects occupy in the life (and death) of human collectives. But while the rapid and dramatic changes in the practices of warfare experienced in the modern era can be directly correlated to the evolutions of technique, we should be wary of simplified linear accounts that all too hastily read developments on the battlefield as incipient to the character of specific technical objects. It is only when these are related back to the wider sociotechnical assemblages in which they are embedded that we can begin to draw out the complex interdependencies and co-constitutive interactions that make up the war machine. Such an intellectual endeavour can contribute to developing more sober and nuanced appreciations of the transformative potential of techno-logical developments than those which have animated RMA enthusiasts and at times intoxicated policy-makers. And, as remote a prospect as it might seem today, it may also be one of the necessary preliminaries to the war machine's eventual disassembly.

Notes

1 It is important to note that the reference to a 'social machine' here is not premised on the notion of a priorly constituted entity of 'the social' that would shape at will technology or any other 'non-social' realm. Within a theory of assemblages, there is no totality of the social, only social assemblages that already combine bodies, material, machines, discourse and so on.

2 This analysis is indebted to the French philosopher of technology Gilbert Simondon (1989, 2011). See also Boever et al. (2012). For related ideas from a Social Construction of Technology (SCOT) perspective, see Chapter 2.

3 The flintlock mechanism was itself already a more integrated ignition mechanism than the earlier matchlock, which lowered a slow-burning match to the flash pan, the lid of which had to be manually lifted by the operator. The flintlock mechanism dispensed with the need for a live match, and used a protruding section of the flash pan (called the frieze) which, upon being struck by the hammer, would provide the spark for ignition as well as lifting the lid of the pan and exposing the priming powder to the spark, all within a single movement.

4 Much the same could be said of the assorted techniques of blood transfusion that developed during the Second World War (see Grove 2015). On the long-standing entanglement of armed conflict and medicine, see Larner et al. (2008).

5 The paucity of general academic accounts of military logistics is revealing in this regard, with Van Creveld (2004) and Lynn (1993) standing as rare exceptions. For a more general treatment of logistics that traces its historical entanglement of military operations and business management, as well as exploring its present role in global manifestations of violence, see Cowan (2014).

6 On the role of technological diffusion from the East in European development, see Hobson (2004).

7 Any catalogue of successful and influential technical innovations would unquestionably be dwarfed by the litany of mostly forgotten failures and dead-ends that have followed from not only obviously flawed or impractical designs but also from the inability of otherwise functional technical objects to secure a sufficient constituency of users due to unpropitious economic, social or cultural conditions. It is hence not uncommon to see previously unsuccessful technologies rediscovered and prospering several decades after their original conception.

8 By 2010, the US military had spent over $17 billion on IED counter-measures, excluding the even higher expenditure occasioned by the procurement of reinforced armoured vehicles (Higginbotham 2010).

9 The drawn-out conflicts in Afghanistan and Iraq occasioned a revival of counter-insurgency doctrine (COIN) that denoted a shift away from NCW's emphasis on high-tempo operations and kinetic force towards the management of populations and winning of 'hearts and minds'. Crucially, however, COIN continued to make extensive use of information and communication technologies, notably in the production of biometric databases of local populations and the computer modelling of societal dynamics (Ansorge 2015).

10 According to one estimate, 'in 1944 it took 108 B-17s dropping 648 bombs to destroy a target. In Vietnam similar targets required 176 bombs. Today, a single PGM [Precision Guided Munition] can destroy the target' (Rip and Hasik 2002: 213).

11 Drone strikes offer the added benefit that the physical elimination of individuals designated as threats to Western security does away with the seemingly insuperable problem created by the capture and detention of 'unlawful combatants'.

References

Acuto, Michele and Simon Curtis (eds). 2014. *Reassembling International Theory: Assemblage Thinking and International Relations*. London: Palgrave.

Adey, Peter. 2010. *Aerial Life: Spaces, Mobilities, Affects*. Oxford: Wiley-Blackwell.

Alberts, David S., John J. Gartska and Frederick P. Stein. 2002. *Network Centric Warfare: Developing and Leveraging Information Superiority*. Washington, DC: CCRP Publications.

Ansorge, Josef. 2015. *Identify and Sort: How Digital Power Changed World Politics*. London: Hurst.

Bachmann, Jan, Colleen Bell and Caroline Holmqvist (eds). 2014. *War, Police and Assemblages of Intervention*. London: Routledge.

Bell, Daniel. 1973. *The Coming of a Post-Industrial Society*. Harmondsworth: Penguin.

Black, Jeremy. 2003. *New Century War: Past, Present, Future*. London: Continuum.

Black, Jeremy. 2008. Was there a Military Revolution in Early Modern Europe? *History Today* 58(7): 34–41.

Boever, Arne De, Alex Murray, Jon Roffe and Ashley Woodward (eds). 2012. *Gilbert Simondon: Being and Technology*. Edinburgh: Edinburgh University Press.

Bousquet, Antoine. 2008a. Cyberneticizing the American War Machine: Science and Computers in the Cold War. *Cold War History* 8(1): 77–102.

Bousquet, Antoine. 2008b. Chaoplexic Warfare or the Future of Military Organization. *International Affairs* 84(5): 915–929.

Bousquet, Antoine. 2009. *The Scientific Way of Warfare: Order and Chaos in the Battlefields of Modernity*. London: Hurst.

Bousquet, Antoine. 2014. Welcome to the Machine: Rethinking Technology and Society through Assemblage Theory. In Michele Acuto and Simon Curtis (eds) *Reassembling International Theory: Assemblage Thinking and International Relations*. Basingstoke: Palgrave Macmillan.

Castells, Manuel. 2000. *The Rise of the Network Society*. Oxford: Blackwell.

Cebrowksi, Arthur K. and John J. Gartska. 1998. Network-Centric Warfare: Its Origin and Future. *Proceedings* 124(1): 28–35.

Chamayou, Grégoire. 2015. *A Theory of the Drone*. New York: New Press.

Chivers, C. J. 2010. *The Gun: The Story of the AK-47*. New York: Simon & Schuster.

Clausewitz, Carl von. 1976. *On War*. Princeton, NJ: Princeton University Press.

Cohen, Eliot A. 1996. A Revolution in Warfare. *Foreign Affairs* 75: 37–54.

Coker, Christopher. 2013. *Warrior Geeks: How 21st Century Technology is Changing the Way We Fight and Think About War*. London: Hurst.

Cowan, Deborah. 2014. *The Deadly Life of Logistics: Mapping Violence in Global Trade*. Minneapolis: University of Minnesota Press.

DeLanda, Manuel. 2006. *A New Philosophy of Society: Assemblage Theory and Social Complexity*. London and New York: Continuum.

Deleuze, Gilles and Félix Guattari. 2003. *A Thousand Plateaus: Capitalism and Schizophrenia*. New York: Continuum.

Dien, Albert E. 1986. The Stirrup and its Effect on Chinese Military History. *Ars Orientalis* 16: 33–56.

Edwards, Paul. N. 1997. *The Closed World: Computers and the Politics of Discourse in Cold War America*. Cambridge, MA: MIT Press.

Fuller, J.F.C. 1998. *Armament and History*. New York: Da Capo Press.

Galison, Peter. 1994. The Ontology of the Enemy: Norbert Wiener and the Cybernetic Vision. *Critical Inquiry* 21(1): 228–266.

Grove, Jairus. 2015. Blood. In Mark B. Salter (ed.) *Making Things International 1: Circuits and Motion*. Minneapolis: University of Minnesota Press.

Guha, Manabrata. 2016. *The Rise and Fall of Network-Centric Warfare*. London: Routledge.

Hall, Bert S. and Kelly R. De Vries. 1990. Essay Review: The 'Military Revolution' Revisited. *Technology and Culture* 31(3): 500–507.

Hardt, Michael and Toni Negri. 2000. *Empire*. Cambridge, MA: Harvard University Press.

Hayles, N.Katherine. 1999. *How We Became Posthuman: Virtual Bodies in Cybernetics, Literature, and Informatics*. Chicago, IL: University of Chicago Press.

Higginbotham, Adam. 2010. U.S. Military Learns to Fight Deadliest Weapons. *Wired* 18(8). www.wired.com/2010/07/ff_roadside_bombs/. Accessed 16 September 2016.

Hildinger, Erik. 2001. *Warriors of the Steppe: Military History of Central Asia, 500 BC to 1700 AD*. Cambridge, MA: Da Capo Press.

Hippler, Thomas. 2013. *Bombing the People: Giulio Douhet and the Foundations of Air-Power Strategy, 1884–1939*. Cambridge: Cambridge University Press.

Hobson, John M. 2004. *The Eastern Origins of Western Civilization*. Cambridge: Cambridge University Press.

Holmqvist, Caroline. 2013. Undoing War: War Ontologies and the Materiality of Drone Warfare. *Millennium: Journal of International Studies* 41(2): 535–552.

Ihde, Don and Evan Selinger. 2003. *Chasing Technoscience: Matrix for Materiality*. Bloomington: Indiana University Press.

Krepinevich, Andrew F. 2002. *The Military-Technical Revolution: A Preliminary Assessment*. Washington, DC: Center for Strategic and Budgetary Assessments.

Larner, Melissa, James Peto and Nadine Käthe Monem (eds). 2008. *War and Medicine*. London: Black Dog.

Latour, Bruno. 1999. *Pandora's Hope: Essays on the Reality of Science Studies*. Cambridge, MA: Harvard University Press.

Lynn, John A. 1993. *Feeding Mars: Logistics in Western Warfare from the Middle Ages to the Present*. Boulder, CO: Westview.

Marcus, George E. and Erkan Saka. 2006. Assemblage. *Theory, Culture and Society* 23(2–3): 101–106.

Mindell, David A. 2003. *Between Human and Machine: Feedback, Control, and Computing Before Cybernetics*. Baltimore, MD: Johns Hopkins University Press.

Owens, Bill. 2001. *Lifting the Fog of War*. Baltimore, MD: Johns Hopkins University Press.

Pape, Robert. 1996. *Bombing to Win: Air Power and Coercion in War*. Ithaca, NY: Cornell University Press.

Parker, Geoffrey. 1988. *The Military Revolution: Military Innovation and the Rise of the West, 1500–1800*. Cambridge: Cambridge University Press.

Phillips, Gervase. 2002. The Obsolescence of the Arme Blanche and Technological Determinism in British Military History. *War in History* 9(1): 39–59.

Pickering, Andrew. 1995. *The Mangle of Practice: Time, Agency, and Science*. Chicago, IL: University of Chicago Press.

Rip, Michael Russell and James M. Hasik. 2002. *The Precision Revolution: GPS and the Future of Aerial Warfare*. Annapolis, MD: Naval Institute Press.

Roberts, Michael. 1967. *The Military Revolution, 1560–1660*. In *Essays in Swedish History*. London: Camelot Press.

Rogers, Clifford J. (ed.). 1995. *The Military Revolution Debate*. Boulder, CO: Westview.

Rose, Gideon. 2013. Generation Kill: A Conversation with Stanley McChrystal. *Foreign Affairs* 92(2): 2–8.

Rumsfeld, Donald H. 2001. Town Hall Meeting, Washington, DC. 9 August.

Rumsfeld, Donald H. 2002. Transforming the Military. *Foreign Affairs*. May/June.

Shachtman, Noah. 2007. How Technology Almost Lost the War. *Wired* 15(12). http://a rchive.wired.com/politics/security/magazine/15-12/ff_futurewar?currentPage=all. Accessed 16 September 2016.

Shaw, Martin. 2005. *The New Western Way of War: Risk-Transfer War and its Crisis in Iraq*. Cambridge: Polity.

Simondon, Gilbert. 1989. *Du Mode d'Existence des Objets Techniques*. Paris: Aubier.

Simondon, Gilbert. 2011. The Essence of Technicity. *Deleuze Studies* 5(3): 406–424.

Singer, Peter W. 2009. *Wired for War*. New York: Penguin.

Toffler, Alvin. 1980. *The Third Wave*. London: Collins.

Van Creveld, Martin. 2004. *Supplying War: Logistics from Wallenstein to Patton*. Cambridge: Cambridge University Press.

Van Creveld, Martin. 2011. *The Age of Airpower*. New York: Public Affairs.

Virilio, Paul. 1994. *The Vision Machine*. Bloomington: Indiana University Press.

Westmoreland, William. 1969. Address to the Association of the US Army. 14 October.

White, Lynn H. 1962. *Medieval Technology and Social Change*. Oxford: Oxford University Press.

Wilcox, Lauren B. 2015. *Bodies of Violence: Theorizing Embodied Subjects in International Relations*. Oxford: Oxford University Press.

10

EXTRA-TERRESTRIAL TECHNOPOLITICS

The politics of technology in space

Columba Peoples

This chapter provides an overview and discussion of the politics of technology in space. Building on the overarching concerns of this volume, a key argument made in the chapter is that space technologies can be understood as *technologies of world politics* in a number of interconnected and overlapping ways. The development of technological means to access and explore outer space[1] has often been presented as an apolitical endeavour pursued in 'the common interest of all mankind [...] free for exploration and use by all States without discrimination of any kind' and as a *res communis*[2] 'not subject to national appropriation by claim of sovereignty'.[3] But even a cursory survey of the historical development of outer space technologies leads quickly to the realisation that such efforts are crucially bound up with terrestrial politics. The design, deployment and use of space technologies are frequently influenced by geopolitical rivalries and competing commercial interests. Understood as artefacts of terrestrial politics, space technologies raise complex questions and issues for the study of world politics. They have been created to observe and sense (most notably via Earth monitoring and Earth remote-sensing satellite technologies) the world to an unprecedented degree. At least initially, hopes abounded that images of the Earth viewed from space as a fragile 'blue marble' or 'dot' set against the darkness of the cosmos would give rise to a greater degree of 'global consciousness' and a unified understanding of the Earth as a single polity rather than divided into distinct territorial units.

While such a degree of political integration has not emerged to the extent that some might have initially hoped, space technologies are nevertheless an increasingly central part of the scientific and technological infrastructures used to monitor and measure changes in the Earth's atmosphere as well as visualising alterations in its topography. And, although space technologies are, in some ways justifiably, seen as the preserve of scientific-political elites as a means to explore the 'unknown' and overcome the 'final frontier' (in language that has by now permeated popular vocabulary), for the many parts of the world dependent on satellite infrastructures to sustain terrestrial communication and navigation systems space technologies now have a more everyday and routine role to play.

The account offered below is underpinned by an engagement with the Critical Theory of Technology as espoused in particular by Andrew Feenberg.[4] As intimated above, space technologies can and arguably should be understood not simply as neutral or apolitical devices that simply extend human control over the cosmos, but rather as forms of technology that embody 'the values of a particular industrial civilization, especially those of elites that rest their claims to hegemony on technical mastery' (Feenberg 1991: v). One way of reading Feenberg's critical project is as an effort to democratise technology, to develop as he puts it 'a democratic politics of technology' (1991: 5) in which extended participation beyond closed groups of technological and political elites is the key to unlocking the 'potentialities' (in Feenberg's terms) of different technologies. In arguably the key phrasing of this approach, Feenberg tells us that:

> Critical theory argues that technology is not a thing in the ordinary sense of the term, but an 'ambivalent' process of development suspended between different possibilities [...] On this view technology is not a destiny but a scene of struggle. It is a social battlefield, or perhaps a better metaphor would be a *parliament of things* on which civilizational alternatives are debated and decided.
>
> *(1991: 14, emphasis in original)*

In many ways, space technologies are a particularly apposite case through which to explore and consider Feenberg's approach. This is not least because the development of outer space technologies has been driven in large part historically by aspirations to extend human civilisation writ large into outer space (as exemplified in manned space missions and, at times, in futuristic visions of human colonies on the Moon, Mars and beyond); it is also because, in relation to world politics, an argument can be made that space technologies simultaneously sustain different possible alternatives: as is discussed in further detail below, some scholars suggest that such technologies simply allow for the transposition of terrestrial nation-state rivalries into outer space, while others make allowance for the potential of space technologies to fundamentally transform our understanding of world politics.

Similarly, while the broader Science and Technology Studies (STS) literature often cites, for understandable reasons, space technologies as the products of closed systems of elite-dominated 'big science', some scholars have begun to think creatively about the ways in which the uses of outer space technologies might already contain the potential for greater public participation and be reformed in more democratic ways. The extent to which this is possible, and the extent to which space technologies in their very design and operation continue to reproduce what Feenberg would call a 'bias' (1991: 65) towards the reproduction of select groups and interests, is of course open to question. But, at the very least, a Critical Theoretic approach to the study of space technologies heightens our awareness of outer space as a 'scene of struggle' in which different 'civilisational alternatives' are advocated, sustained and contested.

The 'space age': above and beyond politics?

When, at 8.52pm Eastern US time on Wednesday 15 July 2015 the National Aeronautic and Space Administration's (NASA) *New Horizons* spacecraft made contact with mission control in Maryland from a successful 'flypast' within 7,750 miles of Pluto, the moment was heralded as 'truly a hallmark in human history' by John Grunsfeld, NASA's associate administrator for science (quoted in Phipps 2015: n.p.). Undoubtedly, the successful passage of the unmanned craft to the furthest reaches of our solar system represented a stunning feat of technological achievement: *New Horizons* had by that point travelled on a journey of 3 billion miles over a duration of nine and a half years. The new images of Pluto beamed back from the craft prompted British cosmologist Stephen Hawking, in a message broadcast on NASA TV, to reflect that: 'We explore because we are human and we want to know. I hope that Pluto will help us on that journey' (quoted in Phipps 2015; NASA 2015a). Then US president Barack Obama later congratulated NASA and the team behind the mission, calling the event 'a great day for discovery and American leadership' in a tweet on social media (quoted in NASA 2015b).

By noting the successful passage of and subsequent contact from *New Horizons* as not only a 'great day for discovery' but also for 'American leadership', President Obama continued a long-standing tradition of nationalising feats of space exploration. Indeed a case can be made that the practice of representing such feats as achieved *both* for the betterment of the human species *and* for the glorification of national cultures has been a staple feature of the political discourse of the 'space age'. When in September 1962 US President John F. Kennedy declared – as both an aspiration and a statement of intent – that 'We choose to go the moon' it was in the context of an assumption that:

> The exploration of space will go ahead, whether we join in it or not, and it is one of the great adventures of all time, and no nation which expects to be the leader of other nations can expect to stay behind in the race for space.
>
> *(Kennedy 1962: 2)*

To assuage the doubts of any listeners who might question the importance of winning this 'space race', and aware of the huge investment it would take, Kennedy identified the mission of being the first state to land a man on the moon as integral to the continuation of American-led technological innovation and moral–political leadership of the world:

> Those who came before us made certain that this country rode the first waves of the industrial revolutions, the first waves of modern invention, and the first wave of nuclear power, and this generation does not intend to founder in the

backwash of the coming age of space. We mean to be a part of it – we mean to lead it. For the eyes of the world now look into space, to the moon and to the planets beyond, and we have vowed that we shall not see it governed by a hostile flag of conquest, but by a banner of freedom and peace. We have vowed that we shall not see space filled with weapons of mass destruction, but with instruments of knowledge and understanding.

(Kennedy 1962: 2)

In effect, Kennedy argued that were the US to opt out of the race to land a man on the Moon, it would not only be abdicating from what he conceived of as a uniquely American heritage in technological innovation, but would also concede global political leadership to a rival state, the Soviet Union, that had already become the first to put an unmanned artificial satellite into Earth orbit (*Sputnik*, on 4 October 1957) and to deliver a man into space (Yuri Gagarin, on 12 April 1961).

Kennedy thus explicitly recognised the space programme as an instrument of American foreign policy (see Slotten 2002) that, while assumed to benefit all humankind by default, was nevertheless crucial to the political competition for global leadership with the Soviet Union. Equally, the Soviet Union and its Communist Party leadership saw its space programme as instrumental to establishing and embedding the assumed superiority of its own political, economic and social values and systems at home and abroad. As James T. Andrews and Asif Siddiqi note (2011: 1), 'The achievements of *Sputnik* and Gagarin were synonymous with a new and dynamic Soviet state no longer hobbled by the devastations of the Great Patriotic War.'[5] In addition the early exploits and achievements of the Soviet space programme – *Sputnik*, the first living being in space (Laika the dog), the first man (Gagarin) and the first woman in space (Valentina Tereshkova), the first probe to impact the surface of the moon (*Luna 2*), to name but a few – all helped inscribe 'a glorious cosmic future into the fabric of popular imagination' where the Communist Party 'closely identified the successes of the space program with the perceived successes of the Soviet state' (Andrews and Siddiqi 2011: 5, 10).

In this sense, the Cold War-era space race can be understood as a political competition in which the US and the Soviet Union contested for leadership. The two states publicly acknowledged the general technological and scientific significance of each other's 'breakthroughs' as contributing to a common human endeavour to explore and better understand space. But they also always placed value on the propaganda and strategic stakes of the space race, and exhibited concern at the possibility of 'falling behind' in that race. In part due to the fact that the White House had announced in 1955 its intention to launch an Earth orbiting satellite, the successful launch of *Sputnik* was generally perceived at the time as a 'shock' to and 'crisis' in US political and media discourse (see Peoples 2008a). Soviet success in rocketry and satellite technologies as manifested in *Sputnik* were taken to equate to US failure, and generated much national soul-searching about why the US scientific, industrial, educational and political system had apparently failed (the event is often taken as being crucial to the creation of NASA, which was established on 1 October 1958 – Garber 2007).

The innovations in rocketry required to deliver *Sputnik* into orbit were also seen as marking a dangerous Soviet advantage over the US in missile technology and its capacity to deliver nuclear weapons, symptomatic of lasting concerns about the potential for overlap between the technologies required to deliver objects and people into space and those required to deliver warheads. Emblematic of this overlap, arguably, was the central role of Wernher von Braun in developing rocketry for use in the US space programme – most notably as a key member of the team that designed and developed the *Saturn V* rocket used to propel the *Apollo 11* astronauts to the Moon.[6] Prior to his incorporation into the US rocketry and space programmes, the German von Braun had previously served in the Nazi war effort during World War II, and is credited as the 'father' of the V-2 missiles (*Vergeltungswaffe* – 'reprisal' or 'vengeance' weapons) used in strikes on Antwerp and London in 1944. Among other reasons, the V-2 was notable for being the first missile to exit and then re-enter the Earth's atmosphere. The V-2 instantiated a debate as to whether weapons that do so (such as modern intercontinental ballistic missiles – ICBMs) should be regarded as 'space technologies' since, strictly speaking, they leave and then re-enter the Earth's atmosphere (see Deudney 1985 for related discussion), a definitional debate with significant implications not least for debates on what constitutes 'space weaponisation' (see Mueller 2003; Peoples 2008b).

Space technologies and the 'closed world' of the Cold War

Sputnik also created fears about the potential for future Soviet capabilities to launch military strikes via space-based orbital platforms that could circumvent US air defences: that space would become a venue for stationing weapons in orbit and not just a medium that missiles might travel through. The latter anxieties were part of President Kennedy's strategic rationale for the mission to land a man on the Moon: 'only if the United States occupies a position of pre-eminence can we help decide whether this new ocean will be a sea of peace or a new terrifying theatre of war' (Kennedy 1962: 2). Kennedy here employed an established trope of conceiving of space as 'essentially a *tabula rasa*, a blank page on which humanity was free to write whatever it chose' (Sheehan 2007: 5), and with the exploration of space consequently cast as a backdrop against which the US and the Soviet Union would project and contest their different 'civilisational alternatives' (in the Feenbergian sense) via demonstrations of technical prowess.

With the *Apollo 11* spaceflight and the landing of Neil Armstrong as the first and Buzz Aldrin as the second man on the Moon on 20 July 1969, the US arguably achieved the position of pre-eminence that Kennedy had earlier aspired to. This was established not only by virtue of the technologies that ferried the astronauts to the Moon and back, but also by the satellite systems that by now afforded the US an enhanced capability to broadcast news of the achievement. As Hugh R. Slotten (2002: 350) notes:

The major television event of the 1960s, the 1969 Apollo moon landing, observed by five hundred million people in forty-nine countries thanks to the Intelsat system, symbolized not only the primary role of the United States in the new global village but also the central role of the space program in the process of globalization.

In turn, dominance of satellite media broadcasting capabilities and weather data as US-supplied global public goods became valuable facets of what Karen T. Litfin (1999: 99) characterises as 'technological anti-communism': while the USSR might have been first to launch a satellite and in manned space travel, the US led the way in terms of meteorological, navigational, electronic intelligence, photo-reconnaissance and communications satellites (see Moltz 2014: 43); and, in meteorology and telecommunications in particular, the US contrasted its 'open' approach to the production and communication of data to the 'secretive' nature of its Soviet counterpart (see Slotten 2002 for discussion).

The Moon landings were thus emblematic as a public manifestation of the space race, but can be regarded as but one of the significant products of much broader Cold War techno-scientific infrastructures that had and continue to have multiple impacts. And, in keeping with broader arguments of the introduction to this volume, the political contestation of the Cold War was a key factor in initiating and sustaining the development of space technologies. While it is of course a counterfactual hypothesis impossible to prove one way or another, it is interesting to consider whether the development of space technologies and space exploration would have developed at the same pace and intensity absent the superpower rivalry. Certainly a persuasive case can be made that the development of rocketry and computer, satellite and communications technologies of the Cold War era, which in turn provided the bedrock for the development of its post-Cold War counterpart, was driven on the part of the US at least by 'global security, big science and advanced capitalism' (Brannon 2013: 273) and, in the case of its Soviet counterpart, by a broadly equivalent set of motors with 'advanced socialism' replacing the last.

But it is also worth noting that the development and applications of those technologies were frequently propelled by complex and contested choices rather than emerging from a seamlessly unfolding process of technological development. When President Kennedy (1962: 2) mused that 'space science, like nuclear science and all technology, has no conscience of its own', he not only made a strong claim to what was assumed to be the neutrality of technology as defined by the purposes that humans put them to, but also in some ways tacitly recognised the influence of cultural factors on the design and use of technologies – the 'conscience' of technology would come from designers and users rather than being inherent in or determined by the technology itself. A number of studies of the 'space age' have subsequently analysed the ways in which cultural variables have influenced the development of space technologies, and vice versa.[7]

One of the best ways of illustrating that point is by reconsidering the choice made by both of the Cold War superpowers (and by multiple states since then, and now private companies as well) to invest in and pursue manned space flight in addition to the development of unmanned technologies in space. For some readers that choice may appear to be an obvious one, and its seeming obviousness might actually be telling in its own right as an indicator of the extent to which manned spaceflight is part of the popular imagination of outer space. Yet in terms of cost and degree of design challenge involved, manned space technologies are not necessarily the optimal choice. Going beyond the Earth's atmosphere by default necessarily takes human beings into an 'airless' realm that is not naturally conducive to human habitability. As was tragically illustrated in examples such as the *Challenger* disaster in January 1986, when the NASA space shuttle orbiter broke apart seconds after take-off, leading to the death of its seven crew members, and the disintegration on re-entry of the space shuttle *Columbia* in 2003, also leading to the death of its seven crew members – the technological challenges involved are significant and high risk. As a result, manned space activity is 'on average ten times more expensive than is unmanned spaceflight, due to using systems with much higher safety margins to "man-rate" the spacecraft … including complex life support systems' (Johnson-Freese 2007: 57).

Gerard DeGroot, in his *Dark Side of the Moon: The Magnificent Madness of the American Lunar Quest*, develops the same basic observation into an argument that, while respectful of the feats of engineering that delivered the first humans into space, nevertheless condemns the general obsession with manned space flight as 'an immensely expensive distraction of little scientific or cultural worth' (2007: xii). He continues:

> Going to the Moon was not just a supreme technological achievement, it was also a magnificent artistic endeavour, requiring huge reserves of imagination, faith and bravery. But all that sublime effort was devoted toward a stunt that had no real purpose other than to kick lunar dust in Soviet faces.
>
> *(DeGroot 2007: xiii–xiv)*

But, while noting the force of such retrospective critiques, the 'human interest' dimension of space technologies became an integral part of the space race (cf. Mindell 2011). Noting the ways in which the first returning cosmonauts and astronauts were hailed as heroes, Johnson-Freese opines that 'nobody throws a parade for robots. Manned space activity captures the imagination in ways that machinery rarely does' (2007: 57). Neil Armstrong and Buzz Aldrin immediately came to be cast as American space pioneers, revered to this day. Gagarin was feted in the Soviet Union on his return to Earth, and Valentina Tereshkova was celebrated as the first woman in space (on 16 June 1963) and was publicly lauded by the Communist Party as emblematic of a more progressive approach to female empowerment in the Soviet space programme as compared to its American counterpart (though in reality, as Sylvester (2011: 197) notes, there was 'no real commitment to robust female participation' in the upper echelons of the Soviet space programme – it would be two decades after Tereshkova before the next female cosmonaut in space).

The enduring fascination with manned space technologies can, though, obscure the additional broader significance of space technologies in producing and sustaining Cold War politics. While the US and the Soviet Union arguably used the race to put men into space and then on the Moon as a kind of proxy for the broader Cold War struggle, developments in rocketry, satellite and associated computing and communication technologies also came to directly underpin the military capabilities and national security infrastructures of both states. The US *Corona* satellite programme – which was launched in 1959 and lasted until 1972 – for example, was used to record images of the Earth on canisters of film which were then ejected from the satellite and retrieved by a plane as they drifted downwards. When in 1995 the US government declassified 800,000 intelligence images from the programme, it attested to the fact that 'The imagery provided unprecedented illumination of key Soviet programs, including missile complexes and test ranges, submarine deployments and operation bases, bombers and fighters, and atomic weapons storage installations' (Deibert 2003: 92).

In this light Paul N. Edwards (1996) argues that the conceptualisation of containment as a concept and a strategy during the Cold War was enabled and sustained not only by high-technology weaponry capable of projecting force at a global level – such as nuclear bombers, submarines and missiles – but also by an accompanying architecture of 'real-time' global monitoring and surveillance enabled in large part by satellite overhead observation. Nuclear weapons and their associated technologies of global surveillance not only became essential to (potentially) prosecuting nuclear war; they also visually framed the world in which such a conflict would take place. The Cold War military and political elite of the US monitored the status quo via surveillance of the Earth, and would 'see' any launch of Soviet missiles represented and mapped on a computer screen before responding (as was imagined and represented to cinemagoers in Stanley Kubrick's 1964 parody *Dr. Strangelove*, where American military planners can be seen underneath a giant computerised map of the world – reportedly modelled on the Pentagon 'War Room' – that lights up as nuclear weapons are launched). As Edwards puts it (1996: 75), the period of the late 1950s onwards witnessed:

> a cascading wave of command-control projects … tied largely to nuclear early warning systems. These systems eventually formed the core of a worldwide satellite, sensor, and communications web that would allow global oversight and instantaneous military response. Enframing the globe, this web formed the technological infrastructure of closed–world politics.

That world was 'closed' in the sense that the meaning of the Cold War conflict was already built into the use, and even the design, of the systems used to visualise the state of Cold War nuclear relations.

The technopolitics of Earth observation from space

As noted above, space-based technologies during the Cold War simultaneously sustained efforts to open up the new frontier of space exploration on the one hand and to enclose the military dimensions of the bipolar superpower rivalry on the other. But many analysts have argued that the post–Cold War era has witnessed rapid diversification of both the range of state and non-state actors developing and using space technologies, and of the functions those technologies now serve and underpin. With the Cold War's end, although the US retained and continues to retain a leadership position in relation to space technologies, it generally became 'less defensible for national security arguments to be used to maintain rigid controls over access to sophisticated satellite technologies' (Deibert 2003: 96; see also Litfin 1998: 205). The Soviet Union's collapse led to greater availability of its satellite imagery for commercial purposes, and the expansion of the range of commercial non-state actors producing and using space technologies – satellites and their attendant systems in particular – has been an especially noteworthy feature of the post–Cold War era.

As Deibert succinctly puts it, the post–Cold War context of space technologies is one in which there is a 'growing and dispersed constituency of private and public actors from around the world in a variety of sectors [that] now depends on, and has a stake in, space-based Earth-monitoring systems' (2003: 101). The 'story' is not as simple, though, as being able to say that a zero–sum game exists in which national security interests have given way to commercial interests; US predominance has given way to rough equality of state power and technological capabilities; or that efforts at manned space exploration have given way entirely to a focus solely on the development of satellite technologies as support systems for terrestrial infrastructures.

By way of illustration, relatively widely available software such as Google Earth has until recently been subject to restrictions that reserved the use of the highest resolution satellite imagery (from satellites capable of distinguishing objects smaller than 50cm in images of the Earth's surface) in the US for military intelligence purposes only. Until June 2014 (when regulations were relaxed) DigitalGlobe – a primary commercial organisation supplying high-resolution imagery to both Google and the US government's National Geospatial-Intelligence Agency (NGA) – was also prevented from selling its imagery to non-US customers on grounds of national security (see Ferster 2014).

Enthusiasm for the pursuit of manned space systems has also arguably dropped off from the heydays of the space race; but it has continued and, most notably, on 15 October 2003 China launched its first manned spacecraft into orbit, *Shenzhou V*, carrying the taikonaut Yang Liwei. The manned dimension of the Chinese space programme attests to the enduring prestige value and attraction of such exploits (see Harvey 2004 for an overview), as do continued pledges and statements of interest from India, Japan, Iran and the European Space Agency (ESA) regarding aspirations to human spaceflight (Moltz 2014: 6). Commercial enterprises are now also part of the manned space picture. SpaceX, one of the leading private companies that manages and launches rockets and spacecraft, declares its intention as being to enable people 'to live on other planets' (SpaceX 2015), which its founder Elon Musk has argued to be the next step in human evolution; and Virgin Galactic aspires to become the world's first commercial 'spaceline', hoping in the near future to 'make space accessible to more people and for more purposes than ever before' and to 'make it possible to see the beautiful planet we call home from a new perspective' (Virgin Galactic 2015a).

Virgin Galactic's enticing invitation to prospective investors and future customers to see the world anew from space through their own eyes is couched within an acknowledgement that satellite technologies already enable humans to view and even sense the Earth vicariously. 'Modern life', the company website notes, would be 'unrecognisable without satellites' (Virgin Galactic 2015b). Images and data beamed back from satellites are used to monitor the global condition from afar (meteorology and environmental monitoring being but two examples), and satellite technologies also form a vital component of modern mapping techniques and global communication infrastructures.

Satellite technologies, in a broad sense, enable a form of Earth observation, surveillance and monitoring not possible in their absence. Space-based remote-sensing systems – roughly, the use of satellite systems to obtain information about objects or areas from a distance by using sensors to record energy that is reflected or emitted from the Earth's surface – are now used in multiple applications ranging from urban planning to geology to climate science. Satellite imagery provides, among other things: a means of viewing the effects of deforestation; the onset of coastal erosion; the melting of ice caps; the location of military facilities and deployments of troops; and the movement and settlement of groups of refugees. And such imagery is not simply limited to photographs or film media – developments in computer programming, processing and graphics have 'allowed the integration of satellite imagery into detailed three-dimensional digital terrain models, which in turn has opened up markets for satellite imagery in a variety of non-military and intelligence areas' (Deibert 2003: 100).

This rapid expansion of applications of space technologies remains relatively under-studied within the disciplinary study of International Relations (although prominent exceptions to that rule include Deibert 2003 and Litfin 1998, 1999). Yet states and international organisations alike now commonly refer to and prioritise 'threats which are not necessarily territorial and dangers which are global and planetary in nature' – such as transnational terrorism, proliferation of weapons of mass destruction, climate change and environmental degradation (Ó'Tuathail 1999: 18); and, simultaneously, space technologies are increasingly relied upon to inform and supplement these understandings of 'global' dangers. Part of the reason for this relative lack of attention might lie in the tendency to assume that the capacity to observe the Earth from space has the effect of erasing the 'lines on maps' that distinguish states from one another as political units (cf. Peoples 2016). Humans who have travelled in Earth orbit have frequently recounted their experience of what has been termed the 'overview effect': coined by Frank White (1998) based on interviews with and writings of astronauts and cosmonauts to describe a change in their consciousness having viewed the Earth as a fragile, 'pale blue dot' from a distance, combined with an almost spiritual sense of awareness of the planet as the shared habitat for the human species rather than territory to be carved up between different nations. The popular reception and appropriation of images of the Earth from space has often echoed this sense of 'globality' that presents an image of the Earth that transcends the modern, statist geopolitical division of the world (see van Munster and Sylvest 2016).

Virgin Galactic's promise of enabling its customers to view the world 'from a new perspective' is but the latest manifestation of this kind of representation (see the work of Robert Poole (2008) and, in particular, of Denis E. Cosgrove (1994; 2001) for more extensive discussion of this theme), and White (1998: 4) argues that even satellites and unmanned space probes 'provide a technological analogue to the Overview Effect and other changes in consciousness that take place during manned flights'. Photos taken by US astronauts aboard the *Apollo 8* mission to orbit the moon in 1968 (often referred to as 'Earthrise' – see NASA 2013a for the image) and from *Apollo 17* in 1972 (often referred to as the 'Blue Marble' – see NASA 2015c), the last American mission to the moon to date, using hand-held 70mm Hasselblad cameras in both instances, are among the most notable examples of images of the Earth from space that have often been associated with attempts to articulate understandings of the planet that transcend terrestrial politics. Once released to the public, they became 'critical to the imaginative reception of the space images and to the totalizing socio-environmental discourse of *One-World* and *Whole-Earth* to which they have become so closely attached' (Cosgrove 1994: 271).

But observation and remote sensing of the Earth have come to play not just a figurative role in informing our 'view' of the Earth; they have also come to underpin scientific understanding of the Earth as a planet and of its atmosphere. When, in July 2015, a NASA camera on the Deep Space Climate Observatory (*Dscovr*) satellite returned its first image of the entire sunlit side of the Earth from a distance of 1 million miles, its import was claimed to represent more than just an aesthetically beautiful image of the planet 'hanging' serenely in space (see NOAA 2015a). NASA administrator and former astronaut Charlie Bolden claimed that:

> Dscovr's observations of Earth, as well as its measurements and early warnings of space weather events caused by the sun, will help every person to monitor the ever-changing Earth and to understand how our planet fits into its neighbourhood in the solar system.[8]

Re-envisioning world politics

Yet, just as it can be argued that the aspirations of the US and the Soviet Union to explore and use space for the benefit of all humankind can be shown to have existed within the context of geopolitical terrestrial rivalries, the multiple uses of Earth observation and monitoring today do not straightforwardly or necessarily provide a benign or unified sense of 'global' or 'planetary' consciousness of the Earth. As Karen T. Litfin puts it, 'At stake is the principle of territorial exclusivity in a world rendered transparent by satellite technology' (1998: 197); and it is not simply the case that the ability to view the Earth as a 'whole' and to 'zoom in' on precise parts of it from space necessarily undermines that principle. Critical geographers studying the use of satellite and Earth observation technologies have been particularly attuned to ways in which such systems can be employed to map, represent and re-inscribe terrestrial borders and boundaries. Data produced by space technologies and their use in remote earth sensing now commonly underpin extensive Geographic Information Systems (GIS): 'relational system[s] of spatial information handling and representation', usually the collection and communication of geographic information using digital technology (Pickles 1995: 3). Typically, such systems take the form of computer programs that present viewers with drop-down menus, sidebars and supplementary video and audio feeds literally and figuratively frame central mappings or images. Many GIS applications aim to capture and relate more localised dynamics and information, but in some instances GIS are also employed to present a 'global' picture. NASA's 'World Wind' for example – which, as the project's website declares, 'overlays NASA and USGS [US Geological Survey] satellite imagery [with] aerial photography, topographic maps and publicly available GIS data on 3D models of the Earth and other planets' (NASA 2015d) – might in this respect be seen as figuratively establishing an explicit link between the American space agency's historic role in providing images of the Earth from space through to embedding those images within already existing and supplementary frames of understanding.

In turn, satellite technology has been crucial to the development of geodesy (see Cloud 2001) – essentially the science of 'accurately measuring and understanding the Earth's geometric shape, orientation in space and gravity field' (NOAA 2015b) – and to the development of practical applications of the Global Positioning System (GPS) for the purposes of mapping coastlines and land boundaries as locative technologies and for improvement of terrestrial navigation. As some of the most ardent advocates of this so-called 'geospatial revolution' would have it:

> Geospatial information influences nearly everything. Seamless layers of satellites, surveillance, and location-based technologies create a worldwide geographic knowledge base vital to solving myriad social and environmental problems in the interconnected global community. We count on these technologies to: fight climate change; map populations across continents, countries and communities; track disease ... enable democracy ... navigate our personal lives.
>
> *(Geospatial Revolution Project 2015)*

Although the benign applications of satellite technologies are emphasised in that characterisation, others contend that such technologies and modes of representation made it possible to 'classify space in terms of dangerousness' during the Cold War, framing territorial spaces in terms of potential risks emanating from particular regions or locales through what Crampton (2003: 140) terms 'geosurveillance'. This interlinkage between military surveillance and geosurveillance continues to be emphasised by critical geographers in particular. In addition to the well-known provenance of civilian satellite navigation now commercially available to individual users in the form of 'satnavs' from military GPS – the American and Russian versions of which, NAVSTAR and GLONASS, both originate in defence programmes from the 1970s – some have pointed to a more general trend in this regard, and go further in suggesting a more substantive relation between militarisation and technologies and practices of visualising the globe even as they migrate beyond explicit military applications and into wider public usage. For example, Crampton 2010: 118) argues that:

> The kind of security desired by the United States and other countries depends on a whole suite of digital spatial mapping and so-called 'locative' technologies. These locative technologies allow people and objects to be geosurveilled, that is, to be tracked, marked, noticed and logged as they move from one place to another [...] Blanket geosurveillance is therefore a logical outcome of the state's representation of its residents as risk factors who need to be controlled, modified and logged.

In other words satellite images and data come to be framed by and overlaid with specific narratives that may be put to use in shoring up and embedding national security and territorial sovereignty rather than necessarily undermining them. Crampton's focus on the monitoring of movement of populations is a good example in this respect, particularly when satellite technologies are employed to track 'flows' of migration, with such flows defined as being politically important precisely when they can be detected crossing state boundaries.

Likewise in the military realm, among multiple examples that might be cited, the NGA (2003) aspires:

> to provide timely, relevant and accurate geospatial intelligence in support of national security objectives [...] we provide geospatial intelligence in all its forms, and from whatever source – imagery, imagery intelligence and geospatial data and information – to ensure the knowledge foundation for planning, decision and action.

By way of illustrating the previous point, though, the NGA explicitly takes the view that such geospatial 'data and information' does not simply speak for itself. Rather, this data has to be translated and interpreted in a step-by-step process in which the NGA distinguishes between 'basic facts' or 'foundations' – 'Physical, political, and ethnic boundaries [...] grid coordinates, latitude and longitude, vectors, altitudes, natural boundaries (mountain ranges, rivers, shorelines) [...] weather, vegetation, roads, facilities, population, languages, social, ethnic, religious, and political factors' – and 'descriptive information' that is then 'layered' on top (so to speak) of those foundations.

As noted above, the 'national security objectives' of the US are the political imperatives around which these processes of translation and interpretation are organised. Not only is it worth noting that the satellite infrastructures and technologies supporting and informing contemporary GIS are the products of particular manifestations of technopolitics rooted in the Cold War and extending beyond that into the contemporary era, then; as in the case of the NGA, the data and information produced by these space technologies is also (often explicitly) put to use in the service of particular political purposes, projects and visions that re-emphasise state boundaries. It is in this sense that Litfin (1998: 197) makes the case that:

> The prohibition of territorial claims on outer space [as a *res communis* in the Outer Space Treaty of 1967] stands in a tense relationship with the efforts of states to enhance their own security through the use of satellites stationed in nonterritorial space.

The democratisation of space technologies?

The NGA's mission to utilise satellite imagery and data to further US national security interests is but one of multiple examples (military reconnaissance and targeting being others) of the ways in which space technologies are now seen to play a vital role in sustaining US military technological superiority even as the role and applications of space technologies have become more dispersed and diverse in the post-Cold War era. Deibert (2003: 100) argues that 'The present configuration of social forces and interests, particularly within US intelligence and defense spheres, could reconsolidate control over Earth remote-sensing activities (ERS) in the event of a global military crisis'; and others have argued that continuing US reluctance to explicitly preclude the deployment of 'space weapons' portends a future in which it will employ space technologies to militarily assert sovereign power and preserve its hegemonic status (see Duvall and Havercroft 2008; Dolman 2002).

Yet, counter to this arguably deterministic vision, a number of scholars have also made the case for the already existing democratic potentialities of space technologies. In relation to Earth remote sensing technologies, for example, Litfin (1998: 203) contends that:

> There is no single straightforward logic to ERS technology. Certainly it still bears the imprint of its origins in military reconnaissance, the root purposes of which was to protect the superpowers' territorial integrity ... Yet the emergence of ERS data on the world market has dramatically eroded the ability of states to control information about the resources within their borders.

In relation to satellite imagery, Brannon relatedly argues that:

> Commercially provided access to imagery gives the public a chance to speak back to the state against its classified legacy [...] This same corporate access can be appropriated by the public as a chance for productive and creative or purely entertaining voyages through the digital landscape, and are sometimes seen as offering a more equalizing platform in the critique of state practices through pointed exposure of secret sites and 'citizen–spying,' which breaks the hegemonic state gaze.
>
> *(Brannon 2013: 289)*[9]

Similarly, Laura Kurgan (2013: 54) suggests that the increasing dissemination and public availability of GIS software, geospatial data and satellite imagery – 'no longer the sole property of governments, militaries and large corporations' – has enabled their 'democratisation'. Kurgan's work aims to show how images and data from satellite surveillance can be used creatively to 'reframe' dominant representations of events as exemplified via her own self-authored 'projects' – such as 'repurposing' satellite images of Ground Zero, the site where the twin towers of the World Trade Center used to stand, to create maps of unofficial memorials to the victims of 9/11 that would take visitors on a significantly different tour of the site than simply paying respects at the official memorial. Indeed Kurgan (2013: 14) goes so far as to suggest that conscious participatory engagement with the applications of space technologies in, for example, the form of GPS, is a necessity: 'Only through a certain intimacy with these technologies – an encounter with their opacities, their assumptions, their intended aims – can we begin to assess their full ethical and political stakes.'

Even if it might not specify the precise details of the kinds of initiatives noted above, Feenberg's Critical Theory of Technology explicitly points towards this kind of normative political endeavour of 'opening technical development to the influence of a wider range of values' as itself a 'technical project requiring broad democratic participation' (Feenberg 1991: 19). At first glance, space technologies might reasonably appear particularly resistant to the kind of democratic impetus Feenberg advocates. Focusing on the examples of the US space shuttle and space station *Freedom* as case studies, W.D. Kay went so far as to put forward the argument that, even in democratic states, space technologies should be categorised as 'super technologies'. As such, space technologies, he argued should be regarded as the products of 'large technological systems' that are 'complex and uncertain', and that this created attendant 'democratic dilemmas': 'under the prevailing norms of democratic decision making – whether defined as popular consent or agreement among elites', Kay argued:

> super technologies present government officials with an apparently inescapable dilemma. Large-scale, expensive, risky and uncertain projects cannot, and many would agree, should not, be undertaken without broad political

consensus. However, procedures which produce this consensus, lower those programs' chances of success by increasing further their scale, expense, risk, and uncertainty. In other words, the traditional democratic political process exacerbates those very features that make development of emerging technologies so difficult in the first place.

(Kay 1994: 147)

In short, Kay can be read as contending that space technologies depend on a kind of trade-off between technocratic and democratic decision-making for the success of their development and deployment: the more technocratic the approach, the higher the chances of success, but with higher risk of accusations that programmes for the development of technologies are closed off from public involvement and democratic oversight; the more democratic and inclusive the approach, the higher the risk that programmes will expand in scope, scale and cost, with a consequently higher chance of failure.

In a related vein, Amy Kaminski notes a fundamental historical tension within the US space programme more generally. The programme was, as she notes, 'born out of an effort to champion the ideal of democracy over the Soviet totalitarian communist regime' (2012: 226). Yet the predominant trend has been that:

A relatively small elite cohort dominates and drives US space exploration's direction: politicians occupied with ensuring US global leadership in space and other techno-scientific arenas but also with meeting the approval of their constituents, whom they hope will support their bids for re-election; scientists interested in the creation of knowledge but also with ensuring their own professional success and livelihood; and private corporations that have the technical abilities to make spaceflight possible but are also driven by the prospects of financial profit from this work.

(Kaminski 2012: 225)

Kaminski is, though, more hopeful than Kay about the prospects for the participation of the 'demos' in shaping the course of US space exploration. The legislation that created NASA, as she notes, mandated that the agency should 'provide for the widest practicable and appropriate dissemination of information concerning its activities and the results thereof'. While this arguably translated into an effort by NASA to 'sell' its human spaceflight initiatives as well as its unmanned space technologies during the Cold War and in the decades after, Kaminski argues that NASA has more recently shifted towards a model of public involvement that goes beyond simply 'dissemination' of information and moves towards substantive public engagement and a 'model of "democratisation"' that sees US citizens as 'not just passive supporters but active participants' (Kaminski 2016: 221). As an example she notes NASA's recent use of crowdsourcing via social media to 'bring ideas and technological solutions into the agency and further space capabilities' (ibid.); and elsewhere Kaminski (2012) has suggested that public hearings, public opinion polling and citizen juries are all ways in which the US space programme (and, conceivably, space programmes in other states) can be further democratised.

Beyond such proposals for formal incorporation of citizen participation in the design, use and future applications of space technologies, a different way of politicizing and possibly democratizing space technologies in a more general sense – or at least a route to opening up that discussion – is by considering space technologies as technologies of world politics that impact upon an ever-greater number of 'users'. The increasing use of satellite systems to underpin terrestrial infrastructure also radically increases the range and number of 'stakeholders' affected by the functioning of space technologies, even if individual users of technologies such as GPS satnavs or satellite-enabled phones may not recognise themselves as such.

In this light, the issue of man-made space debris, for example, takes on a new degree of significance (see NASA 2013b). NASA reports that there are over 500,000 particles of debris orbiting the Earth – pieces of 'space junk' that have been created by, for example: the collision of a French satellite in 1996 with debris from a French rocket that had exploded a decade earlier: from a defunct Russian satellite that crashed into a commercial US Iridium (satellite phone communications) satellite; from the Chinese state's use of a missile in 2007 to shoot down one of its own weather satellites. Although many of these pieces of debris are no bigger than a marble, they all travel at speeds up to 17,500 miles per hour (NASA 2013b), effectively becoming projectiles in their own right and causing serious damage should they collide with manned or unmanned spacecraft.

As orbits become more 'crowded', the risks posed by debris and accidental collisions to satellite systems increase; and, as the Chinese satellite shoot-down – widely viewed as a demonstration of its 'anti-satellite' (ASAT) capability – attests, the risks of destruction to space technologies is not solely limited to unintentional collisions. When thought of in this way, although the advent of space technologies may not lead straightforwardly to the emergence of a single 'global polity' (cf. Corry 2013), it does raise the possibility of considering a wider, global constituency of people affected by and with a potential stake in the interface between space technologies and terrestrial politics.

Conclusion: suspended between different possibilities

Space technologies are physically distant from us when deployed, and yet they have arguably fundamentally changed how humans have come to view and understand the world; and, for an ever-increasing number of people, they are a crucial if often unseen and unnoticed underpinning of modern life. As noted at several points above, the design, deployment and applications of space technologies are also embedded within a 'wider political economy' sustained by a web of military and geopolitical rivalries between states, as well as commercial interests and 'patterns of capital investment, government subsidies, licensing fees and profits' (Dodge and Perkins 2009: 4). Speaking specifically in relation to the production and use of Earth imagery, Dodge and Perkins raise a consequent concern that

'Rather than contributing to a more democratic society, the powerful gaze of satellite imagery at the heart of surveillance infrastructure is likely to deepen the social power of corporations and the state' (ibid.). That concern might be extended to critical analysis of space technologies more generally. When Virgin Galactic notes that 'only 549 people have been to space' (correct as of 27 July 2015) and claims to be 'democratizing access to space for the benefit of life on Earth', it does so in the context of charging a reported $250,000 to each customer who has put their name down in the hope of being carried into suborbital space and back by the company's *SpaceShipTwo* in the future (Wall 2013). Such a restrictive cost (only 580 people have reportedly paid a deposit) necessarily means that Virgin's marketing promise of 'opening space up to the rest of us' has a somewhat hollow ring to it, and could in fact be seen as emblematic of the way in which space technologies have remained largely closed to public participation as the preserve of technical, industrial, political – and, in future possibly, simply wealthy – elites.

A Critical Theoretic approach to space technologies can precisely be attuned to the ways in which such technologies have tended to be predicated on such restricted pools of decision-making and participation, and to the ways in which utopian visions for the future developments of technologies have been part and parcel of the space age. At the same time it can also help highlight the ways in which the range of 'users' of space technologies has widened significantly in recent decades, as well as the role of these technologies in developing our understanding of how the social world works and how the Earth is changing over time. In that sense, space technologies allow for different 'potentialities' (in Feenberg's terms) and enable different visions of the world, even as they arguably exemplify (literally and figuratively) what Feenberg calls 'the *paradox of reform from above*' (1991: 65, emphasis in original): that is, space technologies might be argued to constitute a case in which the design of such technologies to suit the purposes of hegemonic elites means that 'technology is not neutral but fundamentally biased […] all action undertaken within its framework tends to reproduce that hegemony' (ibid.). In that sense, the goal of 'repurposing' space technologies towards a more inclusive and participatory ethos, as discussed above, appears particularly challenging. But the use of space technologies in, for example, viewing, sensing and informing human understanding of climate change as a set of processes affecting the planet as a whole (including the human species) might yet lend sustenance to Feenberg's invitation to consider that 'current scientific and technical knowledge has resources for a very radical reconstruction of the technological heritage if these are appropriated in the right spirit' (1991: 19). In that sense at least, it might be plausible to argue that space technologies remain 'suspended between different possibilities'.

Notes

1 'Outer space' is, in common usage, understood as the physical space beyond the Earth's atmosphere. Although the definition of where the Earth's atmosphere 'ends' and outer space 'begins' is a more complex matter (for discussion, see Strauss 2013), for purposes of

brevity the chapter uses the term 'space' interchangeably with the common definition of outer space (which is as assumed in the Outer Space Treaty that entered into force in October 1967) and 'space technologies' to refer to technologies that enter outer space. United Nations General Assembly, 'Treaty on Principles Governing the Activities of States in the Exploration and Use of Outer Space, Including the Moon and other Celestial Bodies', available at www.unoosa.org/oosa/en/ourwork/spacelaw/treaties/out erspacetreaty.html Accessed 31 July 2015).

2   Public domain or 'common'.
3   Outer Space Treaty 1967: Preamble; Article I; Article II.
4   Initially in Feenberg 1991, cited here as the original formulation, and then later in updated form in Feenberg 1999, 2002; see also Chapter 4 in this volume.
5   The term often used in the Soviet Union and still in Russia and some other post-Soviet states to denote the conflict on the Eastern front in World War II between 1941 and 1945.
6   For an overview and discussion see Peoples (2009).
7   Among others, in the case of the US, see Benjamin (2004) and Sage (2014); in the case of the Soviet Union, the multiple contributions to Andrews and Siddiqi (2011).
8   'Earth from a million miles away: Dscovr satellite sends groundbreaking photo', *The Guardian*, 21 July 2015, available at: www.theguardian.com/science/2015/jul/21/ea rth-from-a-million-miles-away-dscovr-satellite-returns-groundbreaking-picture.
9   See also Dodge and Perkins (2009) and other contributions to the same journal special issue.

References

Andrews, James T. and Asif A. Siddiqi. 2011. Introduction: Space Exploration in the Soviet Context. In James T. Andrews and Asif A. Siddiqi (eds) *Into the Cosmos: Space Exploration and Soviet Culture*. Pittsburgh, PA: University of Pittsburgh Press.

Benjamin, Marina. 2004. *Rocket Dreams: How the Space Age Shaped our Vision of a World Beyond*. London: Vintage.

Brannon, Monica M. 2013. Standardized Spaces: Satellite Imagery in the Age of Big Data. *Configurations* 21: 271–299.

Cloud, John. 2001. Imaging the World in a Barrel: CORONA and the Clandestine Convergence of the Earth Sciences. *Social Studies of Science* 31: 231–251.

Corry, Olaf. 2013. *Constructing a Global Polity: Theory, Discourse and Governance*. Basingstoke: Palgrave Macmillan.

Cosgrove, Denis. 1994. Contested Global Visions: One-World, Whole-Earth and the Apollo Space Photographs, *Annals of the Association of American Geographers* 84: 270–294.

Cosgrove, Denis. 2001. *Apollo's Eye: A Cartographic Genealogy of the Earth in Western Imagination*. Baltimore, MA: Johns Hopkins University Press.

Crampton, Jeremy W. 2003. Cartographic Rationality and the Politics of Geosurveillance and Security, *Cartography and Geographic Information Science* 30: 135–148.

Crampton, Jeremy W. 2010. *Mapping: A Critical Introduction to Cartography and GIS*. Oxford: Blackwell.

DeGroot, Gerard. 2007. *Dark Side of the Moon: The Magnificent Madness of the American Lunar Quest*. London: Jonathan Cape.

Deibert, Ronald J.. 2003. Unfettered Observation: The Politics of Earth Monitoring from Space. In W. Henry Lambright (ed.) *Space Policy in the Twenty-First Century*. Baltimore, MD: Johns Hopkins University Press.

Deudney, Daniel. 1985. Forging Missiles into Spaceships, *World Policy Journal* 2: 271–303.

Dodge, Martin and Chris Perkins. 2009. The "view from nowhere?" Spatial Politics and Cultural Significance of High-Resolution Satellite Imagery, *Geoforum* 40: 497–501.

Dolman, Everett C. 2002. *Astropolitik: Classical Geopolitics in the Space Age*. Portland, OR: Frank Cass.

Duvall, Raymond and Jonathan Havercroft. 2008. Taking Sovereignty out of this World: Space Weapons and Empire of the Future, *Review of International Studies* 34: 755–775.

Edwards, Paul N. 1996. *The Closed World: Computers and the Politics of Discourse in Cold War America*. Cambridge, MA: MIT Press.

Feenberg, Andrew. 1991. *Critical Theory of Technology*. Oxford: Oxford University Press.

Feenberg, Andrew. 1999. *Questioning Technology*. London: Routledge.

Feenberg, Andrew. 2002. *Transforming Technology: A Critical Theory Revisited*. Oxford: Oxford University Press.

Ferster, Warren. 2014. US Government Eases Restrictions on DigitalGlobe, online, available at: http://spacenews.com/40874us-government-eases-restrictions-on-digitalglobe/. Accessed 31 July 2015.

Garber. 2007. Sputnik and the Dawn of the Space Age, online, available at http://history.na sa.gov/sputnik/ Accessed 31 July 2015.

Geospatial Revolution Project 2015. Geospatial Revolution, online, available at: http://geospatialrevolution.psu.edu/project/index.html. Accessed 31 July 2015.

Harvey, Brian. 2004. *China's Space Program: From Conception to Manned Space Flight*. Chichester: Springer-Praxis.

Johnson-Freese, Joan. 2007. *Space as a Strategic Asset*. New York: Columbia University Press.

Kaminski, Amy Paige. 2012. Can the Demos Make a Difference? Prospects for Participatory Democracy in Shaping the Future Course of US Space Exploration, *Space Policy*, 28: 225–233.

Kaminski, Amy Paige. 2016. What Place for the People? The Role of the Public and NGOs in Space Innovation and Governance. In Cenan Al-Ekabi, Blandina Baranes, Peter Hulsroj and Arne Lahcen (eds) *Yearbook on Space Policy 2014: The Governance of Space*. Vienna: Springer.

Kay, W.D. 1994. Democracy and Super Technologies: The Politics of the Space Shuttle and Space Station Freedom, *Science, Technology and Human Values* 19: 131–151.

Kennedy, John F. 1962. Text of President John Kennedy's Rice Stadium Moon Speech, online, available at: http://er.jsc.nasa.gov/seh/ricetalk.htm. Accessed 31 July 2015.

Kurgan, Laura. 2013. *Close Up at a Distance*. New York: Zone Books.

Litfin, Karen T. 1998. Satellites and Sovereign Knowledge: Remote Sensing of the Global Environment. In Karen T. Litfin (ed.) *The Greening of Sovereignty in World Politics*. Cambridge MA: MIT Press.

Litfin, Karen T.. 1999. The Status of the Statistical State: Satellites and the Diffusion of Epistemic Sovereignty, *Global Society* 13: 95–116.

Mindell, David A. 2011. *Digital Apollo: Human and Machine in Spaceflight*. Cambridge, MA: MIT Press.

Moltz, James Clay. 2014. *Crowded Orbits: Conflict and Cooperation in Space*. New York: Columbia University Press.

Mueller, Karl P. 2003. Totem and Taboo: Depolarizing the Space Weapons Debate, *Astropolitics* 1: 4–28.

NASA. 2013a. Earthrise, online, available at: www.nasa.gov/multimedia/imagegallery/ima ge_feature_1249.html. Accessed 31 July 2015.

NASA. 2013b. Space Debris and Human Spacecraft, online, available at: www.nasa.gov/m ission_pages/station/news/orbital_debris.html. Accessed 31 July 2015.

NASA. 2015a. NASA's New Horizons "Phones Home" Safe after Pluto Flyby, online, available at: www.nasa.gov/press-release/nasas-new-horizons-phones-home-safe-after-p luto-flyby. Accessed 31 July 2015.

NASA. 2015b. Professor Stephen Hawking Congratulates the NASA New Horizons Team, online, available at: www.nasa.gov/. Accessed 31 July 2015.

NASA. 2015c. The Blue Marble from Apollo 17, online, available at: http://visibleearth.nasa.gov/view.php?id=55418. Accessed 31 July 2015.

NASA. 2015d. NASA Open Source Software Development, online, available at www.nasa.gov/open/plan/open-source-development_prt.htm. Accessed 31 July 2015.

NGA [National Geospatial Intelligence Agency]. 2013. Four Steps of the Geospatial Preparation of the Environment, online, available at: www1.nga.mil/Pages/default.aspx Accessed 9 July 2013.

NOAA [National Oceanic and Atmospheric Administration]. 2015a. NASA Satellite Camera Provides "Epic" View of the Earth, online, available at: www.nasa.gov/press-release/nasa-satellite-camera-provides-epic-view-of-earth. Accessed 31 July 2015.

NOAA [National Oceanic and Atmospheric Administration]. 2015b. What is Geodesy, online, available at http://oceanservice.noaa.gov/facts/geodesy.html. Accessed 31 July 2015.

Ó'Tuathail, Gearoid. 1999. De-Territorialised Threats and Global Dangers: Geopolitics and Risk Society. In David Newman (ed.) *Boundaries, Territory and Postmodernity*. London: Frank Cass, 1999.

Peoples, Columba. 2008a. 'Sputnik and "skill thinking" Revisited: Technological Determinism in American Responses to the Soviet Missile Threat', *Cold War History* 8: 55–76.

Peoples, Columba. 2008b. Assuming the Inevitable? Overcoming the Inevitability of Outer Space Weaponization and Conflict, *Contemporary Security Policy* 29: 502–520.

Peoples, Columba. 2009. Haunted Dreams: Critical Theory, Technology, and the Militarization of Space. In Natalie Bormann and Michael Sheehan (eds) *Securing Outer Space*. London: Routledge.

Peoples, Columba. 2016. Envisioning "Global Security"? The Earth Viewed from Outer Space as a Motif in Security Discourses. In Rens van Munster and Casper Sylvest (eds) *The Politics of Globality since 1945: Assembling the Planet*. Abingdon: Routledge.

Phipps, Clare. 2015. Pluto: New Horizons Probe Makes Contact with Earth, *The Guardian*, 15 July, online, available at: www.theguardian.com/science/2015/jul/15/new-horizons-pluto-probe-makes-contact-with-earth. Accessed 31 July 2015.

Pickles, John. 1995. Representations in an Electronic Age: Geography, GIS, and Democracy. In John Pickles (ed.) *Ground Truth: The Social Implications of Geographic Information Systems*. London: Guilford Press.

Poole, Robert. 2008. *Earthrise: How Man First Saw the Earth*. New Haven, CT: Yale University Press.

Sage, Daniel. 2014. *How Outer Space Made America: Geography, Organization and the Cosmic Sublime*. Farnham: Ashgate.

Sheehan, Michael. 2007. *The International Politics of Space*. Abingdon: Routledge.

Slotten, Hugh R. 2002. Satellite Communications, Globalization and the Cold War, *Technology and Culture* 43: 315–350.

SpaceX. 2015. About SpaceX, online, available at: www.spacex.com/about. Accessed 31 June 2015.

Strauss, Michael J. 2013. Boundaries in the Sky and a Theory of Three-Dimensional States, *Journal of Borderland Studies* 28: 369–382.

Sylvester, Roshanna P. 2011. She Orbits over the Sex Barrier: Soviet Girls and the Tereshkova Moment. In James T. Andrews and Asif A. Siddiqi (eds) *Into the Cosmos: Space Exploration and Soviet Culture*. Pittsburgh, PA: University of Pittsburgh Press.

van Munster, Rens and Casper Sylvest (eds). 2016. *The Politics of Globality since 1945: Assembling the Planet*. Abingdon: Routledge.

Virgin Galactic. 2015a. 'Who We Are', online, available at: www.virgingalactic.com/who-we-are/. Accessed 31 July 2015.

Virgin Galactic. 2015b. 'Why We Go', online, available at: www.virgingalactic.com/why-we-go/. Accessed 31 July 2015.

Wall, Mike. 2013. Ticket Price for Private Spaceflights on Virgin Galactic's SpaceShipTwo Going Up, online, available at: www.space.com/20886-virgin-galactic-spaceshiptwo-ticket-prices.html. Accessed 31 July 2015.

White, Frank. 1998. *The Overview Effect: Space Exploration and Human Evolution*, 2nd edition. Reston, VA: American Institute of Aeronautics and Astronautics.

11

THE GEOPOLITICS OF EXTINCTION

From the Anthropocene to the Eurocene

Jairus Victor Grove

We humans, as defined by late moderns, are in desperate need of an ecological approach to global politics. By ecological I mean a form of analysis characterized by multi-species encounters and deep relational processes across geographical scales, rather than a form of political thinking that relies on discreteness, causality, and human agency. Hence an ecological approach does not center principally on the environment, what in International Relations is called Environmental Security; nor does it limit global politics to states, international organizations, social movements, or even humans. Instead, I take ecology to mean that all things that make a difference in the vast landscape of global security ought to be included in the geopolitical considerations of contemporary life.

From this ecological perspective, geopolitics has culminated in a planetary epoch in which a particular *anthropos* is capable of making a 'cene.'[1] However, I think the Anthropocene as a philosophical and political crisis has been too quick to forget the geopolitical arrangements of power and violence that have brought us to this point. Not all of 'us' have played an equal part in the making of either the *anthropos* or the Anthropocene. In part, the often narrow focus on climate change and the fever pitch of the contemporary crisis erases the Euro-American role in building and maintaining the current world order. The argument often advanced by great powers and environmentalists alike amounts to 'now that everything is broken it is everyone's problem so pointing fingers just gets in the way of a solution.' Even critical and posthumanist approaches often lose sight of the role of hegemony and power. This is, in part, because of the effort of those lines of thought to decenter the human as the sole locus of thinking, and action is a necessary but insufficient maneuver. This chapter attempts to relax the focus on a narrow human world while holding onto the very specific human, and often national, assemblages that broke this planet.

I do not think I am alone in wanting to open up to the global magnitude of what confronts the planet. And yet in this chapter I want to do so without losing sight of the real differences in politics, geography, history, meaning, and cosmology that modulate how each one of us will confront the end of this epoch. In so doing, I hope to emphasize a refrain that the end of the world is never the end of everything. An apocalypse is always more and less than an extinction; and whatever makes a life out of the mess we are currently in will depend in some ways on how we come to understand the contemporary condition. Ideas matter even if they cannot save us. Stories, explanations, and philosophical adventures are the best of what the human estate has to offer. No matter how desperate things get, someone will still ask why this is happening, and we will share in that question the possibility of thinking together. As William Connolly often says, 'we are distinctive but not unique', and that distinctiveness is connected to a sense of wonder – even when it is a dark wonder.

As we explore the dark fascination with the futures of our species, the catastrophic inadequacy of our dominate form of life becomes more and more apparent. The dominant forms of planetary life display an obsession with warfare and order – part technological hubris, part ecological sabotage – and have ripped their way through every continent on the planet, making a geological mark we could best call the Eurocene. The making of this epoch, the Eurocene, has been created by no single class or nation, much less by a clearly defined agenda. An aggregating and heterogeneous collection of people, things, perspectives, hatreds, malignancies, and creeping global expansions has unleashed our contemporary condition. We live in a moment imperiled by an immature giganticism. All of us experience this moment differently, but a rare few can escape even for a moment the degree to which a weight impinges upon us all. We live in an apocalyptic era unequally created by a minority bent on the accumulation of wealth and a self-interested regenerating political order. However, the 'we' that will bear the burden of this 500-year project of rationalized exploitation is much vaster and includes bumble bees, humpback whales, poison arrow frogs, Hawaiians, wolves, Micronesians, African-Americans, the inhabitants of Flint, Michigan, Syrians, Mayans, Queers, Christians, Muslims, Atheists, Transhumanists, Hipsters, Shamans, Entrepreneurs, homeless veterans, war orphans, albatrosses, elephants …

Unfortunately there is no high ground from which the entire moving arrangement can be seen. Every perspective obscures and reveals some larger or smaller part of the story of how 'we' broke the world. The scale; when? where? magnitude? how long? The connection between each unfolding catastrophe or history of venal will-to-power and presumed superiority shares a connection but not an identifiable cause or choke point that can be isolated and targeted from the heights of rational abstraction. My perspective, my point of view, is from the United States of America, maybe the second to last empire. The U.S. is where I find myself, and it is also where I belong, despite my best efforts to gain distance from such a horrifically destructive and arrogant form of life. To be American is not merely to be a citizen of the U.S.A. It is, rather, to be part of a precarious mixture of European industrial and demographic expansion, a home-grown sense of Christian providence, Liberal institutional development, and a ruthless martial art of extermination and settlement that has continued unabated since its founding. It is in this context that I will try to explore what I think is the character of contemporary geopolitics. For me, in the dying light of the American empire, we face a last great planetary struggle for homogenization.

The character of global extinction: the Anthropocene as geopolitical fact

I would sum up my fear about the future in one word: boring. And that's my one fear: that everything has happened; nothing exciting or new or interesting is ever going to happen again … the future is just going to be a vast, conforming suburb of the soul.

(J.G. Ballard in Vale and Juno 1984: n.p.)

In a world that encourages uniformity, that judges values by their utility, perhaps these animals like so many of their kind, also, are doomed to disappear in favor of some more commercially useful species. Yet, I cannot avoid a bitter sense of loss that, we, born to a world that still held these creatures, are being robbed of a priceless inheritance, a life that welcomes diversity not sameness, that treasures astonishment and wonder instead of boredom.

(Jacques Cousteau)[2]

Every day we are told things are worse than we thought. Sea level rise is happening faster than we thought; species are disappearing faster than we thought; the possibilities for reversal are slimmer and slimmer. And the proposals for human survival gaining traction – geoengineering, the centrally managed super-cities of Stewart Brand's Eco-Modernist manifesto, space colonization, becoming digital beings – resemble the wonders of thriving planetary life less and less (Asafu-Adjaye et al. 2016).[3] On April 20, 2016 *The Washington Post* headline read 'And then we wept.'[4] The news was in and it wasn't good. The Great Barrier Reef, the Amazon rainforest of the world's oceans, was 93 percent bleached. The coral foundation of its vast ecosystem was dead or dying (Mooney 2016). A year to the day before this announcement we were told that the northern white rhino was extinct.[5] The last white rhino, a male named Sudan, is now kept under guard from poachers 24 hours a day, but no army or protection is sufficient for survival as there is no mate remaining. The young men carrying machine guns are Sudan's only company as he waits to perish, a task thoroughly accelerated by human desires for horn.

Each event – a global reef system in Australia, the loss of a singular species in central Kenya, a slow shift in ocean levels – exists in an interregnum between the brutal facts of existence through which all things must pass and the crisis of our contemporary moment that the cycle of passing and renewal has been interrupted by the metabolic rift of modern human animals. Which trajectory we are facing is unclear. Is the sixth great extinction upon us? The difficulty in classifying extinctions is differentiating a normal rise, decline, and extinction of species against which to compare and periodize 'events' of catastrophic and lethal acceleration. Even the five great extinctions took place over unfathomable periods of time.[6] In all of the great extinctions, 'events' are hundreds of thousands of years long. Furthermore, the incomplete nature of the fossil record makes population sampling very difficult. One has to figure out ways to reliably distinguish between whether the absence of evidence is indeed evidence or merely the absence of evidence.

After extensive review of excavations worldwide over at least 150 years of research, one can estimate what is called the 'background' extinction rate. This is the expected rate of species loss over a given period of time. This rate is not definitive. At best, it is a kind of working rule of thumb. That being said, the academic debates over whether or not the current rate of extinction exceeds any version of the background rate is like two kids on the Empire State Building bickering over whether it is the fall that kills you or the certain impact at the bottom (Rockstrom et al. 2009). Even conservative estimates put the loss of species across the plant and animal kingdom at thousands of times the background rate from earlier human and pre-human eras. To put it another way, even if the most conservative estimates are right, we are in real trouble. Thanks to habitat loss and the chytrid fungus, the amphibian extinction rate is 45,000 times higher than the background rate. Amphibians survived four of the five great extinction events in Earth's history, yet one generation of human travel has spiked amphibian extinction rates above what was caused by multiple asteroid impacts, super volcanoes, cataclysmic climate oscillations, and a collision with a comet (Kolbert 2014). In an irony only humans will appreciate, the current apocalypse is marked by a noticeable lack of raining frogs.

Amphibians are not alone in the race to extinction. As recounted by Elizabeth Kolbert (2014), one-third of all reef-building corals, one-third of all freshwater mollusks, one-third of sharks and rays, one-fourth of all mammals, one-fifth of all reptiles, and one-sixth of all bird species are disappearing. What makes this particular era of disappearances unique is not just the rate of extinction but also the distribution. The entire ocean is facing unprecedented instability (Roach 2006).[7] Furthermore, extinctions are occurring globally, even in those areas spared heavy industrialization and development.

While climate change is unlikely to help, the current amphibian apocalypse is driven almost entirely by the human-induced movement of people and things around the planet.[8] The chytrid fungus now affecting the majority of the planet is responsible for mass die-offs of amphibians, depriving them of oxygen and causing heart attacks. While climate change should certainly be central to global political agendas, the already occurring sixth great extinction calls into question more than just the dependence on fossil fuels. Climate change is one manifestation of our global ecological crisis. From the perspective of those forms of life being wiped off the planet, the entire rhythm and circulation of just-in-time globalization enforced by great power navies – one of the most defining characteristics of the Eurocene – is threatening. In so far as an environmental agenda has gained political currency since the mid-1990s, no political party or significant constituency takes seriously the proposition that global travel should come to an end. Freedom of movement is almost unquestionably championed by liberal societies; those that do challenge it are often reactionaries and xenophobes, not environmentalists.

Since the first slow and then accelerating egress from Africa, humans have spread to every continent on the planet. That movement once resembled something like the linearity of osmosis but has reached, for some in the elite, terminal velocity. There are now humans that live in constant motion on permanent-residence cruise ships to avoid taxes, and there is a global class of anxious airport-hopping business elite that resides in no place in particular.[9] The latter are so allergic to friction slowing their circulation that even in this age of security and checkpoints they have been granted special routes and forms of identification to avoid the coagulation of administration now managing planetary circuits (Salter and Mutlu 2012).

This is just one example of how liberal practices come up against McKenzie Wark's reworking of what Marx calls metabolic rift. For Wark, following Marx, the advent of labor which freed humans from the animal world also put humans out of synch with natural process. The result is that humans to be human require too much food, water, and energy for natural cycles to fulfill (Wark 2015: 4). There is no version of the contemporary order that can be egalitarian and sustainable. Disposable consumer-based economies cannot scale for any length of time. So in some sense Wark and Marx are right. The cycles of the Earth and much of its inhabitants are out of synch with humans and their love of labor. For Wark, in particular, this leaves little else to do but accept that any viable human project will have to embrace geoengineering and even space colonization alongside other efforts to build a 'post-scarcity society.' However such concepts should be made more precise in identifying the particular forms of life that are at odds with or exceed multi-species ecological feedback. If humanity is to find itself in another dark age, rather than a unified global project for environmental management there are many possible ways of living that could be sustained within the dynamic equilibrium of earth systems. But the point stands. If we remain within the currently restricted vision of the future of global culture – an America for everyone – the adaptive character of even large Earth systems, such as the hydrologic cycle,[10] will collapse or enter periods of extreme turbulence. To put this another way, the ought of the cosmopolitanism 'good' and the ecological are not consonant.

However you feel about transnational capitalism, it is indisputable that the uninterrupted movement of things and people around the planet comes at an extraordinarily high cost to human animals and non-human animals alike. This is at times difficult to discern as the human population steadily increases and the world seems suffuse with living things. Therefore the problem of the current crisis is not reducible solely to some aggregate of living biomass. What is being lost is the diversity of life that inspires wonder. Apocalypses are not primarily about extinction – they are irreversible transformations.

The often misguided debates over climate change capture this problem quite acutely. In fact, despite how difficult it is to admit that the deniers of anthropogenic climate change may be half right, they are correct that fluctuations are a normal part of the Earth's history.[11] However, what sustains the conservative bent of this claim is the sense of providence that the full argument entails. Those who champion adaptation and 'natural' fluctuation trade on the presumption that the Earth adapts and fluctuates for *us*. Fluctuations will occur and creatures will adapt, but in the past that has meant everything from a world of only single-celled anaerobic bacteria to vast seas of virtually nothing but trilobites. Climate denialism is, ironically, no less anthropocentric than many of its scientifically validated opponents.

The peril of similarity: or, the great homogenization

In addition to extinction level events, the Earth has also experienced a number of monoculture events – that is epochs of great homogenization. Whether by reptiles, plants, or humans, domination by one species has resulted in collapses *and* explosions in creature diversity. It is not without precedent that one form of life could predominate and even spawn a new earthly order, as in the Cambrian explosion 540 million years ago, considered by most geologists as the most innovative period of evolution. The great transformation of the planet by photosynthesis provides another salient example. However, the terraforming accomplished by plants is not likely to be repeated by humans unless an incipient form of life that thrives in a carbon-rich, hot, radioactive, dioxin-saturated environment comes to take over the planet. And even then it is not just the warmer temperature or toxic nature of the Anthropocene that is dangerous to life. Periods of rapid warming and novel additions to the atmosphere have often caused violent feedback such as rapid cooling or, in some cases, ocean stagnation from the loss of ocean currents and upwelling. In such cases the cascading die-offs of creatures great and small can themselves tweak and shift vast planetary cycles in new directions of amplifying and intensifying destructiveness or creativity, depending on the inheritors of the new dynamic equilibrium (Benton 2008).

The problem is also that humans are not innovating or undergoing speciation to fill the gaps left by other forms-of-life, as dinosaurs once did. Diversity is collapsing within the human species as well. Most languages and most ways of life outside the narrow scope of Euro-America are disappearing at an accelerating rate. According to linguist David Harrison (2007) and a number of other linguists working at UNESCO, of the 6,912 languages currently spoken worldwide, fewer than half of them will survive the twenty-first century.

Language extinction is not the loss of words. According to Harrison, each language contains a different cognitive map of the human brain. This claim cannot be overstated. In an example from Harrison's research amongst the Urarina people of Peru, some languages, although very few, place the object of the sentence at the beginning. The action and subject are grammatically organized by the object. According to Harrison (2007: 19):

Urarina places the direct object first, the verb second, and the subject last ... Were it not for Urarina and a few other Amazonian languages, scientists might not even suspect it were possible. They would be free to hypothesize – falsely – that O-V-S word order was cognitively impossible, that the human brain could not process it. Each new grammar pattern we find sheds light on how the human brain creates language. The loss of even one language may forever close the door to a full understanding of human cognitive capacity.

Given the bloody philosophical war that has been waged over the relationship between humans and the objects in the external world they encounter for the entire history of recorded thought, linguistic worlds such as the Urarina's represent possibilities that decades of critique may not be grammatically equipped to produce. Given how bound up our current political and ecological disasters are with the problem of objectification, or why we treat objects so badly, this might be important.

In order to consider Harrison's provocation fully, we have to give up on the idea that there is some kind of formal isomorphism in the basement of all languages. There is no meta-language. Instead, Harrison says, 'languages are self-organizing systems that evolve complex nested structures and rules for how to put the parts of words or sentences together' (2007: 249). Rather than think of language as the way that humans master the world, Harrison says, it is language 'that has colonized our brains' (2007: 225). After a life spent trying to record and hold on to as many of the disappearing languages around the world as possible, Harrison argues that every language is a singular 'accretion of many centuries of human thinking about time, seasons, sea creatures, reindeer, flowers, mathematics, landscapes, myths, music, infinity, cyclicity, the unknown, and the everyday' (2007: viii).

Furthermore, the loss of languages is not an issue of 'multiculturalism.' The loss is not just one of a way of life, like being a hipster, an activist, or an academic: it is the extinction of a form-of-life. With each language that dies we lose a glimpse of the cosmos never to be repeated. As Agamben (2000) has said of the form-of-life, it is a set of practices and conditions of being that is inseparable from being biologically alive. Few cases capture the inextricable relationship between life and living like those groups that have survived 500 years of colonial expansion intact in the forests of Brazil.[12] As they have successfully postponed the virulence of the European world of disease, exposure to 'us' (global culture) will mean certain death. With no inherited immunity, these groups will return to the soil with their cosmic perspective. The primary cause of the displacement of uncontacted peoples in Brazil is logging and drug violence, both part of globalization.

I should be clear about what I mean by 'perspective.' A perspective is not a 'point of view' in the postmodern trivial sense, as if there is no truth and only an 'opinion of the truth.' This kind of consumerist 'common-sense' post-modernism is a dead end. By perspective, I mean what anthropologist Eduardo Viveiros de Castro calls radical perspectivism, whereby the selves of a host of different entities – jaguars, rocks, uncontacted peoples, plants – all experience and theorize the world in heterogeneous alliances not reducible to each other, much less as something like ideology or belief. According to Castro, what we find in comparative cosmologies are the possibilities of human–nature relations that are no less real or material than Western scientific observations, but that organize the world around *feritas* ('wildness') rather than *humanitas* ('culture, humanity') (Viveiros de Castro 1992: 29).

Given how self-destructive and inevitable Euro-American anthropocentrism often feels in contemporary modern life, forms-of-life organized otherwise are more than just curiosities. Instead, other cosmologies and the languages that dwell in them offer the possibility of radical mutation. In the case of French thinker Tristan Garcia, this mutation is an adventure in philosophy and metaphysics that refuses to accept subject/object and human/non-human binaries as inevitable problems of cognition. Instead, Garcia traces what some have called a flat ontology or a way of being where each human is in an egalitarian, give-and-take relationship with things, animals, and other humans for creating meaning about the world. The superiority and sovereignty of self-consciousness for making meaning in the world is ditched to explore something else entirely (Garcia 2014: 221–223).

Garcia's work draws on a minor Continental tradition of philosophy, but it is difficult to imagine the inspired escape from 'the metaphysics of access' in favor of the dignity of things without the cosmologies of Amerindians or without Castro's role as a kind of inter-cosmology diplomat.[13] Consequently, as the linguistic and cosmological differences of the world flatten and merge, it is not just 'background' loss or functional survival of the fittest that is taking place. Humans as the sole inheritors of the hominid legacy are experiencing catastrophic loss, a kind of internal hollowing out. The ecological crisis reaches deep into our material and mental constitutions.

The destruction of perspectives – whether it is those of poison dart frogs, sawfish, Navajo speakers, mpingo trees, bluefin tuna, isolated people of the Brazilian rainforest whose names belong to them alone, or artists and philosophers forced to abandon their creativity in favor of brain-dulling precarious labor – leaves this world less interesting and less complex than it was before. With each loss of these forms-of-life we lose not just a diversity of opinions about the universe, but distinctive practices of tilling the earth, water management, creativity, revolutionary thinking, aquaculture, human–animal ecologies as well as political and ethical practices (Goldberg–Hiller and Silva 2011). More than mere 'points of view,' forms-of-life carry with them means for inhabiting the Earth that in some cases far exceed the mono-technological thinking of contemporary global development. Homogenization entails a restriction of our socio-technical horizons. To be clear, these vital practices are not restricted to the human estate, but also include the North American beaver's river management practices and their ability to combat soil erosion,[14] the duties of megafauna and apex predators to keep grazing creatures on the move and thus prevent overconsumption in prairie ecologies (Manning 2009), and on and on. The expanse of possible human–non-human alliances lost in the singularity of our current apocalypse is unknowable in an unusual way. Each lost alliance or form of life means a future that can no longer come about. The geopolitical advance of homogenization is killing futures as it strangles the present.

Transformation, transcendence, or more of the same: the geopolitics of geoengineering?

Rather than inspire responses adequate to the crisis at hand, Euro-American humans are in large part fighting to continue exactly as we are. For many scientists and modernists, the critical question is how to maintain extraordinarily high levels of economic growth and consumption because they see these practices as necessary conditions for human advancement and innovation. Inheritors of the cybernetics movement of the 1950s, called 'systems thinkers,' see management and governance of the entire Earth system as the next logical step. For many systems thinkers and Ecomodernists, what it is to be human is to alter our environment. Therefore, each step forward means taking greater control of the world around us. The most emblematic of these thinkers was Buckminster Fuller, whose 1968 cult classic *Operating Manual for Spaceship Earth* advocated that the whole planet be seen as a ship that humans must learn to steer just as they learned to navigate the oceans or grow crops.

The next generation of systems theorists came of age at the beginning of the computer revolution in the 1970s when the capability for truly planetary systems management seemed to be on the horizon. Stewart Brand was one of the leaders of that movement, and founded a journal called *Whole Earth Review* which sought to be a forum for planet-wide guided evolution. It is not surprising that, given the interest in engineering and global development, news of the limits of growth would be met with calls for transcending those limits rather than trying to live within them. For Brand and other more explicitly industrial geo–engineers like David Keith, who has become an outspoken advocate for industrial intervention in earth systems, the only solution to the Anthropocene can only be found in its cause – human engineering. To quote the title of a recent article by Keith, the hope is located in the question 'can science succeed where politics has failed?'[15] For Keith and Brand in particular the hope is building what Brand and his collaborators calls in their *Ecomodernist Manifesto* 'A Good Anthropocene' (Asafu–Adjaye et al. 2016). Following proposals made by biologist E.O. Wilson and others, Brand and his team suggest setting aside half of the planet to be rewilded. To do so the management of both human and non-human populations must be greatly intensi-fied to accomplish what Ecomodernists call decoupling. According to the team of mostly Harvard and Oxford scientists working with Brand, modernity has greatly lessened the impact of humans on natural systems. Industrial-style agriculture, nuclear energy, and most of all urbanization reduce the dependence of humans on the environment at large. Following their argument, if humans can be herded entirely into super-cities and human access to the rest of the planet can be restric-ted, then a renewal of the natural world can take place. Food, energy, and other natural resources will then have to be produced by synthetic means made possible by advances in materials engineering such as nanotechnology and extreme forms of recycling which would reprocess and disaggregate all human waste into base materials to be used again.

According to Ecomodernists, if we can let go of the idea that non-modern civilizations 'lived more lightly on the Earth' then we can concentrate and accelerate the *advantages* of highly industrialized societies for the rest of the planet's human population. The Manifesto asserts that 'even developing countries [can] achieve modern living standards' (Asafu-Adjaye et al. 2016). The externalities of these lifestyles, such as carbon emissions which cannot be contained within cities, will have to be ameliorated through vast planet-wide interventions. Solar shielding to regulate sunlight, Albedo modification to alter the color and reflectivity of clouds, mechanical carbon capture and storage, even planet shields of old compact discs are proposed as permanent features of future human existence and governance such that humans and the rest of nature can share a planet while no longer sharing a world. The optimistic version is that these more extreme means of planetary regulation can be replaced in a few hundred years when nuclear power and maybe other alternatives can create 'tens of terawatt' electrical output (Asafu-Adjaye et al. 2016). In a weird resonance with critiques by Donna Haraway, Bruno Latour (1993), Philippe Descola, Jane Bennett (2010), William Connolly, and others who have effectively demonstrated that there is no 'nature' external to humans, Ecomodernists have conceded the point, declaring the need to invent precisely the human/non-human or culture/nature binary of modernist social theory via an unprecedented scale of global governance.

The political or governance side of the vision is significantly less developed than the technical components of the manifesto. In regard to politics, the manifesto merely starts as a kind of disclaimer that: 'We value the liberal principles of democracy, tolerance, and pluralism in themselves, even as we affirm them as keys to achieving a great Anthropocene' (Asafu-Adjaye et al. 2016). So whereas the Manifesto sees a great deal of invention and change for the technical future of the species as a question of governance, history is over and global liberal democracy is its endpoint. Technical issues are not understood as politically charged; nor is this approach understood as a specific socio-technical response to the crisis of the Anthropocene designed to buttress a specific form of consumer capitalism (Keary 2016: 23–24). The existing limitations of 'real existing liberal democracy' are not addressed; nor are there experts on politics or governance included in the who's who of scientists committed to the Ecomodernist project. The challenges to a 'great Anthropocene,' as Brand calls it in the conclusion of the Manifesto, are technical rather than political, future oriented rather than historical, and universal-planetary-species rather than particular. Again, returning to Keith, the goal of Ecomodernism is for science to fix what politics cannot.

Jedediah Purdy (2015) in his book *After Nature: A Politics for the Anthropocene* attempts to fill in where the Ecomodernists have left off. Purdy similarly sees in the 'end of nature' the possibility for a new more equitable nature. Although he diverges from some Ecomodernists on how and to what extent rewilding and urbanization are key components in a good Anthropocene, Purdy shares the commitment that modernism and a break from nature are necessary for achieving survival and any egalitarian future. In a less technocentric vision of geoengineering and managed wild zones, Purdy proposes something like a Roosevelt revolution for resources and global democratic governance. In geoengineering and other technological forms of intervention in the means by which humans survive, Purdy sees the possibility of overcoming scarcity and competition that otherwise undermine democratic principles.

Like Brand and the Ecomodernists, Purdy sees the human character of the Anthropocene as an opportunity rather than just a catastrophe. If humans are capable of destroying the planet and altering the very material conditions of life, then they must be capable via collective action for altering the planet for good; and, like the Ecomodernists, the main obstacle to doing so is a naïve and nostalgic view of nature as 'untouched' or 'untouchable.' Once we accept that there is no nature as such we can better 'spare nature' and live more abundant lives on the planet. In some sense the scale of catastrophe is a kind of windfall as it creates a set of challenges worthy of and inciting a true democratic cosmopolitanism. Political interests in the Anthropocene are synonymous with human interests as planetary survival is at stake.

While global in consequence, the crisis we confront is not singularly global in origin and periodizes in very different ways than suggested by advocates of the Anthropocene. The attempts by Ecomodernists and Purdy alike to 'move on' from history are significantly dangerous for the prospects and success of their future visions for global abundance. The human-induced apocalypse when viewed with an emphasis on the effects of the 1492 landing in the Americas suggests that before the so-called 'great acceleration' after industrialization there is a particular geographic and political rather than species-wide character to the geological era. Advocates for renaming our 'cene' the Anthropocene focus too narrowly on climate change and too expansively when attributing to the whole species that catastrophic transformation of the Earth's atmosphere (Rockstrom et al. 2009). It is telling that so many of those who warn of the dangers of the Anthropocene so quickly use the same scientific evidence to make a case for the 'great powers' of the world to take control of the planet through geoengineering. Ecomodernist proposals both for our new geological epoch and the solution that follows closely with it fail to consider the importance of the geopolitics that have brought our planet to this moment – where nature itself appears as a question for not just human but also Euro-American governance. If we are to meaningfully take on the challenges, and even enemies, of our current apocalypse we must consider carefully the origins of the apocalypse we now face. To do so is to take seriously that there has never been an *anthropos* for which we can now discuss the geological consequences of something like a single human species. Rather, the Euro of the Eurocene designates a vanguard among the European people that developed a distinctively mechanistic view of matter, an oppositional relationship to nature, and a successive series of economic systems bases indebted to geographical expansion. The resulting political orders then measured success by how much wealth could be generated in the exploitation of peoples and resources. The Euro assemblage of hierarchies, racial superiorities, economies, peoples, animals, diseases, and global resettlement is reflected in the geological record. What Mackenzie Wark has called the Carbon Liberation Front was not a global phenomena but a way of technopolitics originating within a narrow geographic region of the world made global by force.[16] Properly named, our era is not the Anthropocene but the Eurocene.

Properly accounting for the origins of our ecological crisis is vital. No political project oriented toward the many possible futures stretching out before us can consider the questions of ecology and justice on a global, much less geological, scale unless we first take on the historical generality of the Anthropocene. The continuing project of Europeanization, now led by U.S. imperial power, is central in how the planet got to this point; and understanding this is essential for how any 'we' worthy of the plurality of the planet can invent something less nasty and brutish than what currently counts as order. A geological history and name that foregrounds the geopolitical confrontation that stands in the way of any such future is required to take the scale of our predicament seriously.

After all, the reason that we need to rename the last 500 or 175 years of the Holocene is based on two claims. The first is that there is significant material evidence on a global scale of human-induced change to the climate system. The second is that renaming the Holocene is essential to raising awareness that climate change and environmental change are more generally anthropogenic. Accuracy and consciousness-raising are the twin urges for renaming. On both counts we should reconsider what we mean by human.

First, the 'human' footprint is much more complex than just CO_2. I think we should do more than acknowledge the vast debates over the various contributions to the geological record, and at the very least consider that on a geological time-scale CO_2 concentration is relatively dwarfed by radioactivity, and comparable to the modern waste product par excellence – plastic.[17] Furthermore, if the claim is that the Anthropocene is meant to name the scale of human effect on the planet, it should include the ability to warm and cool the Earth, as the project of Europeanization has done both at remarkable levels of intensity.

Beginning in 1610, a mini-ice age took hold of the planet. The explanation for this, although debated, is that the 20 million or so people killed by the European invasion of the Americas resulted in vast reforestation of the North and South American continents. The providence that the Conquistadors spoke of was not the blessing of God but syphilis, influenza, and the number of other species that went along for the ride. The first waves of death were in some sense without malice; even if the Conquistadors had been 'friendly' they still would have been contagious. However, the well-armed explorers and settlers that leveraged the apocalypse for their own gain leave no doubt about whether the genocide and terraforming of the Americas was European in cause and intent. There is no way to know how many languages, cities, ideas, cosmologies, and ways of inhabiting the world were lost during the first waves of mass death. Yet we can observe their absence in the Orbis spike, or period of cooling, that took off after 1610 when a wilder arboreal nature took back what had been inhabited land.[18] This was a register of the altered socio-technical order that followed human-bacterial imperialism.

The history of nuclear weapons is more recent but no less lopsided. There is now a distinctive radioactive glow in the layers of earth since July 16, 1945. The bombing of the civilian populations in Hiroshima and Nagasaki is not the end of that story. In the years that followed, more than 2,053 nuclear weapons have been tested. Of those, 97.5 percent have been detonated by European powers. Those detonations do not appear as tests from the perspective of the Marshallese, Western Shoshone, or the thousands of 'downwinders' who experienced the aftermath of radioactivity carried by the shifting air pressures of the atmosphere. A 60-year nuclear war in the form of nuclear testing has spread cancer, incinerated sacred lands, and made other spaces uninhabitable on a temporal scale several orders of magnitude more significant than the 10,000-year lifespan of atmospheric CO_2. And what does the future hold? The nuclear powers of the Eurocene – the U.S., Russia, the U.K., France, and Israel – still maintain 97 percent of the 15,913 nuclear weapons on alert around the planet. Self-annihilation is still a very real possibility despite what would be inferred by the beleaguered state of the arms control agenda.

As for plastic, the Texas-sized trash gyres that swirl in the world's oceans are another reminder of what a cosmology of disposability and synthetic chemistry has wrought. Plastic may not have quite the longevity of CO_2 and irradiated earth, but for hundreds, maybe thousands of years it will continue to circulate, wreaking havoc throughout the food chain. It is hard to imagine the world that now squeezes the last few cents out of the poor with single-serve plastic shampoo pouches or bottled water that is needed because nearby streams have been sold to Coca-Cola without the post-World War II European project of development.

With the survival of the human race at stake, what difference can a concern for naming eras possibly serve? A recounting of the distinctively European history of our geological era is much more than polemical. The Eurocene is a practical problem, as it challenges the very paradigm of equality for a truly global society. For those like Purdy and Brand, who wish to democratize the Anthropocene, the problem of power is at the heart of the matter. Purdy writes: 'In the Anthropocene, environmental justice might also mean an equal role in shaping the future of the planet.'[19]

Contrary to Purdy, I want to suggest that anything resembling environmental justice, or any future at all, will require an unequal role in shaping the planet. In fact, the transformation of the global political system necessary for environmental justice will require significantly constraining, and even repressing, those powers that continue the political-geological project of the Eurocene. Environmental justice will require the kind of struggle taken up by W.E.B. DuBois and Frantz Fanon in the name of self-determination and anti-colonialism, but at a global rather than national scale.

On the eve of the creation of the United Nations at the Dumbarton Oaks conference, DuBois saw the failure of a dream before it had even been fully formed as a thought. DuBois (1975) saw that the vast new international body was little more than the institutionalization of what he called the global color line. The great powers had insisted upon a Security Council with veto powers and a General Assembly subordinate to its nuclear authority. The simple suggestion that the planet could be governed equally ignores that challenging vast systems of injustice will not be welcomed by those that benefit from exploitation. Continued settler-colonialism, continued primitive accumulation, and continued violent power politics all reap enormous rewards for the many in developed countries. To bring those interests to task will require a confrontation with a state-system guarded by great powers that still use 15,000 nuclear weapons to deter change, and now deploy swarms of drones to hunt down those too small for the nuclear option.

Purdy is wrong to say 'There is no political agent, community, or even movement on the scale of humanity's world-making decisions.'[20] The earth has global governance. We share a world governed by a few states with the capability of ending all life on the planet. Those states are, at the international scale, authoritarian in that they rule by economic violence and warfare. That some of those states are liberal democracies domestically is of little consequence to the rest of the world.

The importance of the Eurocene is, as the Anthropocene was intended, to more accurately describe the world we live in and raise awareness of just how unequally that world is and by what means the great homogenization is being carried out. No global environmental justice movement can address justice or the environment in a significant way if it does not take as its starting point our current global environmental crisis as a *geopolitical* crisis.

Purdy and, to a lesser extent, Brand are in a position intellectually and philosophically to take these dangers seriously, even if their policy proposal offers little opportunity for things to turn out otherwise. However there are fellow-travelers within the future-oriented Ecomodernist project that welcome this homogenization as if it were a kind of preordained convergence to truly live up to the promise of the human. For these outreaches of the geoengineering movement hyper-modernization is meant to buy time until the species can escape the planet or escape the organic character of the species. For these more overtly Promethean strains of geoengineering the 'downside' I identify in the trajectory of the Eurocene – total homogenization – is in fact also an opportunity. One such movement even uni-ronically calls its transcendent apocalypse *the singularity*. The Singularitarians follow the dream of Ray Kurzweil (2000), to become 'spiritual machines.' This view of the future finds its salvation in a free market *doxa* that sees human transformation in what is believed to be the limitless innovation of profit-driven market competition. Silicon Valley is now home to a kind of scientific think tank of capital investors and cutting-edge researchers eponymously named Singularity University that is dedicated to a future without limits. The bar napkin description from the website of this so-called university reads: 'Exponential Thinking, Abundance and How to

Create a Mind.'[21] In a perfect Singulatarian future the current ecological crisis will become obsolete because humans will no longer need anything to live other than the energy necessary to power the vast computer servers that will host our digital consciousness. Earthly concerns are treated as quaint and trivial compared to the vast potential of the human mind freed of death and decay. All of life reduced to data, all of experience reduced to knowledge.

It is important to take seriously that other technological lines of development have been marginalized, even driven extinct, not because they are less functional or less innovative but because a particularly abstracted and mechanistic view of technology grounded in the Western Enlightenment got lucky (Mumford 2010). To mistake the fortuitous contagion of 1492 with the superiority of *technē* is as much a failure of facts as ethics. Instead the contemporary line of technological innovation more closely resembles the trilobite explosion just before the Great Dying in which changes in the environment benefitted only one species. The vast homogenization and resulting monoculture resulted in the Earth's third major extinction event some 252 million years ago. The cult of innovation incentivized by the market follows a very limited set of ideas that have varied little since John von Neumann laid out his model of the computer in the 1940s. The computer explosion has followed von Neumann to his logical end but no further (Dyson 2012). The 'breakthroughs' since the early 1990s have basically been technical solutions to the contest between heat and processing speed. In almost eighty years we have not produced *another* computer, and we are already running up against the limits of physics in the advance of the diagram in which we are currently stuck.[22] At this particular moment, humans are like viruses that have plugged a very small number of technical diagrams into the engines of replication and production. As a result we are drowning in a deluge of obsolete cell phones and many other larger and smaller interfaces for computers that do not fundamentally differ from their replacements. Each device, tablet, smartphone, smartwatch, laptop, desktop, smart car, smart refrigerator, and drone is the same device with a different interface for the world. We live in an age of one technical device, the digital computer, and it has 1,000 faces. This is a sign of stagnation, not exponential innovation, a foreclosure by the embrace of the liberal capitalist singularity in modern world order.

Conclusion: an elegy for human transformation

Making his case for minor languages, Harrison questions the virtue and probability of a techno-singularity future:

> Perhaps we will grow plants in greenhouses and breed animals in laboratories and feed ourselves via genetic engineering. Perhaps there are no new medicines to be found in the rainforests. All such arguments appeal to ignorance: we do not know what we stand to lose as languages and technologies vanish because much or even most of it remains undocumented. So, it is a gamble to think that we will never avail ourselves of it in the future. Do we really want

to place so much faith in future science and pay so little heed to our inherited science?

(Harrison 2007: 55)

Rather than see reindeer-herding practices of Siberians as 'localities' or folk knowledge that must be cleared away for some as yet unknown transformation to come, why not see the very complex practices of the Tofa people as a sophisticated science for living in an extreme environment? There is a danger here too, though. The Tofa, as mediated through the work of Harrison, could become yet another noble savage, a mimetic stand-in for what 'we' moderns do not like about ourselves. Castro's advice on the subject is quite useful. To take up the other forms-of-life as provocations for thought means 'refraining from actualizing the possible expressions of alien thought and deciding to sustain them as possibilities – neither relinquishing them as the fantasies of the other, nor fantasizing about them as leading to the true reality' (Viveiros de Castro 2015: 85). There is no guarantee, but we also should not rule out that it may be the Tofa or the Tibetans who will provide the techniques to live on a cold moon with a thin atmosphere. A longer historical view would keep in perspective that fossil fuel-based technics are fizzling out after a measly two centuries, whereas the technologies of the Tofa have been sustainable and innovating for thousands of years. If the goal is a 'jail break'[23] from this planet such an escape will certainly require some combination of techniques that can persist for scales of time that far exceed, by several orders of magnitude, the five-year lifespan of a laptop computer or cell phone. Try making a wafer-thin CPU on an ice moon.

Furthermore, I share Harrison's skepticism. After all, the technics of our technological rut are fragile unto death. The third and fourth industrial revolutions depend upon delicate wafers and rare earth minerals which, when assembled for computation, are fatally allergic to heat and water and entirely dependent on luxurious amounts of electricity. In a world that is getting hotter and wetter, and where energy is scarce, one would hope that other technologies are possible. Instead disposability hovers over all modern technologies. That each object 'innovated' reaches obsolescence before the close of any given financial quarter and is replaced by a nearly identical but improved object follows developmental thinking as much as the consumer products revolutions of the mid-twentieth century (Giedion 2013). Like the aristocracy of the Habsburg Empire, the insular and parochial trajectory of technological thought is replete with recessive traits. A narrow view of industrial and mechanistic technology is, I think, from the perspective of many forms-of-life – whether Mohawks, phytoplankton, humpback whales, Tibetans, or Missourians – *the* social conflict.[24] The prospect of a new hyper-modernity, then, is homogenization.

The danger of homogenization is not new to grand modernization projects. However the prospects for such a global unification of humanity is now so unsustainable that its inevitable failure appears more as farce than tragedy. Like earlier projects for global unifications, the question will be what violence is unleashed in refusing to accept failure. It is unfortunate that advocates of the Singularity join in the long legacy of depriving discontinuous forms-of-life, in particularly indigenous people, of full, meaningful lives.[25] Like imperial, capitalist, and Marxist drives for world integration, calls for unification are little more than calls for homogenization. In the capitalist and Marxist variants of modernization that preceded the Singularity the interest was in primitive accumulation, markets, and labor. As brutal as those processes of integration were and continue to be, the vision and hubris of the Singularity is incomparable. The race for the Singularity, even a failed race, will be extremely resource intensive. In some projections the Singularity is proposed to survive by consuming the entire Sun in a Dyson sphere, a hypothetical device meant to completely surround a star so that all of the solar energy can be captured[26] – and even then there is unlikely to be 'storage' space for everyone. The Ecomodernist variant of modernization is no less catastrophic for obstinate forms-of-life that are put in competition to fight to the death over what little resources remain for those not entrepreneurial enough to dominate other populations for their enrichment. The Singularity does not present an alternative or way out, but instead offers a completion of the geopolitics of homogenization.

Could it be otherwise? Of course. Futures are always unknowable. Furthermore, humanity is not at the helm of history. The many other possibilities we debate in laboratories and parliaments may reflect little more than the provincial plans of a small fraction of just one planetary species. However, what is certain is that 'unleashing' the potential of technics, as promised by the Singularity and other visions of human transformation, is a dead end. If we are to truly accelerate human adaptation it must include the minor and incipient techniques of a world of new and old alliances across cosmologies, creature affinities, even organic and inorganic forms-of-life. Any sufficiently significant change in the nature of life will be a multi-species and multi-cultural endeavor. And still most of us will not make it.

While humans are often the source of technological mutations, whether or not the mutation 'works' is rarely up to the designer. The ecology of each technics, whether the spear or digital consciousness, determines whether a particular arrangement of things is possible and what effect or event it can enter into alliance with. For this reason, technology evolves; but so far its evolution has been tethered to the epigenetic structures of other animals – primarily, but not exclusively, human. Therefore it is necessary to think of each technical object as a kind of exogenous expression of an actual and virtual arrangement of things in a milieu in which humans experiment and replicate but do not control or engineer technics. We are their DNA but little more. The expressive intensity of their existence could quickly leave us behind. Like the Tibetans who inherited the capacity for living in a thin atmosphere from the Denisovans, or the relationship and knowledge of reindeer herding that have enabled the Tofa to live through thousands of long Siberian winters, diversification and not singularity is the history of planetary innovation. The loss of planetary dominance in favor of an-other intelligence is possible, irreversibly catastrophic changes are certain, but extinction is unlikely. What *we* stand to lose as a species in this current apocalypse of homogenization is unimaginable, not because of the loss of life but because of the loss of difference. Who and what will be left of Earth to inspire and ally with us in our creative advance is what is uncertain. If the future is dominated by those who seek to establish the survival of the human species through technological mastery, then whatever human 'we' manages to persist will likely live on or near a mean and lonely planet.

To be clear, we should not throw our weight behind Idle No More, a movement by indigenous and aboriginal people across the world, or behind other practices of indigenous people because we can 'go back to nature.' Indigenous, black, and brown people of the Earth are not the cutting-edge of political struggle because they are more natural, but because they have had front-row seats in the making of this crisis. Furthermore, the Eurocene is not synonymous with all people of European heritage. Many people found in Europe or its colonies continue to live under the harsh violence of the vanguard that leads the worldwide project of Europeanization. There are many minor traditions within the Eurocene that resonate with the need to oppose rather than expand the current geopolitical order. In fact, the categorical murkiness between the Eurocene, and particular Europeans, only intensifies the need to rethink democratization as a political project that demands a new inequality, rather than as a project of incorporation and equalization.

Notes

1 *Anthropos* is the Greek term for 'human'. Anthropocene has been coined to capture the emergence of human beings as a natural force at the geological level.
2 'Jacques Cousteau The Nile 2of6.avi,' YouTube video, 9:15, posted by 'acoustic6strings,' May 4, 2011, www.youtube.com/watch?v=Q47ZVvOelak.
3 Stewart Brand (one of the co-authors) became famous for having founded the Whole Earth Catalogue, a compendium of future-oriented possibilities that could, by the estimation of him and his compatriots, benefit the progress of the human race. Since then Brand has founded the Long Now Foundation with musician Brian Eno, which is focused on extending the survival of the human race. See: http://longnow.org/.
4 www.washingtonpost.com/news/energy-environment/wp/2016/04/20/and-then-we-wept-scientists-say-93-percent-of-the-great-barrier-reef-now-bleached/.
5 www.cnn.com/2015/04/16/africa/kenya-northern-white-rhino/.
6 Apocalypses are definitively what Timothy Morton (2013) calls 'hyberobjects.' The events themselves defy the perceptive and experiential capabilities of humans. One of the shortcomings of the Anthropocene as a concept is the tone of novelty and presentism. Morton rightly points out that climate change and many of the features of the Anthropocene are likely thousands of years old. So the idea that things are 'suddenly' weird is specious – none of us alive have ever lived in 'normal' times.
7 Some scientists argue that these scenarios for collapse are reversible, but that presumes unprecedented political action on a global scale (see Worm et al. 2006).
8 I assume amphibians think of this as the human apocalypse given how much they pre-date our existence.
9 '"The World" Cruise Ship Departing Port Nelson, New Zealand at Night,' YouTube video, 2:56, posted by Nelson Bomber, April 26, 2014, www.youtube.com/watch?v=Xhl51ygXyrE.

10 The hydrologic cycle is what moves moisture around the planet through evaporation and condensation. Changes in the rate of evaporation or the amount of moisture that the air can hold due to increased temperatures can mean the difference between floods and droughts.
11 On how big lies require half-truths, see William E. Connolly, 'The Contemporary Condition: The Return of the Big Lie,' posted December 3, 2011, http://contempora rycondition.blogspot.com/2011/12/return-of-big-lie.html.
12 'Brazil: uncontacted tribe displaced by Amazon logging,' *Argentina Independent*, July 4, 2014, www.argentinaindependent.com/currentaffairs/newsfromlatinamerica/brazil-un contacted-tribe-displaced-by-amazon-logging/.
13 On the importance of diplomats for bridging the cosmological gaps in our current ecological debate, see Latour (2013: 17–19).
14 'Nature's Engineers The Dam Beaver National Geographic Documentary,' YouTube video, 42:56, posted by Documentary Channel, June 16, 2013, www.youtube.com/wa tch?v=aHBCQ_EQ0v0.
15 www.scientificamerican.com/article/stratospheric-pollution-helps-slow-global-warming/.
16 www.e-flux.com/journal/63/60889/molecular-red-theory-for-the-anthropocene-on-a lexander-bogdanov-and-kim-stanley-robinson/.
17 On different approaches to the dating of the Anthropocene, see Zalasiewicz et al. (2015).
18 David Biello, 'Mass Deaths in Americas Start New CO2 Epoch.' *Scientific American*. Accessed May 20, 2016. www.scientificamerican.com/article/mass-deaths-in-america s-start-new-co2-epoch/.
19 http://bostonreview.net/forum/jedediah-purdy-new-nature.
20 Ibid.
21 'Founders,' Singularity University website, accessed August 4, 2014, http://singularityu. org/community/founders/.
22 Tim Worstall, 'DARPA Bigwig and Intel Fellow: Moore's Law Is Ending Soon,' *Forbes*, posted August 29, 2013, www.forbes.com/sites/timworstall/2013/08/29/darpa-chief-a nd-intel-fellow-moores-law-is-ending-soon/.
23 Benedict Singleton, 'Maximum Jailbreak,' *e-flux* 46, no. 3 (2013), www.e-flux.com/ journal/maximum-jailbreak/.
24 A NASA-funded research project concluded that the confluence of intensive social inequality and natural limits to economic growth represents a 'perfect storm' for conflict and the collapse of industrial civilization (see Motesharrei et al. 2014).
25 Glen Coulthard (2014) provides an excellent corrective to Marx by extending the practices of primitive accumulation to the present and insisting that place-based and particularistic forms of political resistance are innovative rather than regressive.
26 https://en.wikipedia.org/wiki/Matrioshka_brain.

References

Agamben, Giorgio. 2000. *Means without End: Notes on Politics*. Minneapolis: University of Minnesota Press.
Asafu-Adjaye, John, Linus Blomqvist, Stewart Brand et al. 2016. *An Ecomodernist Manifesto*. www.ecomodernism.org/. Accessed 13 January 2017.
Bennett, Jane. 2010. *Vibrant Matter: A Political Ecology of Things*. Durham, NC: Duke University Press.
Benton, M.J.. 2008. *When Life Nearly Died: The Greatest Mass Extinction of All Time*. London: Thames & Hudson.
Coulthard, Glen Sean. 2014. *Red Skin, White Masks: Rejecting the Colonial Politics of Recognition*. Minneapolis: University of Minnesota Press.

DuBois, W.E.B.. 1975. *Color and Democracy: Colonies and Peace.* Millwood, NY: Kraus-Thomson Organization.

Dyson, George. 2012. *Darwin among the Machines: The Evolution of Global Intelligence.* New York: Basic Books.

Garcia, Tristan. 2014. *Form and Object: A Treatise on Things.* Edinburgh: Edinburgh University Press.

Giedion, Sigfried. 2013. *Mechanization Takes Command: A Contribution to Anonymous History.* Minneapolis: University of Minnesota Press.

Goldberg-Hiller, Jonathan and Noenoe K. Silva. 2011. Sharks and Pigs: Animating Hawaiian Sovereignty against the Anthropological Machine. *South Atlantic Quarterly* 110(2): 429–446.

Harrison, K.David. 2007. *When Languages Die: The Extinction of the World's Languages and the Erosion of Human Knowledge.* Oxford: Oxford University Press.

Keary, Michael. 2016. The New Prometheans: Technological Optimism in Climate Change Mitigation Modelling. *Environmental Values* 25(1): 7–28.

Kolbert, Elizabeth. 2014. *The Sixth Extinction: An Unnatural History.* New York: Holt.

Kurzweil, Ray. 2000. *The Age of Spiritual Machines: When Computers Exceed Human Intelligence.* New York: Penguin.

Latour, Bruno. 2013. *An Inquiry into Modes of Existence: An Anthropology of the Moderns.* Cambridge, MA: Harvard University Press.

Manning, Richard. 2009. *Rewilding the West: Restoration in a Prairie Landscape.* Berkeley: University of California Press.

Morton, Timothy. 2013. *Hyperobjects: Philosophy and Ecology after the End of the World.* Minneapolis: University of Minnesota Press.

Motesharrei, Safa, Jorge Rivas and Eugenia Kalnay. 2014. Human and Nature Dynamics (HANDY): Modeling Inequality and Use of Resources in the Collapse or Sustainability of Societies. *Ecological Economics* 101: 90–102.

Mumford, Lewis. 2010 [1934]. *Technics and Civilization.* Chicago, IL: University of Chicago Press.

Purdy, Jedediah. 2015. *After Nature: A Politics for the Anthropocene.* Cambridge, MA: Harvard University Press.

Roach, John. 2006. Seafood May be Gone by 2048, Study Says. *National Geographic News,* 2 November. http://news.nationalgeographic.com/news/2006/11/061102-seafood-threat.html. Accessed 13 January 2017.

Rockstrom, Johan, Will Steffen, Kevin Noone, Asa Persson et al. 2009. A Safe Operating Space for Humanity. *Nature* 461(7263): 472–475.

Salter, Mark B. and Can E. Mutlu. 2012. Psychoanlytical Theory and Border Security. *European Journal of Social Theory* 15(2): 179–195.

Vale, Vivian and Andrea Juno (eds). 1984. *J. G. Ballard.* San Francisco, CA: V/Search.

Viveiros de Castro, Eduardo. 1992. *From the Enemy's Point of View: Humanity and Divinity in an Amazonian Society.* Chicago, IL: University of Chicago Press.

Viveiros de Castro, Eduardo. 2015. *The Relative Native: Essays on Indigenous Conceptual Worlds.* Chicago, IL: HAU Books.

Wark, Mackenzie. 2015. *Molecular Red: Theory for the Anthropocene.* London: Verso.

Worm, Boris, Edward B. Barbier, Nicola Beaumont et al. 2006. Impacts of Biodiversity Loss on Ocean Ecosystem Services. *Science* 314(5800): 787–790.

Zalasiewicz, Jan, Colin N. Waters, Mark Williams et al. 2015. When Did the Anthropocene Begin? A Mid-Twentieth Century Boundary Level is Stratigraphically Optimal. *Quarternary International* 383(5): 196–203.

12

CONCLUSION: TECHNOLOGY AND INTERNATIONAL RELATIONS THEORY

The end of the beginning

Daniel R. McCarthy

Contemporary world politics seems mired in a series of complex governance challenges for which no simple answers are present. Whether the problem is climate change, nuclear proliferation, migration, terrorism or economic instability, we increasingly seem to lack the intellectual or political resources to deal with these problems. Divisions of academic labour established in the late nineteenth and early twentieth centuries in which different disciplines focused on their specific sphere of social life – politics, economics, culture, geography – are increasingly struggling to provide adequate explanations for these crises within their own disciplinary terms. As the chapters in this volume have demonstrated, if we want an adequate explanation of the central dynamics in international politics it is necessary to engage in sustained interdisciplinary scholarship; this is a problem-driven rather than a theory-driven endeavour. By integrating Science and Technology Studies (STS) and International Relations (IR) into a productive synthesis we can begin to think through the compound socio-technical character of governance challenges facing our contemporary world.

One of the central premises of this volume has been the relative neglect of technological objects and artefacts as objects of sustained theoretical attention in IR. The field has always reflected upon the materiality of global politics, if at times only implicitly. The disciplinary foundations of IR in the first half of the twentieth century were informed by a number of factors. These included specifically materialist approaches, as in traditions of geopolitical analysis such as Alfred Thayer Mahan's stress on the centrality of the sea or Halford Mackinder's theses about the centrality of the Eurasian heartland (Ashworth 2013); confrontation with complex changes to transportation and communication technologies dating from the Second Industrial Revolution (Osiander 1998; McCarthy 2015: 1–2); and sustained focus on the meaning of the nuclear revolution for world politics (Herz 1950; Craig 2003). Yet, despite this focus, IR has largely treated the politics of technological design and development as marginal to its interests. More interested in how international society is shaped by technology, IR theorists have tended to ignore how technology is shaped by international society. The contributions presented here make the case for paying careful attention to the conceptualization and study of how technology shapes the events, processes and orders of global politics. Looking forward, they also represent an opportunity to close the first chapter in STS-IR scholarship, in which the simple claim that technology is socially constructed gives way to deeper considerations of the ramifications of that claim that are yet to be fully explored. This book should be considered only as an initial sketch of the benefits and potential difficulties that accompany such an exploration.

This concluding chapter will first discuss three central conceptual reconfigurations of IR theory that the integration of IR with STS in this volume propose: a reconfiguration of our concepts of actors and agency; an allied reconfiguration of practical and moral evaluations of power; and, finally, the impact of these two previous moves on our analysis of world order. Second, it will elaborate the similarities and differences between the theoretical approaches discussed in Chapters 2–5. This section will note the general points of agreement in STS-IR syntheses in their approach to technology in world politics prior to clarifying the differences between them, carefully noting that (some of) this terrain is important to avoid the common 'raiding party' practice in IR, in which we cobble together arguments from other fields without careful attention to their controversies in order to support our preferred intellectual positions (Jackson 2011: 10–11, 16; Lawson and Shilliam 2010: 80–82). Finally, the chapter will note how a deeper consideration of the International can benefit the field of STS. For instance, recent scholarship in IR highlights how the division of humanity into multiple political communities operates as an important causal mechanism on processes of social development and is central to any sociological account of the world (Rosenberg 2006, 2016; Buzan and Lawson 2015). For all of the criticism of IR theory outlined in this volume, the discipline has developed a substantial body of scholarship that can deepen and extend work in the field of STS; the continued mixture of STS and IR promises to generate new insights into world politics for some time to come.

Powerful scallops and legitimate networks: practical, moral and evaluative dimensions of STS-IR

The most striking feature of STS-IR scholarship is probably its extension of the range of actors considered as relevant to explaining international politics. That a wide range of actors beyond the state are important to consider in crafting our accounts of how global politics operates is widely accepted across the field; that scallops or the magnetic compass deserve analytical attention no more or less than Portuguese imperialists is probably less so (see Chapter 3). When we start to consider science, technology and nature as central to international relations the number of relevant actors proliferates rapidly. One of the common threads running throughout the contributions to this book is an expanded understanding of who makes global politics.

The authors in this volume have focused on a range of areas of world politics – security and strategic studies, international political economy, and international communications – that have often lent themselves to particularly state-centric analysis. Rather than black box the socio-technical practices that underpin these issue areas, however, STS-IR approaches, in opening up the box, have found that far more actors are involved in producing global politics, at a far wider range of levels and locations, than we normally encounter. Joseph P. Masco, in examining the laboratory politics of nuclear weapons in Los Alamos, tells the story of the scientists, lab technicians and publics crafting America's nuclear weapons policy no less than foreign policy officials or state bureaucrats. Antoine Bousquet's discussion of the revolution in military affairs (RMA) draws out the diversity of actors that constitute militaries and enable warfighting; in this narrative, Alexander Fleming (discoverer of penicillin), Nicolas Appert or Phillipe de Girard (instigators of modern canned-food technologies) feature as centrally as generals, prime ministers and presidents. Columba Peoples, Monroe Price, Alejandro Colás and Jairus Victor Grove all highlight how states, civil society actors, corporations, non-governmental organizations (NGOs) and engineers construct socio-technical orders in the areas of space technologies, information communications technology and the shipping container, respectively.

When technology is no longer black boxed, a series of conceptual cascades are initiated that affect the causal stories we tell about global politics. Crucially, an expanded picture of global political actors has significant ramifications for how we conceptualize power in global politics. STS-IR syntheses thereby directly impact on what is often considered the core of the field of International Relations. As Peter Morriss has noted, when engaged in analyses of power we primarily want to know about the manifestations of power for three reasons: practical, moral and evaluative. Knowing about who is powerful helps us understand what we can do to or for other people, and what they can do to or for us; having this knowledge allows us to allocate moral responsibility for actions taken, or not taken; and these understandings present the opportunity to evaluate how power is distributed within a given social order, national or international (Morriss 2002: 36–42). When we consider a larger number of actors as constituting international relations, answers to where power lies in world politics become more complex and more representative of the complexity of global governance at the same time.

In practical terms, then, STS-IR approaches suggest a rather different picture of who is powerful in global politics from many conventional approaches.[1] For example, the institution of diplomacy is often understood to be in the midst of a significant change. Due to the expansion of information technologies and increased international interaction capacity – the intensity and volume of interactions in a given world order (Buzan and Little 2000) – practices of public diplomacy and citizen diplomacy in which states and publics interact more directly is understood as possible in a way never previously imagined. This has led to suggestions of the emergence of a 'new diplomacy' that is challenging the capacity – the power – of states to adapt (Kelley 2010). Yet this is a rather partial story of the evolution of diplomacy, excluding the power of states to constitute information networks through diplomatic negotiations (Singh 2008; Hills 2007); the power of Internet engineers in setting the agenda to which diplomats are reacting; the power of users to decide for themselves what meaning they will grant the emergent technology. If diplomats lack power within a socio-historical context altered by information technologies, it is useful to know who does have power to shape these processes. And it is, of course, no less useful for diplomats themselves as they adjust to a new environment, knowing that software programmers can design applications to help diplomats talk to their target audiences.

It may seem that many of the issues covered in this volume are academic – disconnected from everyday politics, from policy-makers and their concerns. After all, considering the agency of scallops or what Marx thought about technology is unlikely to be central in policy discussions in Beijing, Delhi, Sao Paolo or Washington. Yet, on closer examination, these are precisely the kinds of questions we must engage if we are to grapple with the complex governance challenges of the twenty-first century.

The STS-IR approaches outlined above do not have any single shared view of power. Just as IR theorists have tended to employ a range of power concepts in their analyses, STS–IR fusions differ on the emphasis they place on the importance of 'power to' versus 'power over' (see Lukes 2005: 35, 69; Barnett and Duvall 2005: 10) as their specific focus of concern, on the precise manifestations of power in social life, and how we may come to know them. It is equally important to note, however, that if STS-IR approaches differ in their understanding of power, they agree that forms of power are both material and ideological. The notion of a divide between these forms of power, still present in some traditionalist approaches to IR (e.g. Mearsheimer 2001; cf. Schmidt 2005), is simply untenable once a nature–culture divide is rejected, as the chapters in this volume have made clear. Each contribution in this volume has emphasized how material practices are structured by ideas, discourses, symbolic representations and scientific imaginaries, and, in turn, how these discourses are already embedded within material contexts. Both ideational and material resources are involved in the politics of socio-technical orders, and both ideational and material forces play constitutive roles in defining where actors sit in these orders.

Barnett and Duvall's typology of power as coercive, institutional, structural and productive is helpful in distinguishing between the distinct takes on power presented in this book. Interestingly, and perhaps somewhat unexpectedly, Actor-Network Theory (ANT's) understanding of power is often closest to a traditional Realist focus on coercive power in International Relations. This concept of power, often termed the 'first face' of power, is defined as the ability of one actor to change the actions or orientation of another actor against their wishes (Dahl 1957; Barnett and Duvall 2005: 13–15). In ANT, this is manifested in claims that humans and non-humans have different capacities to alter the condition of other actants.

When a door with a strong spring-mechanism forces visitors to pass through quickly, it has forced a change of behaviour (see Chapter 3). This form of power is direct, observable in its exercise and centres on changing the condition of an actor.

By contrast, while SCOT, CTT, New Materialisms and posthumanism all employ some notion of coercive power, they also rely on other ideas of power in their analyses. What differentiates STS-IR ideas of institutional power from its traditional treatment in IR is its understanding of technological systems or webs as institutions with rules, norms and decision-making procedures. Institutional power – the ability of an actor to influence others at a distance in space and time – is, for example, central to SCOT treatments of technological closure and momentum. Once closure occurs, large technological systems (LTS) have the capacity to significantly alter the actions of other actors at a distance, as Price demonstrates in his discussion of the social, legal and political ramifications of an American Internet on China (see Chapter 7). Similarly, Colás argues that the shipping container promoted and continues to support the creation of neo-liberal spatial relations in that it creates winners and losers in the global political economy (see Chapter 8). Taking the bias of socio-technical institutions into account widens our understanding of unequal power relations in world politics. Hierarchy is a materialized feature of world order.

Structural power is predominantly restricted to Critical Theory, with its indebtedness to Marxist political economy and its view of capitalism as a structure of social relations. Structural power concerns the internal relations of social structures that produce 'the social capacities of structural or subject positions in direct relation to one another ... The classic examples here are master–slave and capital–labor [sic] relations' (Barnett and Duvall 2005: 18). The power of a master is constituted by his relationship to the slave, just as the slave's disempowerment is constituted by his relationship to the master. Within Critical Theory, structural power relations are viewed as central to defining which actors have the capacity to direct processes of technological design (see Chapter 4). Thus, as we have seen, Peoples' treatment of space politics emphasizes the unequal power capacities held by some actors due to their structural location in the modern capitalist international system (see Chapter 10). Some aspects of structural power also resonate with posthumanist approaches and their stress on capitalist inequalities (Cudworth and Hobden 2013; see Chapter 5). Concepts of structural power rely upon a willingness to black box certain social relations, which the deconstructive impulses of both ANT and New Materialisms do not allow (see below).

Finally, productive power, which is defined by Barnett and Duvall (2005: 20) as 'the constitution of all social subjects with various social powers through systems of knowledge and discursive practices of broad and general scope', also extends across the approaches laid out here, to greater and lesser degrees. ANT, New Materialisms and 'co-productionist' approaches (Jasanoff 2004; Jasanoff and Kim 2015) centrally emphasize productive power, albeit in different ways. Co-productionist accounts tend to stress the role of ideational and discursive meanings in constructing the divisions between science and technology that constitute social orders themselves.

ANT's material semiotics tends not to emphasize productive power quite as strongly, with the physicality of non-human actants presenting a limit to symbolic representations, as in Michel Callon's Brieuc Bay example (see Chapter 3). The direct coercive power of the scallop prevented the Brieuc Bay network from stabilizing, as it were. However, as noted above, symbolic representations and the power of discourse in crafting subjects' identities and technological institutions are important to all the theories in this book. The role of socio-technical imaginaries in the politics of technology should not, therefore, be underestimated. Along these lines, examining how we picture our technological futures as utopian or dystopian in novels, television, films and other cultural products remains a very promising avenue for future STS-IR research (Jasanoff and Kim 2015; Jameson 2005).

The central point is that, in the practical context of power analysis, while each STS-IR approach similarly broadens our understanding of which actors are important in global politics, they do so in different ways. The Critical Theory of Technology, by black boxing capitalism (see below), encourages us to look for powerful actors by noting their social structural location and role. ANT, on the other hand, suggests that no such a priori decision can be made, and that, if we want to know who is powerful in any given context we must get down on the ground and follow the network of associations through which power is exercised. Each approach has its benefits and drawbacks, and each presents potential for productive engagement with the others.

Analysis of power is not limited to simply knowing who can do what, or who holds power over others. Alongside this analytical approach, we want to know who has caused certain social circumstances to come about – who created the Internet, the atomic bomb, the AK-47? – in order to dole out moral praise or blame. Technological determinism, in failing to recognize the agency of human actors to create new technologies with specific social goals in mind, bracketed this question from study in IR. A common thread running through this volume is that, once our scope of relevant actors is broadened, so too are ideas of moral responsibility. If one understands drone technologies to be a humanitarian form of warfighting – by no means a settled or desirable position – we may wish to allocate moral praise to the engineers who created the technology and the political and military actors who authorized their development and deployment over conventional fixed-wing aircraft alternatives. Our understanding of who is responsible is, of course, linked to our practical analysis of power.

Finally, the evaluative dimension of power analysis asks that we examine the broad distribution of power within a social system. This targets one of the central questions of political theory: is the power of rulers legitimate? In IR recent scholarship on legitimacy in (and of) international society has significantly advanced our understanding of these processes at the global level (Clark 2005, 2007; Hurd 1999). STS-IR introduces a further complication through its broadening of relevant actors and its reconfiguration of the concept of power to account for this broadening. As we come to consider a range of actors as more powerful than we had previously – as the American Maritime Association is recognized as possessing coercive, institutional, structural or productive power in relation to the shipping container, and thus the global political economy – questions around what legitimizes this distribution of power emerge. STS-IR syntheses introduce new areas of study for normative international political theory. The ethics of technological development take on a different cast when framed in an international context, with questions of ultimate authority and legitimacy displaced from a focus on a singular national community or set of state institutions to a broader, amorphous notion of international community or world society.

To give one example, assigning responsibility and holding actors to account for violations of domestic law can be complicated by the presence of global transportation and communication infrastructures. In a classic case from 2000, Australian billionaire Joseph Gutnick sought to prosecute the owners of the *Wall Street Journal*, Dow Jones & Company, for libel in Australia's courts. Gutnick had felt that an article on wsj.com had defamed him, and sought redress via Australia's tough libel laws. As Jack Goldsmith and Timothy Wu note, 'Dow Jones argued that Australian courts were legally powerless (or "without jurisdiction") to rule on the legality of information on a computer in the United States, even if it appeared in Australia. The Australian High Court … disagreed' (Goldsmith and Wu 2008: 147). Goldsmith and Wu interpret this case in a positive manner, arguing that it allows for people with different value systems to coexist in international society. This view is, of course, a normative judgement, one very familiar to IR students from English School debates over the nature of international society as either solidarist and cosmopolitan or pluralist and communitarian (Wheeler 1992; Rengger 2015). Questions around legal and moral responsibility may be significantly altered by the development of new technological capacities, and call upon a socio-technical solution in turn – the practice of Internet filtering is a socio-technical solution to precisely this normative problem (see Chapter 7).

The legitimacy of the agents who design and develop technology is, in determinist approaches, underpinned by its non-social character. If these actors do not have the capacity to actively shape technology due to an inherent technological rationale, then the question of legitimacy falls out of our analysis. Once we recognize that some social actors do have this capacity, questions about whether or not their power is legitimate and what makes their power legitimate naturally follow. Answers to these questions are clearer in some instances than in others. In the case of nuclear weapons science at Los Alamos, the legitimate political authority of the United States government to conduct treaty negotiations which subsequently shape the conduct of scientists in the nuclear laboratory is relatively settled. Similarly, classic notions of Westphalian sovereignty may constitute the legitimacy of both the United States and China to pursue a particular vision of the Internet.

Yet, at a deeper level, even these examples ask us to consider why the political legitimacy of the state is given precedence in the constitution of legitimate authority of socio-technical regimes. The sociological recognition that claims to scientific and technological expertise function as a powerful rhetorical resource in winning political battles serves as an important prompt to think through these issues (Ezrahi 1990). Here, the central question about the division between the technological and the social emerges as the object of study; this divide distributes power in specific ways and also can shield it from authorization, understood in conventional terms as either input into decision-making or affecting the distribution of outputs. STS debates over the legitimate scope of expert authority can provide some assistance (see Collins and Evans 2003; Jasanoff 2003; Wynne 2003), but within an international context these questions take on an added dimension. At this stage, STS-IR approaches have not had much to say on these issues. Peoples' work presents perhaps the most sustained engagement from a Critical Theory perspective, as his chapter in this volume makes clear, while New Materialist and posthumanist approaches have evident ethical premises underpinning their critique of certain concentrations of power. Nevertheless, as in STS writ large (Jasanoff 2015: 3, 16–17), these evaluative questions have tended to be sidelined. In sum, if we have good answers to the practical and moral questions, our answers to the evaluative questions at the global level are less developed.

At its highest level of abstraction, then, this book asks us to consider the socio-technical construction of world order in its varied dimensions. Technological artefacts and institutions emerge not as merely secondary characteristics of international order, but as co-constitutive world order as it exists at any given moment in time. While the importance of interaction capacity to the constitution of international systems in world history has been recognized in IR for some time (Buzan and Little 2000; Fritsch 2011), the chapters in this book ask us to consider how, precisely, different socio-technical settlements emerge, are fought over, settled and reproduced. Not every approach to international politics can engage in constructive dialogue with the emerging literature on science and technology in the field – for instance, the sociologically thin account of world politics provided by rational choice approaches cannot be easily integrated with the historically sensitive and interpretive methodologies presented here. For historically and sociologically oriented approaches – Feminism, Postcolonialism, Constructivism, the English School, Marxism, Poststructuralism – significant productive integration is possible and occurring on an ongoing basis.

Similarly different approaches to Science and Technology Studies in International Relations

The perspectives presented in this book are all oriented towards interdisciplinary research in which the intellectual resources of Science and Technology Studies, International Relations, Anthropology, Media and Communications Studies, and Philosophy and Social Theory combine in interesting and novel formulations to illuminate previously obscure dynamics of socio-historical change. In this manner, STS-IR syntheses are moving in tandem with wider trends in International Relations, as IR scholarship has increasingly sought to become an interdisciplinary field defined by its object of study – the 'International' – rather than a focus on an issue area, such as 'politics' narrowly defined (Rosenberg 2016; Buzan and Little 2001: 30).

Importantly, this shift is not driven by a desire to win battles within the discipline of IR, but by the nature of complex global challenges themselves. There are risks, as well as benefits, from this interdisciplinary shift. As Lawson and Shilliam note (2010: 81), 'Interdisciplinarity can engender thinness and sloppiness as well as promote depth and rigour.' It is important to recognize that STS contains a wide range of theoretical positions, points of substantial theoretical agreement and divergence.[2] An awareness of these complexities can help prevent simplistic 'dabbling' in STS in favour of a more sustained and enriching two-way conversation between disciplines and specific theoretical approaches within disciplines.[3]

The most obvious similarity between Social Construction of Technology (SCOT), ANT, CTT, New Materialisms and posthumanism lies in their comprehensive rejection of technological determinism. At the broadest level, each theoretical approach surveyed in this volume could be termed a variant of social constructivism. Such a broad label is not necessarily terribly satisfactory. As noted in the Introduction, nothing about the claim that things are socially constructed tells us much about how this occurs or why things are socially constructed in one way rather than another. Even the claim that 'things could be different' does not necessarily point towards any specific political position.

Underpinning the social constructivisms of STS is the principle of symmetry, first comprehensively outlined by David Bloor (1976) working in the Sociology of Scientific Knowledge (SSK). Traditional divisions between society and technology, nature and culture, humans and non-humans which pervade social theory are rejected by all the approaches outlined above. While the precise nature of symmetry is a significant point of distinction (see below), STS in general attempts to explain the success or failure of technology according to the same criteria. Whereas a common-sense explanation for the success of a technology is that 'it works', it is 'efficient' or another similar claim, STS argues that working/not working must be explained using the same criteria. That is, an explanation for the failure of a technology can often tend towards social explanations – it failed because it was inefficient or too expensive – while successful technologies simply work. In SSK this meant that sociologists only explained the failure of scientific ideas, never their (equally socially defined) successes. If failure is explained by social factors, STS seeks to explain success in the same way.

The focus on social construction and the principle of symmetry underpin the shared orientation to qualitative methods and a non-positivist philosophy of science for SCOT, ANT, CTT and New Materialisms. Interpretation of actors subjective orientations – 'following the actors' – are often favoured in STS, although this is not proscriptive (Jasanoff 2015: 3; Bijker 2010: 67–71). It does suggest, though, that the kind of large-N studies favoured in some strands of IR are not compatible with STS, and highlights the large areas of potential overlap with non-positivist approaches in IR noted above. Because STS does not hold a monolithic picture of what science is, in the same way that IR theory has tended to (Jackson 2011: 189), it is far more comfortable with diverse practices of knowledge production.

Finally, STS approaches generally understand the world in a relational manner. Many approaches in the social sciences do not share this view. For example, it is common to view individuals as their own self-contained units who interact with each other but who do not constitute each other. STS breaks down the methodological individualism that underpins these ideas by suggesting that all social actors – human and non-human – are constituted by the webs, networks of structures of relations, in which they are embedded. That is, what humans and non-humans are is created by their relationships with others. These take slightly different forms, with interest groups, networks, internal relations or assemblages functioning as the key way to conceptualize relations (see Chapters 2–5). Focusing on relations foregrounds processes, change and historical development in a way that other approaches to philosophy or social theory, such as Anglo-American analytical philosophy or rational choice approaches, largely sideline.

These similarities within STS should not be taken for uniformity. While IR's understanding of itself as a discipline often emphasizes its fractured nature, producing significant theoretical anxiety at times (cf. Dunne et al. 2013), it would be misleading to suggest that STS has avoided contentious debates over core epistemological, ontological and methodological issues. SCOT, ANT, Critical Theory and New Materialist approaches are as different as they are similar, and having a clear understanding of these differences is important if we are to avoid an unsophisticated appropriation of STS concepts into IR as a field of study. Core differences lie across several key issues in STS, of which we will concentrate on three: the willingness to black box certain social relations as a starting point of analyses; symmetry understood as a claim about the agency of humans and non-humans; and the boundaries, or absence of boundaries, to social constructivist arguments.[4]

First, then, one of the clearest differences between STS approaches is the willingness to black box certain social relations within their analyses. For example, in the CTT approach developed by Andrew Feenberg, certain core analytical categories are treated as black boxes without significant reflection, with class and capitalism as the clearest examples. This is not to suggest that Feenberg or other Critical Theory work simply deductively picked these categories out of thin air; historical materialism involves an explicit recognition that class is 'socially constructed' as much as any other phenomenon (Thompson 1968; Marx 1976: 873–895). Nevertheless, class is not systematically deconstructed in Critical Theory at every opportunity. SCOT approaches, on the other hand, do not outline the sunk costs that generate momentum as socially constructed, with a generic utilitarian understanding of path dependency underpinning this work (Bijker 2010; McCarthy 2015: 35–37). There is, in both CTT and SCOT, a willingness to accept an account of technological development and diffusion as occurring within an already existing social structure, although this is more explicit in CTT (Feenberg 2002: 30–32; Lynch and Furham 1991). By contrast, ANT has focused on the very production of black boxes such as these, its critique directed towards classic sociology categories such as society, class or culture as mere placeholders for the practical achievement of society or culture as an outcome (Latour 2005). Treating structure as an a priori is understood as merely reintroducing an asymmetry back into our analyses.

The pragmatic requirement to black box some processes or phenomena in order to examine others is relatively well accepted. However, the reasons behind the black boxing remain far more contentious, and indicate different limits to the principle of symmetry between STS approaches. The primary point of contention lies in ANT's attempt to extend the principle of symmetry from its initial formulation by David Bloor and the Strong Programme of STS. Where symmetry as a method was initially formulated to ensure that explanations of the success or failure of a given technological artefact are couched in the same principles of explanation, ANT has extended this principle by focusing on the agency of humans and non-humans. Scallop power thus enters into our analytical frameworks. This appears to extend symmetry from a methodological to an ontological principle, although this understanding is not straightforward due to Latour's tendency to deliberate provocation (Sayes 2014). The central point is that ANT reconfigures concepts of agency. Agency is no longer considered as an already existing quality defined by intentionality or some other quality possessed by humans. Rather, ANT seeks to confer agency to either humans or non-humans on the basis of their ability to make a difference, in causal terms, to an outcome. In concrete terms, ANT can describe a bush pump as central to the construction of Zimbabwe, no less or more important than the usual sociological suspects of colonial administrators or independence activists.

This claim has not gone uncontested in STS. For instance, Bloor (1999) rejects Latour's desire to focus explanations on the co-production of society and nature, stressing that our object of study should be limited to explaining social *beliefs* about science and nature. For Feenberg (2010: 144), the focus on contingent and local settlements which underpins ANT human/non-human symmetry suggests a specific relationship of the local to the global. In this account, the symmetrical treatment of the actants that constitute a network – and are constituted by a network – can sacrifice our capacity for critical normative judgements, a view echoed by other critics of ANT (Sayes 2014). Even very sympathetic accounts of ANT, such as Jane Bennett's version of New Materialism, view this reconfiguration of agency as problematic, with Bennett (2010: 108–109) pulling back from the implications of the 'full Latour' due to its perceived ethical implications.

Disagreement over understandings of agency spill over into perhaps the most significant difference between STS approaches: the limits of social construction itself. Philosophical realism, or at least a particular conception of what realism entails, has formed a central target of STS critiques. Yet each approach in STS draws the line beyond which objects, people or practices are *not* considered to be socially constructed in different places. Feenberg, for example, excludes basic scientific research from his analysis of its social construction; while the specific topics investigated may be socially determined, the results of basic science are not, and remain sufficiently ambivalent that they can be deployed in any form of social order (Feenberg 2002: 34; Wynne 2010: xii–xiii). CTT relies upon a form of philosophical realism in which the natural world is independent of our ideas about that world. SCOT maintains a more ambivalent stance on this issue, with Bijker (2010: 73), for instance, stresses the need for a focus on how technology is made and used, not on its ontological status.

The ramifications of these disagreements are quite substantial and should be carefully noted. This chapter began with a focus on complex global challenges, and perhaps implicitly relied upon a view of complexity as increasing when spatial scales increase. That is, as social, political or ethical issues register at different geographical levels, they take on added complexity: the regional is more complex than the local, and the global is more complex than the regional. Complexity in world politics is, on this view, an emergent property of socio-technical interactions, and the complex global order cannot be reduced to lower levels of explanation – the global is not simply an adding up of the actions of individual actors or states, but different in kind. By contrast, John Law, a central figure in the development of ANT, has stressed the need not to abstract up to the level of the International. Instead, he argues for a 'baroque' sensibility that 'looks down to discover the concrete, and then it discovers complexity within the concrete' (Law 2004: 21; Nexon and Pouliot 2013: 343). Law's central thrust is that we cannot assimilate the multiplicity of local networks, flows and practices into any analytical whole – the whole is only the product of our analytical abstraction from local processes. Law summarizes this point with some force, worth quoting at length:

And if we follow this path, and assume baroque divergence rather than convergence, then the imagination of complexity is not simply vague and in parts 'confused' … It is also (and this is the important additional move) patchy and at best only partially coherent. The implication is that there is no possibility whatsoever of an emergent overview, and this is not simply because it is neither possible nor necessary to make what is known fully explicit – though this is indeed the case. In addition, it is because there is no final coherence. There is no system, global order, or network. These are, at best, partially enacted romantic aspirations. Instead, there are local complexities and local globalities, and the relations between them are uncertain.

(Law 2004: 23–24)

Here, then, is one of the central divisions within STS, apparently even between approaches that are otherwise quite close in complexion, such as ANT and co-productionist accounts (Jasanoff 2015: 16–19). While some scholars urge abstraction in order to gain an overall view of social orders (Klein and Kleinman 2002), others, like Law, caution against the attempt to think away complexity via theoretical abstraction.

To explain the difference between these approaches requires a far more detailed account of STS than can be offered here. Briefly, ANT and New Materialist accounts view the deconstructive impulse as central to diffusing power throughout social and political systems. In highlighting how situations of domination rely on fragile networks to sustain them, these approaches both note the potential for social change and make the case for introducing systems of democratic representation and governance that recognize the diffuse character of power. Think proportional representation, but one that includes non-humans. For critics, identifying historically enduring forms of structural power means we need a view on the 'totality' of a social system: how do the parts fit together to create a larger, irreducible whole? From a consideration of the limits of social construction, then, are derived a set of analytical, normative and political positions which are not easily reconcilable. Again, in order to avoid simple IR 'pillaging raids' careful consideration of these differences within STS is important.

Theorizing the International alongside the technological

Alongside a concern over 'pillaging' other fields, IR scholars have often been anxious about the contribution of International Relations to other disciplines in the social sciences. Thus, while this volume has been centrally concerned with outlining how the field of IR can benefit from engagement with STS, it is important that these conversations are not one way. As Jasanoff (2004: 2) notes, 'Conversations between S&TS and neighbouring fields about the links between knowledge, culture and power are ... urgently needed and could be enormously fruitful.' In this case, as noted in the Introduction, the traffic to date has tended to flow in one direction, from STS to IR. This is not unique for the field of IR – indeed, this predicament is a feature of IR as a discipline (Buzan and Little 2001; Brown 2013; Buzan and Lawson 2015: 330–333; Rosenberg 2016) – but does press those seeking to develop STS-IR syntheses to make the case for retaining the insights of E.H. Carr, Hans Morgenthau or David Mitrany in our studies of the socio-technical construction of world politics.

The central contribution of IR to STS lies precisely in its concern with the International. For all that scholarship in STS notes the global character of technological politics, the precise character of international politics – the relationships between political communities – is often not elaborated in any significant detail. In general, STS has focused on the relationship between state and society within one national context. Even in contexts where STS research questions are explicitly framed around the relationship between science, technology, the state and politics in a global context, the focus is on individual nations (e.g. Jasanoff and Kim 2009, 2015). A strong reliance on comparative research methods reinforces the impression that, for STS, the nation-state is a container of socio-technical orders. In this sense, STS tends to be underpinned by methodological nationalism (Chernilo 2006).[5] Explanations of national technological or scientific cultures thereby rely on what is called an 'internalist' account of social change, in which change is driven through causes internal to the nation-state. Political processes 'external' to the domestic level – the interactions between states or politics taking place in non-state territory, such as the high seas – are often neglected as a result. Thus, even in an era of increasing transnationalism, the field of STS can inadvertently tend to portray the nation–state as a container of social relations. This supposition has been heavily criticized in IR, and in sociology more generally (Hobson et al. 2010: 21; Rosenberg 2005; Chernilo 2006).

As a causal force, the International is underplayed or, when it is noted, under-theorized in STS. In this sense, the role of the International in STS scholarship tends to mirror the incorporation of geopolitics into historical sociology in the 1980s. Sociology as a discipline had traditionally been focused on studying social relations in one state; by the late 1970s, this focus began to shift to a consideration of how the interaction of states can shape societies (Hobden 1998; Hobson et al. 2010). In the process, however, historical sociologists tended to accept a particularly Realist picture of inter-state relations; they understood states as generically driven to compete with each other, and then outlined the consequences for social development inside the state (Giddens 1985; Mann 1986). This approach to inter-state relations ignored how different states relate to each other in a diverse range of ways due to cultural influences, domestic norms and values, economic ties and a range of other factors. As a result, one of the central developments in IR theory – the shift beyond structural Realist constraints – was not effectively incorporated into historical sociology in its turn to geopolitics.

An analogous situation is evident in STS, as inter-state relations are often assumed to be generically about the 'national interest' or security competition (e.g. Dafoe 2016; Salter et al. 2016). As a result, 'international' factors are considered as largely secondary to socio-technical construction, which is driven by what takes place inside the state. Where global processes are considered, this is often in the form of a nod to the generic globalization of science and technology – globalization happens. Attention to the empirical processes of global and transnational flows of technologies and ideas is substantial in STS, but further theoretical elaboration is required.

The contributors to this book have suggested a number of ways in which this picture of technological development is one-sided. Whether noting the diffusion of technological objects from one state to another and the impact this has on the receiving state – as with the Internet (Chapter 7), the role of warfare between states in driving forward specific socio-technical projects within states and the subsequent international ramifications of these (Chapter 9), or the technopolitics that occur in specifically 'international' spaces, such as the high seas or outer space (Chapters 8 and 10) – this book has stressed the need to consider how the International shapes the politics of technology. Similarly, assemblage theory in IR has drawn out the central role of states and borders in constituting global flows of objects and their politics. An 'internalist' account of technopolitics simply misses out too much in this regard.

For STS-IR syntheses, then, it is important to consider how the interaction of multiple political communities occurs in their full socio-technical articulation. These relations may be competitive, focused on domination, security competition, the national interest and power politics in general. Alternatively, they may be cooperative, consensual and cosmopolitan. The texture of these relationships helps shape the development and diffusion of technological objects. How the division of humanity into multiple political communities is created and sustained by specific socio-technical orders is central to the processes that constitute the central empirical focal points of STS.

The engagement with the International need not privilege any specific approach to either International Relations or Science and Technology Studies, although how precisely studies of the International are articulated will vary between approaches. As Hobson et al. (2010: 22–27) point out, IR theorists developing new perspectives on the International embrace a range of viewpoints. They identify three main strands. The first, 'eventful' historical sociology, 'rejects the use of "entities" such as society and civilization in favour of a concentration on how historical events enable social formation to emerge, reproduce, reform, transform and break down' (2010: 25). Second is theories of uneven and combined development, which study how the International is internal to social development (see Chapter 4). Finally, non-Eurocentric or 'global dialogic' processes stress the agency of subaltern and non-Western actors in the constitution of global politics, seeking to recover the agency of actors traditionally excluded from IR. Each approach has resonances with perspectives discussed in this volume. Focusing on historical events and networks, uneven and combined development or non-Eurocentric global dialogues presents just three possible avenues through which ANT and New Materialisms, Critical Theories of Technology and SCOT perspectives, respectively, may approach the International. In turn, it highlights the myriad forms of intra- and interdisciplinary exchange possible in the development of STS-IR. In our attempts to capture the complexity of technopolitics the contributions of IR theory should not be underestimated.

Conclusion: the end of the beginning for STS-IR

This volume started by outlining a strong rejection of the technological determinism that underpins many contemporary accounts of technology in International Relations. This rejection, we noted, is not novel, and has been found in almost all STS-IR syntheses emerging within International Relations since the mid-2000s. While it is necessary to establish why we need to take the politics of technology seriously in our considerations of world politics, the thinness of this claim is also increasingly unsatisfactory. In this sense, this volume hopefully represents the end of the beginning in the emergence of STS-IR scholarship. That technology is socially constructed is well established in IR. A solid foundation has been established on which future research can build.

Contributors to this volume have laid out a range of positions through which this construction can occur. Crucially, the theoretical and conceptual approaches outlined here are problem-driven; STS-IR is interested in producing strong empirical accounts of how world politics operates. At the same time, while STS-IR has been centrally concerned with producing stronger causal explanations of international politics, each approach surveyed also suggests that new moral and evaluative judgements are required once we pay attention to the creation and use of technology. These issues lead naturally into larger questions about the constitution of world order and the place of technology in this process. While the issue areas surveyed here barely scratch the surface of the vast scope of global political technoscience, they indicate precisely how global order is materially created and maintained.

Looking forward, STS-IR syntheses are only one element of the larger trans-disciplinary project required to adequately account for the complexity of our social lives. Whether our focus is on contemporary global politics or the social construction of technology across state systems throughout history, it is clear that arbitrary disciplinary boundaries excessively limit our field of vision. Undertaking inter-disciplinary scholarship is not easy, and its benefits come with significant perils as its practitioners risk academic depth for synthesizing breadth within social sciences defined by discrete fields of study. Nevertheless, this is a road worth travelling.

Notes

1 In Michael Barnett and Raymond Duvall's otherwise exemplary edited volume on power in global governance, socio-technical manifestations of power are not considered at all (see Barnett and Duvall 2005).
2 IR has tended to engage primarily with ANT and New Materialisms, and only secondarily with CTT, SCOT or posthumanism. This limited focus can misrepresent the complexity of STS, leading to the problems noted by Lawson and Shilliam.
3 See Chapter 3 and the forum in International Political Sociology for an example of how IR can engage, or not, with ANT.
4 Please note that these differences are by no means exhaustive, merely indicative.
5 As with all generalizations, there are important exceptions, particularly those emerging from postcolonial approaches. For examples, see Hecht 2002; Anderson 2009; Smith 2014; Miller 2004, 2015; Grant 2016.

References

Anderson, Warwick. 2009. From Subjugated Knowledge to Conjugated Subjects: Science and Globalisation, or Postcolonial Studies of Science. *Postcolonial Studies* 12(4): 389–400.

Ashworth, Lucian M.. 2013. Mapping a New World: Geography and the Interwar Study of International Relations. *International Studies Quarterly* 57(1): 138–149.

Barnett, Michael and Raymond Duvall. 2005. Power in Global Governance. In Michael Barnett and Raymond Duvall (eds) *Power in Global Governance*. Cambridge: Cambridge University Press, pp. 1–33.

Bennett, Jane. 2010. *Vibrant Matter: A Political Ecology of Things*. Durham, NC: Duke University Press.

Bijker, Wiebe. 2010. How is Technology Made? That is the Question! *Cambridge Journal of Economics* 34(1): 63–76.

Bloor, David. 1976. *Knowledge and Social Imagery*. London: Routledge.

Bloor, David. 1999. Anti-Latour. *Studies in the History and Philosophy of Science Part A* 20(1): 81–112.

Brown, Chris. 2013. The Poverty of Grand Theory. *European Journal of International Relations* 19(3): 483–497.

Buzan, Barry and George Lawson. 2015. *The Global Transformation: History, Modernity and the Making of International Relations*. Oxford: Oxford University Press.

Buzan, Barry and Richard Little. 2000. *International Systems in World History: Remaking the Study of International Relations*. Oxford: Oxford University Press.

Buzan, Barry and Richard Little. 2001. Why International Relations Has Failed as an Intellectual Project and What to Do about It. *Millennium: Journal of International Studies* 30(1): 19–39.

Chernilo, Daniel. 2006. Social Theory's Methodological Nationalism: Myth and Reality. *European Journal of Social Theory* 9(1): 5–22.

Clark, Ian. 2005. *Legitimacy in International Society*. Oxford: Oxford University Press.

Clark, Ian. 2007. *International Legitimacy and World Society*. Oxford: Oxford University Press.

Collins, Harry M. and Robert Evans. 2003. The Third Wave of Science Studies: Studies of Expertise and Experience. *Social Studies of Science* 32(2): 235–296.

Craig, Campbell. 2003. *Glimmer of a New Leviathan: Total War in the Realism of Niebuhr, Morgenthau and Waltz*. New York: Columbia University Press.

Cudworth, Erica and Stephen Hobden. 2013. Of Parts and Wholes: International Relations beyond the Human. *Millennium: Journal of International Studies* 41(3): 430–450.

Dafoe, Allan. 2016. On Technological Determinism: A Typology, Scope Conditions, and a Mechanism. *Science, Technology and Human Values* 40(6): 1047–1076.

Dahl. Robert. 1957. The Concept of Power. *Systems Research and Behavioural Science* 2(3): 201–215.

Dunne, Tim, Lene Hansen and Colin Wight. 2013. The End of International Relations Theory? *European Journal of International Relations* 19(3): 3–25.

Ezrahi, Yaron. 1990. *The Descent of Icarus: Science and the Transformation of Contemporary Democracy*. Cambridge, MA: Harvard University Press.

Feenberg, Andrew. 2002. *Transforming Technology: A Critical Theory Revisited*. Oxford: Oxford University Press.

Feenberg, Andrew. 2010. *Between Reason and Experience: Essays in Technology and Modernity*. Cambridge, MA: MIT Press.

Fritsch, Stefan. 2011. Technology and Global Affairs. *International Studies Perspectives* 12(1): 27–45.

Giddens, Anthony. 1985. *The Nation-State and Violence: Volume Two of A Contemporary Critique of Historical Materialism*. Cambridge: Polity.

Goldsmith, Jack and Timothy Wu. 2008. *Who Controls the Internet? Illusions of a Borderless World*. Oxford: Oxford University Press.

Grant, Jenna M. 2016. From Subjects to Relations: Bioethics and the Articulation of Postcolonial Politics in the Cambodia Pre-Exposure Prophylaxis Trial. *Social Studies of Science* 46(2): 236–258.

Hecht, Gabrielle. 2002. Rupture-Talk in the Nuclear Age: Conjugating Colonial Power in Africa. *Social Studies of Science* 32(5–6): 691–727.

Herz, John. 1950. Idealist Internationalism and the Security Dilemma. *World Politics* 2(2): 157–180.

Hills, Jill. 2007. *Telecommunications and Empire*. Chicago, IL: University of Illinois Press.

Hobden, Stephen. 1998. *International Relations and Historical Sociology: Breaking Down Boundaries*. London: Routledge.

Hobson, John, George Lawson and Justin Rosenberg. 2010. Historical Sociology. In Robert A. Denemark (ed.) *The International Studies Encyclopedia*. Malden, MA: Wiley-Blackwell.

Hurd, Ian. 1999. Legitimacy and Authority in International Politics. *International Organization* 53(2): 379–408.

Jackson, Patrick Thaddeus. 2011. *The Conduct of Inquiry in International Relations*. London: Routledge.

Jameson, Frederic. 2005. *Archaeologies of the Future: The Desire Called Utopia and Other Science Fictions*. London: Verso.

Jasanoff, Sheila. 2003. Breaking the Waves in Science Studies Comment on H.M. Collins and Robert Evans, 'The Third Wave of Science Studies' . *Social Studies of Science* 33(3): 389–400.

Jasanoff, Sheila (ed.). 2004. *States of Knowledge: The Co-Production of Science and Social Order*. London: Routledge.

Jasanoff, Sheila. 2015. Future Imperfect: Science, Technology, and the Imaginations of Modernity. In Sheila Jasanoff and Sang-Hyun Kim (eds). *Dreamscapes of Modernity: Sociotechnical Imaginaries and the Fabrication of Power*. Chicago, IL: University of Chicago Press.

Jasanoff, Sheila and Sang-Hyun Kim (eds). 2015. *Dreamscapes of Modernity: Sociotechnical Imaginaries and the Fabrication of Power*. Chicago, IL: University of Chicago Press.

Kelley, John Robert. 2010. The New Diplomacy: Evolution of a Revolution. *Diplomacy and Statecraft* 21(2): 286–305.

Klein, Hans K. and Daniel Lee Kleinman. 2002. The Social Construction of Technology: Structural Considerations. *Science, Technology and Values* 27(1): 28–52.

Latour, Bruno. 2005. *Reassembling the Social: An Introduction to Actor-Network-Theory*. Oxford: Oxford University Press.

Law, John. 2004. And If the Global Were Small and Noncoherent? Method, Complexity, and the Baroque. *Environment and Planning D: Society and Space* 22(1): 13–26.

Lawson, George and Robbie Shilliam. 2010. Sociology and International Relations: Legacies and Prospects. *Cambridge Review of International Affairs* 23(1): 69–86.

Lukes, Steven. 2005. *Power: A Radical View*, 2nd edition. Basingstoke: Palgrave Macmillan.

Lynch, William T. and Ellsworth R. Furham. 1991. Recovering and Expanding the Normative: Marx and the New Sociology of Scientific Knowledge. *Science, Technology and Human Values* 16(2): 233–248.

Mann, Michael. 1986. *The Sources of Social Power, Volume 1: A History of Power from the Beginning to AD 1760*. Cambridge: Cambridge University Press.

Marx. Karl. 1976 [1867]. *Capital: A Critique of Political Economy, Volume One*. London: Penguin.

McCarthy, Daniel R. 2015. *Power, Information Technology, and International Relations Theory: The Power and Politics of US Foreign Policy and the Internet*. Basingstoke: Palgrave Macmillan.

Mearsheimer, John. 2001. *The Tragedy of Great Power Politics*. New York: Norton.

Miller, Clark A. 2004. Climate Science and the Making of a Global Political Order. In Sheila Jasanoff (ed.) *States of Knowledge: The Co-Production of Science and Social Order*. London: Routledge.

Miller, Clark A. 2015. Globalizing Security: Science and the Transformation of Contemporary Political Imagination. In Sheila Jasanoff and Sang-Hyun Kim (eds) *Dreamscapes of Modernity: Sociotechnical Imaginaries and the Fabrication of Power*. Chicago, IL: University of Chicago Press.

Morriss, Peter. 2002. *Power: A Philosophical Analysis*. Manchester: Manchester University Press.

Nexon, Daniel H. and Vincent Pouliot. 2013. Things of Networks': Situating ANT in International Relations. *International Political Sociology* 7(3): 342–345.

Osiander, Andres. 1998. Re-Reading Early Twentieth-Century IR: Idealism Revisited. *International Studies Quarterly* 42(3): 409–432.

Rengger, Nicholas. 2015. Pluralism in International Relations Theory: Three Questions. *International Studies Perspectives* 16(1): 32–39.

Rosenberg, Justin. 2005. Globalization Theory: A Post Mortem. *International Politics* 42(1): 2–74.

Rosenberg, Justin. 2006. Why is There No International Historical Sociology? *European Journal of International Relations* 12(3): 7–40.

Rosenberg, Justin. 2016. International Relations in the Prison of Political Science. *International Relations* 30(2): 127–153.

Salter, Brian, Yinhua Zhou, Saheli Datta and Charlotte Salter. 2016. Bioinformatics and the Politics of Innovation in the Life Sci: Science and the State in the United Kingdom, China and India. *Science, Technology and Human Values* 41(5): 793–826.

Sayes, Edwin. 2014. Actor-Network Theory and Methodology: Just What Does It Mean to Say that Nonhumans Have Agency? *Social Studies of Science* 44(1): 134–149.

Schmidt, Brian. 2005. Competing Realist Conceptions of Power. *Millennium: Journal of International Studies* 33(3): 523–549.

Singh, J.P. 2008. *Negotiation and the Global Information Economy*. Cambridge: Cambridge University Press.

Smith, Frank L. 2014. Advancing Science Diplomacy: Indonesia and the US Naval Medical Research Unit. *Social Studies of Science* 44(6): 825–847.

Thompson, E.P. 1968. *The Making of the English Working Class*. London: Pelican.

Wheeler, Nicholas J.. 1992. Pluralist or Solidarist Conceptions of International Society: Bull and Vincent on Humanitarian Intervention. *Millennium: Journal of International Studies* 21(3): 463–487.

Wynne, Brian. 2003. Seasick on the Third Wave? Subverting the Hegemony: Response to Collins and Evans (2002). *Social Studies of Science* 33(3): 401–417.

Wynne, Brian. 2010. Foreword. In Andrew Feenberg, *Between Reason and Experience: Essays in Technology and Modernity*. Cambridge, MA: MIT Press.

GLOSSARY

Actant

Used in Actor-Network Theory (ANT) to designate human and non-human members of a network. Specifically developed to avoid referring to members of a network as agents, as agency in ANT is a property generated by network assemblages, not a capacity of actors as such.

Affect

Concept in New Materialist approaches to denote the precognitive responses to stimuli. These responses occur prior to any encounter with an individual's defined emotions, in contrast to classic models of rationality. Centrally employed to consider how material networks and processes alter feelings and emotions. See Protevi (2009) and Bennett (2010).

Ambivalence

Refers to the contradictory features within a technological institution to highlight social choice in the further development of one set of features over another. The less complex an object, the more ambivalent its purposes. The Internet, for example, possesses features that may promote or hinder the free flow of information. Highlighting the uncertain future trajectory of technological artefacts and institutions, this may vary according to the complexity of the technological entity. See Bias.

Anthropocene

Used to denote a new era of geological time in which human beings have affected the ecology of the earth at a geological level. Dating of the end of the Holocene and the start of the Anthropocene ranges from the late eighteenth to the mid-twentieth century.

Anthropocentric	A human-centred worldview. A classic example is the idea that the sun revolves around the earth. Often seen as a defining feature of modernist social theory and as partially responsible for the pursuit of human mastery over nature, resulting in deeply negative impacts on the environment. Anti-humanist and posthumanist social theory seeks to replace this viewpoint.
Assemblage	An entity with properties that emerge from the inter-actions of its parts. The whole entity is not reducible to its parts, in contrast to individualist approaches to social theory, and includes humans and non-human objects. Order produced through interaction is con-tingent and non-hierarchical. Derived from the phi-losophy of Gilles Deleuze, see DeLanda (2006) for a clear sustained treatment.
Being	Two separate uses are present in philosophy and social theory. First, being may refer to an ontological claim about what exists in the world – this is the common approach in Anglo-American and analytical philoso-phy. Alternatively, the term is used in Continental philosophy to focus attention on the nature of exis-tence, such as the question of why something rather than nothing exists and the quality of this existence. This second approach is rooted in the philosophy of Martin Heidegger.
Bias	From Feenberg's Critical Theory of Technology – the social and political disposition embedded within a technological object. The bias of an object is a capacity that need not be realized. See Ambivalence.
Biopolitics	The control and regulation of populations through var-ious mechanisms of power. Derived from Michel Foucault's later work, the mechanisms through which biopolitics regulates life is often called biopower.
Black box	Black boxing occurs when we do not enquire into the internal characteristics or make-up of some institution, artefact or social relation, which is described as a black box. Internal workings of the black box are taken for granted, with only inputs and outputs passing through the black box of interest. In International Relations, for example, the state is often treated as a black box, with the internal processes of foreign policy-making and bureaucratic politics sidelined.
Closure	Technological controversies are ended through closure whereby technological objects are accepted as meeting

defined social aims and goals. These need not be the aims set out at the beginning of the design and development process; closure is negotiated amongst social actors throughout the emergence of new technologies. See Pinch and Bijker (1987: 44–46) and Bijker (1995).

Dialectic
At its broadest, this term refers to the relationship between contradictory aspects of a larger totality – for example, the contradiction between the material interests of the working classes and capitalists in a capitalist mode of production. However, dialectic may also refer to a methodology or logical structure of argument or, more strongly, applied as an approach to study the natural world with the claim that the natural world develops through contradictions. For the former, see Lukacs (1971 [1922]) and Ollman (1993); for the latter, see Engels (1940 [1883]).

Epistemic culture
The shared culture of a defined social group concerning the correct or valid ways of acquiring knowledge – similar to the concept of epistemic community in International Relations. See Knorr Cetina (1999) and Haas (1992).

Epistemology
The theory of knowledge. Centred on the study of how we know what we know, such as the definition of what counts as knowledge and the reliability of knowledge claims. Different claims about the nature of valid justified knowledge constitute the ground of debate over epistemology. In IR, debates over epistemology have been important since the 'Third Debate' (see Jackson 2011 and Wight 2006: 226–254). Science and Technology Studies (STS) is rooted in challenges to the traditional picture of the scientific method as a secure ground for valid knowledge claims. For classic early statements, see Kuhn (1962) and Bloor (1976).

Essentialism
Defining the properties of a technological object or artefact according to its (purported) nature or essence. The nature of the object or artefact is not determined by its context, and exists outside of human history or control. One form of technological determinism.

Fetish
Misrecognizing the power of human beings and human action as the power of inanimate objects. Fetishes, and the phenomenon of fetishism, emerged as objects of study through early European imperialist encounters (Ellen 1988: 213–215). Analyses of 'commodity

	fetishism' have been central to the strands of Western Marxism influenced by Gyorgy Lukacs (1971 [1922]).
Forces of production	Tools used in the material production and reproduction of human society. Central to Marxism, the forces of production are often classically conceived as industrial technologies, such as steelworks or Fordist production lines. The boundaries of the forces of production differ between different authors and theoretical positions, sometimes including science or technique.
Idealism	In philosophy an approach that stresses the centrality of ideas as constitutive of reality. This may be either in the strong sense that reality is a form of thought or in the weaker epistemological sense that what we know is what exists. The former position is most associated with George Berkeley and, with very significant qualification, G.W.F. Hegel, while the latter is perhaps most associated with poststructuralist thought. Note, however, that IR theory has also used this term to refer to approaches that stress the possibility of progressive change in global politics, as in the purported 'Realist–Idealist' debate of the 1930s.
Inscription	The process of making events and processes visible in documents, academic papers, diagrams and so forth. An important concept in Actor-Network Theory (ANT), this is part of the process whereby things come to contain meaning and, as a result, affect how other actants behave.
Instrumentalism	The treatment of technology as merely a tool that can be turned to any political or social purpose; the object itself is not understood to carry any bias or shape society in any way. A more subtle version of technological determinism than essentialism.
Intermediator	Element of an assemblage that does not alter the things that pass through it. For example, a garden hose does not alter the water that passes through it within a lawn care assemblage. Distinct from a mediator.
Interpretive flexibility	Used in SCOT approaches to highlight the central role of language and meaning-making in defining what a technological object is and how it can be used. What objects mean is underdetermined and open to contestation. Often used by radical SCOT approaches to suggest that objects do not have politics built into their material form.

Large technical system	Large infrastructural systems composed of human and non-humans; general examples are transportation and communication technologies, such as road and rail networks or the Internet. These systems can include individual technological artefacts, individual human system builders, organizations, books, articles and so forth. LTS research focuses on the evolution and path dependency of systems. See momentum.
Materialism	Philosophical and social theories that prioritize the importance of materiality – physical composition of things and practices – in their explanations of the nature of the world and human social practices. In IR often associated with Realism and a positivist philosophy of science, although this is highly problematic and contrasted to the 'idealism' of Constructivist explanations. For etymology, see Williams (1976: 197–201). In IR, see Wight (2006) and Jackson (2011) for treatments of these and related issues in the philosophy of science.
Mediator	Within Actor-Network Theory this refers to elements of a network that alter the make-up of whatever passes through them. For example, the make-up of water is altered as it passes through a snow machine in the process of creating a ski-slope. Distinct from intermediator. See Latour (2005: 37–42, 106).
Momentum	The role of sunk costs – including money and time – ensuring that a course of technological development, once it reaches a certain threshold, will continue on that path. Reversing development once momentum is attained is too costly, resulting in inertia. Featured particularly in Thomas Hughes's (1983) historical treatment of electrification in Western societies, momentum is similar to the concept of 'path dependency' in political science. See also reverse salient.
Naturalism	The thesis that there is a unity of method between the natural and the social sciences. Use of this approach by the 'Strong Programme' in the field of Sociology of Scientific Knowledge (SSK) points towards an understanding of science as a human practice that can be studied akin to other human practices. This reverses the general terms of the relationship whereby an understanding of science as positivist in nature is then applied to social scientific processes. Bloor (1976; 1981) provides clear statements of this position.

Network
Used in Actor-Network Theory as a topological concept to describe the relationships through which actants are linked via mediators and intermediaries. A metaphorical, not literal, term in ANT, it is distinct from the meaning of network in social network analysis and related sociological approaches.

Neuropolitics
Politics of the human brain's neural networks and structure. This includes the capacities of the brain and how these capacities are constituted on an ongoing basis through our actions in the world. The capacities and structures of neural networks affect the types of politics that may be possible in any given place or time.

Ontology
Refers either to what kind of things exist in the world and their relationship to each other (for example, what are states like and how should we think of their relations) or to the nature of existence as such, with the former approach preferred in Anglo-American philosophy of science and the latter in Continental philosophy. See Being.

Posthumanism
The most straightforward meaning is 'after humanism', a rejection of the humanist tradition of social thought. Stresses human embeddedness in wider systems of nature and technology, challenging ideas of technological and environmental hubris. Not to be confused with transhumanism, referring to the technological enhancement of human biological capacities. See Wolfe (2010).

Realism
In philosophy of science, the claim that reality exists independent of human thought. There are many varieties of philosophical realism. In International Relations scientific or critical realism has been most prominent. Often confused with the political Realism of Hans Morgenthau or Kenneth Waltz, realism need not be Realist, or vice versa. See Wight (2006).

Reflexivity
Refers to the reflection of an observer on their own role in creating or defining an object or process under study. Central to radical constructivist approaches in STS and to strands of Critical Theory and constructivism in IR. See Wyn Jones (1999).

Reification
The treatment of social practices and processes as if they were things. For example, in International Relations 'the State' is often treated as if it were a concrete entity like a car or a house. The concept of reification

	particularly is prevalent in Critical Theory and Western Marxism. See Lukacs (1971 [1922]).
Relational ontology	The claim that entities – people, animals, objects and so forth – are constituted by the relations in which they are embedded. Relations may be understood as networks, as in Actor-Network Theory, or as internal relations within a larger entity, such as those between labour and capitalism within capitalism, as in Marxism.
Relations of production	From Marxist theory, the social relationships between people in a given mode of production, such as the relationship between lords and serfs that defines the feudal mode of production.
Reverse salient	Derived from military terminology and used in studies of Large Technical Systems (LTS), this refers to the uneven growth of different elements of a technical system whereby some parts of the system do not develop as rapidly as others. If salients are not identified and resolved, the success of an LTS becomes problematic. The social definition of reverse salient – the social and political process whereby these problems are identified – is central to the direction and ultimate success of an emerging LTS. The third phase in Thomas Hughes's discussion of LTS development trajectories (1983: 15–16).
Sublime	In the Kantian formulation, the sublime is evoked by a natural object or process whose massive form produces a combination of awe and fear that threatens to obliterate the self. As a sensory experience, the profundity of the sublime is inexpressible, placing it outside of language. See Kant (1986) and Burke (1993).
Symmetry	The principle of using the same method to explain successful and unsuccessful technological designs and artefacts. Developed as a reaction to the non-social explanation of successful technological designs as simply reflecting the essence of how a particular technology must function, Bloor (1976) offers a classic treatment. The extension of symmetry from a methodological principle to an ontological principle – the requirement that all actors be treated as of equal status in creating any social phenomenon – represents a central point of divergence between the 'Strong Programme' in SSK and ANT.
Technoaesthetics	The primarily, but not solely, visual appearance or effect of a technological object. Registered in terms of its

	beauty or ugliness, this refers to the form of a technological artefact rather than its content.
Technological determinism	The idea that technological objects and institutions develop according to their own intrinsic logic, and that these developments are responsible for causing social change. Essentialism and instrumentalism represent two different variants. Often implicit rather than explicit in International Relations and social theory more generally.
Technoscience	The production of science by technological artefacts; used to challenge the idea of a clear distinction between 'basic' and 'applied' science. The term is particularly prominent in feminist approaches in Science and Technology Studies. See Haraway (1997) and Åsberg and Lykke (2010).
Translation	In Actor-Network Theory, a non-causal relation that exists between two mediators. See Latour (2005: 108).

References

Åsberg, Cecilia and Nine Lykke. 2010. Editorial: Feminist Technoscience Studies. *European Journal of Women's Studies* 17(4): 299–305.

Bennett, Jane. 2010. *Vibrant Matter: A Political Ecology of Things*. Durham, NC: Duke University Press.

Bijker, Wiebe E. 1995. *Of Bicycles, Bakelites and Bulbs: Towards a Theory of Sociotechnical Change*. Cambridge, MA: The MIT Press.

Bloor, David. 1976. *Knowledge and Social Imagery*. London: Routledge.

Bloor, David. 1981. The Strengths of the Strong Programme. *Philosophy of the Social Sciences* 11(2): 199–213.

Burke, Edmund. 1993. A Philosophical Enquiry into the Origin of our Ideas of the Sublime and Beautiful. In Ian Harris (ed.) *Pre-Revolutionary Writings*. Cambridge: Cambridge University Press.

DeLanda, Manuel. 2006. *A New Philosophy of Society: Assemblage Theory and Social Complexity*. London: Continuum.

Ellen, Roy. 1988. Fetishism. *Man* 23(2): 213–235.

Engels, Friedrich. 1940 [1883]. *Dialectics of Nature*. London: Lawrence and Wishart.

Haas, Peter M. 1992. Introduction: Epistemic Communities and International Policy Coordination. *International Organization* 46(1): 1–35.

Hughes, Thomas P. 1983. *Networks of Power: Electrification in Western Society, 1880–1930*. Cambridge, MA: The MIT Press.

Jackson, Patrick Thaddeus. 2011. *The Conduct of Inquiry in International Relations: Philosophy of Science and its Implications for the Study of World Politics*. London: Routledge.

Kant, Immanuel. 1986. Analytic of the Sublime. In Ernst Behler (ed.) *Philosophical Writings*. New York: Continuum.

Knorr Cetina, Karin. 1999. *Epistemic Cultures: How the Sciences Make Knowledge*. Cambridge, MA: Harvard University Press.

Kuhn, Thomas. 1962. *The Structure of Scientific Revolutions*. Chicago, IL: University of Chicago Press.

Latour, Bruno. 2005. *Reassembling the Social: An Introduction to Actor-Network Theory*. New York: Oxford University Press.

Lukacs, Georg. 1971 [1922]. *History and Class Consciousness*. London: Merlin Press.

Ollman, Bertell. 1993. *Dialectical Investigations*. New York: Routledge.

Pinch, Trevor J. and Wiebe E. Bijker. 1987. The Social Construction of Facts and Artifacts: Or How the Sociology of Science and the Sociology of Technology Might Benefit Each Other. In Wiebe E. Bijker, Thomas P. Hughes and Trevor Pinch (eds) *The Social Construction of Technological Systems: New Directions in the Sociology and History of Technology*. Cambridge, MA: The MIT Press.

Protevi, John. 2009. *Political Affect: Connecting the Social and the Somatic*. Minneapolis: University of Minnesota Press.

Wight, Colin. 2006. *Agents, Structures and International Relations: Politics as Ontology*. Cambridge: Cambridge University Press.

Williams, Raymond. 1976. *Keywords: A Vocabulary of Culture and Society*. London: Fontana Press.

Wolfe, Cary. 2010. *What is Posthumanism?* Minneapolis: University of Minnesota Press.

Wyn Jones, Richard. 1999. *Security, Strategy and Critical Theory*. Boulder, CO: Lynne Rienner.

GUIDE TO FURTHER READING

This volume has brought into conversation a number of disciplines, and it is not possible to provide a comprehensive survey of literature that touches upon the issues raised. This guide notes only particularly high-profile books and articles, and only those in English. As a result, this is only intended as indicative of the wider terrain of the field and as a useful prompt to further investigation, not as final accounting of what is and what is not important in these fields.

General readings in Science and Technology Studies and the Philosophy of Technology

Introductory works to Science and Technology Studies (STS) are numerous. Sergio Sismondo, *An Introduction to Science and Technology Studies*, 2nd edition (London: Wiley-Blackwell, 2009), is a model introductory text to the field. Steven Fuller, *New Frontiers in Science and Technology Studies* (Cambridge: Polity, 2007) is more advanced and puts forward more contentious claims, in Fuller's typically entertaining fashion. Harry Collins and Trevor Pinch, *The Golem: What You Should Know about Science*, 2nd edition (Cambridge: Cambridge University Press, 2012) is clear and easy to read, and is particularly useful in outlining science as a practical skill.

Thomas S. Kuhn, *The Structure of Scientific Revolutions* (Chicago, IL: University of Chicago Press, 1962) is a foundational text for STS and the Philosophy of Science more generally. The impact of its claim that science is an historical practice on the social sciences cannot be underestimated. Robert K. Merton, *The Sociology of Science: Theoretical and Empirical Investigations* (Chicago, IL: University of Chicago Press, 1973) and Karl Mannheim, *Ideology and Utopia: An Introduction to the Sociology of Knowledge* (New York: Harvest, Brace & World, 1927) are classic texts in the treatment of scientific knowledge that nevertheless never escape the distinction between nature and culture. David Bloor, *Knowledge and Social Imagery* (London: Routledge, 1976) and Barry Barnes, *Scientific Knowledge and Sociological Theory* (London: Routledge and Kegan Paul, 1974) are cornerstones in the development of the 'Strong Programme' in STS. Critical engagement with their work is found in Martin Hollis and Steven Lukes (eds), *Rationality and Relativism* (Oxford: Blackwell, 1982).

The Philosophy of Technology has often been unable to steer past the twin determinisms outlined in the Introduction. Lewis Mumford, *Technics and Civilization* (New York: Harcourt & Brace, 1934), Jacques Ellul, *The Technological Society* (New York: Knopf, 1976 [1964]) and Marshall McLuhan, *Understanding Media: The Extensions of Man* (New York: McGraw-Hill, 1964) are indicative mid-twentieth-century treatments of technology in philosophy and social theory. While limited in their determinism, each still contains suggestive insights. The field has made significant strides since the mid-1980s. Don Ihde, *Technics and Praxis: A Philosophy of Technology* (Boston: Reidel, 1978) is an important text in its revitalization. Langdon Winner, *Autonomous Technology: Technics-out-of-Control as a Theme in Political Thought* (Cambridge, MA: MIT Press, 1977) provides a survey of political theorists understanding of technology. Donna Haraway, *Simians, Cyborgs and Women: The Reinvention of Nature* (London: Free Association, 1989) is the central text in the development of feminist approaches in the field. Ian Hacking, *The Social Construction of What?* (Cambridge, MA: Harvard University Press, 1999) provides a clear consideration of the meaning of 'social construction' and its application to a variety of social and natural phenomena – students of IR will find it particularly helpful in relation to the claims of Constructivism in philosophy and social theory. As noted in Chapter 4, Andrew Feenberg's body of work remains the standout philosophical account from a critical perspective.

The history of technology was traditionally not theoretically oriented, but this changed with Steven Shapin and Simon Schaffer, *Leviathan and the Air-Pump: Hobbes, Boyle, and the Experimental Life* (Princeton, NJ: Princeton University Press, 1985). Shapin and Schaffer's work is exemplary – necessary reading for political theorists, historians of science and STS scholars alike. Less theoretically informed, yet nevertheless valuable in terms of their historical detail and depth, are William H. McNeill, *The Pursuit of Power: Technology, Armed Force, and Society since A.D. 1000* (Chicago, IL: University of Chicago Press, 1982), with particular relevance for the history of warfare, and David Headrick, *Power Over Peoples: Technology, Environments, and Western Imperialism 1400 to the Present* (Princeton, NJ: Princeton University Press, 2012), which develops Headrick's earlier work and speaks to the creation and maintenance of hierarchy in global politics. Jared Diamond, *Guns, Germs and Steel: The Fate of Human Societies* (New York: Norton, 1997) is a popular history of environmental and material determinants of human history, although subject to significant criticism from academics, particularly anthropologists. David Edgerton, *The Shock of the Old: Technology and Global History since 1900* (Oxford: Oxford University Press, 2011) is a useful correction to the general focus in popular culture (and elsewhere) on the impact of novel technologies on the course of the twentieth century, and is easy to read.

Finally, a wide range of academic journals publish material from these research areas. *Science, Technology and Human Values* and *Social Studies of Science* are the standout titles for the field of STS. In IR, *Millennium: Journal of International Studies*, *International Political Sociology* and *Security Dialogue* have been at the forefront of publishing STS-IR scholarship, although journals throughout the discipline increasingly feature such work. *Diplomatic History* has substantively engaged with a material turn in international history since the turn of the century and is particularly relevant to students of IR. Finally, Mark Salter (ed.), *Making Things International 1: Circuits and Motion* (Minneapolis: University of Minnesota Press, 2015), Mark Salter (ed.), *Making Things International 2: Catalysts and Reactions* (Minneapolis: University of Minnesota Press, 2016) and Maximilian Mayer et al. (eds), *The Global Politics of Science and Technology, Volume 1* (Heidelberg: Springer, 2014) provide comprehensive coverage of STS-IR scholarship from a range of perspectives, and serve as an indication of the emergence of STS-IR as a significant point of engagement for IR scholarship in general.

The Social Construction of Technology

The central text in the development of the SCOT approach is, as noted in Chapter 2, Wiebe E. Bijker et al. (eds), *The Social Construction of Technological Systems: New Directions in the Sociology and History of Technology* (Cambridge, MA: MIT Press, 1987). Other seminal works from the first phase of SCOT's development include Thomas P. Hughes, *Networks of Power: Electrification in Western Society, 1880–1930* (Baltimore, MD: Johns Hopkins University Press, 1983); Donald MacKenzie, *Inventing Accuracy: A Historical Sociology of Nuclear Missile Guidance* (Cambridge, MA: MIT Press, 1990); and Wiebe E. Bijker and John Law (eds), *Shaping Technology/ Building Society: Studies in Sociotechnical Change* (Cambridge, MA: MIT Press, 1992).

As SCOT has continued to develop and flourish, the initial focus on micropolitics or specific national technological cultures has expanded to a broader consideration of global processes, although without any significant engagement with IR theory. Only a very small sample of this work can be suggested here. Contributors to James Delbourgo and Nicholas Dew (eds), *Science and Empire in the Atlantic World* (London: Routledge, 2007) explore the role of science and technology in the process of colonization of the new world. Gabrielle Hecht (ed.), *Empire and Technopolitics in the Global Cold War* (Cambridge, MA: MIT Press, 2011) explores the role of technology in maintaining hierarchies in global politics, examining the impact of hegemonic science and technology upon postcolonial states during the Cold War. Shelia Jasanoff and Sang-Hyun Kim (eds), *Dreamscapes of Modernity: Sociotechnical Imaginaries and the Fabrication of Power* (Chicago, IL: University of Chicago Press, 2015) employ Jasanoff's central concept of 'sociotechnical imaginaries' to examine the relationship between technology, power, and hierarchy in contemporary forms of global governance.

Actor-Network Theory

In addition to those mentioned in Chapter 3, other classic ANT texts include Bruno Latour, *The Pasteurization of France* (Cambridge, MA: Harvard University Press, 1987) and *We Have Never Been Modern* (Cambridge, MA: Harvard University Press, 1993). The second half of the former book is essential reading to grasp Latour's theoretical project, while the latter provides a fascinating argument challenging conventional distinctions about the modern and the non-modern, particularly relevant to attempts in political theory and IR to develop non-Eurocentric approaches to global politics. Of secondary engagement with Latour's version of ANT, Graham Harman, *Prince of Networks: Bruno Latour and Metaphysics* (Melbourne: re.press, 2007) is an excellent discussion of Latour's ontology and 'object-oriented' philosophy, although Harman's *Bruno Latour: Reassembling the Political* (Chicago, IL: University of Chicago Press, 2014) is less successful. Among other treatments or developments of ANT, John Law and John Hansard (eds), *Actor Network Theory and After* (Oxford: Blackwell, 1999) provides a good overview and summary of ANT from key contributors in its initial phase of development.

Applications to global politics extend across a range of disciplines alongside IR, including geography, anthropology and organization studies. For a sample of work explicitly engaging with the global or international, see Tony Porter et al., 'Global Benchmarking Networks: The Cases of Disaster Risk Reduction and Supply Chains', *Review of International Studies* 41(5) 2015: 865–886; Jonathan Luke Austin, 'Torture and the Material-Semiotic Networks of Violence across Borders', *International Political Sociology* 10(1) 2016: 3–21; Mikkel Flyverbom, 'Hybrid Networks and the Global Politics of the Digital Revolution: A Practice-Oriented, Relational and Agnostic Approach', *Global Networks* 10(3) 2010: 424–442; and, in an interesting reflection on knowledge production practices in STS and science policy, including reflexive insights on ANT itself, Tereza Stockelova, 'Immutable Mobiles Derailed: STS, Geopolitics and Research Assessment', *Science, Technology and Human Values* 37(2) 2012: 286–311.

Critical Theories of Technology

As noted in Chapter 4, the work of Karl Marx and Friedrich Engels is foundational to Critical Theories of Technology, and their *The Communist Manifesto* (London: Penguin, 2002 [1848]) remains important in capturing central dynamics of modernization from a Marxist perspective. Engels' *Dialectics of Nature*, found in their *Collected Works, Volume 25* (London: Lawrence & Wishart, 1987), introduced a problematic dialectical ontology that led to some of the difficulties found in later orthodox Marxist treatments of technology. Chris Wickham and Chris Harman present alternative views of the role of technology in the feudal mode of production, a debate that serves as a wider platform for theoretical disagreements about the classical or orthodox Marxist approach to the forces and relations of production. See Chris Wickham, 'Productive Forces and the Economic Logic of the Feudal

Mode of Production', *Historical Materialism* 16(2) 2008: 3–22 and Chris Harman, 'Chris Wickham's Framing the Early Middle Ages', *Historical Materialism* 19(1) 2011: 98–108. While valuable, neither approach delves into the micro-politics of technological development in any detail.

Valuable discussions of Marx's conception of nature and society are found in Neil Smith, *Uneven Development: Nature, Capital, and the Production of Space* (Athens: University of Georgia Press, 2012 [1984]); and Maurice Godelier, *The Mental and the Material* (London: Verso, 1986) from the perspectives of human geography and anthropology. A suggestive (and only suggestive) development of a Marxist approach to culture, technology and modernity is found in Walter Benjamin's 'The Work of Art in Its Age of Mechanical Reproduction' in *Illuminations* (Glasgow: Fontana/Collins, 1977): 219–253. Raymond Williams, *Culture and Materialism* (London: Verso, 2005 [1980]) is similarly suggestive, and both repay careful engagement.

While specific studies on capitalist social relations have not been central in STS, there are some very interesting studies on a range of topics that work from a Marxist-influenced perspective. See, for example, Kaushik Sunder Rajan, *Biocapital: The Constitution of Postgenomic Life* (Durham, NC: Duke University Press, 2006) and the special issue 'STS and Neoliberal Science', *Social Studies of Science* 40(5) 2010. Edward J. Hackett, 'Academic Capitalism', *Science, Technology and Human Values* 39(5) 2014: 635–638, is a call for sustained research into the capitalist structuring of social studies of science and technology from Marxists and non-Marxists alike.

New Materialisms, posthumanism

New Materialist scholarship has roots in poststructuralist continental philosophy, particularly the work of Gilles Deleuze. Alongside Jane Bennett's work, mentioned in Chapter 5, William Connolly, *Neuropolitics: Thinking, Culture, Speed* (Minneapolis: University of Minnesota Press, 2002) and *A World of Becoming* (Durham, NC: Duke University Press, 2010) and Manuel DeLanda, *A New Philosophy of Society: Assemblage Theory and Social Complexity* (London: Bloomsbury, 2006) have been particularly influential. Significant strands of scholarship have emerged detailing the role of emotion and affect in world politics, although these extend beyond specifically new materialist approaches. For the most sustained treatments to date, see Emma Hutchison, *Affective Communities in World Politics* (Cambridge: Cambridge University Press, 2016) and the forum in *International Theory* 6(3) 2014.

Posthumanist scholarship looks to a more diverse range of inspirations, drawing, at times, on poststructuralist and postcolonial thought – see Rosi Braidotti, *The Posthuman* (Cambridge: Polity, 2013) – but also on systems theory and political ecology, as in the work of Erika Cudworth and Stephen Hobden, *Posthuman International Relations: Complexity, Ecologism, and Global Politics* (London: Zed Books, 2011) or Cary Wolfe, *What is Posthumanism?* (Minneapolis: University of Minnesota Press, 2010). For overviews of New Materialism and posthumanist social theory, Rick Dolphijn and Iris van der Tuin (eds), *New Materialism: Interviews and Cartographies* (Ann Arbor, MI: Open Humanities Press, 2012) is quite helpful, while Ashley Barnwell, 'Method Matters: The Ethics of Exclusion', in Vicki Kirby (ed.), *Sociology Under the Skin* (forthcoming) offers a critical survey of these approaches.

The politics of nuclear weapons

The literature on nuclear weapons in International Relations is, of course, vast. Campbell Craig, *Glimmer of a New Leviathan: Total War in the Realism of Niebuhr, Morgenthau, and Waltz* (New York: Columbia University Press, 2003) does a great job in tracing the impact of nuclear weapons on IR theory. Rens van Munster and Casper Sylvest, *Nuclear Realism: Global Political Thought during the Thermonuclear Revolution* (London: Routledge, 2016) deepens our understanding of this impact through an examination of international theory outside the 'canon' of IR.

Treatments of nuclear weapons integrating insights from IR, STS, historical sociology and anthropology have produced a rich range of material. Donald MacKenzie, *Inventing Accuracy: A Historical Sociology of Nuclear Missile Guidance* (Cambridge, MA: MIT Press, 1990) provides a detailed account of the micro-politics of nuclear weapons and remains a classic work. Graham Spinardi, *From Polaris to Trident: the Development of US Fleet Ballistic Missile Technology* (Cambridge: Cambridge University Press, 1994) was an early demonstration of the potential for IR–STS syntheses, drawing, as MacKenzie does, particularly on SCOT approaches. Columba Peoples, *Justifying Ballistic Missile Defence: Technology, Security and Culture* (Cambridge: Cambridge University Press, 2010) advances a critical theory of technology perspective, pushing forward Richard Wyn Jones' remarks in *Security, Strategy and Critical Theory* (Boulder, CO: Lynne Rienner, 1999). Nick Richie, *A Nuclear Weapons Free World? Britain, Trident, and the Challenges Ahead* (Basingstoke: Palgrave Macmillan, 2012) is strong in laying out the distinct policy drivers of UK foreign policy, particularly the role of identity in nuclear weapons policy for a post-imperial state. Daniel Deudney, *Bounding Power: Republican Security Theory from the Polis to the Global Village* (Princeton, NJ: Princeton University Press, 2008) provides the most sophisticated technologically determinist reading of nuclear weapons and their relationship to forms of world order.

Global transportation and communication infrastructures

In addition to the literature on transportation infrastructure is a range of other studies on technology and the materialization of the global political economy and world politics in general. Keller Easterling, *Extrastatecraft: The Power of Infrastructure Space* (London: Verso, 2014) provides a popular introduction to the role of infra-structure in creating the geography of the global economy. Donald MacKenzie, *An Engine, Not A Camera: How Financial Models Shape Markets* (Cambridge, MA: MIT Press, 2006) traces the emergence of modelling and its impact on the global financial system, although without significant reference to its international political dynamics. Human geographers have produced the best work on the materialization of the global economy processes from critical theory and ANT perspectives, as a brief scan of *Antipode: A Radical Journal of Geography* will indicate, although, again, explicit engagement with the IR literature is relatively muted.

Standard setting for goods is an important source of conflict and power in the global political economy. Tim Buthe and Walter Mattli, 'Setting International Standards: Technological Rationality or the Primacy of Power?', *World Politics* 56(1) 2003: 1–42, discusses standard setting on manufactured goods and provides a solid account from a World Society perspective; Kenneth W. Abbot and Duncan Snidal, 'International "Standards" and International Governance', *Journal of European Public Policy* 8(3) 2001: 345–370, approaches standard setting from a rational choice perspective. Stephen Krasner, 'Global Communications and National Power: Life on the Pareto Frontier', *World Politics* 43(3) 1990: 336–366 outlines how state power shapes regimes governing technological development. All provide insights into these processes, although with no engagement with the STS literature or the micro-politics of technological design and use.

There is a range of work on a range of topics that is beginning to engage with the politics of infrastructure in global politics in greater depth. Allison Loconto and Lawrence Busch, 'Standards, Techno-Economic Networks, and Playing Fields: Performing the Global Market Economy', *Review of International Political Economy* 17(3) 2000: 507–536, integrates insights of ANT with International Political Economy. Peer Schouten, 'The Materiality of State Failure: Social Contract Theory, Infrastructure and Governmental Power in Congo', *Millennium: Journal of International Studies* 41(3) 2013: 553–574, traces the relationship between infrastructure and state failure. Claudia Aradau, 'Security that Matters: Critical Infrastructure and Objects of Protection', *Security Dialogue* 41 (5) 2010: 491–514, is an important intervention into security studies, and represents an early example of a flourishing body of work on critical infrastructure, borders, bodies and cartography, often also published by the same outlet. Finally, Maximilian Mayer and Michele Acuto, 'The Global Governance of Large Technical Systems', *Millennium: Journal of International Studies* 43(3) 2015: 660–683, is a strong example of the potential for STS-IR syntheses to examine the relationship between global governance and global infrastructure.

Global politics of Internet governance

While initial treatments of the place of the Internet in global politics were quite sociologically thin, this is certainly no longer the case. A number of IR-STS syntheses exist that take the politics of technological design seriously. See, among others, Laura DeNardis, *Protocol Politics: The Globalization of Internet Governance* (Cambridge, MA: MIT Press, 2009); Milton L. Mueller, *Networks and States: The Global Politics of Internet Governance* (Cambridge, MA: MIT Press, 2010) and Madeline Carr, *US Power and the Internet in International Relations: The Irony of the*

Information Age (Basingstoke: Palgrave Macmillan, 2016). Carr's work is of particular relevance, engaging with IR theory in some depth. On the political economy of Internet governance, see Shawn M. Powers and Michael Jablonski, *The Real Cyberwar: The Political Economy of Internet Freedom* (Urbana: University of Illinois Press, 2015).

There are a number of historical treatments of the development of the Internet, but quality in this area is quite varied. Katie Hafner and Matthew Lyon, *Where Wizards Stay Up Late: The Origins of the Internet* (New York: Simon & Schuster, 1998) is a popular account that is good on some details but theory-light and somewhat dated. Janet Abbate, *Inventing the Internet* (Cambridge, MA: MIT Press, 2000) is stronger on integrating social and cultural influences, drawing on SCOT approaches, while Miles Townes, 'The Spread of TCP/IP: How the Internet Became the Internet', *Millennium: Journal of International Studies* 41(1) 2012: 43–64, is the best historical account from an IR perspective.

Less theoretically explicit but nevertheless invaluable are the series of works dealing with Internet freedom and censorship from the Open Network Initiative: see Ronald Deibert et al. (eds), *Access Denied: The Practice and Policy of Global Internet Filtering* (Cambridge, MA: MIT Press, 2008); *Access Controlled: The Shaping of Power, Rights, and Rule in Cyberspace* (Cambridge, MA: MIT Press, 2010); and *Access Contested: Security, Identity and Resistance in Asian Cyberspace* (Cambridge, MA: MIT Press, 2012). Any study of Internet filtering and competing Internet foreign policies should carefully engage with these pathbreaking volumes.

As cyberwar has emerged as an area of international concern, books and journal articles have poured forth. Richard Clarke, *Cyber War: The Next Threat to National Security and What to Do about It* (New York: Ecco, 2010) should be avoided due to its fondness for hyperbole and scaremongering. However a very good introductory treatment of the topic can be found in P.W. Singer and Allan Freidman, *Cybersecurity and Cyberwar: What Everyone Needs to Know* (Oxford: Oxford University Press, 2014). The seminal take is surely Thomas Rid, *Cyber War Will Not Take Place* (London: Hurst, 2013), while Tim Stevens, *Cyber Security and the Politics of Time* (Cambridge: Cambridge University Press, 2015) is a valuable and theoretically sophisticated look at the broader concept of cybersecurity.

The revolution in military affairs

New approaches to materiality and technology in IR have made the most significant impact in the study of war. The burgeoning literature on drone warfare is perhaps the best example: for a sample, see Caroline Holmqvist, 'Undoing War: War Ontologies and the Materiality of Drone Warfare', *Millennium: Journal of International Studies* 41(3) 2013: 535–552; William Walters, 'Drone Strikes, Dingpolitik and Beyond: Furthering the Debate on Materiality and Security', *Security Dialogue* 45(2) 2014: 101–118; and Mary Manjikian, 'Becoming Unmanned: The Gendering of Lethal Autonomous Warfare Technology', *International Feminist Journal of Politics* 16(1) 2014: 48–65. All three take their cues from a mixture of ANT and SCOT approaches.

New and emerging technologies have received the most coverage from IR-STS syntheses – work on more mundane (and more lethal) older conventional weapons has not kept pace with new theoretical developments. Mike Bourne, 'Guns Don't Kill People, Cyborgs Do: A Latourian Provocation for Transformatory Arms Control and Disarmament', *Global Change, Peace and Security* 24(1) 2012: 141–163, is very interesting from an ANT perspective, and is one of the few examples of theorization of small arms from an IR-STS approach. Neil Cooper, 'Humanitarian Arms Control and Processes of Securitization: Moving Weapons along the Security Continuum', *Contemporary Security Policy* 32(1) 2011: 134–158, outlines the re-emergence of small arms as objects of controversy, without explicitly drawing on STS. Gautam Mukunda, 'We Cannot Go On: Disruptive Innovation and the First World War Royal Navy', *Security Studies* 19(1) 2010: 124–159, discusses the impact of new technology on naval practices from a management and organizational studies perspective.

Space politics

The literature on the politics of space and technology is interdisciplinary in nature, which prevents any easy summation. Scholarship draws on STS, but also on broader fields of social theory, particularly anthropology and political geography, which feature the most sustained engagements. Alison J. Williams, 'Beyond the Sovereign Realm: The Geopolitics and Power Relations in and of Outer Space', *Geopolitics* 15(4) 2010: 785–793, reviews parts of the literature and discusses central points of focus; and Lindy Newlove-Eriksson and Johan Eriksson, 'Governance Beyond the Global: Who Controls the Extraterrestrial?', *Globalizations* 10(2) 2013: 277–292, traces the rise of private authority in outer space governance, shifting analysis away from classic Realist and Liberal views of space technopolitics. Etienne Benson, 'One Infrastructure, Many Global Visions: The Commercialization and Diversification of Argos, a Satellite-Based Environmental Surveillance System', *Social Studies of Science* 42(6) 2012: 843–868, offers a fine-grained analysis of the commercialization of space technologies.

STS scholarship has engaged in a sustained way with the politics of outer space in a number of registers relevant to world politics. Peter Redfield, *Space in the Tropics: From Convicts to Rockets in French Guiana* (Berkeley: University of California Press, 2000), traces the complex relationship between space exploration and terrestrial politics between the global North and the global South. The symbolic construction of space and its impact on earthly politics is examined in Lisa R. Messeri, *Placing Outer Space: An Earthly Ethnography of Other Worlds* (Cambridge, MA: MIT Press, 2016) and Daniel Sage, *How Outer Space Made America: Geography, Organization, and the Cosmic Sublime* (London: Routledge, 2016), with the latter developing a Deleuzian approach to the constitution of American identity via space exploration and the technological sublime. See also Katerina Damjanov, 'Of Defunct Satellites and Other Space Debris', *Science, Technology and Human Values* 42(1) 2017: 166–185.

Climate change

The politics of climate change extend across all human and natural sciences, and the social science literature reflects this scope. Here we will only note work that explicitly centres on International Relations or geopolitics and the technological politics of climate change. Matthew Patterson, *Automobile Politics: Ecology and Cultural Political Economy* (Cambridge: Cambridge University Press, 2007) is an excellent study of the cultural and socio-technical politics of the automobile, and the impact of these on global politics, from a critical IR perspective, albeit with little explicit engagement with STS perspectives as such. Joshua B. Horton and Jesse L. Reynolds, 'The International Politics of Climate Engineering: A Review and Prospectus for International Relations', *International Studies Review* 18(3) 2016: 438–461, surveys Realist, Liberal, Institutionalist and Constructivist IR theories approaches to geoengineering, providing a useful overview and basis for further research, although it tends to reinforce the division between the social and the technical.

Shannon O'Lear and Simon Dalby (eds), *Reframing Climate Change: Constructing Ecological Geopolitics* (London: Routledge, 2016), bring together an interdisciplinary array of scholars in an effort to shift our understanding of climate change from an environmental issue to the framework within which global politics is now embedded. Anthony Burke et al., 'Planet Politics: A Manifesto from the End of IR', *Millennium: Journal of International Studies* 44(3) 2016: 499–523, set out a case to reconsider IR as a whole through confrontation with the contemporary ecological crisis, with the concept of the Anthropocene as a central frame for the project.

Bentley B. Allan, 'Producing the Climate: States, Scientists, and the Constitution of Global Governance Objects', *International Organization* FirstView, outlines a co-productionist approach to climate governance, as does Clark A. Miller's work – see his essays in Sheila Jasanoff (ed.), *States of Knowledge: The Coproduction of Science and the Social Order* (London: Routledge, 2004) and Shelia Jasanoff and Sang-Hyun Kim (eds), *Dreamscapes of Modernity: Sociotechnical Imaginaries and the Fabrication of Power* (Chicago, IL: University of Chicago Press, 2015). Finally, Paul N. Edwards, *A Vast Machine: Computer Models, Climate Data, and the Politics of Global Warming* (Cambridge, MA: MIT Press, 2012) outlines how modelling practices shape our conception of the global and climate politics. His study traces the history and contemporary politics of these processes, and effectively balances philosophical realism and social constructivism.

INDEX